THE RESTORATION OF THE KINGDOM TO ISRAEL

by

Ronald R. Wlodyga

Copyright 1992 by Ronald R. Wlodyga, all rights reserved, including the right to reproduce this work or any portion thereof by any means whatsoever.

Library of Congress Catalog Card Number: 92-90857

Published by Teach Services, Brushton, New York 12916

Revised Print by Ingram, 2021

Acknowledgements

I am truly grateful to Bill Koehn who took the pictures on the Jacket cover and for Eric Wilbers who helped in the formatting.

FOREWARD

Prophecy has been one of the most fascinating subjects to Christians of all ages. Yet it is one of the most complex subjects and I doubt if anyone has put every detail together in it's proper perspective to date. I will be the first one to admit that I don't have all the pieces of this fantastically intricate puzzle in it's entirety—but for purely educational purposes, my opinions are stated.

In all cander, the only thing I want to be *dogmatic* about in this book, is that speculative aspects in regard to *my opinion* of prophetic events *are not to be interpreted dogmatically*! I do not want to speak with authority where there is no definite word of scripture to guide.

However, like the Beureans who searched the scriptures day and night to see if these things be so—it is my hope that this book will inspire you to do the same, and perhaps together we can put the final pieces of this end-time prophetic puzzle together.

Furthermore, speculative aspects contained in this book, as well as the sequence of end-time events are my thoughts, and do not represent any Church, nor am I sponsored or endorsed by any religious organization.

If my opinions turn out to be correct, it is because God inspired them. If they are wrong or misleading, I hope you will not judge me too harshly, for I like you, will be judged by Jesus Christ.

I do not profess to be a prophet, nor have I received special revelation from God concerning the end-time prophecies. I am merely a student of prophecy and would like to share with you the results of my research for your enjoyment, edification and consideration.

Though I do not press points of speculation as doctrine, I do give my opinion for reproof, for correction and instruction in righteousness (11 Tim. 3:16). As Paul said in 1 Corinthians 14:3: **"He that prophesieth speaketh unto men to *edification* and *exhortation* and *comfort.*"** Concerning those who have the gift of prophecy, Paul said: **"Having then gifts differing according to the grace that is given to us, whether prophecy, let us prophesy according to the proportion of faith...(Rom. 12:6).**

Oftentimes prophecy seems to be obscure or contradictory, yet God says, **"The secret things belong unto the LORD our God: but those things which are *revealed* belong unto us and to our children for ever that we may do all the words of this** law" (Deut. 29:29). "Surely the Lord GOD will do nothing, but he *revealeth* his secret unto *his servants* the prophets" (Amos 3:7). "For whatsoever things were written aforetime were written *for our learning,* that we through patience and comfort of the scriptures might have hope" (Rom. 15:4).

In order to weather the "spiritual storms" up ahead—it is my hope that this book will enable you to foresee the "handwriting on the wall."

INTRODUCTION

At Mount Sinai, God set up an organization. At that time God's people—the only people on earth who were the people of God were formed into a nation. As such, they had laws, and government. They were *a kingdom on earth*!

This was both a civil and ecclesiastical government and the start of God's Church! The ancient Israelites were known as "The Church in the Wilderness" (Acts.7:38).

When God first set up this kingdom on earth, the people who formed this organization were *married* to the Lord. It was this marriage that bound the Eternal God to His people, notice (Jeremiah 3:13) where the Eternal declares: **"Turn O backsliding children, saith the Lord, for I am *married unto you*."**

Yes, the Old Covenant was a marriage compact! However, because the Israelites failed to keep their part of the covenant and committed spiritual adultery by serving heathen gods—the Eternal found it necessary to divorce His wife (see Isa. 50:1; 59:1-2; Jer. 3:6,8).

During Jesus' day, His disciples understood that the kingdom, with all authority to govern, whether civil or Church government had been taken away from their people, and turned over to the Gentiles. Recall how they asked Him, **"Lord will thou at this time *restore again the kingdom to Israel*" (Acts 1:6).**

When Israel went after the ways of other nations, breaking the Commandments—God divorced Israel, and gave over the government [which included Church and State government] to the Gentile kingdoms symbolized by Daniel's image and the four "beasts." He gave the government into the Gentile *hands* until the government shall be *restored* to the nation of Israel upon Christ's return.

In the interim, God has begun a process through the New Testament Church to reestablish His government on earth. The parable of the Vineyard in (Matthew 21) is very graphic in explaining the transfer of the Kingdom to another nation [the Church].

God shows in (Romans 11) through the analogy of wild olive trees [Gentiles] that they can now be grafted into branches that were broken off [Israelites]. And that the branches that were cut off [Israelites] can also be grafted back into His new kingdom.

Thus, some day all Israel shall be saved (Rom. 11:26).

The New Testament Church then—is God's spiritual nation composed of both Jews and Gentiles hand selected and chosen by God the Father—for the express purpose of *restoring* God's government to the earth.

But *when* is the *restoration* of God's government going to *occur* on earth? And *how* will it come about? And *who* will be responsible for bringing it about? These questions will be answered in the remaining pages of this book.

The *Jews* were the leading tribe of the 12 tribes of Israel and God uses them in the third chapter of Romans to represent the *Israelites*. The gospel was preached to the *Jew* first, and also to the Greek [or Gentile] (Rom. 1:16).

Those who are now called, and do repent, who do receive Christ as their personal Savior, will eventually be married to Christ under the New Covenant and *rule* with him as kings and priests in his newly established kingdom (Rev. 5:10, 20:6).

After His return as King over the nations, sitting on the throne of His glory, then shall Christ say to the overcomers: **"Come, ye blessed of my Father, inherit the kingdom (Matt. 25:31-34).**

But prior to His return, Christ said of the Jewish nation:

> **Behold, I will send you Elijah the prophet before the coming of the great and dreadful day of the Lord, And he shall turn the heart of the fathers to the children, and the heart of the children to their fathers, lest I come and smite the earth with a curse (Mal. 4:5-6).**

This verse has a *dual* meaning as we shall see. But its spiritual meaning implies the return of the nation of Israel to God their Father, thus the grafting back into His Vineyard.

Prior to Christ's second coming—God is going to pour out His Spirit upon the nation of Israel as Joel prophesied:

> **And it shall come to pass afterward, that I will pour out my spirit upon all flesh; and *your sons* and *your daughters* shall prophesy, *your old men* shall dream dreams, *your young men* shall see visions: (Joel 2:28).**

On the Day of Pentecost, Peter said that this event [the conversion of 120 devout *Jews*] was a *partial fulfillment* of Joel's prophecy (Acts 2:16-17).

Realize that Jesus [the God of the Old Covenant] came to His own first [the Jew] or to His wife (Jn. 1:11). All of the apostles were Jews! Jesus said He was sent to the house of Israel (Matt. 15:24). The early Church was composed solely of *Jews* on the Day of Pentecost (Acts 2:5). (See also Acts 3:25, 26; 13:36).

The start of *restoring the kingdom of God* on earth begins with *the restoring of the nation of Israel* back to God! It will involve their repentance, construction of a Temple in Jerusalem, the restoration of animal sacrifices, the testimony and killing of the "Two Witnesses" in Jerusalem, the pouring out of God's Holy Spirit on Jews as occurred on Pentecost, the fleeing into the wilderness from Jerusalem, the sealing of 144,000 Israelites, the treading down of Jerusalem by Gentile armies, the intervention of Jesus Christ to cleanse the Temple, and take His chosen people out of captivity and restore them in the land of Palestine as His model nation once again.

Several of God's Feast Days *picture* the end time scenario of Israel's repentance and forgiveness at which time God will intervene and lead them out of captivity. Through a study of the *types* we will also learn a great deal concerning Israel's future.

Truly, the time is fast approaching when Jesus will restore all things to this earth, including *the kingdom of God to Israel* (Acts 3:2)

TABLE OF CONTENTS

Page

Chapter One
God's Promise to Abraham

1. The Old Covenant...6
2. Israel's first King.. 8
3. Identity of Jacob's Sons 11
4. Jeremiah's Commission 12
5. Judah taken captive 13
5. Marks of Israel's Identity 16

Chapter Two
The Old Covenant Marriage

1. The Lord Divorced His Wife 22
2. Jesus was Married to Israel 23
3. Jesus came to His Wife..23
4. The Pruning of God's Olive Tree 24
5. Christ to Marry His Wife...26
6. The Bride and Bridegroom.....................................27
7. The "Mystery" of Christ's Body 29
8. The "Mystery" Solved 33

Chapter Three
Daniel's Seventy Weeks Prophecy

1. The first 69 Weeks...35
2. The 70 Years National Captivity............................38
3. Daniel's 70th Week..41
4. The 70th Week and Christ.....................................43
5. The Anti-Christ Version 44
6. The "Times of Jerusalem" 52

Chapter Four
Shaddows of Israel's Future

1. Israel—a type of God's Kingdom...........................58
2. Cyrus—to set the Captives free............................60
3. Zerubbabel—a type of Christ 61

4. Israel—a type of Christ 67
5. Antiochus—a type of False Prophet 68
6. The "Man of Sin" 75
7. The Three Judas's 76

Chapter Five
Types of the Two Witnesses

1. Moses and Aaron 81
2. "Two Olive Trees" and "Two Candlesticks" 82
3. Zerubbabel and Joshua 83
4. John the Baptist 89
5. Clothed in Sackcloth 93
6. Not Moses and Elijah. 94
7. Levitical Types 96

Chapter Six
Parables of Israel's History

1. The Wicked Husbandmen 101
2. The Parable of the Two Sons. 104
3. The Barren Fig Tree Accursed 105
4. The Barren Fig Tree 106
5. The Changing of Administration 108
6. Israel in Tribulation 110

Chapter Seven
Evangelistic Parables

1. The Ten Virgins 117
2. The Royal Marriage Feast for the Kings Son. 119
3. Marriage or Marriage Feast 120
4. A lesson in Hebrew Espousal 122
5. Biblical Weddings—a type of the Church 123
6. The Lost Sheep 130

Chapter Eight
Prophetic Parables

1. The Parable of the Fig Tree 133
2. The Marriage Supper of the Lamb. 134

3. The Bride becomes Christ's Army 135
4. The Harvest of Souls 136
5. Who will populate the Millennium? 137
6. "One shall be taken" 139
7. The Winepress 141
8. When the New Covenant will be made.......................... 144

Chapter Nine
God's Judgment Upon False Religion

1. The Future Passover 148
2. God's Judgement on False Religion............................... 149
3. The Year of Jubilee.. 153
4. A decade of Jubilees 156
5. Pentecost and Jubilee.. 160

Chapter Ten
God's "Seven Times" Punishment

1. The Handwriting on the Wall... 163
2. A Restoration to Sanity 166
3. 2520 Years to World Peace 166
4. Israel's "Seven Times" Punishment................................ 167
5. Ezekiel's Living Legend 169
6. Sabbatical Cyclers 172

Chapter Eleven
Pentecost And Firstfruits

1. God's Covenant with Israel 174
2. Israel Commits Idolatry 177
3. God's Promise of Future Retribution 178
4. God to Circumcize Israel's Heart 181
5. The Start of the New Testament Church....................... 182
6. The New Covenant with Israel....................................... 184
7. The New Covenant for Gentiles..................................... 186
8. Repoting the Nation of Israel 187
9. Spiritual Meaning of Annual Harvests 189

Chapter Twelve
Jacob's Trouble

Trumpets

1. Jacob's Trouble. 193
2. Assyria—the Rod of God's Anger................................ 197
3. Israel's Enemies to be Punished.................................. 198
4. A Symbol of War.. 198
5. The Atonement Money... .199
6. The Silver Trumpets and Redemption. 200

The Day of Atonement

1. The Spiritual meaning 202
2. The Azazel Goat 204
3. The Cleansing of the Sanctuary 206
4. The Spiritual fulfillment 208
5. Jacob's Cleansing... .210
6. The Future Atonement 213

Chapter Thirteen
The Feast of Tabernacles

1. Israel to Dwell in Tents again.................................... 216
2. A Remnant Returns 218
3. The Day of the Lord 219
4. Israel's Second Exodus 221
5. Israel to Rule over their Oppressors.......................... 221
6. Pictures the Millennium.. 223
7. Israel—a type of God's Family.................................. 224

The Last Great Day

1. God to Pour out His Spirit 226
2. Salvation—Past—Present—Future............................ 230
3. Israel's Blindness.. 231
4. A Day of Salvation .... .233
5. Three Periods of Judgment....................................... 236
6. The Great White Throne Judgment........................... 241

Chapter Fourteen
The Temple to be Rebuilt?

1. The Abomination of Desolation 247
2. The Daily Sacrifice taken away 250
3. The 2300 Prophetic Days. 251
4. The "Holy Place" 258
5. The Sanctuary 260
6. The Millennial Temple 264
7. The Levitical System Restored 265
8. God's Glory to Reappear 269

Chapter Fifteen
Jews Have Hope

1. Jewish Complications. 275
2. In Search of the lost Ark. 278
3. The Ark to Reappear 279
4. The Ethiopian Connection. 281
5. A new Archaeological discovery 287

Chapter Sixteen
The Gathering of the Elect

1. God's Spirit upon Jerusalem 294
2. The "Remnant" "Elect" "Woman" "144,000" 297
3. The 144,000 of Revelation 7 & 14 300
4. The Woman and the Manchild 301
5. The Grafting back of Israel 305
6. Israel—God's Firstborn 308
7. The start of the N.T. Jewish Church 310

Chapter Seventeen
God's End-Time Protection

1. The Hour of Temptation 313
2. The Petra Controversy 317
3. Double Indemnity 319
4. The Mysterious Eagle 323
5. To be on Earth. 325
6. Four Types of the Church. 329

7. One Place of Safety. 331
8. The Model—Solomon's Temple 332

Chapter Eighteen
The Restoration of Israel

1. The Restoration of all things. 337
2. The 1290 and 1335 day Controversy 339
3. The 1290 Days..342
4. The 1335 Days..343
5. The Valley of Dry Bones..346
6. The Wise shall understand...348
7. Israel's Four Returns...349

Chapter Nineteen
Satan Chained 1,000 Years

1. Saints to Reign with Christ 358
2. Nations to keep Feast of Tabernacles............................359
3. Gog and Magog attempt Coup. 360
4. Nations to learn War no more 363
5. Israel to build Waste Places..366
6. Israel—a "Light to the World". 368
7. The Millennium's Beginning...373
8. Millennial Life 375
9. Satan's Fate..377

Chapter Twenty
The New Heaven and Earth

1. The Marriage of the Church. 381
2. Overcomers comprise New Jerusalem.........................382
3. Tabernacles and God's Dwelling..................................384
4. The Eternal Tabernacle of God.....................................386
5. God and Man Reconciled. 390
6. The Eighth Day and Eternity..391
7. Entering the "Holy of Holies" 392
8. "Spiritual Firstfruits"..394
9. To Rule over Nations..397

Chapter One

GOD'S PROMISE TO ABRAHAM

Now there was one man in early times that did obey God—that was Abraham: **"Abraham obeyed his voice and kept his charge, his commandments, his statutes, and his laws" (Gen. 26:5),** and therefore Abraham received the promises on which the salvation of every person through Christ is based. He is called the father of the faithful [humanly] (Gal. 31:7).

God actually made *two* separate promises to Abraham, notice: **"Now from thy kindred and from thy father's house, unto a land that I will show thee: and I will make thee a great nation...And in thee shall all the families of the earth be blessed" (Gen. 12:1-3).**

There are *two* separate and distinct promises God made to Abraham:

1. THE BIRTHRIGHT PROMISE:

"I will make thee a Great nation..." This was a promise of national wealth and prosperity to Abraham's descendants. This promise is further elaborated upon in chapter 17 of Genesis. God said: (Vs.2) And I will make my covenant between me and thee, and will multiply thee exceedingly. (Vs. 6) And I will

> make thee exceeding fruitful, and I will make nations of thee, and kings shall come out of thee. (Vs. 7) And I will establish my covenant between me and thee and thy seed after thee in their generations for an everlasting covenant, to be a God unto thee, and to thy seed after thee. (Vs. 8) And I will give unto thee, and to thy seed after thee, the land wherein thou art a stranger, **ALL THE LAND OF CANNAN, FOR AN EVERLASTING POSSESSION; and I will be their God.** (Vs. 9) And God said unto Abraham, Thou shalt keep my covenant therefore, thou, and thy seed after thee in their generations [*emphasis mine*].

Eventually the material land blessings were also promised to Abrahams's flesh and blood seed as indicated by "**...and thy seed, after thee in *their* generations.**"

The Birthright promise is one *race* and the identity of the modern nations that have become the recipients of this promise is of vital importance to the understanding of prophecy!

But notice the land of Canaan [present day Israel] was to be of special importance to God. That's why Jerusalem is called **"the apple of God's eye" (Zech. 2:4,8).** We will learn more of the reasons for this special city later on!

Concerning the importance of the perpetual Palestinian Covenant, Pentecost writes:

> **Great importance is attatched to this covenant (1) in that it reaffirms to Israel, in no uncertain terms, their title deed to the land of promise. In spite of unfaithfulness and unbelief, as manifested so frequently in Israel's history from the time of the promise to Abraham until that time, the covenant was not abrogated. The land was still theirs by promise** (*Things to Come,* p. 96).

2. THE SCEPTRE PROMISE:

"And in thee shall all the families of the earth be blessed"—The spiritual promise of *grace*. This same promise is repeated in Genesis 22:18; **"in thy seed shall all the Nations of the earth be blessed."**

This particular **"one seed"** refers to Christ as made evident in (Galatians 3:8,16). This is a *spiritual* promise of *grace* or salvation through Jesus Christ, mankind's Messiah. This is our only hope of eternal life independent of nationality.

ISAAC AND ISHMAEL

Both the Birthright and Septre promise were unconditionally made to Abraham. These same promises were re-promised to Abraham's son Isaac, notice:

> **...I will be with thee, and will bless thee; for unto thee, and unto thy seed, I will give all these countries, and I will perform the oath which I sware unto Abraham thy father; And I will make thy seed to multiply as the stars of heaven, and will give unto thy seed all these countries; and in thy seed shall all the nations of the earth be blessed (Gen. 26:3-4).**

Generally, the eldest son of each family automatically inherited the Birthright, unless God intervened by divine providence, which He did three times.

Ishmael was Abraham's eldest son born of Hagor, Sarah's Egyptian handmaid and therefore the legal Birthright inheritor. Although Abraham desired Ishmael to have the Birthright promise, God chose Isaac to inherit both promises. Thus, **"Abraham gave all that he had unto Isaac" (Gen. 25:5).**

But God had mercy upon Ishmael and made a separate promise to him as recorded in Genesis 17:19-21:

> **And God said, Sarah thy wife shall bear a son indeed; and thou shalt call his name Isaac: and I**

> will establish my covenant with him for an everlasting covenant, and with his seed after him. And as for Ishmael, I will make him fruitful, and will multiply him exceedingly...and I will make him a great nation. But my covenant will I establish with Isaac...

The angel of the Eternal told Hagar what was going to be the characteristic of the nation to come from Ishmael: **"..he will be a wild man; his hand will be against every man, and every man's hand against him; and he shall dwell in the presence [to the east] of all his brethren" (Gen. 16:12).**

Let's summarize: 1) Ishmael's descendants were to become a great nation but the Birthright nations were to be greater and, 2) they were to dwell to the east of their brethren—that is of Isaac's descendants who had the Birthright. The children of Ishmael have become the Arabs of today as most Bible students realize. The Birthright nations must dwell geographically West of the Arab nations and be larger, wealthier and more powerful. Few realize that the contention in the Middle East today is the same struggle over the Birthright between Jews and Arabs that existed between Isaac and Ishmael.

Finally, the promise of Birthright and Septre were confirmed and elaborated upon to Isaac's son Jacob as we read in Genesis 35:9-12:

> And God appeared unto Jacob...And God said unto him, Thy name is Jacob: thy name shall not be called any more Jacob, but Israel shall be thy name: and he called his name Israel. And God said unto him, I am God Almighty: be fruitful and multiply; and *a nation* and *company of nations* shall be of thee, and kings shall come out of thy loins. And the land which I gave Abraham and Isaac, to thee I will give it, and to thy seed after thee will I give the land.

Here we find that the **"many nations"** to spring from Abraham are to culminate into *one* supreme, wealthy, powerful nation and a company or group or *commonwealth* of nations!

Esau and Jacob were twins, born of Isaac's wife Rebekah.

Esau was the firstborn and therefore the legal inheritor of the Birthright, but he sold it to his brother for a bowel of pottage.

Previous to their birth, God had chosen Jacob to inherit the Birthright and Septre promises, but impatient Jacob, encouraged by his mother, deceived Esau into selling his Birthright for a measly bowel of pottage.

God had already revealed the character of the two nations to descend from these brothers to their mother, God said: **"Two nations are in thy womb...the one people shall be stronger than the other people; and the elder [Esau] shall serve the younger"** (vs. 23).

Just as the two brothers were different in physical characteristics [Esau was hairy and red], so would be the manner of the nations descending from them (vs. 25).

The nation to come out of Esau can be determined from the story in which he sold his Birthright; let's read it:

> **And the boys grew: and Esau was a cunning hunter, a man of the field; and Jacob was a plain man, dwelling in tents. And Isaac loved Esau, because he did eat of his venison: but Rebekah loved Jacob. And Jacob sod pottage [boiled porridge—see** *Fenton's* **translation]; and Esau came from the field, and he was faint: and Esau said to Jacob, Feed me, I pray thee, with that same red pottage; for I am faint: therefore was his name called** *Edom* **(Gen. 25:27-30).**

As most Bible scholars realize, the nation of Edom refers to the Turkish nation of today, Esau's descendants.

The very name Jacob means "supplanter" and depicts the very deceptive nature in which he acquired the Birthright promise from Esau. If Jacob had trusted in God to secure the Birthright for him, he would have received it in a more honorable way. But after several years of testing Jacob; God changed his name from Jacob, meaning "supplanter", to Israel, meaning "overcomer with God."

Jacob's character had changed as indicated by the wrestling match with God in which he "prevailed" all night (Gen. 32:24-29).

This entire intriguing account of Jacob and Esau is recorded in (Genesis 25:21-34).

THE RESTORATION OF ISRAEL

JUDAH AND JOSEPH

Now comes a most interesting surprise. After God had given *both* Birthright and Septre promises to Abraham, Isaac and Jacob, He now separated these two promises. Jacob or "Israel" had 12 children which became known as "the children of Israel." God now gave the Sceptre promise to Jacob's son Judah (Gen. 49:10) and the Birthright promise to Jacob's son Joseph (1 Chron. 5:2).

So, the Sceptre promise of GRACE through Jesus Christ was given to Judah in which the kingly line of the House of David would conceive the Messiah.

Here is an amazing truth that very few understand and yet is the *key* to understanding all prophecy. The only tribe of the children of Israel that became known as "Jews" was that of Judah. It was Judah's nickname. King David descended from this line as well as did Jesus Christ. That's why Christ was called a Jew!

But the Birthright promise did not go to the tribe of Judah. It went to the tribe of Joseph who were not Jews!

Although Jacob's firstborn was Reuben by his first wife Leah; he forfeited the Birthright to Joseph, eleventh-born of Jacob, but firstborn of Jacob's second wife Rachel. Reuben defiled his father's bed and therefore lost the Birthright (1 Chron. 5:1-2).

THE OLD COVENANT

Joseph had been Jacob's favorite son and the envy of his eleven brothers (Gen. 37:3). One day, Joseph told his father of some wrong things his brothers had done, and this only added more fuel toward their burning animosity toward Joseph. Besides this, Joseph had told them of visions he had in which he was going to be a very prominent individual some day and that his brothers would look to him as a leader of great importance (Gen. 37:5-11).

It wasn't long after these things took place that Joseph was sold by his brothers without their father's knowledge, to a caravan of Midianites on their way to Egypt. He was sold to the Midianites for twenty pieces of silver (Gen. 37:28) and resold to Potiphar, an officer of Pharaoh's army in Egypt (Gen. 37:36).

Joseph wasn't in Egypt very long before he was recognized as one who had great understanding in the interpretation of dreams (Gen. 40).

One day the Pharaoh had a dream in which Joseph was called

upon to interpret it. Joseph told the Pharaoh that there was going to be seven good years followed by seven years of famine in the land. Quickly realizing Joseph's talent for understanding dreams, the Pharaoh appointed Joseph second in rank under Pharaoh and he was given the authority to implement a plan for the stockpiling of grain in granaries. This plan proved to save thousands of lives during the seven years of famine (Gen. 41).

This famine was widespread in all the lands, yet in Egypt there was plenty of food (Gen. 41:54). Soon other nations came to Egypt to buy corn (vs. 57).

Shortly after, Joseph's brothers came to buy food in Egypt as Joseph had envisioned; and they did look to him as a person of prominence. Amends were made between the brothers in a happy reunion (Gen. 45:1-2).

Before long, Jacob and all his sons and their families journeyed to Egypt for permanent residence (Gen. 45:27-28).

While in Egypt, the children of Israel numbered near two and three million people in about two and a quarter centuries.

But despite all the good Joseph had done for the Egyptians, the children of Israel became slaves to the Egyptians after Joseph's death:

> **And Joseph died, and all his brethren, and all that generation. And the children of Israel were fruitful, and increased abundantly, and multiplied, and waxed exceedingly mighty; and the land was filled with them. Now there arose a new king over Egypt, which knew not Joseph. And he said unto his people, Behold, the people of the children of Israel are more and mightier than we: Come on, let us deal wisely with them; lest they multiply, and it come to pass, that, when there falleth out any war, they join also unto our enemies, and fight against us, and so get them up out of the land. Therefore they did set over them taskmasters to afflict them with their burdens. And they built for Pharaoh treasure cities, Pithom and Ramses. But the more they afflicted them, the more they multiplied and grew. And they were grieved because of the children of Israel. And the**

> Egyptians made the children of Israel to serve with rigour: And they made their lives bitter with hard bondage, in morter, and in brick, and in all manner of service, wherein they made them serve, was with rigour (Ex. 1:6-14).

Finally, Moses was chosen of God to lead His people out of this bondage and into the land He promised Abraham. The children of Israel left Egypt with about 600,000 men (Ex. 12:37-39).

God made a covenant with Israel when they reached Mt. Sinai in the peninsula wilderness. Thus, the Old Covenant was made, establishing Israel as God's chosen nation among all the nations of the earth.

Israel's government was a theocracy [a government of a state by immediate divine guidance by it's leaders]. It contained civil, spiritual and religious laws dictated from God via Moses and the priestly Levite tribe.

GOD WAS ISRAEL'S FIRST KING

Israel's first king was God and He instituted His laws through a system of judges for 450 years (Acts 13:20). Then Israel desired a physical king that they could see; so God obliged by giving them Saul.

After Saul was removed from office because of rebellion (1 Sam. 15:23) God raised up David to be Israel's new king (Acts 13:22).

During this time, each tribe was independent, yet united they formed *one* nation in the same manner the United States is one nation composed of separate states.

When king David died, his son Solomon succeeded him to rule over Israel. But Solomon did not keep God's covenant or statutes, so God told him:

> ...I will surely rend the kingdom from thee, and give it to thy servant. Notwithstanding in thy days I will not do it for David thy father's sake: but I will rend it out of the hand of thy son. Howbeit I will not rend away all the kingdom; but will give *one tribe* to thy son for David my

THE OLD COVENANT MARRIAGE

servant's sake, and *for Jerusalem's sake which I have chosen* (1 Kings 11:11-13).

Notice the special significance God places upon Judah and Jerusalem! Except for *one tribe* [Judah] to carry out the Sceptre promise, God was going to rend the kingdom of Israel. We read in (1 Kings 11:26) where Jeroboam, the son of Nebat, an Ephraimite was made ruler over the "house of Joseph."

The northern 10 tribes became known as Israel—with Jeroboam as it's king, while the southern nation composed of Judah, Benjamin and some of the priestly Levites intermingling—became known as the nation of Judah. Solomon's son Reoboam was Judah's king, maintaining the kingly line as God had said *one tribe* would fulfill his promise to David.

Therefore, the name "Jew" became associated with the nation of Judah. The fact that the nation of Israel was not Jewish is clearly revealed in (11 Kings 16:6), where the nation of Israel was fighting "Jews." Israel and Judah remained separate nations with their own kings for many years.

The nation of Israel was taken captive in 721 B.C. by the Asseryians (11 Kings 17:23) while the nation of Judah was taken captive in 606 B.C. by the Babylonians (11 Kings 23:27).

JEWS AND ISRAELITES

The Septre promise of the kingly line to progenate the Savior of mankind would stem from the tribe of Judah.

No place in the Bible does the term "Israel" refer to the Jews exclusively. When the sense is not national but individual, the term "Israel" alone, or "children of Israel," or "men of Israel," may, and sometimes does refer to or include the Jews. Such an expression, for instance, as "Ye men of Israel," as frequently occurs in the New Testament, refers to Israelites as individuals in a collective sense, not a national sense. It usually refers to Jews as individual descendants of the patriarch Israel [Jacob].

Technically, Moses, Abraham, Isaac, Jacob, Adam and Noah were not Jews! Moses was a Levite and Abraham was a Hebrew (Gen. 14:13). Only the tribe of Judah which descended from Jacob's son Judah are "Jews" racially. The tribe of Benjamin and the scattered priestly tribe of Levi became "Jews" nationally when they became part of the nation of Judah.

THE RESTORATION OF ISRAEL

Just as all New Yorkers are Americans, but not all Americans are New Yorkers, so all Jews are Israelites, but not all Israelites are Jews!

Further, the Birthright promise of national wealth and prosperity to a great nation and a commonwealth of nations— was promised to the tribe of Joseph.

EPHRAIM AND MANASSEH

The descendants of Joseph as well as the Birthright promise finally culminated in the two tribes Ephraim and Manasseh, the two sons of Joseph.

When Jacob [Israel] was on his death bed, he placed his hands on the head of Ephraim and Manasseh and said:

> **...and let my name be named on them, and the name of my fathers Abraham and Isaac; and let them grow into a multitude in the midst of the earth. And when Joseph saw that his father laid his right hand upon the head of Ephraim, it displeased him: and he held up his father's hand, to remove it from Ephraim's head unto Manasseh's head. And Joseph said unto his father, Not so, my father: for this is the firstborn; put thy right hand upon his head. And his father refused, and said, I know it, my son, I know it: he also shall become a people, and he also shall be great: but truly his younger brother shall be greater than he, and his seed shall become a multitude of nations (Gen. 48:16-19).**

THE NATIONAL IDENTITY OF JACOB'S SONS

Remember there were twelve original sons from Jacob's four wives. Joseph was one of his original twelve sons. Jacob adopted Joseph's two sons, Ephraim and Manasseh and gave his name, Jacob or "Israel" to them [Ephraim and Manasseh].

THE OLD COVENANT MARRIAGE

GOD'S COVENANT WITH DAVID

God's Covenant with David was that there would never be a generation when a descendant of David's would not sit on God's Throne ruling over the House of Israel (11 Sam. 23:1, 5 and 11 Sam. 7:4-5, 12-16). Where?

Where David was to build God's house or Temple (11 Sam. 7:5). Notice further that once established, God said of His people:

> **...moreover I will appoint a place for my people Israel, and will plant them, that they may dwell in a place of their own,** *and move no more*; **neither shall the children of wickedness afflict them any more, as beforetime (11 Sam. 7:10).**

Clearly, God was going to place David's descendants in Jerusalem for an everlasting inheritance! This covenant relates to the promise to Abraham; but is a separate promise between David and God for his obedience!

CHRIST THE ONE SEED

1 Sam.18:4-9 — Israel's first King was God or the personage that later became Jesus Christ. He sat on Israel's throne first and He will sit on Israel's throne last! See also (Jn. 1:1-2,14; 17:5;1 Cor. 10:4).

Rev. 22:16 — Christ is both the root and offspring of King David therefore:

Lk. 19:12 — Jesus is pictured as a nobleman who went into a far country [heaven] to get Himself a kingdom and then to return.

Lk. 1:31-33 — Jesus Christ will then take over the throne He left, the throne of David FOREVER!

THE RESTORATION OF ISRAEL

JEREMIAH'S COMMISSION

Jer. 1:5   The Bible mentions only three men who were sanctified [set apart] for a chosen office before their actual birth. They are John the Baptist, Jesus and Jeremiah.

Jer. 1:9 10   Of Jeremiah's commission we read: ."..And the Lord said unto me, Behold, I have put my words in thy mouth. See, I have this day set thee over the nations and over the kingdoms, to root out, and to pull down, and to destroy, and to throw down, to build, and to plant." Jeremiah's commission was to 1) pluck up or root out or pull down or to overthrow, 2) to build and plant.

Jer. 1:2   Jeremiah was God's prophet to warn the nation of Judah of their transgressions against God's government and ways. If they did not repent, God would have them taken captive!

Jer. 1:14   "Then the LORD said unto me, Out of the north an evil shall break forth upon all the inhabitants of the land." God was going to use "an evil out of the north" to destroy Judah.

JUDAH TAKEN CAPTIVE BY BABYLON

11 Kings 17:18   After Israel's captivity by Asseryia in 721 B.C. only the nation of Judah remained.

11 Kings 23:27   But Judah went the same way as Israel, therefore God said, ."..I will remove Judah also out of my sight, as I have removed Israel, and will cast off *this city Jerusalem which I have chosen*, and the house of which I said, My name shall be there." Judah was taken in three sieges by Babylon; the first in 604 B.C. and the last 19 years later in 585 B.C.

THE OLD COVENANT MARRIAGE

Jer. 39:1-7   The last king of Judah before their captivity to Babylon was Zedekiah. King Nebuchadnezzar of Babylon had his eyes put out and all of Zedikiah's sons killed.

Jer. 52:1-11   King Zedekiah died in prison. Thus, the first part of Jeremiah's commission was accomplished as Judah was "pulled down" or "overthrown."

TO BUILD AND TO REPLANT

Jer. 39:11-12   The next part of Jeremiah's commission was to "replant." Jeremiah was one of the Jewish captives at Jerusalem, not Babylon. Nebuchadnezzar, the king, gave charge concerning Jeremiah to his guard Nebuzaradan, saying: "Take him, and look well to him, and do him no harm; but do unto him even as he shall say unto thee."

Jer. 40:1-5   Nebuzaradan gave Jeremiah money and let him go. Jeremiah went to Mispah (near Jerusalem) unto Gidaliah who had been made governor of Mispah by Nebuchadnezzar. Mispah was the headquarters for the remaining Jews after Jerusalem was finally destroyed. But the king of Ammon plotted with a Jew named Ishmael to assassinate Gedaliah. The plot was executed; the governor and part of the Jews were slain. Jeremiah was among the survivors. See also (Jer. 40:6).

Jer. 41:10   "Then Ishmael carried away captive all the residue of the people that were in Mizpah, even *the king's daughters*, and all the people that remained in Mizpah, whom Nebuzaradan the captain of the guard had committed to Gedaliah the son of Ahikam: and Ishamel the son of Nethaniah carried them away captive, and departed to go over to the Ammonites."

Jer. 42:2-3   Johanan replaced Ishmael as leader and feared

THE RESTORATION OF ISRAEL

	reprisals from Nebuchadnezzar and wanted to flee Egypt.
Jer. 42:7-16	Jeremiah tried to tell the people that God would protect them if they did not enter into Egypt. But if they did, then the sword would overtake them.
Jer. 43:2-4	But Johana said Jeremiah was lying and convinced the people to go.
Jer. 43:4-7"	So Johanan the son of Kareah, and all the captains of the forces, and all the people, obeyed not the voice of the LORD, to dwell in the land of Judah. But Johanan the son of Kareah, and all the captains of the forces, took all the remnant of Judah, that were returned from all nations, whither they had been driven, to dwell in the land of Judah. Even men, and women, and children, and *the king's daughters*, and every person that Nebuzardan the captain of the guard had left with Gedaliah the son of Ahikam the son of Shaphan, and Jeremiah the prophet, and Baruch the son of Neriah. So they came into the land of Egypt: for they obeyed not the voice of the LORD..."
Jer. 44:10-28	"Therefore thus saith the LORD of hosts, the God of Israel Behold, I will set my face against you for evil, and to cut off all Judah. And I will take the remnant of Judah, that have set their faces to go into the land of Egypt to sojourn there, and they shall all be consumed...For I will punish them that dwell in the land of Egypt...(Verse 28): "Yet a small number that escape the sword shall return out of the land of Egypt into the land of Judah, and all the remnant of Judah, that are gone into the land of Egypt to sojourn there, shall know whose words shall stand, mine, or their's."
Jer. 45:2-5	Baruch was one of the remnant that was to

escape of the house of Judah to fulfill God's purpose of "bearing fruit upward."

Isa. 37:31, 32   "And the remnant that is escaped of the house of Judah shall again take root downward, and bear fruit upward: For out of Jerusalem shall go forth a remnant, and they that escape out of mount Zion: the zeal of the Lord of hosts shall do this." See also (11 Kings 19:30).

THE MYSTERIOUS "BREACH"

Jacob's son Judah to whom the Sceptre promise fell, had twin sons, Zarah and Pharez. As with the Birthright promise, the firstborn would be "royal seed" through which the Sceptre promise would be delivered.

The delivery of these two twins is most interesting and is recorded in (Genesis 38:27-30). It portrays what was to befall the two brothers in prophecy years later.

The account states that prior to the birth of the twins, one of them **"put out his hand: and the midwife took and bound upon his hand a scarlet thread, saying, 'This came out first': But the child drew back his hand"**, and the other was actually born first.

Said the midwife: "How hast thou broken forth? This breach be upon thee: [margin-wherefore hast thou made this breach against thee?]. This twin was named Pharez, meaning "Breach", while the other twin was named Zarah.

This was indeed an unusual event that occurred in biblical history, yet this mysterious breach was to be healed between Zarah and Pharez or their descendants in the future.

This healing never occurred in their lifetime, but Zarah of the scarlet thread had five sons as recorded in (1 Chronicles 2:6). A descendant of the Zarah lineage did finally rule on the house of King David, thus *healing* the breach.

King David and king Zedekiah were all of the Pharez line as was Jesus Christ. Therefore, this breach was not healed at this time.

The breach or transfer of the Sceptre promise from the Pharez line to the Zarah line had to occur sometime after Judah's last king [Zedekiah] was dethroned!

Because David's line [Pharez] was to remain on the throne for

THE RESTORATION OF ISRAEL

ALL generations [FOREVER], the healing of the breach could only happen by a marriage between the Pharez heir to the throne and one of the Zarah line, thus healing the breach!

MARKS OF ISRAEL'S IDENTITY

The "Nation" and "Commonwealth of Nations" promised Abraham must contain the following scriptural description:

1) Israel must be a "Nation and a Company of Nations" (Gen. 35:11).
2) Israel must exist as a "nation" for ever (Jer. 31:35-37; 33:20-26).
3) Israel must have a nation springing from them yet entirely independent of them (Gen. 48:19).
4) Israel must be an island nation (Jer. 31:10; Isa. 41:1; 42:12; 11:11; 24:14-15; 49:1,3,12).
5) Israel's islands must be North and West from Palestine (Jer. 3:12, 23:8; Isa. 49:12).
6) Israel would always have a descendant of David reigning over them forever (1 Chron. 22:10; 2 Chron. 13:5; Jer. 33:17, 19-26; 2 Sam. 7:13-16).
7) Israel would be as the sand of the sea or have a great population (Hosea 1:10; Gen. 22:17; 32:12).
8) Israel would be as the sand of the sea or have a great population Gen. 22:17;32:12).(Hosea 1:10;
9) Israel must be extremely wealthy (Deut. 8:18).
10) Israel would lend to outside nations but never borrow from them (Deut. 15:6).
11) Israel must have abolished slavery (Isa..58:6).
12) Israel must have the finest fruit and cattle of the earth (Deut. 28:4).
13) Israel's national emblem must include the Lion and the Unicorn (Num. 24:8,9).
14) Israel must be a great missionary people (Isa. 27:6; 43:21; Matt. 7:20, Mk. 16:15).
15) Israel must speak another language other than Hebrew (Isa. 28:11).
16) Israel must be a Christian nation (Hosea 1:10; Isa. 9:2,8; 45:17-19, 25; 48:20; 49:3).
17) Israel must posses the gates of their enemies (Gen.

THE OLD COVENANT MARRIAGE

22:17,18).
18) Israel must be a very powerful nation (Isa. 41:11, 12).
19) Israel must be successful in war (Numbers 24:8).
20) Israel's preservation will be due to Divine intervention and protection against her foes (Psalm 124; Isa. 54:15,17).
21) Israel was to be used in war to destroy heathen nations (Jer. 51:20, Dan. 2:44).
22) Dan to leave a serpents trail (Gen. 49:17). The dying Jacob prophesied this would be a characteristic of the tribe of Dan in the last days (Gen. 49:1). Dan named places after their father as they traveled (Judges 18:11-12, 29, Joshua 19:47).

In Hebrew, there are no vowels as in the English language and therefore vowels were added by others. Dan, Din, Den, Dun and Don are all corruptions of the Hebrew name for Dn. Before the captivity of Israel, the tribe of Dan occupied *two* different districts or provinces in the Holy land (Judges 5:17). One of these colonies lived on the sea coast of Palestine, Notice: "Dan remain [abode] in ships."

There is speculative history that when Assyria captured Israel, these Danites struck out in their ships and sailed west through the mediterranean, and north to Ireland. Irish annals and history show that the new settlers of Ireland, at around 700 B.C. were the "Tuatha de Danaans," which means "Tribe of Dan." Dan's serpent trail is all over Ireland in such names as "Dans-Laugh", "Dan-Sower",'Dun-dolke","Dun-drum","Dan-egal Bay", "Dun-glow",
"Lon-donderry", "Dun-gle", "Duns-more" [meaning, more Dans].

AN ALLEGORY OF THE TWO COVENANTS

There is an allegory of the two Covenants found in (Galatians 4:22-31), notice:

> **For it is written, that Abraham had two sons, the one by a bondmaid, the other by a freewoman. But he who was of the bondwoman [Ishmael born of Hagar] was born after the flesh...**

Notice, the Old Covenant is described as a fleshly Covenant. A carnal Covenant for fleshly, physical carnal people without

God's Holy Spirit, and human nature to conquer.

The Old Covenant was based on physical promises [of protection, food, etc.] if they would keep the physical part of the Ten Commandments [the letter of the Law].

It had physical men [the Levites] carrying out the administration to teach them *obedience* to God's Laws. They used physical ritualistic ceremonies [sacrifices, meat and drink offerings]—carnal fleshly ordinances to teach a physical carnal minded nation obedience to God's Laws. They were a schoolmaster—and like any *schoolmaster* they teach people obedience or discipline! The Old Covenant was based on the promise to Abraham [Birthright], purely temporal, physical, and national!

Continuing in Galatians 4:3:

> **...but he of the freewoman was by promise. Which things are an allegory: for these are the two Covenants, the one from the mount Sinae, which gendereth to bondage, which is Hagar." (Vs. 28): "Now we, brethren, as Isaac was, are the children of promise.**

Isaac was promised to Abraham when Abraham was 100 years old—and under the New Testament, Christians are promised better promises! (Heb. 8:6-10, 9:15). We are promised God's Holy Spirit that gives Eternal Life! The New Covenant was based on the Septre promise to Abraham, of Grace through Jesus Christ, and the gift of Eternal Life!

SUMMARY

God made a two-fold promise to faithful Abraham, that of Birthright and Septre. The Birthright and Septre promise was given to Isaac, then Jacob. Finally, these promises divided and the Septre promise was given to Judah, while the Birthright promise was given to Joseph.

The Birthright promise was further separated into Manasseh [a Great nation] and Ephraim [a Commonwealth of nations], the two sons of Joseph. Several books have been written that have speculated the promises of Birthright were fulfilled in the United States and the British Commonwealth (*Judah's Sceptre and*

THE OLD COVENANT MARRIAGE

Joseph's Birthright by J.H. Allen).

Birthright, as defined, has only to do with national wealth and prosperity to flesh and blood seed by right of birth. As this promise was passed down to generations, it eventually becomes a national inheritance.

The Septre promise that the Messiah would come out of "the seed" of Abraham was fulfilled in the House of David, the kingly line from Judah. Although eternal life would come from the seed of Judah, no one could receive eternal life as an inherent right of nationality.

If this were possible, salvation would not be of grace but of natural birth. Only material possessions can be acquired by heredity through RACE, but GRACE is a spiritual blessing independent of nationality.

There is yet a vital difference between Birthright by Race and eternal life by Grace. There are no stipulations on the eldest son inheriting the physical birthright blessing of his father. He is the recipient with no strings attached and has done nothing to earn it or qualify for it.

The gift of eternal life however, DOES have stipulations and qualifications. Grace means undeserved or unmerited pardon and you do not have a right to receive the gift of eternal life except by God's GRACE. Can you imagine the consequences of giving someone eternal life as a result of nationality?

Part of the Birthright promise to Abraham was the land of Palestine, as we read in Genesis 12:6-7: ."..**and Abram passed through the land unto the place of Sichem, unto the plain of Moreh. And the Canaanite was then in the land. And the Eternal appeared unto Abram, and said, unto thy seed will I give this land.**" So the promise was the inheritance of the Land of Palestine. "**And the Eternal said unto Abram...Lift up now thine eyes and look from the place where thou art Northward, and Southward, and Eastward, and Westward; For all the land which thou seest, to thee will I give it, and to thy seed Forever.**"

The land where Abram was, is the land of Canaan, called Palestine today. That, then, is the promised land—that's why it's called the promised land! That's why it's called "the apple of God's eye" and will be the focal point of God's end-time prophecies!

But for how long? Forever! The inheritance is to be an eternal inheritance, which of necessity involves and includes Everlasting

THE RESTORATION OF ISRAEL

Life!

Upon reading the promises God made to Abraham, and studying the prophecies dealing with the preservation of these promises, we may draw the following conclusions and end-time observations: 1) the nation of Israel will be plucked out of her land because of rebelliousness (Deut. 28:63-68); 2) there will be a future forgiveness and atonement of the nation of Israel (Deut. 28:63-68; 30:1-3); 3) Israel's deliverer [Messiah] will return (Deut. 30:3-6); 4) the nation of Israel will be brought back to her God-given land (Deut. 30:5); 5) conversion of the nation of Israel will transpire (Deut. 30:4-8; Rom. 11:26-27); 6) Israel's enemies will be judged and punished (Deut. 30:7); 7) finally the nation of Israel will be a blessed people, receiving her rightful blessing (Deut. 30:9).

To Israel, the Jubilee Year envisioned the time when the Messiah would restore again their kingdom—by allowing them to maintain possession of the land promised their father Abraham.

Daniel's Seventy Weeks Prophecy has tremendous importance in this regard, and is a pivotal prophecy in the Bible. We will study many aspects of this prophecy throughout this book. This will be the fulfillment of the Jubilee in their future Messianic Kingdom!

Throughout the remainder of this book, we shall read how God has revealed the way for Israel's regeneration, repentance, forgiveness, justification, and the pouring out of His Holy Spirit. We will read *how* God will RESTORE His holy nation to the place where He blessed Abraham—all founded on the ministry, and blood of our Savior Jesus Christ.

Chapter Two

> *Turn, O backsliding children, saith the LORD; for I am married unto you: and I will take you one of a city, and two of a family, and I will bring you to Zion...*
> —*Jer. 3:14.*

GOD'S MARRIAGE TO ISRAEL

At Mt. Sinai, God set up an organization. At that time God's people—the only people on earth who were the people of God were formed into a nation. As such, they had laws, and government.

They were literally a *kingdom on earth*!

First of all, they formed a civil government. But in this government, God also placed certain church governments, giving them the rituals, ceremonies, and sacrifices of the "law of Moses." Church and state were inseparable.

This was the start of God's Church, **"The Church in the Wilderness" (Acts 7:38).** A fact that many have failed to notice is that the Old Covenant was also a MARRIAGE COMPACT!

When God first set up an organization on earth, the people who formed this organization were MARRIED to the Lord. It was this marriage that bound Him and His people together! In (Jeremiah 3:14) the Lord warned His wife: **"Turn O backsliding Children, saith the Lord, for I am *Married unto You."***

The making of the Old Covenant, as recorded in the 24th

THE RESTORATION OF ISRAEL

chapter of Exodus, was the *marriage ceremony*. If anyone may doubt this, let us merely ask, *when*, if not here, did the Lord ever enter into a marriage ceremony, joining Himself and His people together as Husband and wife? Where else, in all the Bible, can you find any account of a marriage ceremony?

The *marriage ceremony* was the Old Covenant ceremony! They are one and the same! It was this marriage, then, that established *organization* and *government* among God's people!

Every marriage is based on law—else it would not be legal. The 10 Commandments, God's statutes and judgments were only the terms and conditions—the basis—of that marriage contract.

The Eternal [Lord] of the Old Covenant, as the Husband, promised to provide for and protect the nation or congregation of Israel. The nation Israel in turn agreed to remain faithful always to Him. God agreed to perform the duties of a husband, to provide for and bless her. The people of Israel accepted the terms that God gave them. They bound themselves by the Old Covenant to refrain from any adulterous or whorish relations with the false gods of other nations—and to remain chaste and acceptable to their own "husband" (Ex. 34:12-17).

THE LORD DIVORCED HIS WIFE

In the space of at least nine short months after Israel had agreed to the covenant, the people had failed so badly to live by the conditions of the covenant that the Lord, her husband, found it necessary to correct His wife.

The Israelites, being without the Spirit of God, were constantly rebelling—sinning—against their "husband"—and the 10 Commandment Law He had given them (Ezek. 20:13).

The Eternal then added temporary "ritualistic laws" for them to keep because of their rebellion, to impress upon them the weakness of their own inherent *human nature* in respect to keeping God's Law (Lev. 1:1-9).

But ancient Israel continued to be disobedient and UNFAITHFUL to her husband. She broke her part of the marriage contract! She turned from worshipping God, and followed the customs of the heathen—serving other gods! She broke her part of the marriage covenant by committing *spiritual adultery*!

Because God is Holy, He does not "co-exist" with sin! Therefore, He was forced to separate His "wife"—ancient Israel,

THE OLD COVENANT MARRIAGE

from Himself (Isa. 50:1; 59:1-2; Jer. 3:6,8).

Even though God had given Israel a bill of divorcement for her sins, God was, however, not free to "marry" again, according to the marriage Law! Adultery is not necessarily a cause for the dissolution of a marriage. That's why the Eternal said, **"I am (still) married unto you" (Jer. 3:14).**

JESUS WAS MARRIED TO ISRAEL

Jesus Christ is the Father's Spokesman—the "Word" of the God family. Realize that Jesus is the "Lord" of the Old Covenant—the One who did the speaking at creation! God the Father planned the universe and Jesus—before His human birth—spoke, and the creation was done by the power of the Spirit of God!

Jesus—the Word—therefore created everything (Jn. 1:3; Col. 1:16). He made the first man and woman and He established the marriage relationship (Gen. 2:21-25).

It was the One who later came as Jesus Christ, the "Lord" who spoke the Ten Commandments on Mount Sinai (Ex. 20:1-2)—for no man has ever seen or heard the Father (Jn. 1:18; 5:37; 6:46; 4:20).

It was the Word that became Jesus Christ that followed Israel (1 Cor. 10:4).

The Lord—the human Jesus Christ of the New Testament, was still bound by His part of the conditions of the marriage contract. That is one reason why Christ never got married when He was in the flesh—for He was already married!

These conditions were, however, limited by death! Only the death of one of the partners of a marriage covenant can sever the marriage relationship—for marriage is binding until death!

JESUS CAME TO HIS WIFE

Jesus' disciples understood that the *Kingdom*, with all authority to govern, whether civil or church government, had been taken away from their people, and turned over to Gentiles. You'll remember how they asked Him, **"Lord, wilt thou at this time restore again the kingdom to Israel?" (Acts 1:6).**

Jesus came to His own [the nation of Israel] first, or to His wife! (Jn. 1:11). Realize, all the apostles were Jews! The gospel was to go to the Jew first (Rom. 1:16). Jesus said He was sent unto

THE RESTORATION OF ISRAEL

the house of Israel! (Matt. 15:24). He told His disciples not to go to the Gentiles or the Samaritans—but to *the house of Israel*! (Matt. 10:5). The early Church was composed solely of Jews on the day of Pentecost! (Acts 2:5). See also (Acts 3:25, 26; 13:36).

The parable of the Vineyard in (Matthew 21) is very graphic in explaining the transfer of the Kingdom to another nation [the Church]. Jesus said to them,

> **Did you never read in the scriptures, The very stone which the builders rejected has become the head of the corner; this was the Lord's doing...Therefore I tell you *the kingdom of God will be taken away from You and given to a nation producing the fruits of it* (Matt. 21:42-43).**

This parable graphically shows that God had given a kingdom to the Israelites (notice vs. 45—the chief priests and Pharisees knew Jesus was talking about them) who had killed God's servants [the prophets He sent them including His Son], and so now God was going to give the kingdom over to a nation that would bring forth fruit [spiritual works].

God sent Moses, Isaiah and many other prophets to Israel (Rom. 10:1821; 11:1-3), but they were still disobedient and killed God's prophets (Matt. 23:37).

When Israel went whoring after the ways of other nations, breaking the Commandments—God DIVORCED Israel, and gave over the government [which included Church government as well as state] to the Gentile kingdom's *symbolized* by Daniel's image and the four "beasts." He gave the government into Gentile hands for 2520 years *until* the second coming of Christ—when the government, church and state, shall be *restored* to Israel!

THE PRUNING OF GOD'S OLIVE TREE

The expression, "times of the Gentiles," refers to the entire period of Gentile supremacy, dating from Nebuchadnezzar's Babylonian invasion and captivity of Judah in 606 B.C. to the time when a supernatural Stone from heaven [Jesus Christ] smashes the image on its toes. Upon Jesus' second advent, He will restore the government of God to Israel! But that process has already begun starting in 1948 when the Jews were allowed to return to their

THE OLD COVENANT MARRIAGE

homeland!

The Tribulation period, lasting forty-two months, or three and one half years, will be the most severe period of Gentile rule and treading down of Israel. God's holy city will be invaded by Gentile forces killing thousands of God's people in Jerusalem!

The apostle Paul points out in (Romans 9) that even though God made a promise to Abraham and his seed [the children of Israel]—He could have mercy on Gentiles and make them His people also (vss. 24-26).

In (Romans 11), God shows that the Gentiles can be adopted into His family through the *analogy* of wild olive trees (Gentiles) being grafted into branches that were broken off [Israelites]. Furthermore, the branches that were "cut off" [Israelites] can also be "grafted back" into God's Vineyard or Kingdom. And so all Israel shall some day be saved (vs. 26).

Thus, Gentiles can be grafted in or adopted into God's family, through the *acceptance* of Jesus Christ and thereby become the seed of Abraham spiritually (Gal. 3:29).

Gentiles become "spiritual Jews" by having a converted heart (Rom. 2:17-29; Gal. 5:1-12). Paul answers the question, "who are Israelites?" in (Romans 9:4). He says that not all that are of Israel [physical Israelites] are Israel (vs. 6), but the Children of Promise (vs. 8).

Make no mistake, the Church is *Israelitish*! Not just a Gentile Church just *called* "Israel"—it is ISRAEL! It is a spiritual nation, composed of individuals *personally* selected by God the Father!

They have become heirs of the same promises given to the nation of Israel. But those who do not come by faith, and who are disobedient, are *cut off*, [natural born Israelites] while Gentile converts, through Christ, are *adopted* into Israel. Thus, spiritually speaking, Israel is THE CHURCH!

Very few indeed understand this vital truth, and fewer understand the *purpose* for the Church. Basically, there are two reasons *why* Jesus built His Church. The two-fold purpose for the Church can be summarized as follows:

1) To preach the Gospel into all nations as a witness, which is the good news of God's soon coming Kingdom or restored government to the earth (Matt. 24:14).

2) To prepare individuals to *rule* with and under Christ in

God's Kingdom over all the nations of the earth. These individuals will be a chosen people comprising God's *family* who will judge angels as well as those resurrected under the White Throne Judgment (Rev. 2:26-27; 5:10; 19:16; 20:4).

CHRIST TO MARRY HIS WIFE

Jesus Christ's death on the stake at Golgotha freed Him from His first marriage contract with ancient Israel. Thus, the Old Covenant was ended and so was the marriage. Israel is free to marry again! Jesus' first coming was to *redeem* Israel, not to *restore* it.

Now to *whom* will Christ be married, at the Marriage of the Lamb? Notice it, in your own Bible—Revelation 19:7:

> **Let us be glad and rejoice, and give honor to him: for the marriage [supper] of the Lamb is come, and his wife hath made herself ready.**

And who will the New Covenant be made with? Read Hebrews 8:8 ."**..Behold, the days come, saith the Lord, when I will make a *new covenant with the house of Israel and with the house of Judah*."** Jesus is going to make a new covenant with the same wife He made the first covenant with, but later divorced!

Then He shall *restore* the Kingdom to Israel—both Church government, as well as state! The Church of the living God shall then become the Kingdom of God. It is the Church, composed of Jew and Gentile which shall be married to the Lamb, establishing God's government on earth, *restoring* the Kingdom to Israel!

So, the Church is God's instrumentally for overcoming the *fault* of the Old Covenant. That fault was *disobedience*. The New Covenant will be made with those in whose minds and hearts God's Law has been written, by His Holy Spirit! (Heb. 8:10).

Let's read some New Testament scriptures that prove the New Testament Church will become Christ's Wife. Paul marshals in impressive evidence concerning this subject in Ephesians 5:27:

> **That *he might present it to himself a glorious Church*, not having spot, or wrinkle, or any such thing, but that it should be holy and without blemish.**

THE OLD COVENANT MARRIAGE

Now, let's move to 11 Corinthians 11:2 for more proof:

> **For I am jealous over you with godly jealousy: for** *I have espoused you to one husband,* **that I may present you as a chaste virgin to Christ.**

Paul pounds the final nail into the coffin on this subject in Romans 7:4:

> **Wherefore, my brethren, ye also are become dead to the law by the body of Christ;** *that ye should be married to another, even to him who is raised from the dead,* **that we should bring forth fruit unto God.**

THE BRIDE AND THE BRIDEGROOM

There has been some confusion in recent years as to the identification of "the Body of Christ." The most common belief is that the New Testament Church will become "the Body" and "the Bride" of Christ spiritually. Others believe this would be impossible since "the Body" of Christ [the Bridegroom] is to marry "the Bride."

How then could they represent the same entity?

Still more confusing is the fact that ancient Israel was called "the Bride" of God (Isa. 5:6-8; 62:4-5; Jer. 3:14; Hosea 2:19,26). These and other passages clearly prophesy that *an election of Israel* shall be "the Bride."

We have already seen that had ancient Israel repented and turned to the Lord (Acts 3:18-19), there would have been no need to start the New Testament Church. All of the Old Testament prophecies concerning the Bride would have been fulfilled in ancient Israel!

Who then is going to be "the Bride" of Christ—Old Testament Israel or the New Testament Church? There cannot be TWO BRIDES for this would be spiritual polygamy!

THE RESTORATION OF ISRAEL

WHAT EKKLESIA MEANS

The Greek word for Church in the New Testament is *ekklesia*. This same Greek word is used 75 times in the *Septuagint* Translation of the Old Testament in describing five different Hebrew words.

However, it is used 70 times in describing the Hebrew word CAHAL, from which we have our English word "call." It simply means "to call together", "to assemble", or "gather together." This Hebrew word CAHAL occurs 123 times and is rendered; "congregation" 86 times; "assembly" 17; "company" 17; and "multitude" 3 times.

Its first occurrence is in (Genesis 28:3) in describing the Nation of Israel as "a called out people." Israel was a people "called out" and assembled from all other peoples.

When Jesus said, ."..**upon this rock I will build My Church**" [Greek *ekklesia*], He did not use this word in any "spiritual" sense, but rather that He was "calling out an assembly of people" for Himself.

This same Greek word *ekklesia* is used in (Acts 19:32) to also describe "unbelievers" who assembled together, proving that this word itself has no spiritual connotation. Thus, both ancient Israel and the New Testament Church were "called out peoples."

THE BODY OR BRIDEGROOM

There are many New Testament scriptures which show the New Testament Church to be represented spiritually as "the Body of Christ" as well. A case in point is found in 1 Corinthians 12:12-13:

> **For as the *body* is one, and has many members, and all the members of that *one body*, being many, are *one body*: so also is Christ. For by one spirit are we all baptized into *one body*, whether we be Jews or Gentiles, whether we be bond or free: and have been all made to drink into one spirit. For the body is not one member but many. (Vs. 27)** *Now we are the body of Christ,* **and members in particular. See also (Rom. 12:4-5; Eph. 4:16; Col. 1:24-27).**

Jesus Christ is the invisible head of the Body, notice:

> **...and hath put all things under His feet, and gave Him to be the head over all things to the Church [Greek *ekklesia*], which is *His body*, the fullness of Him that filleth all in all (Eph. 1:22-23—see also Col. 2:19).**

This New Testament Body is *symbolically* described in (Ephesians 4:13) as becoming unto "a perfect man."

THE "MYSTERY" OF CHRIST'S BODY

Jesus Christ had been promised to come as the Messiah by the Old Testament prophets (Rom. 1:1-2). But the MYSTERY of the Body of Christ had never been revealed, and did not therefore form the subject of Old Testament prophecy. It was the subject of a special revelation to the apostles and New Testament "Church of God" through the apostle Paul—to whom this MYSTERY was first announced.

Paul lets the spiritual genie out of the bottle in regards to this *mystery* in Colossians 1:24-27:

> **Who now rejoice in my sufferings for your sake, and fill up on my part that which is lacking of the afflictions of Christ in my flesh *for His body's sake, which is the Church*; whereof I was made minister according to the dispensation [marg. stewardship] of God which is given to me to you-ward, to fulfil [A.V. marg. fully preach] the word of God, even the mystery [i.e. the secret] *which hath been hid from all ages and generations*: but now hath been manifested to His saints, to whom God was pleased to make known what is the riches of the glory of this *mystery* [or secret] among the Gentiles, which is Christ in [A.V. marg. among] you, the hope of glory, whom we proclaim, admonishing every man and teaching every man in all wisdom.**

In chapter 2:2 of Colossians, the apostle Paul further states of this mystery:

> **That they being knit together in love, and unto all riches of the full assurance of understanding that they may know [or have full knowledge of] the mystery [or secret] of God, even Christ, in whom are all the treasures of wisdom and knowledge hidden.**

Here, we learn that this "secret" had *never* before been made known, and that to make it known was to "fully preach the Word of God." Hence, today, the Word of God is not "fully preached" unless the *secret* be proclaimed. Paul makes more flagrant remarks of this *mystery* in Romans 16:25, 26 (R.V.):

> **Now to Him that is able to stablish you according to my gospel and the preaching of Jesus Christ, according to the revelation of the *mystery* [i.e. the secret] *which had been kept in silence through times eternal*, but now is manifested and by [margin, through] the scriptures of the prophets according to the commandment of the eternal God, is made known unto all nations unto obedience of faith [i.e. on the principle of faith-obedience].**

Here, observe, that the same *secret* is referred to as being made known by a special silent *revelation*, and as having been kept in eternal silence, not a word having been breathed concerning it before!

The great secret of the MYSTERY is revealed by Paul in Ephesians 3:1-7:

> **For this cause, I Paul, the prisoner of Christ Jesus in behalf of you Gentiles—if so be that ye have heard of the dispensation [marg. stewardship] of that grace of God, which was given me to you-ward; how that by revelation was made known unto me the mystery [i.e. the secret], as I wrote afore in few words, whereby,**

> when ye read, ye can perceive my understanding in the mystery [or secret] of [or concerning] Christ; which in other generations was not made known unto the sons of men, as it hath now been revealed unto His holy apostles and prophets in [or rather 'by', as A.V.] the Spirit; to wit, *that the gentiles should be fellow-heirs, and fellow-partakers of the promise in Christ Jesus*, according to the gift of the grace of God which was given me through the Gospel whereof I was made a minister, according to the working of His power.
>
> Unto me, who am less than the least of all saints, was this grace, given, to preach unto the Gentiles the unsearchable [the untractable] riches of Christ; and to make all men see [Greek, to enlighten all as to] what the mystery [secret] which from all ages hath been hid in God, who created all things, to the intent that now unto the principalities and the powers in the heavenly places might be made known through the Church the manifold wisdom of God, according to the eternal purpose (marg. purpose of the ages) which He purposed in Christ Jesus our Lord.

The "mystery" that was revealed by the apostle Paul and unknown to the Old Testament prophets, is that: *the Gentiles could now become* members of the "Body" of Christ—His Church (Gr. *ekklesia* or called out ones).

Had Israel obeyed the call in (Acts 3:19-21) and repented when Jesus came, there is not a prophecy in the Old Testament that would not have been fulfilled!

WHY WAS THE SECRET KEPT?

But first let us ask, "why was the great doctrine of the *mystery* concerning the grafting in of Gentiles to God's Kingdom ever kept secret at all"? Why did God hide it in Himself, so that no one could possibly discover it till He chose to reveal it?

THE RESTORATION OF ISRAEL

The reason is clear!

Had it not been kept secret, the Jews would have had a reason for their rejection of Christ. They could have pleaded "a stacked deck", and that they were only fulfilling the prophecies—and would have lost at once all their responsibility.

True, the rejection of Christ was foretold, but there was not one word about their rejection of the renewed offer of the King and the Kingdom, which was made authoritatively after Christ's Ascension.

THE WIFE OR BRIDE

We have already shown the many passages which clearly prophesy Old Testament Israel to be the Bride of the Messiah. But can the New Testament Church also be called the "Bride?"

While all the promises to Israel as a nation were *earthly*, there were always those who lived "by faith" and "died in faith", and were "partakers of the heavenly calling" (Heb. 3:1). They looked for no earthly portion, but they looked forward with a heavenly hope to a heavenly blessing.

> **These all died in faith, not having received the promises, but having seen them afar off, and were persuaded of them, and embraced them, and confessed that they were strangers and pilgrims on the earth. For they that say such things declare plainly that they seek a country...a better country, that is an Heavenly: wherefore God is not ashamed to be called their God; for He hath prepared for them a CITY" (Heb. 11:13-16). And of Abraham it is said, "he looked for a CITY, which hath FOUNDATIONS, whose builder and maker is God (vs. 10).**

Now when we turn to (Revelation 21:9), we read that one of the seven angels said to John: **"Come hither, I will shew thee the BRIDE, the Lamb's wife."**

> **(Vs. 27) And he carried me away in the spirit to a great and high mountain, and shewed me that great CITY, the holy Jerusalem descending out**

of heaven from God, having the glory of God; and her light was like unto a stone most precious.

What are we to understand but that this CITY—which is declared to be the BRIDE, the Lamb's "wife," is the city for which all those who were partakers of the heavenly calling looked; and that these *elect* saints of the Old Testament will form part of this new Bride. This "Holy Jerusalem" also contains the "Church of God" or Body of Christ. It will also form the Bride, inasmuch as "the Lord God Almighty, and the Lamb, are the Temple of it", and "the Lamb is the Light thereof" (Rev. 21:22).

It will be noted that the names "ON THE GATES of the city" are "the names of the *twelve tribes of the children of Israel"* (Rev. 21:12), while the names "IN THE FOUNDATIONS" are "the names of *the twelve apostles* of the Lamb" (vs. 14).

The apostles form a part of the Body of Christ, [the Church] or the Bridegroom. But the apostles also form a part of the Bride! However, although the Bride and the Bridegroom though in a sense are ONE, they are yet surely distinct!

THE "MYSTERY" SOLVED

Ancient Israel was an *ekklesia* or called out people that formed a *nation* with definite laws and government that was God's *Kingdom* on earth. They had an agreement with God to set the example to other nations that was a covenant which was also a *marriage* agreement. This covenant promised Israel to become a kingdom of *priests*—an holy nation!

But because Israel rebelled against God—her Husband had to divorce her and turned the organization or *government* over to the Gentiles until Christ returns.

When Jesus came in the flesh, He came to give His wife an opportunity to repent—but instead, she crucified Him! It was at this precise time that God called out an *ekklesia,* a different people to become His Bride. The apostle Paul was the first one to understand this MYSTERY—that Gentiles could now become a part of ISRAEL—the WIFE and BRIDE of Christ!

Paul explains how Gentiles could become grafted into Israel. That a Jew or Israelite was a person that had a converted heart inwardly, and no longer was one who was circumcised through heredity. Paul calls this "circumcision of the heart."

Both Old and New Testaments contain an *ekklesia,* [individuals that have been called out] to be a chosen generation, a royal priesthood, an holy nation, a peculiar people (Ex. 19:5,6; 1 Pet. 2:5,9; Rev. 5:10). They will form the spiritual nation of Israel—a holy city—the Bride of Christ!

We cannot apply the *analogy* of the New Testament Church solely becoming the Body of Christ or Bridegroom, anymore than the apostle Paul to be the "father of the Church" (1 Cor. 4:15), and also its "mother" (Gal. 4:19).

To say that all *analogies* must be taken literally is a fallacy. Jesus Himself is called our husband, brother, and friend. The Church is called the "wife of Christ"; yet individual members are "sons of God." God is our Father, yet if Christ were our husband and brother, this would be spiritual incest and a fallacy in the literal sense.

Chapter Three

DANIEL'S SEVENTY WEEKS PROPHECY

Prophecy in general and Daniel's Seventy Weeks prophecy in particular has been one of the most confusing and debatable prophecies ever written. Yet it is a "key" prophecy that "unlocks" a number of other prophecies including *when* the Kingdom would be returned to Israel.

Virtually all Bible scholars recognize that these "seventy weeks" are to be understood using the day for a year principle as recorded in (Ezek. 4:3-6, and Numbers 14:34).

For example, every day the Israelites searched the land of milk and honey, even forty days, they were punished forty years for their sins. Therefore, the 70 weeks equal (70 x 7) = 490 days or 490 years prophetically. The angel Gabriel told Daniel:

> **Seventy weeks are determined upon thy people and upon thy holy city, to finish the transgression, and to make an end of sins, and to make reconciliation for iniquity, and to bring in everlasting righteousness, and to seal up the vision and prophecy, and to anoint the most Holy. Know therefore and understand, that from the going forth of the commandment to restore and to rebuild Jerusalem unto the Messiah the Prince [Christ] shall be seven weeks, and threescore and two weeks [a total of 69 weeks or (69 x 7)= 483 prophetic years] the street shall be built again, and the wall, even in troublous times. And after threescore (60) and**

THE RESTORATION OF ISRAEL

two weeks (a total of 62) shall Messiah be cut off, but not for himself... (Dan. 9:24-26).

Henry Halley summarizes Daniel's Seventy Weeks Prophecy by stating in his handbook, "The 70 weeks is subdivided into 7 weeks, 62 weeks, and 1 week (25, 27). It is difficult to see the application of the "7 weeks"; but the 69 weeks (including the 7) equal 483 days, that is, on the year-day theory (Ezekiel 4:6), which is the commonly accepted interpretation, 483 years" (p. 349).

In other words, the entire time period involved is exactly specified as *Seventy Weeks* (24); and these Seventy Weeks are further divided into three lesser periods: first a period of *seven weeks;* (7 x 7 = 49) after that a period of *three-score and two weeks;* (62 x 7 = 434) and finally, a period of *one week* (1 x 7 = 7), a total of 490 years (49 + 434 + 7) (25, 27).

To put Daniel's prophecy in modern vernacular, 483 years from the time the commandment or decree given to restore and to rebuild Jerusalem—or after the "threescore (60) and two weeks", which follows the first seven weeks (69 weeks) the Messiah would make His triumphant entry into Jerusalem and present Himself as the Messiah of Israel, and shortly thereafter would be "cut off" or be crucified..

Take note, the Hebrew word for weeks in this prophecy is *shabua* which means "seven", thus the scripture should read, "Seventy sevens are determined upon thy people and upon thy holy city..." These "sevens" have reference to God's "seven sabbaths" of years or Jubilee year. We will cover more of the significance of Daniel's Seventy Weeks Prophecy in relationship to the Jubilee in a later chapter.

WHICH COMMANDMENT?

But which commandment do we begin counting from? The starting point from which the 70 weeks were to be counted, was the decree or commandment to rebuild Jerusalem. But several decrees were issued by Persian Kings during the course of time with many discrepancies. Thus, a further point of clarification must be made in order to calculate the 69 weeks prophecy.

If we use the traditional date of 457 B.C. as the Persian decree and count 483 calendar years, we would arrive at the date of Christ's beginning ministry in A.D. 27. This would make the crucifixion (3 1/2 years later) in A.D. 31.

Failure to distinguish between Judah's national captivity for 70 years, beginning in 606 B.C., and the time period beginning the seventy weeks prophecy [69 weeks from the decree to restore Jerusalem to the Messiah being "cut off"] known as the "Desolations" has led to additional error!

ISRAEL'S 430 YEAR PUNISHMENT

Few indeed realize that the 430 years of Israel's punishment was prophesied 430 years earlier to Abraham on Nisan 14, the very day the nation of Israel prepared to leave their Egyptian taskmasters. The Eternal made a promise to Abraham that his descendants would inherit the land of Canaan or the promised land.

Scriptural evidence suggests that God's covenant with Abraham, when he circumcised all the males of his household was on Nisan 14 (Gen. 17:10-11). Four-hundred and thirty years later, God gave Moses instructions that no male could partake of the Passover feast unless they were circumcised (Joshua 5:2-5).

At this time God also told Abraham his descendants would be in physical bondage for 430 years prior to this, notice Genesis 15:13:

> **And he said unto Abram, know of a surety that thy seed shall be stranger in a land that is not their's, and shall serve them four hundred years.**

Concerning God's promise to Abraham, the apostle Paul stated Israel's 430 year servitude in Canaan and Egypt:

> **And this I say, that the covenant, that was confirmed before of God in Christ, the law which was four hundred and thirty years after, cannot disannul, that it should make the promise [to Abraham] of none effect (Gal. 3:17).**

Because of their rebelliousness and lack of faith—God made Israel wonder in the wilderness aimlessly for an additional forty

THE RESTORATION OF ISRAEL

years, before they could cross over to the promised land of milk and honey (Heb. 4:6).

Once Israel rejected God as their King and wanted a visible king that they could see like all of the heathen nations around them—the Eternal allowed king Saul to rule over them in 1096 B.C. During this time, Israel did not keep seventy of God's land Sabbaticals or "seventy sevens" or a period of 490 years. A Sabbatical land rest occurred every 7th year, therefore 70 x 7= 490 years.

Exactly 490 years from Solomon's reign in 1096 B.C. God allowed the Babylonian king Nebuchadnezzar to conquer the nation of Judah in 606 B.C. in fulfillment of Leviticus 26:34,35.

The year 606 B.C. was a Jubilee Year in which king Zedekiah, Judah's last ruling king made a last ditch effort to plead with the nation of Israel to repent, notice Jeremiah 34:8:

> **This is the word that came unto Jeremiah from the LORD, after that the king Zedekiah had made a covenant with all the people which were at Jerusalem, to proclaim liberty unto them.**

But Judah refused to hearken unto the Eternal's command, and therefore God sent them into captivity for seventy years. Let's read God's judgment in Jeremiah 34:17:

> **Therefore thus saith the LORD; Ye have not hearkened unto me, in proclaiming liberty, every one to his brother, and every man to his neighbor: behold I proclaim a liberty for you, saith the LORD, to the sword, to the pestilence, and to the famine; and I will make you to be removed into all the kingdoms of the earth.**

How appropriate, that after Daniel's people had served seventy years of punishment for violating God's land Sabbaths, God was going to begin a new cycle of "seventy sevens" or 490 years of their punishment through the seventy weeks prophecy.

THE 70 YEARS NATIONAL CAPTIVITY

"In the third year of the reign of Jehoiakim king of Judah

DANIEL'S SEVENTY WEEKS

came Nebuchadnezzar king of Babylon unto Jerusalem, and besieged it" (Dan. 1:1). This occurred in 606 B.C. Along with the royal seed of King Jehoiakim, and the princes, came men who were skilful in wisdom, knowledge, and science [the intellectuals] chosen to teach the Babylonian ways to the Jewish captives in Jerusalem (Dan 1:3-5).

Among the bright captives, was Daniel, Hananiah (Shadrach), Mishael (Meshach) and Azariah (Abed-nego) (Dan. 1:6-7). Soon these four men would be recognized for their exceptional understanding in all dreams and visions (Dan. 1:17-20). Recall how Daniel had interpreted Nebuchadnezzar's dream of the great image (Dan. 2). They soon found favor in the king's sight, and were appointed very lofty positions as the king entrusted them with the affairs of the Empire. Daniel was elevated to the rank of minister in the king's cabinet.

However, after being in the Babylonian Empire for 20 years, these three faithful men found themselves in the fiery furnace. These men were uncompromising in their religious convictions and would not bow down to the kings idolatrous command (Dan. 3:10-11).

The prophet Ezekiel was also a captive in Babylon. He was carried to Babylon in 597 B.C., 11 years before Jerusalem was destroyed, and 9 years after Daniel arrived. Ezekiel may have been Jeremiah's pupil, as he was preaching the same warnings in Babylon as Jeremiah was in Jerusalem!

The seventy years national captivity of Judah is calculated by subtracting 606 B.C. [Jerusalem taken captive by King Nebuchadnezzar] from 536 B.C. [Cyrus' decree] allowing the exiles of Judah to return from Babylon to rebuild the Temple in Jerusalem. Thus, 606 - 536 = 70 years!

However, the period known as the "Desolations" of Jerusalem, beginning the "seventy weeks" prophecy [not the beginning of the counting to the Messiah] were a result of further warnings of the prophets Jeremiah and Ezekiel—while Daniel was still in exile in Babylon.

THE "DESOLATIONS" OF JERUSALEM

Meanwhile, back in Jerusalem, the prophet Jeremiah pleaded with the rebellious nation,:"**..this whole land shall be a desolation and an astonishment, and these nations shall serve**

the king of Babylon seventy years" (Jer. 25:11). Realize, these "seventy years" of "Desolations" were to begin as a result of *disobedience* and *rebellion* against the authority of the divine decree given to Nebuchadnezzar during their captivity—not as a result of it! Observe:

> **And now have I given all these lands into the hand of Nebuchadnezzar the king of Babylon, my servant; and the beasts of the field have I given him also to serve him...And it shall come to pass, that the nation and kingdom which will not serve the same Nebuchadnezzar the king of Babylon, and that will not put their neck under the yoke of the king of Babylon, that nation will I punish, saith the LORD, (Jer. 27:6,8).**

Now notice the time element of this prophecy. It is when Zedekiah is king of Judah (Jer. 27:12-15). It is a prophecy and warning to Zedekiah and those remaining in Jerusalem after the first siege, notice Jeremiah 27:20:

> **Which Nebuchadnezzar king of Babylon took not, when he carried away captive Jeconiah the son of Jehoiakim king of Judah from Jerusalem to Babylon, and all the nobles of Judah and Jerusalem (including Daniel).**

This same prophecy is repeated in Jeremiah 38:17-21:

> **Then said Jeremiah unto Zedekiah, Thus saith the LORD, the God of hosts, the God of Israel; If thou wilt assuredly go forth unto the king of Babylon's princes, then thy soul shall live, and this city shall not be burned with fire; and thou shalt live, and thine house:**

Realize also, that these "seventy weeks" of "Desolations" were to begin during the reign of Zedekiah—Judah's last ruling king! Judah's servitude of 70 years began in 606 B.C. and ended in 536 B.C. with the decree of Cyrus to rebuild the Temple, not the city.

DANIEL'S SEVENTY WEEKS

However, the period of time known as the "Desolations" in (Daniel 9:25), began in 589 B.C. when Jerusalem was besieged the third and final time by the Babylonians in fulfillment of Jeremiah's prophecy. It had been besieged a 2nd time, 9 years earlier in 598 B.C.

In 589 B.C. the city of Jerusalem was ransacked and destroyed by the invading Babylonian army. This date, beginning on the tenth of Tebeth was in the ninth year of king Zedekiah (11 Kings 25:1).

Therefore, counting seventy prophetic years of 360 days = 70 x 360 = 25,200 prophetic days from 589 B.C. brings us to 520 B.C. This date was the second year of king Darius the Persian, in which the foundation of the second Temple was laid (Hag. 2:18,19).

DANIEL'S 70TH WEEK

Much understanding about Israel's restoration as a government can be understood from the 70 weeks prophecy [a multiple of 7] in (Daniel 9:24-27) in particular the 70th week.

As already noted, most Bible scholars agree the first part of this prophecy [69 weeks] refers to Jesus the Messiah [when He would be crucified], but there are vast differences of opinion concerning the interpretation of the last part of this prophecy.

One school of thought believes that this prophecy is speaking exclusively about Jesus Christ, while the other school of thought believes the last part of the prophecy beginning in (verse 26) refers to the "False Prophet." They reason, in (verse 25), it speaks of Jesus, the "Messiah" (capital letters...where small letters are used in (verse 26) to describe "the people of the prince"), who will come and destroy the city and the sanctuary and the end thereof shall be with a flood, and unto the end of the war desolations are determined. Here's how Daniel 9:27 reads:

> **And he shall confirm the covenant with many for one week (7 years): And in the middle of the week (3 1/2 years) he shall cause the sacrifice and the oblation to cease, and for overspreading of abominations he shall make it desolate, even until the consummation, and that determined shall be poured upon the desolate.**

The crux of this disagreement revolves around WHO confirms this covenant for *seven* years—Christ or Anti-christ?

As noted earlier, virtually all Christian expositors believe the first 69 weeks of this prophecy applies to the *anointing* and crucifixion of Jesus Christ. It is this final 70th week or last seven years that brings about a vast difference of opinion.

Many have reasoned that the 70th week of Daniel refers to Jesus being "cut off" after 3 1/2 years of His public ministry and that He still has 3 1/2 years remaining. That He will use these 3 1/2 years through the "Two Witnesses," who will be preaching the gospel at Jerusalem prior to Christ's return.

They feel Jesus used the first 3 1/2 years to *confirm* the covenant [New Covenant] and by His death caused the sacrifice to cease.

Others believe this covenant is confirmed for only 7 years, while the New Covenant is *everlasting*, and therefore could not be referring to Jesus Christ.

Those who believe in this exegesis believe this cannot be the Messiah, nor is it the Messiah who causes "the sacrifices and oblation to cease" in the midst of the last week [which is still future], as is clear from (Daniel 8:11-13; 11:31; and 12:11), which it is also connected with the setting up of the "abomination of desolation."

They contend the 26th verse describes the present dispensation from the crucifixion of Christ to the rise of the Antichrist, while the 27th verse describes the last week [or seven years of Antichrist's actings], divided as it is into two parts of 1260 days, (3 1/2 years or 42 months). Advocates of the *seven years* of the "False Prophet" ask: "why would Jesus and His people destroy the city of Jerusalem and the sanctuary?"

To support their argument, "seven year False Prophet proponents" point out that practically every Bible [including the Companion, Cambridge, Scoefield, International] and Bible commentaries have marginal references or appendixes that explain the last week or seven years of Daniel's seventy weeks as relating to the Anti-christ.

Two major events are said to transpire after the sixty-ninth week and before the seventieth week, namely, 1) the "cutting off" or crucifixion of the Messiah, and 2) the destruction of the city and the Temple in Jerusalem. As we have observed, the crucifixion of our Lord took place within a few days after He entered Jerusalem and presented Himself as Israel's Messiah, or when the sixty-ninth week ended.

However, the destruction of the Temple did not occur until 70 A.D.—or until 40 years after the termination of the sixty-ninth week when the Roman general Titus entered Jerusalem and destroyed the Temple and the city.

From our understanding of the *types*—it seems apparent that there is another *duality* between Jesus Christ and Satan presented in this prophecy. Satan is a master *counterfeiter* and duplicates everything in God's plan. It seems evident that he would also duplicate God's end-time seven year plan for Jesus Christ.

Assuming that the 70th week applied to Jesus Christ only, undoubtedly the Devil would also desire seven years to counterfeit God's plan!

THE SEVENTIETH WEEK AND CHRIST

As noted earlier, virtually all Christian expositors believe the first 69 weeks of this prophecy have found its fulfillment to the letter in Jesus Christ's first Coming. It is this final 70th week or *last seven years* that brings about a vast difference of opinion. The following reasons are given by advocates who believe Jesus fulfilled the remaining seventieth week:

- Jesus confirmed a covenant for one week (7 years) and in the midst of it (after 3 1/2 years) was "cut off" by being killed. A prophecy concerning Christ's death is found in (Isaiah 53:8) which states: "**..He was *cut off* out of the land of the living...**" The covenant Jesus confirmed of course was the New Covenant.

- There is no mention of "Anti-christ" in this scripture, but only "Most holy", "Messiah", and "Prince."

- Nothing is said of a covenant restoring sacrifices or breaking a covenant.

- Christ confirmed the New Covenant as mentioned in (Matthew 26:28; Malachi 3:1, and Hebrews 8:6; 12:24).

- Jesus did cause the sacrifice of animals to cease by becoming

THE RESTORATION OF ISRAEL

the only true sacrifice for sin (Hebrews chapters 9 and 10:18,26).

- This prophecy is continual and does not allow for a 2,000 year gap of time.

THE ANTI-CHRIST VERSION

This is the more popular view and is held by many television evangelists including Jack Van Impe, Hal Lindsey, Howard Estep and prophetic writers Salem Kirban, John F. Walvoord, and Allen Beechick to name a few. Actually, this belief is nothing new, and was written about in the first part of this century by H.A. Ironside and Sir Robert Anderson. But this concept dates even further than this century, and is as old as the writings of the Ante-Nicene Fathers which included Irenaeus.

Proponents of this view contend, trying to fit 7 years of prophecy into 3 1/2 years is like trying to put a size 10 foot into a size 5 shoe!

Here's what the *Companion Bible* says of this 70th week in (Appendix 89 & 90):

> **There are five specific periods of "time" and "days" mentioned in the Book of Daniel (7:25; 8:14; 12:7,11,12). In addition to these five, we have the great period of the "seventy sevens" (or weeks) of years in chapter 9.** *Sixty-nine* **of these were completed at the "cutting off" of the Messiah; the last or "seventieth seven" is yet to come. All the other five periods of time in the book are to be referred to, and are** *standardized*, **so to speak, by this last "seven." The "seventy weeks" (sevens) are confessedly to be reckoned as** *years*. **Therefore, on the basis of a Jewish year of 360 days, one "seven" is 360 x 7=2,520 days. The** *terminus a quo* **is manifestly determined by the term "in the midst of the week" (the last "seven" of years), of the** *standard*, **that is 1,260 days, or 3 1/2 years from either end of the column.**

"The prince that shall come" (Antichrist) "will make a covenant with many for one week" (i.e. *seven years*) (9:27). After 3 1/2 years, on grounds not stated, he breaks this covenant (or "league", 11:23), the daily sacrifice is "taken away", the "abomination" set up, and "Jacob's trouble" (Jer. 30:7) commences and continues for the remainder of the "seven", vis: for the 1,260 days or 3 1/2 years. It is this "midst of the week" that determines both the *a quo* and the *adquem* of these Numbered Days.

In 8:14 it is stated, "then shall the Sanctuary be cleansed." With regard to this "cleansing", all the periods synchronize at the end, while the last two columns are *extended* and prolonged beyond the close of the 1,260 days by two significant periods of days, viz. 30 days and 75 days, respectively. The first of these, 1,290 days is 1,260 + 30. And the 90 days here may be taken as a "Ve-Adar" or intercalary month of 30 days of "cleansing" following directly after the destruction of the false Messiah; and the break up of his confederacy. These *thirty* days may possibly be the period allotted for the construction of the new and glorious "Sanctuary" of Ezekiel 40-43, which is to be erected *after* the destruction and removal of the Jewish temple which will have been built by the sons of Israel some time previously to its profanation by the Antichrist—as the antitype of Antiochus Epiphanes. With regard to the 1,335 days of 12:12: This 1,260 days with an excess of 75 days. This again being an excess of 45 days beyond the 1,290 of 12:11. 1,335 is, therefore 1,260 + 30 + 45. If the 30 days are occupied with the "cleansing", i.e. with the "justifying" or "making righteous" a new and glorious "Sanctuary", then it may be that the further 45 days, over and above the 1,290, will cover the preparation time for the fulfillment of

THE RESTORATION OF ISRAEL

the forty-fifth psalm (such preparation including the resurrection to life of those concerned in 12:2), in order that the nuptials of the king may be celebrated as described in such wonderful and minute detail in that psalm (Ap. 89 & 90).

THE GAP THEORY

The beginning of the first 69 weeks began with the commandment to rebuild Jerusalem, which was issued by the Persian king Artaxerxes in 445 B.C.

From this well established date, to the coming of the Messiah as Israel's "Prince" would be exactly 69 prophetic weeks or 483 years. This event has already occurred as both schools firmly believe!

But now we come to what one school of thinking calls the *continuous* interpretation of this prophecy, while the other school labels the separation of the 69th and 70th weeks as the *gap* interpretation.

Those who believe in the continuous interpretation, contend there is no division of time lapse between the 69th and 70th week of Daniel's "Seventy weeks" prophecy—and therefore the prophetic events mentioned here have already been fulfilled!

Contrary to this view of thinking are the advocates of the *gap* interpretation of the 70th week, who maintain that there is a division of thousands of years between the 69th and 70th week, and the 70th week therefore is yet future!

Advocates of this exegesis contend that a great parenthesis of time between the 69th and 70th week is made evident from several related passages, which our Lord Himself inspired.

This is the viewpoint held by H.A. Ironside and A.J. McClain as summarized by Pentecost on pp. 247-48 of his book, *Things to Come*.

To disprove the *continuous* interpretation of this prophecy, *gap* enthusiasts point out that the events which led to Jerusalem's destruction in A.D. 70 along with the Temple and Sanctuary were nearly *forty years after* the fulfillment of the first 69 weeks!

History informs us that the invading Roman legions of General Titus destroyed Jerusalem around A.D. 70. For this to be the interpretation of the *continuous* theory would prove in actuality a *gap* between the 69th and 70th week. Surely, if even one year would be acknowledged longer than the last two weeks of this prophecy, it would be an admission to the gap interpretation!

Since Christ came in A.D. 27 and died 3 1/2 years later—this leaves an obvious gap of nearly forty years to the supposed fulfilment of this prophecy by Titus in A.D. 70. This is a definite problem for advocates of the continuous philosophy to reckon with!

P. Mauro rebukes this concept for the following reasons, as he states:

> **...there is "an absolute rule", admitting of no exceptions, [namely] that when a definite measure of time or space is specified by the number of units composing it, within which a certain event is to happen or a certain thing is to be found, the units of time or space which make up that measure are to be understood as running continuously and successively (*The Seventy Weeks, Leviticus, and the Nature of Prophecy* p. 23).**

Furthermore, proponents of the gap interpretation ask: "When did God ever "finish the transgression"—""make and end of sins"—"make reconciliation for iniquity"—"bring in everlasting righteousness"—"seal up the vision and prophecy" and "anoint a most holy place" (A.R.V. margin) for Israel?

This most certainly was not done within a prophetic week (7 years) after Christ's death! There is no mention of such things occurring in the book of Acts! Contrariwise, we find the apostle Paul grafting in Gentiles to the Church because of Israel's sins! There is no mention of forgiveness to Israel here—rather mercy extended to the Gentile!

Now one final point is given by *gap* proponents to prove their interpretation is the correct one. They refer to the prophecy in (Isaiah 61:1-2), in which our Lord quoted from in (Luke 4:18,19). This refers to His public ministry of preaching the gospel and healing the sick—to a 2,000 year gap in which he would fulfill the last part of the prophecy by delivering the captives of Israel out of slavery!

THE RESTORATION OF ISRAEL

THE SEVENTY WEEKS AND ISRAEL

John F. Walvoord, gives his interpretation of the Seventy Weeks prophecy as it relates to the nation of Israel:

> **The seventy weeks of Daniel, properly interpreted, demonstrate the distinct place of the Christian church and Israel in the purposes of God. The seventy weeks of Daniel are totally in reference to Israel and her relation to Gentile powers and the rejection of Israel's Messiah. The peculiar purpose of God in calling out a people from every nation to form the church and the program of the present age are nowhere in view in this prophecy (Is Daniel's Seventieth Week Future?,** *Bibliotheca Sacra,* **101:30, January, 1944).**

SUMMARY OF THE ANTI-CHRIST VERSION

The following are points of difference between the advocates who believe Daniel's 70th week refers to the coming of Anti-christ and is yet future:

- This covenant is confirmed for only *7 years*, while the New Covenant is *everlasting!*

- The entire prophecy deals with the nation of Judah and Jerusalem as (verse 24) refers to *Daniel's people* and *Daniel's city!* (see also verses 2,7,12,16,18,19,25).

- There indeed is a *gap* from the 69th to the 70th week, for the death of the Messiah and the destruction of Jerusalem nearly 40 years later in A.D. 70 by the invading armies of Titus were not a continuous prophetic year! There is a further 2,000 year gap between our Lord's first and second Coming!

- Two different "princes" are alluded to as the "Messiah the *Prince"* refers to Jesus Christ (vs. 25)—but "the *prince* that shall come" describes a different prince—the "False Prophet" or "little horn."

- The fulfilment of the events in (verse 24), "to finish the transgression", "to make an end of sins", "to make reconciliation for iniquity", "to seal up the vision and prophecy", "to anoint a most holy place" (A.R.V. margin), have not happened to the Jewish people or their city as yet!

- The death of Christ did not cause the sacrifices to stop—for they continued until the city and the Temple were destroyed by Titus' Roman legions nearly forty years later! Since the death of Christ in the middle of the week did not stop the sacrifices, this prophecy could not be referring to the Messiah the Prince!

- Only when Christ returns in power and glory can specific great blessings be poured out upon Judah! This can only happen *after* the "seventy weeks" have been fulfilled! Upon Christ's return, He will institute a place of Temple worship with sacrificial system for all nations to worship Him properly! This is when He will "anoint a most holy place" for the Millennial Temple!

- Daniel 7,8,9,11,12 all refer to the Anti-christ ("little horn") taking away the daily sacrifice, setting up the Abomination of desolation, and making war with God's people. Why assume that in the middle of these chapters any change of thought occurs?

- The close of the seventieth week was to bring full blessings to Judah resulting from the Messiah's death. But Judah's transgression is yet to be restrained, and his sins to be sealed up. The Hebrew verb *caphar* [to make atonement or reconciliation] means literally "to cover over" sin. It implies the removal of the punishment between the sinner and God, or the obtaining of forgiveness for the sin. This verb *caphar* is used in (Exodus 32:30) in reference to doing away with a charge against a person by means of bloodshedding. This same word was used in (Genesis 6:14) for "pitch" in reference to "covering" Noah's Ark. This was a *type* of "covering" or "atonement" for sin that protected the individual inside the Ark. In all references where the

THE RESTORATION OF ISRAEL

Hebrew word *caphar* is used, it means "atonement" or "forgiveness" (Girdlestone's *Synonyms* O.T., p. 214). But the time of "atonement" for Israel and complete "forgiveness" of her sins will only occur upon the return of the Messiah when He fulfills the Day of Atonement!

- The seven year end-time plan is revealed by God through the *types*. The 7 years of famine in Egypt during the time of Joseph is merely a *type* of the 7 years of famine coming prior to Christ's return. King Nebuchadnezzar's "seven times" punishment and "seven years" of actual insanity is a *type* of the Gentile madness that will exist in the Babylonian system at the end of this age (Dan. 4:25). Ironically, a "seven times" punishment was stipulated to the nation of Israel if they became disobedient and rebellious (Lev. 26:14-28). Bible students are aware that a "time" is God's day for a year principle in prophecy (Ezek. 4:4-6; Num. 14:34). Both of these prophecies [the Gentile domination, and the removal of Israel's power] dovetail each other and add up to a duration of 2520 years. After this time, God will restore His kingdom to the nation of Israel.

- The prophecy has to do with the anointing of "the most holy" (margin: Most Holy Place). The "Most Holy Place" can only refer to the Holy of Holies in the Temple. Since the Temple was destroyed in A.D. 70 by the Roman General Titus—there has not been a "Most Holy Place" in Jerusalem because there has not been a Temple!

- In (Daniel 11:31), speaking of the evil Antiochus Epiphanes, who is a *type* of the Beast to come, we read that his forces will "pollute the *sanctuary of strength,* and shall take away the daily sacrifice, and they shall place the abomination that maketh desolate." Antiochus polluted the Temple of God, and placed a statue of himself in the "Holy of Holies." Since this was a *type* of the coming Beast, then he must do the same type of things. For this to occur, a Temple or sanctuary must exist in our time with a "Holy of Holies"!

- If the 69th week has a literal interpretation, then it follows

DANIEL'S SEVENTY WEEKS

that the 70th week would also be taken literally.

JOSEPH IN EGYPT AND 7 YEARS OF FAMINE

Many Bible students are aware that Joseph is a *type* of Christ—now we shall show how the famine conditions that existed in the days of Joseph were a *prototype* and a *prelude* to the famine to occur in these last days!

After being sold into slavery by his jealous brothers into Egypt, Joseph became renowned as an interpreter of dreams. One night, Pharaoh had a remarkable dream that disturbed him tremendously. When Pharaoh's chief counsellor's magicians, soothsayers, and priests failed in their attempt to interpret his dream—he called upon the services of Joseph.

Pharaoh had dreamed that seven fat cows fed in a meadow, but after them seven lean cows ate up and consumed the seven fat cows! After this he dreamed again, and this time seven fat ears of wheat came up on one stalk, full and goodly to behold; but then seven thin ears came up, blighted with the east wind, and devoured the seven fat and full ears. The lean cows, Pharaoh told Joseph, were so skinny that they were **"such as I never saw in all the land of Egypt for badness."**

This was a most incredible dream, and this was Joseph's interpretation for the Pharaoh:

> **The dream of Pharaoh is one: God hath shown Pharaoh what He is about to do. The seven good cows are *seven years*; and the seven good ears are *seven years*: the dream is one. And the seven thin and ill favored cows that came up after them are *seven years*; and the seven empty ears blighted with the east wind shall be *seven years* of famine.**

Joseph explained to the Pharaoh of Egypt that there was coming a time in which there would be seven years of great plenty throughout all the land of Egypt, followed by seven years of famine.

What few realize, is that this *seven years of famine* in the days of Joseph, as well as the last seven years of the *"times of the Gentiles"* pictured by Nebuchadnezzar's temporary insanity, represent the *seventieth week* of (Daniel 9:27). This was merely a *type* of what is going to happen on this planet, before the glorious return of Jesus Christ!

THE "TIMES OF JERUSALEM"

We have just examined several interrelated prophecies concerning the nation of Judah which correlate to the holy city of Jerusalem. Coincidentally, all of these prophecies dovetail into one theme—the termination of the Gentile powers rule on earth known as "the times of the Gentiles" and the reestablishment of the nation of Israel as God's supreme nation upon the earth.

These prophecies can best be summarized as follows:

- **The "times of the Gentiles"**—the nation of Israel was God's chosen nation over the hierarchy of the nations upon the earth. Israel was to be a "model nation" for all the world to see and emulate. They were a kingdom literally "set on a hill" [Jerusalem] to be a shining example for the Gentile world around them.

However, due to spiritual infidelity, the Lord divorced His wife and sent her into captivity. Judah and Jerusalem would be *synonymous* as they possessed the holy land and were the last tribe to go into captivity (1 Kings 11:11-13). They would also be the tribe to progenate the Messiah!

At this point, the Eternal had now decided to transfer the kingdom to the Gentile powers pictured by the two visions of king Nebuchadnezzar of Babylon as recorded in (Daniel 2 and 7).

The vision of Nebuchadnezzar's great image (Dan. 2) and the lion, bear, leopard and beast with iron teeth and ten horns (Dan. 7) both *portray* the succession of Gentile powers on the earth until Christ would return and *restore* again the kingdom to Israel.

During Jesus' day, His disciples understood that the kingdom, with all authority to govern, whether civil or Church government had been taken away from their people, and turned over to the Gentiles. Recall how they asked Him, **"Lord will thou at this time restore again the kingdom to Israel" (Acts 1:6).**

As already inferred, the "times of the Gentiles" began in 606 B.C. when God decided to send Judah into captivity by the first Gentile power (Babylon) represented by Nebuchadnezzar's dreams.

The "times of the Gentiles" will end upon Christ's second Advent when He returns as the supernatural "stone made without hands" to smite the final Gentile power represented by Nebuchadnezzar's dreams (Roman).

Jesus Christ will at this time *restore* the kingdom of God to Israel once again as they will be His model nation to begin the Millennium.

- **Israel's "seven Times Punishment"**—because the nation of Israel had become disobedient to her husband [Jesus Christ] they were going to be punished for 7 TIMES or 2520 prophetic years (Lev. 23:24; 26:14-28; 27:28). In other words, they would be under Gentile domination for a period of 2520 biblical years of 360 days.

After seventy years of servitude, a partial return of the nation of Judah was allowed to return to their homeland by king Cyrus the Persian in 536 B.C. Therefore, if we count 2520 prophetic years from 536 B.C. we would arrive at the very significant year of 1948—the year in which Israel was "reborn" as a nation and established in their homeland!

- **The Gentiles "seven Times Punishment"**—after the captivity of God's chosen people, king Nebuchadnezzar of Babylon became very proud and haughty. God was going to cut him down to size. This should be a lesson to all of us as, "Pride goeth before destruction" (Prov. 16:18).

The 4th chapter of Daniel describes the fate of Nebuchadnezzar in a dream of the great tree. The dream was a warning to the king that his empire was about to crumble and he would become as a wild beast for seven years.

This seven years of literal insanity was characteristic of "seven Times" or 2520 years of Gentile insanity, after which a brief restoration to sanity would occur prior to our Lord's return. We will study this prophecy in it's entirety in a later chapter.

- **Daniel's Seventieth Week**—as already mentioned, Daniel's seventy weeks prophecy was a decade of Jubilees! It was upon the breaking of God's Jubilee cycles that the

THE RESTORATION OF ISRAEL

"desolations of Jerusalem" were calculated. In the course of breaking seventy sabbatical years, ten Jubilee cycles were also violated!

Therefore, God was going to punish Judah *sevenfold* or "seven Times" or 490 prophetic years (70 x 7 = 490) till their land would be returned to them. Then the Messiah would "make an end of Israel's sins" and "bring in everlasting righteousness" and "anoint the most holy place"—Jerusalem!

The year 2,000 A.D. is also the 70th Jubilee year (3450 calendar years) from 1451 B.C. when the nation of Israel crossed over the Jordan to settle in the land of Canaan [present day Jerusalem] when they began to break God's sabbatical cycles.

God had promised Abraham that his descendants through the lineage of Judah would inherit the birthright promise which includes the land of present-day Palestine.

Prior to entering the promised land, God sent this rebellious nation into 70 years captivity for breaking His land Sabbaths during the coarse of 490 years. Then, God gave them an additional 490 year sentence before the kingdom would be restored again to Israel. The land was restored to them in 1948! When the Messiah returns, the Kingdom will be restored again to Israel in fulfillment of God's promise to Abraham. This is the capstone of all the prophecies of the Bible!

After sixty-nine prophetic weeks of Daniel's prophecy, the kingdom was offered once again to Israel by Jesus Christ—but they rejected Him! At that time they could have inherited their land and the kingdom would have been restored to them!

However, because of their rejection of the Messiah—their is a gap between the 69th and 70th week of Daniel's Seventy Weeks prophecy until they will fulfill this prophecy. Then, Jesus will say to them—"Come ye, inherit the kingdom that has been prepared for you."

After sixty-nine prophetic weeks of Daniel's prophecy, the kingdom was offered once again to Israel by Jesus Christ—but they rejected Him! At that time they could have inherited their land and the kingdom would have been restored to them!

However, because of their rejection of the Messiah—there is a gap between the 69th and 70th week of Daniel's Seventy Weeks prophecy until they will full this prophecy. Then, Jesus will say to them, **"Come ye, inherit the kingdom that has been prepared**

DANIEL'S SEVENTY WEEKS

for you."

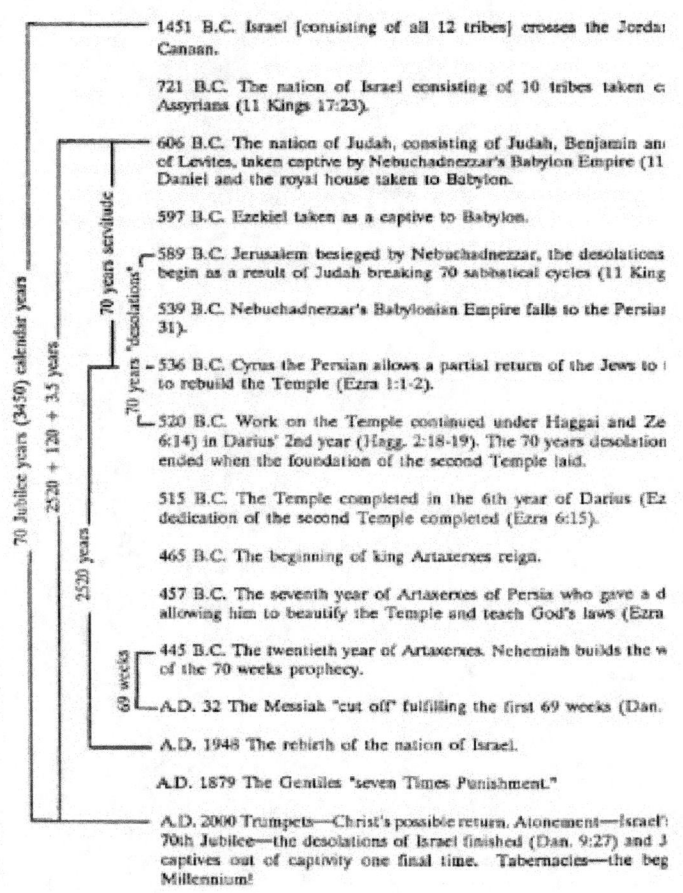

THE DESOLATIONS OF ISRAEL

1451 B.C. Israel [consisting of all 12 tribes] crosses the Jordan Canaan.

721 B.C. The nation of Israel consisting of 10 tribes taken c Assyrians (11 Kings 17:23).

606 B.C. The nation of Judah, consisting of Judah, Benjamin an of Levites, taken captive by Nebuchadnezzar's Babylon Empire (11 Daniel and the royal house taken to Babylon.

597 B.C. Ezekiel taken as a captive to Babylon.

589 B.C. Jerusalem besieged by Nebuchadnezzar, the desolations begin as a result of Judah breaking 70 sabbatical cycles (11 King

539 B.C. Nebuchadnezzar's Babylonian Empire falls to the Persia 31).

536 B.C. Cyrus the Persian allows a partial return of the Jews to to rebuild the Temple (Ezra 1:1-2).

520 B.C. Work on the Temple continued under Haggai and Ze 6:14) in Darius' 2nd year (Hagg. 2:18-19). The 70 years desolation ended when the foundation of the second Temple laid.

515 B.C. The Temple completed in the 6th year of Darius (Ez dedication of the second Temple completed (Ezra 6:15).

465 B.C. The beginning of king Artaxerxes reign.

457 B.C. The seventh year of Artaxerxes of Persia who gave a d allowing him to beautify the Temple and teach God's laws (Ezra

445 B.C. The twentieth year of Artaxerxes. Nehemiah builds the w of the 70 weeks prophecy.

A.D. 32 The Messiah "cut off" fulfilling the first 69 weeks (Dan.

A.D. 1948 The rebirth of the nation of Israel.

A.D. 1879 The Gentiles "seven Times Punishment."

A.D. 2000 Trumpets—Christ's possible return. Atonement—Israel' 70th Jubilee—the desolations of Israel finished (Dan. 9:27) and J captives out of captivity one final time. Tabernacles—the beg Millennium!

Chapter Four

SHADDOWS OF ISRAEL'S FUTURE

Every word of God's Holy book is in its right and proper place. Sometimes it may appear to be out of order—but the *lock* and *key* are there. The lock may be in one place and the key in another. The key may be hidden in a *number*, feast *day*, *duality* or *parable*.

This only proves that no one person, group or organization could have planned such a marvelous work. Securing such uniformity in consistency of thought would have been absolutely impossible without a "guiding hand." Though many different writers *penned* the Bible—God Almighty was its Pen!

Types, *analogies*, *dualities* or *symbols* of one age may convey a literal interpretation of some part of God's plan of the future. This is a spiritual tool to help us better understand and appreciate the plan of God, rather than an acting agency.

As we scrutinize God's word under a spiritual microscope—we shall see the *perfection* of God's wonderful work. The seemingly *insignificant* will become highly relevant.

In the *types* we will see a jig-saw puzzle of God. Each set of *pictures* or *emblems* forms a piece of this intricate and fantastic puzzle. It is God's kindergarten method of instructing His children in the understanding of salvation through Jesus Christ! God uses *types,* etc., like a cartoonist uses his imagination to express truth by a *picture*.

By a *type*, in a Biblical sense, is meant a *picture* or object lesson by which God taught His people concerning His grace and redemptive power. A *type* is a person or thing that *prefigures* a future person or thing.

THE RESTORATION OF ISRAEL

The Old Covenant and New Testament bring out this *dual* relationship. Abraham was chosen of God to be the "father of the faithful" *spiritually*. God's plan began with Abraham, the patriarch of the Old Testament nation of Israel, which became known as "the church [Gr. *ekklesia,* "called out ones"] in the wilderness" (Acts 7:38).

ISRAEL—A TYPE OF GOD'S KINGDOM AND FAMILY

Every Government, or Kingdom has essentially (4) basic characteristics:

- a King that rules over them.
- people, subjects or citizens.
- a definite jurisdiction or territory with
- laws and an organized system of administering them.

Ancient Israel was also a FAMILY! A Family of the Children of Israel or "Jacob." And so we see how "Israel" was a family of the Father's [Jacob's] Children [Jacob's 12 sons who became known as the "Children of Israel"] and a wife [Israel was married to Christ] (Jer. 3:14).

Thus, God used the nation of Israel, a physical nation to give us a SPIRITUAL understanding of His SPIRITUAL KINGDOM AND FAMILY which we can enter into!

But we, like the ancient Israelites may not enter the Kingdom of God [God's Spiritual Promised Land, not a physical promised land] if we are not loyal to God (Heb. 4:11).

Notice what God says of Israel's heart:

> **Forty years long was I grieved with this generation, and said, It is a people that do err in their heart, and they have not known my ways: Unto whom I sware in my wrath that** *they should not enter into my rest* **(Ps. 95:11).**

Yes, God uses ancient Israel as an example for us today (1 Cor. 10:6).

The theme of (Isaiah 58) is God's Kingdom yet future. The Kingdom will be the RESTORATION of all things (Acts 3:21). Notice verse 12:

> And they that shall be of thee shall build the old waste places: thou shalt raise up the foundations of many generations; and thou shalt be called, The *repairer* of the breach, The *restorer* of paths to dwell in.

Isaiah 66 refers to the time when Jesus Christ will set up God's Kingdom here on earth. At that time the Sabbath will be restored to the world:

> For as the new heavens and the new earth, which I will make, shall remain before me, saith the LORD, so shall your seed and your name remain. And it shall come to pass, that from one new moon to another, and from one *Sabbath* to another, shall ALL FLESH come to worship before me, saith the LORD (verses 22-23).

God also told the Israelites to let their land rest every *seventh* year (Lev. 25:1-7). This resting of the land is also typical of the *earth resting* during the 1,000 year reign of Jesus Christ as depicted by the *seventh* day Sabbath!

CYRUS—A TYPE OF CHRIST

It is difficult to imagine that God would use a Gentile king as a *type* of Christ—but as we examine the prophecy given to Cyrus the Persian king in (Isaiah 45), that is the only conclusion we can reach!

Cyrus, like Jesus Christ was named and prophesied to come even before he was born, notice: **"I am the LORD, and there is none else, there is no God beside me; I girded thee, though thou hast not known me" (vs. 5)**.

Cyrus was the subject of many prophecies of Isaiah concerning the restoration of the nation of Judah from Babylon, and the rebuilding of Jerusalem and the Jewish Temple after the captivities (Isa. 44:28; 45:1).

THE RESTORATION OF ISRAEL

TO SET THE CAPTIVES FREE

In verse one of (Isaiah 45), we read of Cyrus: **"Thus saith the LORD *to his anointed,* to Cyrus, whose right hand I have holden, to subdue nations before him, and I will loose the loins of kings..."** This verse should immediately ring a bell in connecting Christ as *God's anointed*, who will subdue all nations as King of Kings upon His return!

Continuing in verse two: **"I will go before thee, and make the crooked places straight: I will break in pieces the gates of brass, and cut in sunder the bars of iron."** The typical fulfillment of this verse occurred in 538 B.C. when Cyrus broke through the brass gates of the impregnable city of Babylon, and shortly afterwards set "the crooked places straight" by allowing the Jews to return to their homeland. Jesus Christ will fulfill this verse as God's "anointed Shepherd" when He returns to *set the captives of Israel free*, and straighten out this crooked world!

Again, the *duality* between Cyrus and Christ surfaces in verse 13:

> **I have raised him up in righteousness, and I will direct all his ways: he shall build my city, and he shall *let go my captives,* not for price nor reward, saith the LORD of hosts.**

The book of Jeremiah explained that the captivity would last 70 years, and then the Jews would be allowed to return. Other details about this deliverance were given in the book of Isaiah, which was probably among the "books" that Daniel studied. The prophecy in Isaiah is especially significant in this connection, for it revealed the *name* of the man that would set the captives free and cause Jerusalem to be built again. His name would be CYRUS.

It was Cyrus who led the armies that overthrew the Babylonian empire on the night the mysterious "handwriting on the wall" appeared. The 70 "weeks" prophecy of Daniel 9 was to begin with **"the going forth of the commandment to restore and to build Jerusalem."** The evidence is clear from secular history that it was Cyrus who gave the decree [although not the actual commandment] which restored the people to Jerusalem so that it could be rebuilt—both city and the Temple!

According to Bible prophecy, Cyrus was to be the one that

would speak the word which would cause the city of Jerusalem to be rebuilt, as well as the Temple:

> **He [Cyrus] is my shepherd, and shall perform all my pleasure: even saying to Jerusalem, Thou shalt be built; and to the Temple, Thy foundation shall be laid (Isa. 44:28).**

Continuing Isaiah's prophecy of Cyrus: **"I have raised him up in righteousness, and I will direct all his ways: HE SHALL BUILD MY CITY, and shall let go my captives, not for price nor reward" (Isa. 45:14).**

As we journey through more of the *types* and *antitypes* throughout the remainder of this book, these verses and the *parallels* between Christ and Cyrus will become more apparent.

ZERUBBABEL—A TYPE OF CHRIST

The book of Haggai contains several prophecies concerning Zerubbabel that very few are indeed familiar with. Some prophetic interpreters go so far as to say that the entire book has already been fulfilled—but based on sound scripture and history, we shall prove that these prophecies are yet future.

Zerubbabel was in fact a *type* of a spiritual leader to arise in the last days, *both* of which will be *types* of Christ! To understand these end-time prophecies, let's go back to the days of Zerubbabel, and review what occurred to him and the nation of Judah.

Cyrus, the king of Persia had conquered the Babylonian empire in 539 B.C. Previously, Babylon had taken captive the Jewish nation in 606 B.C. God had declared 70 years of national punishment before the nation of Judah would be released for it's sins! This ties in with Daniel's "Seventy Weeks" Prophecy concerning Judah's *seven times* punishment in the desolations of Jerusalem.

Cyrus, being a wise king, always endeavored to secure peace and cooperation of conquered nations by granting them religious freedom. It was to this humanitarian aspect, that the spirit of God led Cyrus to grant the Jewish exiles their return to Zion, *to rebuild their Temple* (Jer. 29:10 14; Isa. 44:28; 45:1).

However, approximately 50,000 persons took advantage of Cyrus' generosity (Ezra 2:64-65). Only seventy-four Levites

THE RESTORATION OF ISRAEL

heeded this opportunity, along with four of the twenty-four orders of the priests [4,289] (1 Chron. 24:3; Ezra. 2:40; 7:13,14; 8:15).

Why did so few Jews want to leave Babylon?—because it offered them material prosperity and security of new homes and jobs. They were afraid of the long and dangerous journey back to a land that laid desolate. In other words, they chose to live in exile as rich slaves, rather than as free men in a poor country!

Is there a parallel to today's Christian experience? Are the majority of people desirous of coming out of the MENTAL SLAVERY of spiritual Babylon in favor of worldly riches—or do they seek the spiritual truths and blessings contained in another country (heaven)? As we continue our explanation of the *types,* the parallels between ancient Judah under Zerubbabel, and today's Church age under Christ will become more apparent.

To faithful Israelites, the rebuilding of the Temple was the *symbol* of God's presence in their midst, the outward expression of faith, and a manifestation of true repentance towards the service of God.

THE REINSTITUTION OF GOD'S FEAST DAYS

The first task of the returning exiles was to build the altar of God on the ancient foundations and to *re-institute God's solemn feast days in the seventh month.* The book of Ezra helps to clarify the time setting of Haggai 2:1: **"In the seventh month, in the one and twentieth day of the month, came the word of the LORD by the prophet Haggai saying."**

Now notice the third chapter of Ezra:

> **And when the seventh month was come, and the children of Israel were in the cities, the people gathered themselves together as one man to Jerusalem. Then stood up Jeshua [Joshua] the son of Jozadak, and his brethren the priests, and Zerubbabel the son of Shealtiel, and his brethren, and builded the altar of the God of Israel, to offer burnt offerings thereon, as it is written in the law of Moses the man of God"** (Ezra 3:1-2).

Continuing the account in Ezra: **"They kept also *the feast of***

Tabernacles **as it is written...and all the set feasts of the LORD...But the foundation of the temple of the LORD was not yet laid" (Ezra 2:4-6).**

The date given in (Haggai 2:1) [the 21st day of the seventh month] as to when the word of the Lord came, corresponds exactly with the last day of the Feast of Tabernacles (Lev. 23:33).

The Feast of Tabernacles was a joyous festival commemorating the nation of Israel's *deliverance* from Egyptian bondage (Lev. 23:42 43). This inspiring feast also envisions the government of God ruling over the entire earth during Christ's glorious 1,000 year rule.

Haggai and Zechariah were prophets during the time God was going to *restore* God's feast days and His Temple. Haggai means "My Festival," and Zechariah means "Remembered of God." Through these Hebrew names, God revealed that He had not "forgotten" nor "forsaken" His people.

The dedication of Solomon's rebuilt Temple occurred during this time as recorded in Ezra 6:16: **"And the children of Israel, the priests, and the Levites, and the rest of the children of the captivity, kept the dedication of this house of God with joy."**

Zerubbabel was a governor, and Joshua a priest, representing the entire nation of Israel. But the call to rebuild the Temple goes out to prophet, governor, priest and lay people alike!

The Church of Jesus Christ (Matt. 16:18) is compared to Christians being "living stones" building God's "spiritual Temple" (1 Pet. 2:5). The Church of the living God is, **"...built upon the foundation of the apostles and the prophets, Jesus Christ Himself being the Chief Corner Stone, in whom all the building fitly framed together groweth unto a holy temple in the Lord" (Eph. 2:20,21).**

The *rebuilding of the Temple* was a prerequisite before Christ's first coming, and completion of *God's spiritual house* is a prerequisite before Christ's second advent! Unlike the physical Temple, Christian Stones hewn out of the quarry of this world must become converted by God's Holy Spirit, the mortar that incorporates us into God's living Temple!

Prior to the building of the Temple, God asked His nation this pertinent question: **"Now therefore thus saith the LORD of hosts,** *consider your ways"* **(Hag. 1:5,7).**

THE RESTORATION OF ISRAEL

ISRAEL HAD WILLING HEARTS

The returning exiles of Israel, considered their evil ways and:

Then Zerubbabel the son of Shealtiel, and Joshua the son of Josedech, the high priest, with all the remnant of the people, *obeyed the voice of the LORD their God,* **and the words of Haggai the prophet, as the LORD their God had sent him,** *and the people did fear* **before the LORD (Hag.1:12).**

Everyone began pitching in with willing hearts to build God's physical Temple—and the same is true regarding God's spiritual Temple!

After the people REPENTED, notice what happened:

And the LORD stirred up the spirit of Zerubbabel the son of Shealtiel, governor of Judah, and the spirit of Joshua, the son of Josedech, the priest, and they came and did the work of the LORD of hosts, their God (Hag. 1:14).

God had stirred up the spirit of Cyrus to allow the captive Israelites to return to their homeland. God then stirred the people to repent, and the entire nation to want to build the Temple! The same is true today! Christians have been "stirred up" to do the work of the LORD of hosts—and the modern nation of Israel will soon be stirred up to offer up sacrifices to their Great God!

It wasn't long after work on the Temple began, when some of the older Israelites began comparing it with Solomon's Temple. God again asked them:

Who is left among you that saw this house in her first glory? And how do you see it now? Is it not your eyes in comparison of it as nothing? (Hag. 2:3).

Solomon's Temple was truly a magnificent edifice (1 Kings 6:22-32; 7:48-50). And to those who saw both Temples, the second deemed inferior to Solomon's. The ark, cherubim, tables of stone, the pot of manna and Aaron's rod that budded, were all pillaged in the Babylonian seige.

The Holy of Holies was empty without the SHEKINAH, or cloud of glory hovering over it, indicative of God's Holy presence. The sacred fire was gone as well as the Urim and Thummim. Even the high priest's official dress with the stones of the breastplate was missing. Many of the older people lamented over the missing Temple furniture, and spread remorse and gloom to the others.

If you are an older member in God's Church today—are you spreading *discouragement* to newer members by comparing today's Church age to apostolic times? Have you despised the day of small things like some of the older people of Israel? (Hag. 4:10).

It would have been easy to get depressed by comparing the two Temples, yet God encouraged His servants:

> **Yet now be *strong*, O Zerubbabel, saith the LORD, and, be *strong* O Joshua, the son of Josedech, the high priest, and be *strong*, all ye people of the land, saith the LORD, and *work:* For I am with you, saith the LORD of hosts (Hag. 2:4).**

"CHRIST" THE ULTIMATE "SIGNET BEARER"

Haggai's prophecy then skips to the end-time as the *duality* of the two Temples [physical and spiritual] culminate in Christ's return:

> **For thus saith the LORD of hosts; yet once, it is a little while, and I will shake the heavens, and the earth, and the sea, and the dry land (Hag. 2:6).**

This "shaking of the nations" shall put an end to the corrupt satanic inspired kingdoms of this world and usher in God's eternal kingdom. This is the time when the powers of heaven shall be shaken, and then shall appear the sign of the Son of man in heaven (Matt. 24:7, 29, 30). **"And in the days of these kings shall the God of heaven set up a kingdom, which shall never be destroyed" (Dan. 2:44; Rev. 19:11-21).**

Some so called Bible scholars have gone to great lengths to present scholarly exegesis to prove that these prophecies were fulfilled in Zerubbabel, but we might ask: "were the kingdoms of this world overthrown, and did the Messianic age start with Zerubbabel holding a high office?"

Therefore, I think you will agree that Zerubbabel is merely a *type* of Christ, who is also of the royal house of David.

Haggai, the messenger of the Lord, continually said to Zerubbabel, "be strong" and have "courage", and do the work! What was Zerubbabel's reward for completing his commission:

In that day, [when Christ intervenes to shake the nations] saith the LORD of hosts, will I take thee, O Zerubbabel, my servant, the son of Shealtiel, saith the LORD, and will make thee as a *signet*: for I have chosen thee, saith the LORD of hosts (Hag. 2:23).

Zerubbabel was to be a *signet* to God. A *signet* was a *ring* that contained the king's POWER and AUTHORITY to endorse his seal. The king's seal was a mark of authenticity and *authority* to royal commands. It marked the formal ratification of a covenant as proof of deputed authority and power by an official mark of ownership. This stamp of approval elevated the bearer to a position of *dignity* and *high esteem.* The Pharaoh of Egypt ordained Joseph by such an ordination (Gen. 41:42).

Because of Judah's rebellion, the Eternal sentenced them to seventy years of Babylonian captivity and transferred the "signet ring" from king Jehoiachin ["through Coniah", the son of Jehoiachin the last king of Judah] to Zerubbabel and his family (Jer. 22:24). Therefore, the Messianic promise to David, was transferred to Zerubbabel, who was of the royal house of David.

Thus, the preservation of the dynasty of David was restored by Zerubbabel and his family. He is a *type* of Christ, the ultimate "signet ring" bearer, who will fulfill the Messianic promise made to David! God the Father, in a spiritual sense as King, gives His stamp of approval to His Son Jesus Christ with His "signet ring." In essence, He is saying, **"This is my beloved Son, in whom I am well pleased"** as He did when Jesus was baptized in the Jordan river (Matt. 3:17).

When Christ returns in full power and glory, He will fulfill the Messianic expectation of Israel, and like Zerubbabel as *prototype*—He will lead the nation of Israel out of captivity of Gentile powers.

Then, also like Zerubbabel, who rebuilt the physical Temple with 50,000 exiles—Christ will build His *Millennial Temple* with the Israelite slaves from the second exodus!

The ultimate fulfillment of the prophetic words of Haggai are primarily SPIRITUAL and not found in the physical fulfillment. Jerusalem, will have a new physical Temple, and also the foundations of the spiritual Temple will be formed. The "spiritual stones" for completing the Temple structure will be shaped throughout the Millennium! Finally, God the Father, and Jesus Christ will *dwell* together as "the Lord God Almighty and the Lamb are THE TEMPLE of it [the holy city] (Rev. 20:21).

During Christ's reign on earth, the "shekinah glory" will be retored in the Temple, as God's ministers will also replace the "Urim and Thummim" as God's *guides* to the people!

Then, **"...they shall bring the glory and honor of the nations into it" (Rev. 21:26).** As the spiritual Temple of God finally comes to fruition, the ultimate fulfillment of Haggai's prophetic announcement: **"The glory of this latter house shall be greater than of the former, saith the LORD of hosts..."** will come to pass.

In anticipation of that great and wonderful day—let us heed the admonition of Haggai and "be strong and work" to complete God's glorious house!

ISRAEL—A TYPE OF CHRIST

There is a most fascinating *typology* between the experience of the nation of Israel and the life of Jesus the Messiah as prophesied by the prophet Hosea, **"When Israel was a child, then I loved him, and called my son out of Egypt" (Hos. 11:1).**

Here we find a most interesting parallel to the happenings of the nation of Israel to that of the baby Jesus as foretold by Matthew, **"When he arose, he took the young child and his mother by night, and departed into Egypt: And was there until the death of Herod: that it might be fulfilled which was spoken of the Lord by the prophet [Hosea], saying, Out of Egypt have I called my son" (Matt. 2:14-15).**

These verses clearly verify the nature of *typology* in the Word

THE RESTORATION OF ISRAEL

of God. Both Jesus and the nation of Israel were called God's "son" and as such were entitled to very special blessings. Both were led out of Egypt, Israel during the exodus, and Jesus after the death of Herod.

Therefore, Jesus becomes the *antitype* or fulfillment of Hosea's prophecy and becomes the embodiment of the nation of Israel—or in fact *personifies* the nation of Israel!

In other words, Jesus relived what the nation of Israel did, [or should have done in lifestyle], by going back into Egypt, and fulfilled the exodus deliverance. Jesus' personal deliverance from Herod was the *antitypical* fulfillment of Hosea's prophecy and demonstrates the typological relationship between Jesus and the nation of Israel, both of whom were "sons" called out of Egypt.

In another typological relationship, Christian "sons of God", are also *types* of Christ and Israel coming out of spiritual Egypt or sin. This relationship will be more fully explained as we continue our study of typology.

ANTIOCHUS—A TYPE OF THE FALSE PROPHET

Antiochus IV (Epiphanes), whose name means "God Manifest" ruled the Seleucid dynasty of Syria from 175-163 B.C. Antiochus made a covenant with apostate Jews, who favored him politically, and encouraged them to forsake God's laws. Even the high priest acquiesced to his demands. This *rebellion* began around 171 B.C.

In his attempt to Hellenize the Jews, he stopped the sacrifices, and sacrificed a pig instead. Then this ruthless king committed a most abominable act by sprinkling pigs blood on the Holy of Holies in the Temple. This "swine" forbade circumcision observance of the holy Sabbath, and destroyed all of the Old Testament books he laid his hands on (*The Pictorial Bible,* Tenney, p. 421).

Anyone found possessing a copy of the holy scriptures was killed by decree! A great slaughter followed! As a result of these repugnant acts by this insolent monarch, these Syrian armies were eventually defeated by the gallant Judas Maccabeus (1 Macc. 1:10; 6:16).

This intriguing story is found in the first two books of the Maccabees in the Apocrapha. The Jewish uprising began in 168 B.C. when Mattathias, an aged priest, struck down a royal commissioner and an apostate Jew, who were about to offer heathen sacrifice in the town. Mattathias leveled the altar, and fled to the hills with his sons Eleazor, John, Judas, Jonathan and Simon.

Therefore, we may only conclude that Antiochus Epiphanes is only a *archetype* of the being known as the "Beast" who will perform similar heresies.

After a few months of guerrilla warfare, Mattathias died and his sons Eleazor and John were killed. Mattathias' other three sons continued the insurrection as Judas became the leader and was nicknamed Maccabee, meaning "the Hammerer."

Being a fine soldier and loyal patriot for Jewish independence— Judas organized a battalion consisting of Galieans that defeated major Syrian militia sent against them in 166-165 B.C. Finally, in December of 165 B.C. Judas formally "cleansed the temple" of Syrian pollution and celebrated the event with a great festival. This celebration became a permanent commemoration, falling on December 25, and lasting eight days (1 Macc. 4:52-59; 11 Macc. 10:6; Jn. 10:22).

THE CLEANSING OF THE TEMPLE

This event also had been prophesied in the book of Daniel. In (Daniel 8:13 14), *New International Version,* God revealed:

Then I heard a holy one speaking, and another holy one said to him, 'How long will it take for the vision to be fulfilled—the vision concerning the daily sacrifice, the rebellion that causes desolation, and the surrender of the sanctuary and of the host that will be trampled underfoot'? He said to me, It will take 2,300 evenings and mornings; then the sanctuary will be reconsecrated.'

In other words, there would be 2,300 evening and morning sacrifices that would not be offered—a period of 1,150 days or just a little more than three years till God would permit restoration of the sacrifices.

Those three years were to be among the most trying in Jewish history. Jews were forced to eat pork and worship pagan gods. Those who refused were mercilessly killed.

Many of them therefore acquiesced to adopting Hellenistic

customs, notice: "**Many also of the Israelites consented to his [Antiochus'] religion, and sacrificed unto idols, and profaned the sabbath (I Macc. 1:20-53).** But when the Maccabees liberated Jerusalem, they tore down the pagan gods from the Temple Mount and relit the lights of the Menorah.

To this day the Jewish eight day winter festival of Hanukkah, or Festival of Lights, recalls the cleansing of the Temple in the days of the Maccabees.

In all probability it had been 1,150 days or 2,300 evenings and mornings since Antiochus had forbidden Jewish sacrifices. What happened to the Jews in the days of the Maccabees was merely a *type* of what is yet to happen to them once again in the last days. The *Critical, Experimental Commentary* provides additional information concerning this travesty:

> **This horn is explained (vs.23) to be a 'king of fierce countenance,' etc. Antiochus Epiphanes is meant. Greece, with all its refinement, produces the first—ie., the Old Testament ANTICHRIST. Antiochus had an extraordinary love of art, which expressed itself in grand temples. He wished to substitute Zeus Olympius for Jehovah at Jerusalem. Thus, first, heathen civilization from below and revealed religion from above came into collision. Identifying himself with Jupiter, his air was to make his own worship universal (cf. v.25 with ch. 11:36): so mad was he in this that he was called Epimanes (maniac) instead of Epiphanes (illustrious). None of the previous world rulers...had systematically opposed the Jews' religious worship...He is the forerunner of the final Antichrist, standing in the same relation to the first advent of Christ that Antichrist does to His second coming...He not only opposes God's ancient people, but God Himself.** *The daily sacrifice*—**one lamb was offered in the morning and another in the evening (Exo. 29:38,39).** *was taken away*—**by Antiochus (***Critical Experimental Commentary***, by Jamieson, Fausett and Brown, vol. 1, p. 427).**

The Jews thought that the *Abomination of Desolation* in (Daniel 11:31) was fulfilled in 186 B.C. by Antiochus Epiphanes. This detestable king erected an idolatrous altar on the altar of the Temple in Jerusalem and sacrificed a pig to the heathen god Jupiter Olympus (1 Macc. 1:54; 6:7; 11 Macc. 6:2; Josephus *Antiquities*, 12:5,4; 7,6).

But Jesus said in 31 A.D. that the Abomination of Desolation spoken by Daniel had not yet occurred (Matt. 24:15)!

Today, there are many religious observers watching Europe believing that a future leader will emerge out of a "United States of Europe" and fulfill the prophecy in Daniel.

If Antiochus Epiphanes is a *type* of the "Beast" to come, such an individual would have to be *contemptible*, who comes without *warning!* (Dan. 11:21,24).

Recall also that the kingdom was already formed when Antiochus came on the scene—as will occur when the already formed 10 nations give their power to the "Beast" (Rev. 17:12-13). These men may be instrumental in forming the future organization—but may not be the actual man who will be the coming "Beast."

Such a man will come with *flatteries* and without *warning* to take the kingdom! He may be the least likely man! The "Beast" will be someone who wouldn't offend anyone! He will be a man that nobody takes seriously!

THE "SON OF PERDITION"

Were you aware that the term "son of perdition" is only used *twice* in all the Bible? Most are aware that Judas Iscariot was called "son of perdition" (Jn. 17:12). It was this infamous character who betrayed our Lord during the night of the Passover.

But did you know that this phrase is also used in describing the "man of sin" in the last days? This account is found in (11 Thessalonians 2:3), notice:

> **Let no man deceive you by any means: for that day shall not come, except there come a falling away first, and that *man of sin* be revealed, the *son of perdition.***

There are two ways that people have interpreted this scripture: 1) the "man of sin" comes from an apostate system that never was a part of God's true Church, and 2) the "man of sin" would be a deceiver within the Church, and would cause a "falling away" of true believers.

We shall now view the most generally accepted and most logical explanation. First, we must understand *who* the apostle Paul was addressing this prophecy to, and the conditions that then existed.

Although his assessment of the end-time is correct, Paul thought these events would happen in his life time (vs. 2). Now, if we know what events were happening in Paul's lifetime, we can relate it to the end-time.

Paul said there would, **"come a falling away [Gr. *apostasia*], first"**—notice it does not say as some suppose, "A GREAT FALLING AWAY!"

The Greek word *apostasia* means "rebellion," "forsaking," "defection from the truth," "apostacy," (*Thayers Greek-English, Lexicon*). *The International Bible Commentary* says *apostasia* means" revolt or rebellion against God. It is not stated whether the rebellion occurs among Jews, in the Church, or is a general refusal by men to acknowledge the Creators authority.

The word "apostasy" as used in the Septuagint and NT points to a deliberate abandonment of a former professed position (Thomas, *New Commentary on the Whole Bible*, by Tyndale).

The "man of sin" or "man doomed to destruction", or "man of lawlessness", or "man of rebellion" (NIV), is identical with "Antichrist", and like Antiochus will make claim to divine authority, as he takes over the rebuilt Temple. The "man of lawlessness" will supplement true Christian teaching just as Antiochus was a type.

Next, realize Paul said that this event was already existent, and referred to it as **"the mystery of iniquity" (vs. 7)**. As an historical fact, Simon Magus, was chief leader of the "Babylonian Mysteries," an *apostate* system beginning in 33 A.D. Paul wrote this letter in 51 A.D. Iniquity means "lawlessness" or "opposed to God's law."

This false Babylonian system turned people away from God's laws by substituting pagan counterfeits!

Now notice what else Paul says this "son of perdition" will do during the end of the age: **"Who opposeth and exalteth himself** above all that is called God, or that is worshipped; so that he as God sitteth in the temple God, shewing himself that he is God" (vs. 4).

During the apostle Paul's day, the Temple in Jerusalem was still in existence, and wasn't destroyed until 70 A.D. That is why Paul thought that an individual would fulfill this event in *antitype* of what Antiochus Epiphanes did some 100 years previously. Paul was very familiar with the Old Testament prophecies and what Jesus said in regards to the "Abomination of Desolation."

Jesus indicated that the "Abomination of Desolation" spoken of by Daniel the prophet had not yet occurred in His day, and had something to do with the "holy place" [possibly the holy of holies in the Temple] (Matt. 24:15). Paul realized that the fulfillment of this prophecy would be similar to what occurred during Antiochus' reign.

Realize also, that the very name Epiphanes means "God manifest," from which the Catholic "Feast of Epiphany" is derived. Epiphany, is a festival held on January 6th commemorating Christ to the Gentiles as represented by the Magi. Truly, to commit the abominable acts of Antiochus, one would have to think he was God!

Paul was well acquainted with the prophecies in Daniel that spoke of a time in which and individual would come described by Daniel as "a Little Horn" who would "wear out the saints of the most high," and "change times and laws" (Dan. 7:25). Paul also knew this individual would plant his palace [Temple] in the glorious land of Palestine (Dan. 11:45), and come to his end when he stood against the Prince of Peace [Jesus Christ] after "magnifying himself in his heart" [proclaimed himself as God] (Dan. 8:25).

Notice that the fate of the "man of sin" is the same as that of Daniel's prophecy (11 Thess. 2:3-8). Most likely, Paul believed these Beings to be one and the same!

"The son of destruction" (i.e., destined to destruction), a title given only one other person [Judas, the traitor], is the Antichrist who will come up out of the earth "with two little horns like those of a lamb but a fearsome voice like the Dragon's" (Rev. 13:11. TLB). He will be an imposter!

Realize also the *parallels* between the book of Daniel and the book of Revelation that describes the "False Prophet," or "Image of the Beast," to the "Man of Sin" and "Little Horn." The "Little

THE RESTORATION OF ISRAEL

Horn," "Image of the Beast," and "False Prophet," have power for 3 1/2 years prior to Christ's return (Dan. 7:25; Rev. 11:2; 13:5,14,16).

TO DECEIVE THE ELECT?

The "Little Horn" comes by "flatteries" (Dan. 11:21,32,34), while the "Man of Sin," "Image of the Beast," and "False Prophet," all perform "false miracles" to deceive people (11 Thess. 2:9; Rev. 13:14; 19:19). But this deception is to deceive them that are in the world, not a wholesale deception of the Church! They make war with the Saints (Dan. 7:25; Rev. 13:15-16; 19:29). All come to their end by Christ's return (Dan. 8:25; 11:45; 11 Thess. 2:3-8; Rev. 13:16; 14:9-10; 16:14; 17:14; 19:19-20).

Now let us take a closer look at a very interesting Greek word that describes those that are to be "deceived" by the "lying wonders" or "false miracles" of the "Man of Sin" whose working is after Satan the devil (11 Thess. 2:9-10). These individuals are to "perish" [Gr. *apollumi*] because they received not the love of the truth that they might be saved, and for this cause God sent them strong delusion that they should believe a lie (11 Thess. 2:10-11).

Realize that in most instances, the Greek word *apollumi* refers to people who have never been converted and are lost until they receive the knowledge of our Savior! These are people who have been deceived by Satan, who deceives the whole world (Rev. 12:9). This same Greek word is used in (1 Cor. 1:18 and 11 Cor. 2:15) in describing two groups of people, 1) those that are in the process of being saved, and 2) those that are *deceived* and are *perishing*.

These "lying wonders" will cause "strong delusion" to those in the world to be deceived—not the Elect or Church! God has never purposely sent His people a deception [God does not tempt His people with evil] (Jas. 1:13).

Some have applied this coming deception to the true Church, quoting (Matthew 24:24) and believing this verse pertains to a "select special group" withing the Church. Here's how (Matthew 24:24) reads: **"For there shall arise false Christs...and shall shew great signs and wonders; insomuch that if it were possible, they shall deceive the [very] elect."**

However, we must realize that the word "very" [Gr. *kai*] is a poor translation, and is translated as "even" in the *King James*

Revised Standard Version, The New King James Version, Phillips, and Interlinear Bibles. In Vines, *An Expository Dictionary of New Testament Words*, under "very" it says regarding (Matthew 24:24): 4) Sometimes it translates the conjunction *kai*, in the sense of "even," e.g. Matt. 10:30; in 24:24, A.V., "very" (R.V., "even"; Luke 12:59). Clearly, this verse is not referring to a "select group" of God's true Church that will not be deceived during the end-time by the "lying wonders" of the "man of sin"—but that it is not going to be possible to deceive [even] the Elect.

"THE MAN OF SIN"

Perhaps we can now better understand what Paul meant when he said: **"For the mystery of iniquity doth already work: only he who now letteth [Gr. *restrains*] will let [*restrain*] until he be taken out of the way" (vs. 7).** With most of the apostles martyred, the apostle Paul and John were the only ones left to restrain the "mystery of iniquity" or apostasy that was now entering into the Church to change God's laws!

Let's review why this interpretation appears to be the most logical: 1) the "Mystery of Iniquity" was already in existence during Paul's day, and did not refer to something that would only occur at the end-time, 2) the Temple was in existence during Paul's time, and he thought these events would occur then, and were related to Daniel's prophecies describing the "Little Horn," 3) this prophecy is related to the book of Revelation describing the identical events as pertaining to the "False Prophet."

Clearly, the "Little Horn," "False Prophet," "Man of Sin," and "Antichrist" are all of the same character!

Most of the commentaries have assumed this scripture is referring to the individual known as the "Antichrist," and the "falling away" would be from religion in general. However, some have thought this verse is referring to yet another Judas [traitor] within the midst of God's true Church—that could cause the "falling away" of God's people? They believe it would not be possible for Antichrist to deceive God's own elect?

Furthermore, they believe this verse is referring to a "spiritual Temple" [the Church] and not a literal Temple in Jerusalem. They claim, because Paul referred to the Temple as, "The Temple of God," this could only refer to the Church, as God will never designate the *apostate* anti-Christian Church as "The Temple of

God." It is true that the original Greek word for Temple can be interpreted in a literal or spiritual sense [we will cover this subject in more detail later]. Therefore, the word "sitteth" could imply his occupying the place of power and majesty.

What would precipitate such an event? Certainly his title "man of sin" would indicate that this individuals character had been misleading and concealed. Once the identity of his sins became public—many would be offended and leave God's true Church! However fascinating as this scenario may seem, it appears hard to fathom because of the other events that this "man of sin" would do, such as declare himself as God. Who would be deceived by him in God's Church?

If history is to repeat itself in *duality*—another "son of perdition" may in fact be found in God's true Church. This individual could have a high position in God's Church—even as Judas was the *treasurer* and head of financial affairs for the early Church. However, to fit the *duality* of past types, this individual would not be the leader of the Church, even as Judas and Ahithophel. They were "friends" or close associates, but not leaders!

Although this seems to be an unlikely possibility—anything is possible and only time will tell. Then again, perhaps the *antitype* of this fulfillment has already occurred!

THE THREE JUDAS'S

The name "Judas" has commonly been used in modern vernacular to connotate a *traitor*—and rightly so. Certainly everyone is familiar with the account in which Judas Iscariot, one of the original twelve apostles betrayed our Lord on the night of the Passover.

What you may not know however, is that there is a *duality* to this betrayal in the Old Covenant.

Now realize, there is a duality between the life of King David to that of Christ. Jesus said of His betrayer:

> **I speak not of you all: I know whom I have chosen: but that the scripture may be fulfilled,** *He that eateth bread with me* **hath lifted up his heel against me (Jn. 13:18).**

This is practically a direct quote from (Psalm 41:9) which was written by King David. Let's read it: **"Yea, mine own familiar friend, in whom I trusted, which did eat of my bread, hath lifted up his heel against me."** This Old Testament Judas actually ate at David's table and later betrayed him. David reveals more about this individual's personality in Psalm 55: 12-14:

> **For it was not an enemy that reproached me; then I could have borne it: neither was it he that hated me that did magnify himself against me: then I would have hid myself from him: But it was thou, a man mine equal,** *my guide, and mine acquaintance.* **We took sweet council together, and walked unto the house of God in company.**

Who was this ancient Benedict Arnold that was David's trusted friend, counselor and adviser? His name was Ahithophel which means "foolishness." The entire account is found in (11 Samuel 17 through 19).

The Bible does not reveal *why* Ahithophel turned on King David—but by understanding human nature, perhaps we can speculate. The following facts may give us a clue to this ancient turn coat. From (11 Samuel 23:34; 11:3) it can be determined that Ahithophel was Bathsheba's grandfather.

Very possibly, Ahithophel plotted a way in which he could become part of David's royal family through the seduction of Bathsheba. Perhaps he persuaded her to take a bath on her rooftop so David would see her and be enticed. Bathsheba may have been innocent of all this herself.

When David gazed upon the voluptuous Bathsheba—his heart was filled with passion. David eventually conspired to have Bathsheba's husband Uriah killed in battle. David wanted to marry Bathsheba more than anything in the world.

But finally, David's sanity returned to him and he deeply repented of his heinous sins. When Ahithophel saw this, he threw in his lot with David's ambitious son Absalom. Recall how Absalom desired to usurp his father's throne. Perhaps Ahithophel thought, "Maybe Absalom will give me a high office in his new government?" Whatever Ahithophel's reasoning was—one thing is for sure—these two were in cahoots! More of this conspiracy is found in 11 Samuel 15:12:

> **And Absalom went for Ahithophel the Gillonite, David's counsellor, from his city, even from Giloh, while he offered sacrifices. And the *conspiracy* was strong; for the people increased continually with Absalom.**

Absalom had stolen the hearts of the people, probably with the advice of Ahithophel (verse 6). When Absalom moved against Jerusalem with an army, David fled for his life (verses 13-14).

The story continues in verse 31:

> **And one told David, saying, Ahithophel is among the conspirators with Absalom. And David said, O Lord, I pray thee, turn the counsel of Ahithophel into foolishness.**

Upon fleeing Jerusalem, David met his long time friend and adviser Hushsi (11 Sam. 15:32). These two began a plot of their own to regain the throne. David asked Hushai to return to Jerusalem instead of fleeing into the wilderness with him. David said to Hushai:

> **But if thou return to the city, and say unto Absalom, I will be thy servant, O king; as I have been thy father's servant hitherto, so will I now also be thy servant: then mayest thou for me defeat the counsel of Ahithophel (verse 34).**

Faithful Hushai did as David requested and gave Absalom counsel diametrically opposite that of Ahithophel's. Absalom heeded the advice of Hushai and this eventually led to David's return to power.

Ahithophel foresaw the "handwriting on the wall" for Absalom—as David's forces began regrouping because of Absalom's procrastination of attack. If Absalom was defeated—Ahithophel knew he would be revealed as a traitor and punished severely. The thought of disgrace and shame to his family was too much for Ahithophel to cope with. Ahithopel realized his rope had run out for him—and went home and hanged himself (11 Sam. 17:23).

Here is an amazing *duality* that vividly parallels "the last supper." This account portrays Ahithophel as a traitor like Judas. And like Judas, he committed suicide when he became mentally depressed.

But this story also *parallels* Hushai as a true friend—even as the apostles were true and loyal friends of Jesus.

Chapter Five

TYPES OF THE "TWO WITNESSES"

And I will give power unto my two witnesses, and they shall prophecy a thousand two hundred and threescore days, clothed in sackcloth. These are the two olive trees, and the two candlesticks standing before the God of the earth. And if any man will hurt them, fire proceedeth out of their mouth, and devoureth their enemies: and if any man will hurt them, he must in this manner be killed (Rev. 11:3-5).

Although it is impossible to forecaste the exact identity of *who* will be the "Two Witnesses", there is a great deal we can learn about them from the *types*, such as *what* their message will be, *who* they will preach to, and *where* they will preach.

God's "Two Witnesses" will exist at the same time the "Beast" and "False Prophet" will be in power. They will be God's comtemporary Moses and Aaron withstanding Satan's idolatrous system.

They are *cameos* of Moses and Aaron who performed MIGHTY MIRACLES in the sight of Pharaoh through the power of the Almighty God.

Even as Moses and Aaron warned Pharaoh of the impending plagues if he would not let God's people go—so will these two servants of God. The apostle John writes of their supernatural powers in Revelation 11:6 :

THE RESTORATION OF ISRAEL

These have *power* to shut heaven, that it rain not in the day of their prophecy: and have *power* over waters to turn them to blood, and to smite the earth will all *plagues*, as often as they will.

"TWO OLIVE TREES" AND "TWO CANDLESTICKS"

But why are these "Two Witnesses" labeled as *"two olive trees"* and *"two candlesticks"* as well? What could these *symbols* possibly represent?

In (Revelation 1:12), the apostle John saw a vision in which he saw a *seven branched golden candlestick*, [a "minorah"] and in the middle of the seven candlesticks one like unto the Son of man. The explanation of the seven candlesticks are explained in (Revelation 1:20), as being *God's seven Churches* or era's. In other words, God's Church would exist throughout the ages, as Christ said His Church would never die (Matt. 16:18).

Of course the Son of Man who sits [in authority] in the middle of the candlesticks is Jesus Christ, who is the invisible head of the Church (Eph. 5:23). Jesus is the invisible head of the Church, even as Satan is the invisible head of the false church! There are also seven stars which are angels [Gr. *messengers*] over the Churches (Rev. 1:20).

Therefore, since "seven candlesticks" represent God's seven Church eras, and because the "Two Witnesses" are two candlesticks, the only logical conclusion we can draw is that they *symbolically* represent two Church era's!

Symbolically, these messengers *symbolize the leaders of the last two eras*, as God has most likely chosen a person to represent each era based on his character. For example, the leader of the Philadelphia era will be a person who God finds little fault with (Rev. 3:10), whereas the leader of the Laodicean era will be a person who is *lukewarm* in character [until repentant] (Rev. 3:16).

The Laodiceans will have to go through the *Tribulation* [fire] in order to qualify to be in God's Kingdom (Rev. 3:18). Because the Philadelphia messenger [leader] is promised protection from the Tribulation, some have therefore felt it would be impossible for him to represent one of the Witnesses. Only time will tell!

TYPES OF THE TWO WITNESSES

TYPES OF ZERUBBABEL AND JOSHUA

And the angel that talked with me came again, and waked me, as a man that is wakened out of his sleep. And said unto me, What seest thou? And I said, I have looked, and behold a candlestick all of gold, with a bowl upon the top of it, and his seven lamps thereon, and seven pipes to the seven lamps, which are upon the top thereof. And two olive trees by it, one upon the right side of the bowl, and the other upon the left side thereof (Zech. 4:1-3).

Immediately we recognize that John's prophecy of the "Two Witnesses" is related to the prophecy concerning Zerubbabel and Joshua of the Old Testament as recorded in the book of Zechariah. Zerubbabel was the governor and prince of ancient Judah (B.C. 520) and Joshua was the high priest as we have already learned.

Zerubbabel led God's people out of captivity in Babylon to build God's house in Jerusalem. The very name Zerubbabel means "out of Babylon." Working along side Zerubbabel was Joshua the high priest of Judah.

Symbolically, God's Word uses oil [olive] as one of the *types* to describe God's Holy Spirit. In these last days, God is going to *anoint* His "Two Witnesses" with the power of His Holy Spirit to perform *mighty miracles* once again!

Likewise, a modern-day Zerubbabel will lead His people out of "spiritual Babylon." He will thunder God's warning, **"Come out of her, my people, that ye be not partakers of her sins, and that ye receive not of her plagues " (Rev. 18:4)**.

This end-time Zerubbabel will help build God's "spiritual house" and his *counterpart* in the nation of Israel most likely will be instrumental in building a religious center in Jerusalem in the last days.

Just as Joshua and Zerubbabel began a "new work", **not by might** [Heb. *hayel*, i.e., sheer force of labour], **nor by power** [Heb. *koah*, i.e., ability], **but by my Spirit** [Heb. *ruah*], so will the Two Witnesses!

This will be a "new work" in Jerusalem performed by God's Holy Spirit working in and through them. It will be a unifying Spirit, the same Spirit that worked in many of the prophets of old that will bring about the glorious completion of God's work! God used Moses and Aaron, Elijah and Elisha, and Joshua and Zerubbabel to help us better understand what events will occur in the last days!

Although there are many similarities in Joshua and Zerubbabel to the end-time "Two Witnesses", there are also many differences. That is why so many scholars have tried to piece together the main lessons to be learned from them.

In John's vision we see seven stars, and seven golden candlesticks which are interpreted as seven angels and seven churches (Rev. 1:20). The resurrected and glorified Jesus, (the Son of Man) sits in the middle of the golden single branched Menorah (vs. 13-15) as head of His Church. In Zechariah's lampstand we see a bowl, seven golden pipes, seven lamps, two olive trees, and two olive branches that transfer olive oil to God's two anointed ones that stand by the Lord of the whole earth (Zech. 4: 11-14).

Because the book of Revelation was not written as of yet, the visible church giving light to the world at the time of this prophecy was the *ecclesia* or called out people of the Jews. The sons of oil, that stood by the Lord of the whole earth at that time were Joshua and Zerubbabel.

Most scholars agree that the "branches" of the trees are the channels through which a continual flow of oil goes into the bowl of the lamps at the top of the candlestick (Zech 4:2), and that this is the purpose for which the two olive trees stand beside the candlestick. This "candlestick of gold" symbolizes the Light of the world. The two olive trees supply an unlimited amount of oil to the bowl without any human agency. Zerubbabel's task would not be because of his own power or might, but by the power of the Holy Spirit.

The work of Zerubbabel was a *type* of what Jesus would do through grace, not through personal effort, notice Zechariah 4:7: "Who art thou, O great mountain? Before Zerubbabel thou shalt become a plain: and he shall bring forth the headstone thereof with shoutings, crying, Grace, grace unto it." The angel was stating that no obstacle will be able to stop the completion of the temple in Zerubbabel's time or in God's kingdom reign.

This unifying and completing end-time work is also symbolic of the capstone mentioned in (Zech. 13:2), which completes and unifies the physical and spiritual Temple.

In (chapters 3,4 and 6 of Zechariah) we find additional information concerning the "Two Witnesses." Jesus Christ, the

TYPES OF THE TWO WITNESSES

head of the Church is represented as a candlestick of all gold with a bowl upon it (Zech. 4:2)—and has seven lamps thereon and seven pipes to the seven lamps. These seven lamps could represent God's seven Church eras, even as the seven candlesticks did in (Revelation 1:20).

The seven pipes leading to the lamps, could represent the connection to Jesus Christ by which His Holy Spirit [in the form of oil] can flow to His Church (Zech. 4:12). It is by this medium that the "Two Witnesses" will receive their power (Zech. 4:6).

These "Two Witnesses" will have power to shut heaven that it rain not, and turn water into blood and to smite the earth with all plagues. They will have *power* and *authority* to kill anyone who tries to overcome them (Rev. 11:6 7). They are the Lord's anointed Ones that stand by the Lord of the whole earth (Zech. 4:1; Rev. 11:4).

THE LAST TWO ERAS

These "Two Witnesses" will be very instrumental in building God's "spiritual Temple." Joshua and Zerubbabel built God's physical Temple after the Jews were released from their captivity in Babylon in 536 B.C. God uses them *symbolically* to show what the "Two Witnesses" will also do in these last days.

Although the historical context of the book of Haggai and Ezra is to rebuild the "physical Temple", the book of Zechariah is primarily directed towards building God's "spiritual Temple."

During the time of the rebuilding of the Temple—Haggai, Zechariah and Malachi were God's living prophets. But it wasn't until 400 years after Malachi, that Israel had another prophet through the preaching of John the Baptist.

During this interval of time, the Temple was not filled with God's shekinah glory! God's Holy Spirit was *among* them, but not *in* them! God's glory only returned *symbolically* to the Temple when Jesus Christ entered with the LIGHT of truth!

Speaking to the *spiritual* Zerubbabel, God says he will help lay the foundation of His house and finish it (Zech. 4:9). Concerning God's "spiritual Temple," Jesus Christ is the ultimate fulfillment of laying the foundation. Other apostles throughout the ages have helped Jesus Christ build the spiritual Temple, including the apostle Paul (1 Cor. 3:11).

Because the "Two Witnesses" represent two Church eras, it

seems evident that they will *symbolize* the Philadelphia and Laodicean eras—as these will be the last two eras in time sequence prior to Christ's return. However, they will not be the only eras in existence!

Zerubbabel appears to represent the Philadelphia era as it will have little strength (Rev. 3:8; Zech. 4:6). Joshua who has "filthy garments" [symbolic of sin] needs to repent and go through the Tribulation (Zech. 3:2-4). Notice, God's inspired wording: **"...is not this a brand plucked out of the fire?" (3:2).** This appears to correspond to the Laodicean character. Notice the words "the true and faithful *witness"* in (Revelation 3:14) to the leader of the Laodicean Church.

Once this individual repents as well as those representative of this era [his fellows—Zech. 3:8], they will qualify to become *judges* in God's Kingdom (Zech. 3:7). This also corresponds with the Laodiceans as they will sit with Christ in His throne (Rev. 3:21). This is *symbolic language* for their responsibility, meaning they will be doing what Christ does. Jesus will be a *judge* over the nations (Acts 10:42; 1 Pet. 4:5; Jn. 5:22,27).

Jesus indicated in (Luke 7:41-50) the relationship of one who had many sins also had much love, because they also knew how much they needed forgiveness. Certainly, this type of individual would be more qualified as a judge, since they have firsthand experience in repentance and mercy. God chastens every son He loves, and He loves repentant Laodiceans (Rev. 3:19).

Zechariah 3:8 speaks of these "fellows" as "men wondered at" [Heb. "men of wonder" margin]. These "men of wonder" or repentant Laodiceans will reign with Christ, the BRANCH (Zech. 3:8) who is building God's "spiritual Temple" (6:12).

It is also fitting that the Philadelphia era will have the responsibility of being the *educators* in God's Kingdom—because they are represented spiritually as *pillars* that hold up God's Temple (Rev. 3:12). A physical pillar is a structural support.

Because prophecy is often *dual* to the nation of Israel and the Church, there most likely will be a physical *counterpart* in the nation of Israel to spiritual Joshua and Zerubbabel.

These converted Israelites may be instrumental in building God's physical Temple in the last days (Zech. 6:11-13,15). This Temple would be in Jerusalem, the holy city (Rev. 11:1-3). No doubt this would cause a great deal of confusion since the "False Prophet" is also associated with God's Temple (11 Thess. 2:4).

TYPES OF THE TWO WITNESSES

JOSHUA'S "FILTHY GARMENTS"

Joshua's "filthy garments" (Zech. 3:3) *symbolized* the sins of Israel as well as his own. Notice Isaiah's parallel wording to the national sins of Israel:

> **...behold, thou art wroth, for we have sinned: in those is continuance, and we shall be saved. But we are all as an unclean thing, and all our righteousness are as** *filthy rags...* **(Isa. 64:5-6).**

The changing of Joshua's garments characterizes the RESTORATION, and moral cleansing of the nation of Israel! Under Zerubbabel, 4,289 priests returned to restore the Temple service. Previously, the priesthood had become corrupted and the offerings polluted (Mal. 2:5-9). Thus God "cleaned up" the nation of Israel and Judah at this time, and made them ceremonially clean to rebuild the Temple!

This moral cleansing of the physical nation of Israel may also *parallel* the spiritual cleansing of the last church era under spiritual Joshua. After Zerubbabel died, the priesthood became corrupt, and the people turned away from God. Realize, God does things in DUAL stages. Zerubbabel and Joshua worked side by side building the *material Temple* of stone, wood and other materials, and are *forerunners* or *types* of God's end-time *spiritual Temple*!

Could it be that two close associates building the Church in the last days would parallel the lives of Zerubbabel and Joshua. Remember, the problem with the Laodicean's is in their attitude producing lukewarm works! God commands them to repent and be zealous [Gr. *zeo*], meaning "to boil." These "works" would have to begin *prior* to the Tribulation, as it is these "lukewarm works" that has caused them to be sent into the Tribulation! Therefore, we may conclude that the Laodicean era will exist at the same time, and may even be affiliated with the Philadelphia era.

Zechariah 3 and 4 detail the characteristics of Joshua, and may very well be a *type* of spiritual Joshua. Here we find that Joshua was God's chosen leader and then Satan found his weakness, and overpowered him (Zech. 3:1). After Joshua repented, he was given a new mitre [a symbol of government] and new garments (Zech. 3:5). Clearly, Joshua had a problem following God's government that had been previously layed down and enforced by

Zerubbabel.

Those who are "his fellows" have a similar problem, and will also have to go through the great Tribulation to "open their eyes" (Zech. 3:8). In other words, they were not walking in God's ways! (Zech. 3:7).

Just as God has always had a *duality* between the physical and the spiritual—there may also be a *duality* between Spiritual Joshua and Zerubbabel of the Church and their *counterpart* in the physical nation of Israel. Two Witnesses may be instrumental in building a physical Temple in Jerusalem in the last days as did the literal Joshua and Zerubbabel (Zech. 6:11-13, 15).

Lest there be any doubt that a remnant of Israelites will form a part of the Laodicean Church and be "plucked out of the fire," let's read Amos 4:11: **."..ye [Israel] were as a firebrand plucked out of the burning: yet have ye not returned unto me, saith the LORD."**

During "Jacob's trouble" in the last days, when the nation of Israel is held in captivity in the Great Tribulation—a remnant of Israel will repent as the Eternal pours out His Holy Spirit! When Jesus Christ returns to the earth, He will lead them out of captivity, and back to their land!

Now here is something interesting concerning the changing of Israel's filthy garments!

On the Day of Atonement, the high priest entered the Most Holy Place in the Temple, not in his ordinary golden garments, but in a *white linen* dress with matching girdle. Although his mitre was the same shape, it was of a different material than he ordinarily wore.

Thus, on this most sacred and solemn day, the high priest appeared, not as the *Bridegroom* of our Lord, but *symbolically* as the *Bride!* White linen is the *symbol* of righteousness (Rev. 3:4,5; 4:4; 7:9,13; 15:6; 19:8,14).

The removal of Joshua's "filthy garments" and the clothing of him with a change of righteous clothing was *emblematic* of the perfect purity that will eventually happen to Israel and the Church—Christ's "spotless Bride"!

TYPES OF THE TWO WITNESSES

JOHN THE BAPTIST
A TYPE OF THE PROPHET ELIJAH

Malachi the prophet, who lived about the time of Zechariah the prophet, declared:

> **Remember ye the law of Moses my servant, which I commanded unto him in Horeb for all Israel, with the statutes and judgments. Behold, I will send you Elijah the prophet before the coming of the great and dreadful day of the Lord: and he shall turn the heart of the fathers to the children, and the heart of the children to their fathers, lest I come and smite the earth with a curse (Mal. 4:4-6).**

Elijah, of course, was the greatest prophet of God in ancient times. In his days, as in our modern times, the people had strayed far from the knowledge of God. King Ahab, the wickedest king who ever lived, sat on the throne of Israel, and Jezebel, his wicked and treacherous wife, ruled with him. Israel had fallen into paganism, and Baal worship was rife. In fact, the prophets of Baal outnumbered the servants of God 450 to one!

Says *Unger's Bible Dictionary*, "Ahab had taken for wife Jezebel, a Canaanite woman, daughter of Eth baal. Of a weak and yielding character, he allowed Jezebel to establish the Phoenician worship on a grand scale—priests and prophets of Baal were appointed in crowds—the prophets of Jehovah were persecuted and slain, or only escaped by being hid in caves. *It seemed as if the last remnants of true religion were about to perish*" (art; "Elijah", p. 302).

In the face of stiff persecution and the threat of violent death at the hands of Jezebel's police, Elijah, under inspiration of God, proclaimed with dynamic power:

> **As the Lord God of Israel liveth, before whom I stand, whose constant servant I am, there shall not be dew nor rain these years, but according to my word.**

Elijah had the same power as the "Two Witnesses" described

THE RESTORATION OF ISRAEL

in (Revelation 11)!

For three years and six months [a time, times, and half a time!] there was no rain (Jas. 5:17). The full horrors of famine, caused by crop failure, descended on Samaria and the northern Ten-Tribed Kingdom.

Then Elijah returned from hiding out, and confronted Ahab and Jezebel once more. Before Ahab, he challenged the prophets of Baal to the supreme test, that the controversy as to who really represented the true God, and who was the true God, would be resolved once and for all time!

Unger's Bible Dictionary relates:

> **There are few more sublime stories in history than this. On the one hand the servant of Jehovah, attended by his one servant, with his wild, shaggy hair, his scanty garb, and sheepskin cloak, but with calm dignity of demeanor and the minutest regularity of procedure. On the other hand the prophets of baal and Ashtaroth—doubtless in all the splendor of their vestments (11 Kings 10:22), with the wild din of their 'vain repetitions' and the maddened fury of their disappointed hopes—and the silent people surrounding all; these form a picture which brightens into fresh distinctness every time we consider it. The Baalites are allowed to make trial first. All day long these false prophets cried to Baal, they leaped upon the altar, and mingled their blood with that of the sacrifice—but all is in vain, for at the time of the evening sacrifice the altar was still cold and the bullock lay stark theron- 'there was neither voice, nor any to answer, nor any that regarded.'**
>
> **Then Elijah repaired the broken altar of Jehovah, and having laid thereon his bullock and drenched both altar and sacrifice with water until the trench about it was filled, he prayed, 'Lord God of Abraham, Isaac, and of Israel, let it be known this day that thou art God**

> in Israel, and that I am thy servant, and that I have done all these things at thy word.' The answer was all that could be desired, for 'the fire of the Lord fell, and consumed the burnt sacrifice, and the wood, and the stones, and the dust, and licked up the water that was in the trench.' The people acknowledged the presence of God, exclaiming with one voice, 'The Lord, he is God; the Lord he is God' (*Unger,* p. 303). See (1 Kings 18:38).

Elijah also had power to kill his enemies as will the "Two Witnesses" (Rev. 11:5). However, Elijah was not perfect. His faith weakened at times. He had "like passions" as we do (Jas. 5:17). Even after this mighty miracle, after which the prophets of Baal were all slain, Jezebel sent him a threatening letter and he fled for his life! In the wilderness, he sat down under a juniper tree, discouraged, depressed, and despondent.

John the Baptist was a voice crying out in the *physical* wilderness of the Jordan River, preparing the way for Jesus' First Coming. This Coming was to a *material* Temple and to a *physical* nation (Judah). This *physical* Coming was but a *prototype*, or forerunner to Jesus' second Coming, in which one in the "spirit and power" of John and Elijah will prepare the way for Jesus' second Coming.

Spiritual Elijah will cry out amidst today's *spiritual wilderness* of sin and religious confusion, announcing Christ's Second Coming to His *spiritual* Temple (the Church). This time Jesus will be coming in a *glorified* spiritual body, not a *physical* body!

The Elijah to come in these last days, before the second coming of Christ, will be a prophet in the "spirit and power" of Elijah—not Elijah himself. John the Baptist fulfilled this role before Jesus' first coming. Zacharias, the father of John the Baptist, was told by an angel that his son would:

> ...be great in the sight of the Lord, and shall drink neither wine nor strong drink; and he shall be filled with the Holy Spirit, even from his mother's womb. And many of *the children of Israel* shall he turn to the Lord their God. And

THE RESTORATION OF ISRAEL

> he shall go before him [the Messiah] *in the spirit and power of Elias [Elijah],* to turn the hearts of the fathers to the children, and the disobedient to the wisdom of the just; to make ready a people prepared for the Lord' (Lk. 1:15-17).

Who will fulfill this role in these last days?

Who will turn the hearts of the nation of Israel to their Father in heaven? This end-time messenger will turn the hearts of them of Judah in Jerusalem as did Elijah and John the Baptist (Mal. 3:4-6). He will convert 144,000 hearts of the nation of Israel back to God! Once again, this prophecy is *dual* to the nation of Israel.

Notice a little more about the precise role John the Baptist, the "Elijah" of his day, was to fulfill as his father Zecharias, inspired by God's Holy Spirit announced:

> And thou, child shalt be called the prophet of the Highest; for thou shalt go before the face of the Lord to prepare his ways; to give knowledge of salvation unto his people by the remission of their sins, through the tender mercy of our God; whereby the day-spring from on high hath visited us, to give light to them that sit in darkness and in the shadow of death, to guide our feet into the way of peace (Lk. 1:76-79).

When the Pharisees asked him, John himself said he was not Elijah (Jn. 1:21). His answer was, **"I am the voice of one crying in the wilderness, Make straight the way of the Lord, as said the prophet Isaiah"** (vs. 23).

But Jesus plainly said of John, **"And if ye will receive it, this is Elias [Elijah], which was for to come"** (Matt. 11:7-14). Later, the disciples had forgotten Jesus' words, so they asked Him again:

> And his disciples asked him, saying, 'Why then say the scribes that Elias must first come' And Jesus answered and said unto them, Elias truly shall first come, *and restore all things.* But I say unto you, That Elias is come already, and they knew him not, but have done unto him whatsoever they listed. Likewise shall also the

TYPES OF THE TWO WITNESSES

Son of man suffer of them. Then the disciples understood that he spake unto them of John the Baptist (Matt. 17:10-13).

CLOTHED IN SACKCLOTH

Although the substance of their preaching is not revealed by scripture, the message of the "Two Witnesses" is suggested by the clothing of these end-time messengers:

And I will give power unto my two witnesses, and they shall prophesy a thousand two hundred and threescore days, clothed in sackcloth (Rev. 11:3).

Thayer defines this sackcloth [Gr. *sakkos*], as follows:

a coarse cloth, a dark coarse stuff made especially of the hair of animals: a garment of the like material, and clinging to the person like a sack, which was wont to be worn by mourners, penitents, suppliants...and also by those, who, like the Hebrew prophets, led an austere life (*A Greek-English Lexicon of the New Testament*, p, 566).

Here are more startling facts between the *dual* lives of Elijah and John the Baptist. Both were crude men dressed in sheepskin (11 Kings 1:8; Heb. 11:37) and camels's hair (Matt. 3:4). Interestingly, Joshua, another *type* of the "Two Witnesses" had unusual [filthy] garments (Zech. 3:3).

Both men were audacious and rebuked kings. Elijah rebuked king Ahab of Israel, while John the Baptist reprimanded king Herod. Both were preachers of righteousness and acquired the animosity of a queen, whose king tried to kill them. Jezebel and Herod's wife are *types* of the false church while Ahab and Herod are *types* of the "False Prophet."

Elijah was well known to the nations around him. One thing more is worth speculating upon. When Elijah's work on earth was over, he passed his mantle to Elisha. Once spiritual Elijah completes his work on the earth, one has to wonder if there will be an Elisha work afterwards?

Someone, on the earth in these last days will fulfill this tremendous prophecy. He will restore the true worship of God, and turn the hearts of the fathers to their children, and "restore all things" preparing a people to meet God, proclaiming the good news of the coming Kingdom of God to the nations of the world!

Both Elijah and John the Baptist were prophets sent to the house of Israel in a time of apostasy, to call the nation to REPENTANCE! With the ministry of the "Two Witnesses," we see once again the sign of their message in their very special clothing—hair cloth, which was a SIGN of national mourning and repentance!

It may therefore be concluded, from their distinctive dress, that the "Two Witnesses" are announcing the same message as did John—that of *repentance* because the Messiah is coming!

NOT MOSES AND ELIJAH

According to the literalist theory, the "Two Witnesses" will be Moses and Elijah. They base their claims on several scriptural references.

Literalists assume that Elijah will be one of the "Two Witnesses" because it is predicted in (Malachi 3:1-3; 4:5-6) that Elijah would come before the second coming of Christ, and since he did not appear to experience physical death (2 Kings 2:9-11).

It is true that there are many similarities between the life of Elijah and the "Two Witnesses", including power to withhold the rain for 3 1/2 years (1 Kings 17:1; Rev. 11:3,6), and power to kill their enemies (Rev. 11:5).

Literalists also identify Moses as one of God's end-time messengers because Moses appeared with Elijah in the transfiguration (Matt. 17:3), and he performed similar miraculous feats such as turning water into blood (Ex. 7:19-20; Rev. 11:6).

Now the theory continues. Moses' body was preserved by God so that he would be restored (Deut. 34:5-6; Jude 9) as one of the Witnesses [representing the Law], with Elijah [representing the Prophets], in witnessing and proclaiming the coming of the Messiah!

However, there are several fallacies with this theory. The "transfiguration" was a *vision* of the Kingdom of God, and not a resurrection of Moses since Christ is the firstfruit of the

TYPES OF THE TWO WITNESSES

resurrection (1 Cor. 15:20,23). The answer to this perplexing scripture is found in (Matthew 17:9), where Jesus told them, "Tell the VISION to no man." A vision is not a material reality, but a supernatural picture observed by the eyes.

The "Witnesses" have mortal bodies and are subject to death. Elijah and Moses on the Mount of transfiguration evidently did not have mortal bodies, for they "appeared in glory." Therefore, it is hardly likely that they would be given mortal bodies again.

EZEKIEL'S MESSAGE—A TYPE FOR THE END TIME

God used the prophets, naming them Isaiah, Ezekiel, Hosea and Joel, to warn Israel about punishments He would bring upon them for their constant rebellion against His laws. These prophets were to use their voices like trumpets to blare their warnings to God's people.

Notice, for example, God's instruction to Isaiah:

Cry aloud, spare not, lift up thy voice like a trumpet, and shew my people their transgression, and the house of Jacob their sins (Isa. 58:1). See also (Hosea 5:8 and Joel 2:1).

Portions of the prophets' warnings were fulfilled in *type*, by ancient Israel's captivity. Yet many of these prophecies are *dual*, having both ancient and modern fulfillments. Such is the case with the message of the prophet Ezekiel.

God set Ezekiel as a watchman to Israel. Ezekiel, through his message, *symbolically* blew a trumpet of warning to God's people (Ezek. 33:1-7).

Ezekiel's warning, however, did not reach the house of Israel, because they had already gone into captivity! Ezekiel's visions of Israel's impending destruction were given "in the fifth day of the month, which was the fifth year of king Jehoiachin's captivity" (Ezek. 1:2). Jehoiachin went into captivity in 597 B.C. or about 125 years after the removal, to Assyria, of the last of the northern tribes, which occurred from 721-718 B.C.

If Ezekiel's message did not reach ancient Israel—for whom was it intended?

God's warning through Ezekiel was intended for the modern descendants of ancient Israel—the peoples of Israel scattered throught the United States, Britain and northwestern Europe today!

LEVITICAL TYPES

Over the years, there have been many different interpretations as to the identity of these two exalted individuals known biblically as the "Two Witnesses." Theologians have speculated these two end-time miracle workers to be everyone from the resurrected Moses and Elijah, to angelic beings! Although it would be preposterous to give actual names of the "Two Witnesses", their nationality and origin can be safely speculated upon, based on our previous knowledge of the *types* and scripture!

Note this first of all!

Whoever these "Two Witnesses" of God will be, they definitely will be human! Scripture is emphatic on this point because they are *killed* in the holy city (Rev. 11:7,8).

Because a Levitical system is yet to emerge in Jerusalem with a sacrificial system and probable Temple—it is my personal belief that these two end-time servants of God will be of Israelite origin. This understanding is also based upon our knowledge of past *types* of the "Two Witnesses." As already mentioned, there may be a *duality* between the "Two Witnesses" in Jerusalem representing the physical nation of Israel and the spiritual Church.

Also, as already shown, Moses, Aaron, Joshua, and Zerubbabel, Elijah and John the Baptist were all *types* of the "Two Witnesses." The first *type* of the "Two Witnesses" were Moses and Aaron—who turned water into blood and caused a devastating drought (Ex. 7:17). The "Two Witnesses" will perform similar feats (Rev. 11:6).

Realize this important truth—both Moses and his brother Aaron were Levites!

Next, we come to Elijah who brought fire down from heaven (1 Kings 18:38) and prophesied a 3 1/2 year drought (1 Kings 17:1; Jas. 5:17). Again, these are identical powers the "Two Witnesses" will receive (Rev. 11:5,6).

Although the Bible does not give Elijah's nationality, other than he was a Tishbite of Gilead—he is believed to be a Levite. For him to erect an altar and make a sacrifice without being a Levite (1 Kings 18:31-38)—would have been an abomination to the Eternal! Also, because our Savior said that John the Baptist

TYPES OF THE TWO WITNESSES

was a *type* of Elijah (Matt. 17:12,13)—and John was a Levite (Lk. 1:5,13).

In these last days—a third *type* of Elijah is yet to come, **"Behold, I will send you Elijah the prophet before the coming of the great and dreadful day of the Lord" (Mal. 4:5).**

What is this coming Elijah to do? Let Christ give us the answer: **."..Elijah truly shall come first, and *restore all things"* (Matt. 17:!1).** This was also prophesied by Peter in Acts 3:20-21:

> **And he shall send Jesus Christ, which before was preached unto you: whom the heaven must receive until the times of *restitution* [restoring] of all things...**

But what things are the coming Elijah to *restore* before Christ returns? He will begin to *restore* the Kingdom to Israel! The apostles were well aware that this would someday occur as they inquired of Christ: **."..Lord, wilt thou at this time *restore again the kingdom to Israel?* (Acts 1:6).**

Now we come to the final *type* of the "Two Witnesses" to learn *what* will be *restored* by the coming Elijah!

The account of Joshua and Zerubbabel *parallels* what the "Two Witnesses" will do to a tee! They, like the "Two Witnesses" were God's "two olive trees" that stood before God on earth.

Now what did Joshua and Zerubbabel do? They *restored* the Aaronic *priesthood* and *sacrificial system* in a *rebuilt Temple!* Because they *symbolically* stood on each side of the seven branched candlestick in the holy place of the Temple (Zech. 4:2,3)—they must be Levite priests! Scripture tells us that Joshua was a high priest (Zech. 3:8). No Gentile or other Israelite tribe was permitted to enter the Holy Place in the Temple where the seven branched candlestick was located (Ex. 30:27).

Let's notice further similarities between Joshua and Zerubbabel, and the "Two Witnesses."

Both are called "two olive trees" and "two candlesticks" or "two anointed ones" that stand by the Lord of the whole earth (Zech. 4:2,3,14; Rev. 11:4).

Both have something to do with measuring a Temple in Jerusalem! Notice the resemblance in wording:

THE RESTORATION OF ISRAEL

> **Therefore thus saith the LORD, I am returned to Jerusalem with mercies:** *my house* **shall be built in it, saith the LORD of hosts, and a line shall be stretched forth upon Jerusalem...I lifted up mine eyes again, and looked, and behold a man with a** *measuring line* **in his hand (Zech. 1:16; 2:1).**

Zerubbabel is then seen with a *plummet* in his hand [a carpenter's tool for making walls perpendicular] to *measure* and complete God's house [Temple] (Zech. 4:9,10). Now notice the similar wording of (Revelation 11) in reference to the "Two Witnesses":

> **And there was given me [John]** *a reed like unto a rod***: and the angel stood, saying, Rise, and** *measure the temple of God***, and the** *altar***, and them that worship therein. But the** *court* **[court of the Gentiles] leave out, and** *measure* **it not; for it is given unto the Gentiles: and the holy city shall they tread under foot forty and two months (Rev. 11:1,2).**

Undoubtedly there are spiritual implications of this Temple to God's Church—however, to "spiritualize" the entire context as applying to a "spiritual Temple" is a gross error!
Consider!

Joshua and Zerubbabel were *types* of the "Two Witnesses" and built a *literal* Temple! Gentiles will *literally* tread down God's holy city of Jerusalem for forty two months [3 1/2 years] (Lk. 21:24). If this Temple is "spiritual"—why connect the "court of the Gentiles" to it which is *literal*, and will be *literally* trodden under foot by Gentile armies? The "court of the Gentiles" can only be interpreted in a literal sense—for what is it's spiritual implication?

After viewing the *types* of the "Two Witnesses"—we can only come to one possible conclusion. They will be of Israelite origin, and be instrumental in building a house for the Lord in Jerusalem. Most likely one of them will be of priestly origin as was Aaron, Joshua, Elijah and John the Baptist.

Jerusalem is to be the focus of attention in these last days. It

TYPES OF THE TWO WITNESSES

is where the "Two anointed" servants of God will perform mighty miracles that will convert thousands in Israel! This will be similar to what John the Baptist did and Peter on the Day of Pentecost (Acts 2:41: 21:20).

So great will be the conversion of Israel that 144,000 Israelites (12,000 from each tribe) will be protected from the seven last plagues of God (Rev. 7:1-8). Unbelievable miracles are about to occur in Jerusalem, and in fact may parallel what happened during the first century. Notice Jesus' prophetic words:

> **But ye shall receive power, after that the Holy Spirit is come upon you: and ye shall be witnesses unto me both in Jerusalem, and in all Judaea, and in Samaria, and unto the uttermost part of the earth (Acts 1:8).**

This will be the time that all things will be *restored* in Jerusalem including a Temple, Levitical priesthood and sacrificial system. This will occur in Palestine as a result of the conversion of thousands of Jews to a *type* of Jewish Christianity that was experienced during the first Century!

Chapter Six

PARABLES OF ISRAEL'S HISTORY

THE PARABLE OF THE WICKED HUSBANDMEN

There was a certain householder, which planted a vineyard, and hedged it round about, and digged a winepress in it, and built a tower, and let it out to husbandmen, and went into a far country: And when the time of fruit drew near, he sent his servants to the husbandmen, that they might receive the fruits of it.

And the husbandmen took his servants, and beat one, and killed another, and stoned another. Again, he sent other servants more than the first: and they did unto them likewise. But last of all he sent unto them his son, saying, They will reverence my son. But when the husbandmen saw the son, they said among themselves, This is the heir; come, let us kill him, and let us seize on his inheritance. And they caught him, and cast him out of the vineyard, and slew him. When the lord therefore of the vineyard cometh, what will he do unto those husbandmen? (Matt. 21:33-44).

THE RESTORATION OF ISRAEL

The parables of Israel's history demonstrate the common theme: "The Change of Administration" from Jew to Gentile. This can only be understood by comprehending the parables of Israel's history as a nation. Not only can God's plan for the *present* dispensation be clearly defined from these parables—but also His plan for the future of the world and Israel's part in it.

The parable of *The Wicked Husbandmen* is an extension of the parable of *Two Sons*. The householder in this parable is Christ who went away to a far country (heaven).

The husbandmen in this parable is *symbolic* of the nation of Israel—who has continuously REJECTED God's chosen *servants* throughout history—as well as their own transcendental purpose. They have *killed* God's servants, the prophets through *beatings* and *stonings!*

Ancient Israel stoned Jeremiah; cut Isaiah in two; clubbed Amos to death; allowed the head of John the Baptist to be a gift on a silver platter; and stoned Steven! See (Jer. 20:1,2; 37:15; 38:6; 26:20-23; l Kings 18:13; 22:24; 11 Kings 6:22,31; Matt. 23:29-37; Acts 7:5; 11 Chron. 24:2; Heb. 11:36-38).

Jesus cries out because of these atrocities in Matthew 23:37: **"O Jerusalem, Jerusalem, thou that *killest* the prophets, and *stonest* them which are sent unto thee..."** How Jesus would have loved to see His chosen people repent, so He could take them under His wing—even as a mother hen gathering her chicks (vs. 37).

It was this same stiff-necked nation through the leadership of the Pharisees that killed the householders son (Jesus Christ). When Jesus returns as lord of the vineyard, He will destroy those who have rejected Him (vs. 41-42).

Ironically, the Pharisees failed to perceive this parable was directed at them personally, and unwittingly pronounced their own condemnation. When they realized Jesus spoke of them—they wanted to kill Him then and there (vs. 46). There was venom in their hearts and minds!

Therefore, *the Kingdom of God* was *temporarily* taken from them and given to other nations [Gentiles] that will bring forth fruit (vs. 43). Paul mentions the transfer of the Vineyard [rulership over His goods] to include Gentiles in (Romans 11:15-23). Here, Gentiles are envisioned as "a wild olive tree" grafted into God's Vineyard which originally only included Israelites.

Now, a *holy nation* is being prepared by God which includes converted Jews and Gentiles to rule over His Vineyard (1 Pet. 2:9; Rev. 1:6). This will be a nation of people consisting of many different nationalities—yet all with the same willing heart of faithfulness.

They will be eager to OBEY God's way of life and *repent* of their sins. These servants will not desire to crucify their Master, rather they will want to help Him cultivate His Vineyard and implement His plans for making the Vineyard fruitful!

Though these be few in number as "the harvest is great, but the laborers are few," they will be desirous in helping God convert the world! Incidently, this is the *only* parable that vividly describes our Lord's death!

For further proof that this parable referred to Israel's past history, all we need do is turn to (Isaiah 5) where it is evident that this is almost identical wording. If there be any doubt as to the interpretation of the Vineyard's identity through *symbolism*—Isaiah explains: **"For the *vineyard* of the LORD of hosts *is the house of Israel,* and the men of *Judah* his pleasant plant..." (Isa. 5:7).** See also (Hosea 10:1; Ps. 80; 81).

Ironside sums up Israel's past and future history:

> **By and by, the vine is going to be replanted in Palestine. In fact, we may go further and say, The vine is being replanted in Palestine. The Jews are going back to their own land; it stirs one's soul as Scripture is being fulfilled before our eyes. They are being replanted in their own vineyard, but replanted for what? For the vintage of the wrath of God. A remnant will be gathered out, separated to the Lord, but the rest will be given up to unsparing judgment in the time of Jacob's trouble. Fleshly Israel, the vine of the earth, can produce no fruit for God. But, in that day of distress, the clusters of the vine of the earth will be cast into the great winepress of the wrath of God (*Lectures on the Revelation,* p. 267).**

The cultivation of God's Vineyard, or Israel's early history began when the Vineyard was transplanted from Egypt to the fertile soil of Palestine. Further, the tiling or removal of Israel's enemies from the land to enhance rapid growth are all outlined in the eightieth Psalm.

All through the Word of God, the nation of Israel is *figuratively* labeled as God's Vine! Sometimes Israel is called an olive tree, sometimes a fig tree. See (Hosea 10:1; Joel 1:7).

The Eternal is now in the process of *restoring* His Vineyard back to "the house of Israel." This process began in 1948 when the nation of Israel became a nation once again!

THE PARABLE OF THE TWO SONS

> *But what think ye? A certain man had two sons; and he came to the first, and said, Son, go work today in my vineyard. He answered and said, I will not: but afterward he repented, and went. And he came to the second, and said likewise. And he answered and said, I go, sir: and went not. Whether of them twain did the will of his father? They say unto him, The first. Jesus saith unto them, Verily I say unto you, That the publicans and the harlots go into the kingdom of God before you. For John came unto you in the way of righteousness, and ye believed him not: but the publicans and the harlots believed him: and ye, when ye had seen it, repented not afterward, that ye might believe him (Matt. 21:28-32).*

This true to life story struck deep in the heart of the Pharisees who rejected Jesus' teachings. It is aimed at all religious leaders garbed in HYPOCRISY who reject the message of Christ. Like the parable of *The Wicked Husbandmen*, it gives hope to the common people who accept Him joyfully!

The second son is a *portrait* of all kinds of super sanctimonious religious types—who worship God through lip service—but deny Him in works of repentance! The first son depicts the worst of sinners who at first defiantly *refuse* to repent of their heinous sins, but later in life accept this calling. These are the penitent sinners [publicans and harlots] that Jesus referred to and delighted in their works of repentance.

Contraiwise, the Pharisees openly mutinied against the proclamation of repentance by John the Baptist, but the common sinners believed in his message. To those who *repent* like the first son, will be granted the Kingdom of God. Those who rebel like the second son will be thrust out of the Kingdom and there will be "weeping and gnashing of teeth."

The deeper implication of the "two sons" in this parable are *types* of the nation of Israel and the New Testament Church—composed of repentant Gentile sinners (publicans and harlots).

Notice the wording of Jesus to His Old Testament wife: **"For John came unto you [Israel] in the way of righteousness and ye believed him not."**

THE PARABLE OF
THE BARREN FIG TREE ACCURSED

> *And on the morrow, when they were come from Bethany, He was hungry: And seeing a fig tree afar off having leaves, He came, if haply He might find anything thereon: and when He came to it; He found nothing but leaves; for the time of figs was not yet. And Jesus answered and said unto it, No man eat fruit of thee hereafter forever. And His disciples heard it. (Mk. 11:12-14).*

The question we want to answer here is WHY did Jesus curse the fig tree, and *how* does this parable apply to the nation of Israel. In (verse 15 of Mark 11) Jesus says:

> **And they come to Jerusalem: and Jesus went into the temple, and began to *cast out* them that sold and bought in the temple, and overthrew the tables of the money changers, and the seats of them that sold doves; And would not suffer [permit] that any man should carry any vessel through the temple. And He taught, saying unto them, Is it not written, My house shall be called of all nations the house of prayer? but ye have made it a den of thieves.**

Like the parable of *the Wicked Husbandmen*, this parable was especially aimed at the Pharisees and stood as a stern WARNING

THE RESTORATION OF ISRAEL

to the nation of Israel. Immediately after Jesus cursed the fig tree, He stormed into the Temple and threw out the hypocritical Pharisees!

These disciples of Satan were turning God's House into a religious carnival. Jesus had warned these Pharisees on several occasions, that the Kingdom would be taken from them and they would be *cast* into outer darkness.

He said there would be "weeping and gnashing of teeth" (Matt. 8:12). Jesus asked them, **"Ye serpents, ye generation of vipers, how can ye escape the damnation of hell?" (Matt. 23:33).**

As we have read, the nation of Israel is pictured as a *fig tree* in the Bible. Jesus' physical hunger in this parable was only *superficial* of a deeper spiritual hunger He had for Israel's refusal to repent as a nation.

Israel showed outward leaves of piety, but inwardly they did not bear the fruit of *faith* in God!

Christ cursed the fig tree [Israel] to bear no more fruit forever [for the age] in (Mark 11:12-14), as He declared Israel's infertility for the remainder of this age. Then after Israel's 2520 years punishment, God will begin to restore her as far as producing fruit in converting other nations!

During the Millennium, Israel will once again bring forth fruit for other nations to emulate and enjoy!

THE PARABLE OF THE BARREN FIG TREE

> *He spake also this parable; A certain man had a fig tree planted in his vineyard; and he came and sought fruit thereon, and found none. Then said he unto the dresser of his vineyard, Behold, these three years I come seeking fruit on this fig tree, and find none: cut it down: why cumbereth it the ground? And he answering said unto him, Lord, let it alone this year also, till I shall dig about it, and dung [fertilize] it: And if it bear fruit, well: and if not, then after that thou shalt cut it down (Lk. 13:6).*

PARABLES OF ISRAEL'S HISTORY

Jesus describes in this parable what will happen to fig trees that do not bear fruit. This is the *third* time in which Jesus used a fig tree to describe an object spiritual lesson. Each account speaks of a different fig tree.

It takes time for spiritual fruit to be born in most peoples lives. Our just and loving Father gives us plenty of time to change. He even *cultivates* us with special care [fertilizer] so we have no excuse not to grow. God gives us every advantage!

But when we fail to produce spiritual fruit after sufficient time—God will cut us down like a barren fig tree! Turn your Bible to (John 15:1-6) to see the fate of those who fail to grow spiritually!

There, Jesus confers:

> **I AM the true vine, and my Father is the husbandman. Every branch in me that beareth not fruit He taketh away: and every branch that beareth fruit, He purgeth it, that it may bring forth more fruit. Now ye are clean through the word which I have spoken unto you. Abide in me, and I in you. As the branch cannot bear fruit of itself, except it abide in the vine, ye are the branches: He that abideth in me, and I in him, the same bringeth forth much fruit: for without me ye can do nothing. If a man abide not in me, he is cast forth as a branch, and is *withered*; and men gather them, and *cast them into the fire*, and they are burned.**

The *fire* Jesus is referring to—is "the lake of fire" that will CONSUME rebellious and sinful beings like a dead fig tree at the end of the age. See also (Jn. 3:9; Matt. 7:16-19; Heb. 6:7-9). God makes no bones about our fate if we *neglect* our Christian calling!

Christians who become *sterile* spiritually in the form of *love* and *repentance* stand in danger of the death penalty! Any Christian who does not grow spiritually and OVERCOME sin in this life, except for God's mercy, will be thrown into the lake of fire like a dead tree!

The Barren Fig Tree in Luke's account is also a direct reference to the *fruitless* nation of Israel. Notice the "three years" in which the Lord [God] gave the fig tree [Israel] to produce fruit.

This is the approximate time of Jesus' ministry, after which Israel was still spiritually barren!

THE CHANGING OF ADMINISTRATION

Paul explained very graphically in (Romans 11) that the Gentiles [wild olive branches] could be grafted into the Jewish olive tree! God's Vineyard or work had now been entrusted to them temporarily!

The witness-bearing and fruit-bearing were now given to the Gentiles primarily—although some of the natural branches [Jews of the early Church] would remain!

However, just prior to our Lord's return, the Vineyard will once again be given to the nation of Israel—for an end-time witness upon the earth to all nations! This is made vivid in Paul's exhortation of the dispensational change in Romans 11:1-2: **"I say then, Hath God cast away His people? God forbid..*God hath not cast away His people* which He foreknew"**!

J. Dwight Pentecost, Professor of Bible Exposition, Emeritus, at Dallas Theological Seminary where he has served since 1955 explains this transformation to the Church:

> **The fact that God was going to form Jews and Gentiles alike into one body was never revealed in the Old Testament and forms the mystery of which Paul speaks in Ephesians 3:1-7; Romans 16:25-27; Colossians 1:26-29. This whole mystery program was not revealed until after the rejection of Christ by Israel. It was after the rejection of Matthew 12:23-24 that the Lord first makes a prophecy of the coming church in Matthew 16:18. It is after the rejection of the Cross that the church had its inception in Acts 2. It was after the final rejection by Israel that God called out Paul to be the Apostle of the Gentiles through whom this mystery of the nature of the church is revealed.**
>
> **The church is manifestly an interruption of God's program for Israel, which was not brought into being until Israel's rejection of the**

offer of the Kingdom. It must logically follow that this mystery program must itself be brought to a conclusion before God can resume His dealing with the nation of Israel, as has been shown previously He will do. The mystery program, which was so distinct in its inception, will certainly be separate at its conclusion. This program must be concluded before God resumes and culminates His program for Israel (*Pretribulation Rapture Theory*, p. 201).

Now a quotation from Alva J. Mclain's book entitled *Daniel's Prophecy of the Seventy Weeks*, p. 8:

> More than one expositor has stumbled over the ultimatum of Christ, 'I was not sent but unto the lost sheep of the house of Israel.' The only adequate explanation is to see, what our Lord understood clearly, the contingent nature of His message of the Kingdom. To put the matter in a word: *the immediate and complete establishment of His Kingdom depended upon the attitude of the nation of Israel*, to whom pertained the divine promises and covenants...

Peters offers this rendition of the mission of Christ:

> The Kingdom was offered to the nation in good faith, i.e. it would have been bestowed *provided* the nation had repented. The foreknown result made no difference in the tender of it, so far as the free agency of the nation is concerned; that result flowed from *a voluntary choice.* The national belief did not change God's faithfulness, Rom. 3:3. It would be derogatory to the mission of Christ to take any other view of it, and *the sincerity and desire* of Jesus that the nation might accept it, is witnessed in His tears over Jerusalem, in His address to it, in His unceasing labors, in sending out the twelve and the seventy, and in His works of mercy and love. It

follows, then, that the Jews had *the privilege* accorded to them of accepting the Kingdom, and if the condition annexed to it had been complied with, *then* the Kingdom of David would have been most gloriously re-established under the Messiah (*The Theocratic Kingdom*, I, 377).

ISRAEL IN TRIBULATION

There is going to come a time when the Great God of heaven will once again intervene in the course of human affairs—and restore again His Kingdom to the nation of Israel.

Jeremiah's prophecy describes this time setting as "Jacob's trouble" (Jer. 30:7), and Stanton explains the Jewish attitude during this crucial period:

> **The tribulation is primarily Jewish. This fact is borne out by Old Testament Scriptures (Deut. 4:30; Jer. 30:7; Ezek. 20:37; Dan. 12:1; Zech. 13:8-9), by the Olivet Discourse of Christ (Matt. 24:9-26), and by the book of Revelation itself (Rev. 7:4-8; 12:1-2; 17, etc). It concerns 'Daniel's people,' the coming of the 'false Messiah,' the preaching of the 'gospel of the kingdom,' flight on the 'sabbath,' the temple and the 'holy place,' the land of Judea, the city of Jerusalem, the twelve 'tribes of the children of Israel,' the 'song of Moses,' 'signs' in the heavens, the 'covenant' with the Beast, the 'sanctuary,' the 'sacrifice and the oblation' of the temple ritual—these all speak of Israel and prove that the tribulation is largely a time when God deals with His ancient people prior to their entrance into the promised kingdom. The many Old Testament prophecies yet to be fulfilled for Israel further indicate a future time when God will deal with this nation [Deut. 30:1-6; Jer. 30:8-10, etc.]** (*Kept From the Hour*, p. 30-31).

From these multitude of very definite scriptures, it is very clear that the main intention of the Great Tribulation is to bring about the conversion of a multitude of Jews and Israelites.

Let's read some of these prophecies:

> **When thou art in *tribulation*, and all these things are come upon thee, *even in the latter days*, if thou turn to the Lord thy God, and shall be obedient unto his voice;...he will not forsake thee, neither destroy thee, nor forget the covenant of thy fathers which he sware unto them (Deut. 4:30,31).**

> **And they shall go into the hole of the rocks, and into the caves of the earth, for fear of the Lord, and for the glory of his majesty, when he ariseth to *shake terribly* the earth (Isa. 2:19).**

> **Alas! for the day is great, so that none is like it: it is even *the time of Jacob's trouble*, but he shall be saved out of it (Jer. 30:7). And he shall confirm the covenant with many for one week: and in the midst of the week he shall cause the sacrifice and the oblation to cease, and for the overspreading of abominations he shall make it desolate, even until the consummation, and that determined shall be poured upon the desolate (Dan. 9:27).**

> **And at that time shall Michael stand up, the great prince which standeth for the children of the people: and there shall be *a time of trouble*, such as never was since there was a nation even to that same time...(Dan. 12:1).**

> **Alas for the day! for the day of the Lord is at hand, and as a *destruction from the Almighty* shall it come (Joel 1:15). See also (Joel 2:1-2; Amos 5:18,20; Zeph. 1:14-15, 18).**

During this very dreaded time, Israel will be told by the "Two Witnesses" that they are about to enter into the blessings of the kingdom and experience the fulfillment of all Israel's covenants. The "Two Witnesses" will preach the "good news" that the Messiah is about to return and deliver them and restore the Kingdom of God to them (Matt. 24:14).

One walking in the spiritual footsteps of John the Baptist will declare the identical message, and prepare Israel for the return of their Messiah. Spiritual Elijah will proclaim this truth to Israel in preparation of Christ's return, even as John prepared them for Christ's first coming, notice:

> **Behold, I will send you Elijah the prophet before the coming of the great and terrible day of the Lord: And he shall turn the heart of the fathers to the children, and the heart of the children to their fathers, lest I come and spite the earth with a curse (Mal. 4:5-6).**

Pentecost writes of this prophetic announcement:

> **This witness is seen to be effective in that multitudes of Jews are converted during the tribulation period and are waiting for the Messiah (Rev. 7:1-8) and the wise virgins of (Matt. 25:1-13). It is also God's purpose to populate the millennium with a multitude of saved Gentiles, who are redeemed through the preaching of the believing remnant. This is accomplished in the multitude from 'all nations, and kindreds, and people, and tongues' (Rev. 7:9) and in the 'sheep' (Matt. 25:31-46) that enter the millennial age. God's purpose, then, is to populate the millennial kingdom by bringing a host from among Israel and Gentile nations to Himself (*Things To Come* p. 237-238).**

Grant Jeffrey further clarifies the relationship between the two Israel's of God in his book *Messiah*:

> **One of the fundamental roles of Israel was to be a 'light to the Gentiles' (Isa. 42:6) and to manifest God's nature and teach His Law, the**

> Torah, to the Gentile nations. That is why there was a Court of the Gentiles in the Temple. That is why the prophet Jonah was sent to the Gentile nation of Nineveh with the astonishing result that the entire city repented in a revival that has never been equaled...(p. 258-259).
>
> But God's Word will be fulfilled in another way regarding His command that the Jews would be a light to the Gentiles. During the terrible period of the Great Tribulation, Israel will finally fulfill its prophesied role as the Two Witnesses and the 144 thousand Jewish witnesses evangelize the entire world...(p. 260).
>
> If we substitute the Church for Israel in the detailed prophecies of Daniel, Matthew 24, and Revelation 4 through 19, we will never understand how God will accomplish His prophecies that Israel will be a light to the nations during the terrible days of the Tribulation...(p. 262).
>
> Also, such a misunderstanding will result in a failure to appreciate the final redemption and reconciliation of Israel to their rejected Messiah at the close of the Great Tribulation period. If we understand the specific roles which Israel, the Church, and the Gentile nations will play in prophecy, God's whole plan becomes much clearer to the believer...(p. 263).

THE BARREN FIG TREE TO BEAR FRUIT

God will start His plan with a *remnant* of physical Israelites according to His grace (Rom. 11:5). It is highly probable that this remnant will consist of 144,000 physical *firstfruits* of Israel (Rev. 7), as well as those brought back out of captivity. However, these may be different than the 144,000 *firstfruits* in (Revelation 14:1,4) who speculatively may represent the Gentile Church in *duality* and are Tribulation Saints!

THE RESTORATION OF ISRAEL

It will be at this moment that *the barren fig tree of Israel* will once again become a *fruitful Vineyard* of the Lord! These "firstfruits" of Israel will be the start of God's refurbishing the nation of Israel for His Kingdom's glory!

Consequently, during this present dispensation—God has taken the fruitfulness of His Kingdom from Israel! This is made explicit from the striking words of our Lord in the parable of the Wicked Husbandmen: **"Therefore say I unto you, the kingdom of God shall be *taken* from you, and *given* to a nation bringing forth the fruits thereof" (Matt. 21:43).**

Israel is *pictured* as the Father's Vineyard in the parable of *The Wicked Husbandmen.* He entrusted Israel to produce luscious fruit as His earthly witness—but they neglected His Vineyard!

Then the Father sent His Son to be the Husbandman over His Vineyard. There is a prophecy in (Zechariah 13:5) in which the Messiah is described as "an husbandman"! Christ, as keeper of His Father's Vineyard, tried to promote spiritual growth in Israel for 3 years—but to no avail! (Lk. 13:7).

Finally, Jesus became the Vine Himself and the source of *all* fruit-bearing (Jn. 15). Jesus had been sent to the lost sheep of the house of Israel (Matt. 15:24). His commission to His disciples was: **."..Go not into the way of the Gentiles...But go rather to the lost sheep of the house of Israel" (Matt. 10:5-6).**

But from the time Israel rejected her King—the call became: **"Go not to the lost sheep of the house of Israel—but into the highways of the Gentile world" (Matt. 22:9-10; Acts 13:46).**

The parables of the *Marriage Supper* and *Great Feast,* clearly distinguish between those who were bidden [Israel] because of their refusal, and those now invited. This new invitation was the start of a new dispensation of grace to the Gentile!

Along with a change of administration came the blessings of the first-born as Paul clarifies:

> **As he saith also in Osee, [Hosea] I will call them my people; and her beloved, which was not beloved. And it shall come to pass, that in the place where it was said unto them, Ye are not my people: there shall they be called the children of the living God (Rom. 9:25-26).**

This was a quote from (Hosea 1:10).

PARABLES OF ISRAEL'S HISTORY

This was the promise to Israel which Paul now reiterates and claims for the Church! Paul now shows us the change in dispensations carries with it the same blessings!

To assume that these were only privileges and blessings to Old Testament Israel is a blatant mistake. For now these blessings have been engrafted into the new dispensation which includes Gentiles! The Church now takes on the responsibilities of Israel as "light bearer" and also the *blessings* that go along with it!

The prophets spoke of Israel's captivity and respite of sacrifice (Hosea 3:4); of the desolation of their land, and divinely imposed blindness (Isa. 6:9-12; Jn. 12:38-41).

There are also references to the times of blessings of Gentiles, of tribulation in the last days, and of Christ's imminent return to establish His Kingdom in Israel. But we look in vain for any light on Israel's fate during the present dispensation!

The New Testament establishes God's purpose for the Church—both Jew and Gentile alike. However, the purpose for the Gentiles was NOT known previously by the prophets! But God shall yet have mercy on Jacob, and will yet choose Israel, and set them in their own land (Isa. 14:1). He **"shall choose Jerusalem again" (Zech. 2:12).** For the present, God is making no distinction between Jew and Gentile (Rom. 10:12).

The present age, unannounced by the prophets, must be completed before God resumes His plans for His ancient people. There is a distinct break in the text between the "cutting off" of the Messiah, and the events to transpire during the last seven years of Israel's history—such as the setting up of the "abomination of desolation" (Dan. 9:26-27).

When Jesus began His public ministry, He read the Messianic prophecy of Isaiah which declared **"...the acceptable year of the Lord, and the day of vengeance of our God" (Isa. 61:1-2; Lk. 4:16-21).**

After reading only the first part of the scripture, Jesus stopped reading at the comma between the two phrases. The reason is that He had come to proclaim **"the acceptable year of the Lord"** during which time the Gentiles could come to God [as well as the Jews]—but not the day of vengeance. This must await the end of the age, plainly showing that Jesus recognized the time element by the correct punctuation. This is a good illustration of how dispensations of prophecy are divided by a simple comma.

Once again, during this current dispensation, the Church is a chosen generation—as God inspired Peter to write: **"But *ye* are a chosen generation, a royal priesthood, an holy nation...which in time past were *not* a people, but now *the* [not a] people of God" (1 Pet. 2:9-10).**

Thanks be to God for His marvelous truths and wonderful plan—that allows for all of mankind to become a part of His eternal ruling family!

Chapter Seven

EVANGELISTIC PARABLES

THE PARABLE OF THE TEN VIRGINS

Then shall the kingdom of heaven be likened unto ten virgins, which took their lamps, and went forth to meet the bridegroom. And five of them were wise, and five were foolish. They that were foolish took their lamps, and took no oil with them: But the wise took oil in their vessels with their lamps. While the bridegroom tarried, they all slumbered and slept. And at midnight there was a cry made, Behold, the bridegroom cometh; go ye out to meet him. Then all those virgins arose, and trimmed their lamps. And the foolish said unto the wise, Give us of your oil; for our lamps are gone out.

But the wise answered, saying, Not so; lest there be not enough for us and you: but go ye rather to them that sell, and buy for yourselves. And while they went to buy, the bridegroom came; and they that were ready went in with him to the marriage: and the door was shut. Afterward came also the other virgins, saying, Lord, Lord, open to us. but he answered and said, Verily I say unto you, I know you not. Watch therefore, for ye know neither the day nor the hour wherein the Son of man cometh (Matt. 25:1-13).

The ten Virgins in this parable most likely represent the TRIBULATION SAINTS being made ready for the Bridegroom [Jesus Christ]. Oil in the Bible is *analogous* to God's Holy Spirit as we have read under the *types.*

Here then are 50 percent of the last era of God's Church on earth unprepared for the returning Jesus Christ! Why? Because they were "lukewarm" in applying and utilizing God's Holy Spirit which must be *stirred up day by day!* In the second and third chapters of the book of Revelation, God's seven Church eras are given.

These have existed since apostolic times down unto the end of the age. Jesus said the gates of hell [Greek, *hades*, meaning the grave] would never prevail against His Church. In other words, it [Christ's Church] would *never* die out!

However, this is not to say the Church would always remain "unspotted" in character. The last two eras of God's Church at the end of the age are the Philadelphia and Laodicean. The Philadelphians will be granted PROTECTION from the Great Tribulation because of their *faithfulness* in applying God's way of life (Rev. 3:10).

This is not evident with Laodiceans who are "lukewarm" in faithfulness , and will therefore have to be *tried in fire* [Great Tribulation] to learn some very bitter lessons (Rev. 3:18). These individuals have let the cares of this world [riches, etc. vs. 17], *choke* God's Word to the point they have become unfruitful! They will be slumbering spiritually—but 50 percent of them (5 of 10) will wake up in time to meet the Bridegroom!

Jesus incites the Laodiceans to *repent* and wake up out of their slumber: **"Behold, I stand at the door, and *knock:* if any man hear my voice, and open the door, I will come in to him, and will *sup* with him, and he with me" (Rev. 3:20).** Those who fail to hear this call will not make it to the marriage supper of the Lamb, and hence into the Kingdom of God!

THE PARABLE OF
THE ROYAL MARRIAGE FEAST
FOR THE KING'S SON

The kingdom of heaven is like unto a certain king, which made a marriage for his son, And sent forth his servants to call them that were bidden to the wedding: and they would not come. Again, he sent forth other servants, saying, Tell them which are bidden, Behold, I have prepared my dinner: my oxen and my fatlings are killed, and all things are ready: come unto the marriage. But they made light of it, and went their ways, one to his farm, another to his merchandise: And the remnant took his servants, and entreated them spitefully, and slew them. But when the king heard thereof, he was wroth: and he sent forth his armies, and destroyed those murderers, and burned up their city. Then saith he to his servants, The wedding is ready, but they which were bidden were not worthy. Go ye therefore into the highways, and as many as ye shall find, bid to the marriage (Matt. 22:1-14).

This graphic illustration entails the principles of *The Great Supper; The Wicked Husbandmen; and The Ten Virgins* all rolled up into one. Our magnanimous Dad is preparing a SPOTLESS BRIDE for His Son Jesus Christ through the Church. In the parable of *The Wicked Husbandmen,* God the Father was the Householder. Here He is featured as a King preparing a *royal wedding feast* for His son whom He loves.

Throughout the ages, our heavenly King has bidden [invited] many guests through His *servants* to the wedding feast. Israel, of old, refused their invitation from God's Old Testament prophets and instead killed them. Once again God bid for guests to fill His marriage feast chambers through the invitation of New Testament servants whom they also killed!

This was too much for the King to bear, so He sent forth *armies* to destroy those wicked murderers and *burned* their city (vs. 7). In A.D. 70, Roman soldiers under General Titus stormed and completely ransacked the city of Jerusalem, destroying the

Temple and fulfilling this prophecy.

When the nation of Israel failed to respond to God's generous invitation to the marriage of His Son—He called Gentile nations (from the *highways* of the world). It was the nation of Israel that *slew* God's servants the prophets, who bid them to be the first ones in the Kingdom of God (Jer. 37:15; 38:6, 26:20-23; 11 Chron. 24:21; Matt. 23:37).

When Christ returns in full glory, He will destroy those who have rejected Him and His servants (vs. 7).

What a rude awakening!

But now there is a stern warning to those newcomers invited to the marriage feast to be diligent, lest they meet this same fate. Like the parable of *The Ten Virgins*—Christ warns those who would not take their calling seriously. If anyone thinks he can make it to the marriage feast of the Lamb [and hence into the Kingdom] without developing GODLY CHARACTER by utilizing God's Holy Spirit—he has been bamboozled! This is depicted by the 5 *foolish* Virgins in (Matthew 25) who had insufficient oil [Holy Spirit] in their lamps [lives], and by the proper wedding apparel required in this parable.

God the King, began inviting Gentiles as His wedding guests after Israel refused their calling. But observe, these guests included both *good* and *bad*—distinguishable only by their garments. Those who do not have on the *garments of righteousness* spiritually, shall be cast into outer darkness—for truly there shall be **"weeping and gnashing of teeth" (vs. 13).**

MARRIAGE OR MARRIAGE FEAST?

The first part of this parable is straight forward and easy to decipher. The Jewish people received the first and second invitation to God's MARRIAGE FEAST. This invitation was given under Moses and the Old Covenant and before the crucifixion!!

Although the actual marriage feast was well into the future, the Jews were offered a part in the first resurrection beginning Christ's Kingdom [and beginning the 1,000 year marriage feast]!

But they rejected Christ's message!

The beginning of the *marriage feast* is announced by an angel in (Revelation 19). This announcement is followed by a

EVANGELISTIC PARABLES

description of Christ's Bride arrayed in white linen ready for the battle of Armageddon.

A major problem in trying to make some sense as to *who* is "Christ's Bride", the "wedding guests" and *when* "the marriage will occur"—is due to a biblical mistranslation!

When the translators deciphered the Greek into English, they decided to interpret the Greek word *gamos* [*Strong's* #1062, nuptials, marriage, wedding], as "marriage" in (Revelation 19:7). But they translated this identical word *gamos* as "marriage supper" in (Revelation 19:9). This same Greek word is used to describe the *marriage feast* for the King's Son in the parable of (Matthew 22) and the *marriage feast* of the 10 Virgins! (Matthew 25).

Conclusively, the Greek word *gamos* means "marriage feast" and should have been translated as such in (Revelation 19). Consequently, this scripture should read: **"Let us be glad and rejoice, and give honour to him: for the *marriage feast* of the Lamb is come..." (Rev. 19:7).**

But what is this marriage feast *for* and *who* will be the Bride? To better understand, we must comprehend the physical espousal period. This *spiritual* marital relationship with Christ is *pictured* by the *physical* Hebrew custom of marriage.

Concerning this millennial marriage feast, Pentecost writes:

> **The wedding supper, then, becomes the parabolic picture of the entire millennial age, to which Israel will be invited during the tribulation period, which invitation many will reject and so they will be cast out, and many will accept and they will be received in. Because of the rejection, the invitation will likewise go to the Gentiles so that many of them will be included. Israel, at the second advent, will be waiting for the Bridegroom to come from the wedding ceremony and invite them to that supper, at which the Bridegroom will introduce His bride to His friends...(*Things To Come*, p, 227-228).**

As to the interpretation of the "marriage feast" and "marriage supper," Pentecost has this to say:

> Inasmuch as the Greek text does not distinguish between marriage supper and marriage feast, but uses the same word for both, and since the marriage supper consistently is used in reference to Israel on earth, it may be best to take the latter view and view the marriage of the Lamb as that event in the heavens in which the church is eternally united to Christ and the marriage feast or supper as the millennium, to which Jews and Gentiles will be invited, which takes place on the earth, during which time the bridegroom is honored through the display of the bride to all His friends who are assembled there (*Things to Come*, p. 228).

A LESSON IN HEBREW ESPOUSAL

In Biblical times, the Hebrews had lengthy engagements of a different character than our engagements of today. The announced intention to become husband and wife began a period in which legal authority of the coming union was already in force.

Before the couple became man and wife, there was a "day long" marriage feast! This was evident in the marriage of Jacob and Leah (see Gen. 29:22). Jacob did not know that the bride was Leah until the next morning! If Leah had been there during the entire wedding feast, surely Jacob would have known she was not Rachel!

There was actually three stages a prospective bride and groom encountered. Oftentimes the parents of the future couple pre-arranged a marriage contract [covenant] while they were still children. A payment of a suitable dowry was also included as part of the agreement. For all intent and purpose, the couple was legally married at this point.

When the couple reached adulthood—the marriage ceremony took place, following a "wedding feast" in which the *friends* of the bride and groom were invited. This wedding feast was similar to the one Christ attended at Cana (Jn. 2:1-12).

EVANGELISTIC PARABLES

BIBLICAL WEDDINGS—TYPES OF THE CHURCH

Perhaps you have not given it much thought before—but did you ever stop and think *where* today's modern marriage customs originated? Biblical weddings were quite different from the elaborate white gown ecclesiastical ceremonies performed by a priest or rabbi of today! In fact, there is no Biblical evidence that any such type of ceremony was ever performed by an Old Covenant [Levite] or New Testament [minister] priest of God!

When Adam and Eve were united in marriage—there is no Biblical evidence that they recited any vows to God as an officiating minister! Eve did not wear a white gown and there is no evidence of a "big splash" of a wedding reception afterwards!

Assuredly, the Bible is not suggesting for one moment that it is wrong to have a minister perform a marriage ceremony—on the contrary, for their counsel and advice beforehand is encouraged by Paul in (1 Corinthians 7). This should be done by every Christian couple to better understand their Christian responsibilities (Eph. 5).

During Patriarchal times we know that marriages were oftentimes pre-arranged by parents, as was the case of Isaac. Because Isaac and his wife Rebekah are a *type* of the marriage between Christ and His Church—perhaps we can learn more about the marriage of the Church through them.

Recall, Abraham is a *type* of God the Father who chose Isaac's wife for him (Gen. 24:3-4). After having his servant seek out a proper wife for Isaac from his household, a wedding gift [Heb. *mohar*] was given to Rebekah's parents (vss. 10-24).

A suitable "dowry" was then negotiated between the two consenting parents which became a part of the wedding contract or agreement (vss. 28-50). Upon consulting with the bride-to-be [in some cases], and after she consented to the conditions of the contract—she and her parents were given a *mohar* (type of dowry—vss. 53-58).

The marriage was finally consummated when Rebekah was taken to Isaac's home (tent—vss. 61-67).

Concerning the Hebrew marriage ceremony, the *Expository Times* contributes:

When we hear of a wedding today, certain questions immediately occur to us. Where did

> the marriage ceremony take place? Was it held in a church or at a registry office? If the former, in what church, and who was the officiating minister?...To the Jew of Biblical times these questions would have been meaningless. No marriage occurred in a 'place of worship', except in so far as the Jews regarded all their customary practices as shot through and through with religious significance...There was no officiating minister... (*Expository Times* April, 1975, Vol. LXXXVI, No. 7).

THE BASIC WEDDING PATTERN

As time passed, the Hebrew wedding ceremonies became more elaborate and formalized from that of Isaac and Rebekah. However, the general format remained the same, namely:

- The bride was generally chosen by the groom's parents, without the groom's prior knowledge.
- A suitable dowry was negotiated between the parents of the bride and groom which became a formal contract.
- The groom and his friends took a wedding gift *[mohar]* to the house of the bride, and presented it to her parents. Then a celebration took place in the home of the bride.
- The wedding procession composed of the bride and groom's friends marched to the house of the groom. This was often done in the evening accompanied with lit torches.
- Upon arriving at the home of the groom, the bride was formally accepted into the groom's family, and a wedding feast began. The wedding celebration would last anywhere from a day to a week.
- Finally, the marriage was consummated when the groom took the bride to his home.

On page 271 of his book, *The Revelation of Jesus Christ*, John F. Walvoord explains the three phases of the Eastern marriage customs:

> **Though marriage customs varied in the ancient**

world, usually there were three major aspects:

1) The marriage contract was often consummated by the parents when the parties to the marriage were still children and not ready to assume adult responsibility. The payment of a suitable dowry was often a feature of the contract. When consummated, the contract meant that the couple were legally married.

2) At a later time when a couple had reached a suitable age, the second step in the wedding took place. This was a ceremony in which the bridegroom accompanied by his friends would go to the house of the bride and escort her to his home. This is the background of the parable of the virgins in Matthew 25:1-13.

3) Then the bridegroom would bring his bride to his home and the marriage supper, to which guests were invited, would take place. It was such a wedding feast that Christ attended at Cana as recorded in John 2:1-12. The marriage symbolism is beautifully fulfilled in the relationship of Christ to His church. The wedding contract is consummated at the time the church is redeemed. Every true Christian is joined to Christ in a legal marriage. When Christ comes for His church at the rapture [Christ's second Advent, *emphasis mine*], the second phase of the wedding is fulfilled, namely, the Bridegroom goes to receive His bride. The third phase then follows, that is, the wedding feast.

THE BETROTHAL

The BETROTHAL period is designated as that period of time between the giving of the *mohar* and the actual marriage union. This generally took a whole year. Actually, negotiations over the terms of the contract was the most difficult part to resolve, and oftentimes took a year or longer to come to an agreement (Hastings, *Dictionary of Christ and the Gospels,* article, "Betrothal." This is evident from the seven year agreement Jacob made with Laban over Rachel (Gen. 29:20).

Assuredly, the Hebrew *betrothal* period was quite different from our modern-day engagement period. For all practical purposes, the couple was legally married at this point.

Should a betrothed person die prior to the consummation, the remaining partner was labeled a "widow" or "widower." Divorce proceedings were necessary, should one party decide to back out prior to the consummation.

You will recall how Joseph wanted to put Mary away [divorce her] before they were actually married, when he suspected sexual impropriety (Matt. 1:19). This only proves that the Hebrew marriage custom, was a *covenant* or contract between two consenting parties prior to actual sexual relations!

Sexual copulation is what actually bound the marriage or made the two "one flesh" (1 Cor. 6:16; Matt. 19:5). On the night of consummation, hymeneal blood was collected by the groom on a cloth to prove the bride's virginity. The mother-in-law of the groom waited in an adjoining room, to make sure there was no "hanky-panky" by the groom in the event he wanted to conspire against her for prior sexual misconduct (Deut. 22:15-20).

This momentous event was humorously portrayed in the movie "Yentl" starring Barbara Streisand. Clearly, the legality of the marriage was binding prior to the actual coming together in sexual relations!

The *Encyclopedia Biblica* offers this in regards to the act of betrothal:

> **Legally considered, the marriage relation was formed by the act of betrothal that is to say, by the payment, on the bridegroom's part, of the *mohar* to the parent or guardian of the bride, with this she passed into the possession of her husband. To betroth a wife to oneself, meant simply to acquire possession of her by payment of the purchase money...The girl's consent is unnecessary...the arrangements about the marriage, and especially about the *mohar*, belonged to the province of the father or**

EVANGELISTIC PARABLES

guardian [Gen. 24:50 ff; 29:23; 34:2] (*Encyclopedia Biblica,* 1914 edition, Vol. 1, Cheyne & J.S. Black, London).

THE BETROTHAL OF THE CHURCH

Plainly, there is a difference between the betrothal, feast and marriage! Applying the Hebrew marriage custom to the Church—it is now BETROTHED to Christ! According to the understanding of the Hebrew custom, after Christ returns with His Bride, the marriage feast could take place spiritually for 1,000 years!

Jesus made this abundantly evident when He prophesied to His disciples: **"But I say unto you, I will not drink henceforth of this fruit of the vine, until that day [at the marriage feast], when I drink it new with you in my Father's kingdom" (Matt. 26:29).**

Now do you suppose God would have a WEDDING FEAST without any wine? I think not! The final proof that this feast will occur on earth after Christ returns, is because that is where God's Kingdom will be! How clear!

At the present time, the Church is in the betrothal stage. Next, in sequence with the Hebrew custom, she will enjoy the one thousand year wedding feast ruling with Christ in His Kingdom. Finally, the Church is to be "joined in one" to Christ *after* the Millennium as "bone of His bone and flesh of His flesh."

Now, we are not disputing the fact that Israel will also be the Bride in the future (Jer. 3:1,8,14,20). Both history and geography have been determined by God's purposes towards Israel (Deut. 32:8-9).

While it is quite apparent that the Church is not *synonymous* with Old Testament Israel, we must not assume there is no connection! Jesus is not God the Father—but to say they are not both God is a fallacy!

It might just as well be said that the Church is not Old Testament Israel—but to say it is only Gentile because of this privileged Gentile dispensation would also be a grave fallacy!

THE MILLENNIAL BANQUET

The MARRIAGE FEAST could be another way of describing the millennial reign of Jesus Christ with His *espoused*

THE RESTORATION OF ISRAEL

Bride on earth! This entire one thousand year courtship period of Jesus and His Bride will culminate in marriage! But the marriage will be at the *end* of the Millennium! Remember, an espoused Bride is not yet a wife!

It is only then that we see "New Jerusalem" descending as the Lamb's Wife! This will come *after* the 1,000 year [day-long feast] of the Millennium! Recall how God's days are a thousand years (11 Pet. 3:8).

"New Jerusalem" is a part of a new creation—and far more glorious than the present "Jerusalem Above"! But it comes down to earth out of heaven *after* the Millennium is finished!

Yes, Jesus is coming back to present to Himself a glorious Church without spot or wrinkle! But this will happen *after* the Millennium when *New Jerusalem* becomes His Wife!

WHO ARE THE WEDDING GUESTS?

Ah! Now we come to the nitty gritty! Granted, we have a Bride in the New Testament Church. Granted, that the wedding supper occurs on earth at Christ's return!

But where does Israel fit into the picture, and *who* are the wedding guests mentioned in the parable of The Royal Marriage Feast?

There is no contest that Israel was the Bride of Christ through a previous marriage. But that marriage ended in divorce (Jer. 3:1,8,14,20). There is also no question about the fact that Christ will one day remarry His former wife—the only question is when? The remarriage of Israel need not correspond to the marriage of the New Testament Church in time!

Could it possibly be that those invited as wedding guests of the Bride, will be tribulation Saints as well as Old Testament Israel! Let's read Revelation 19:9: **"And he saith unto me, write, Blessed are they which are called unto the marriage supper of the Lamb [as guests]."**

It should be apparent that the "Ten Virgins" of (Matthew 25) are not the same group as form the Bride during the feast! Christ comes for a Bride (singular) not virgins (plural). How can they be Bridesmaids and the Bride at the same time?

In view of the *types* and double *symbolism* running throughout God's Word—it is quite likely that the wedding guests who are called to the marriage supper (Rev. 19), the wise virgins

(Matt. 25), and the Bride herself—will include both Israelites and Gentiles comprising the New Testament Church!

To say that the Levites were priests who administered service to God in the Temple would be an absolute truth. But to say that they were not a part of the nation of Israel would be a misnomer! Each tribe had a specific function—yet all were Israelites! In other words all Levites were Israelites, but not all Israelites were Levites!

This concept may also parallel the two Church dispensations! There may be different groups such as Old Testament Saints, N.T. Gentile Saints, Tribulation Saints, Millennial Saints, etc. all under the banner of "Church" forming the eventual Wife of Christ!

All will comprise the Wife of Christ at the Millennium's conclusion—but in the interim they are distinctly classified!

SUMMARY

The ancient Hebrew wedding ceremony is a *picture* of the relationship of Christ to His Church. There were three phases of courtship.

First, there was the lengthy engagement period which outlined the legality of the marriage. This is similar to the contract [New Testament] the Church is currently under during its *espousal* period.

Next, a "day-long" *marriage feast* preceded the actual coming together as man and wife. This corresponds to the Millennial reign of Jesus Christ ruling with His Bride.

During the Millennium, both houses of Israel will be reunited into one fold in preparation of the marriage (Jn. 10:16). Judah and Israel will be one during the Millennium, with one Shepherd [Christ] ruling over them (Ezek. 37:22-26). This will be the time the New Covenant will be made with them (Heb. 8:8; Jer. 31:31-33).

Finally, at the Millennium's conclusion, "New Jerusalem", that holy spiritual city composed of all overcomers during all ages—will be joined with Christ as "bone of His bone" and "flesh of His flesh" forevermore!

THE PARABLE OF THE LOST SHEEP

> *And he spake this parable unto them, saying, What man of you, having an hundred sheep, if he lose one of them, doth not leave the ninety and nine in the wilderness, and go after that which is lost, until he find it? And when he hath found it, he layeth it on his shoulders, rejoicing. And when he cometh home, he calleth together his friends and neighbors, saying unto them, Rejoice with me; for I have found my sheep which was lost. I say unto you, that likewise joy shall be in heaven over one sinner that repenteth, more than over ninety and nine just persons, which need no repentance (Lk. 15:3 7).*

Once we have willingly undertaken the journey towards salvation, Jesus will do everything in His power to keep us on that straight and narrow path. At times we may wander and stumble along the way—but as long as we continue to pick ourselves up, *forgiveness* will be given time and time again!

This is parabolically illustrated by the three parables of *The Lost Sheep, Recovery of the Lost Coin, and Return of the Prodigal Son*. This chapter is a companion to *The Sinful Woman* of (Luke 7:36-50) and *The Adulterous Woman* in (John 8:1-11).

In the parable of *The Lost Sheep*, God shows how very precious each Christian is to Him as our "Good Shepherd." Through the analogy of a shepherd caring for the one stray in 100—God demonstrates His concern for us and will do everything possible to recover strayed sinners from His flock. When sinners return—our loving Dad is exuberant with joy and wants the faithful to rejoice with Him!

This parable also describes the time when the nation of Israel will be brought back into God's fold. Christ said of this event: **"And other sheep I have which are not of this fold: them also I must bring, and they shall hear my voice; and there shall be one fold, and one shepherd" (Jn. 10:16).**

Jesus had been sent to the lost sheep of the house of Israel (Matt. 15:24). His commission to His disciples was: ."**..Go not into the way of the Gentiles...But go rather to the lost sheep of the house of Israel" (Matt. 10:5-6).**

EVANGELISTIC PARABLES

Christ had come to His own nation of Judah (Jn. 1:11), but they had rejected Him! Israel and Judah had both rejected the gospel message and the commission then became: "Go not to the lost sheep of the house of Israel—but into the highways of the Gentile world" (Matt. 22:9-10; Acts 13:46).

But there is coming a time when a new covenant will be made with the houses of Israel and Judah when God will write His laws in their hearts (Jer. 31:31-33; Heb. 8:8). At this time both houses will be reunited under Christ the Chief Shepherd! (Ezek. 37:22-26). Thus the "other sheep" of Israel will be brought back into the "fold" of Judah!

The restoring of God's "fold" began in 1948 when the Jews once again were restored in their homeland. Soon God will begin pouring out His Holy Spirit on Jerusalem and begin the conversion process of Israel. A few sheep will return to His fold at this time (144,000)—later during the Millennium, the entire flock will be brought back into God's fold!

THE RESTORATION OF ISRAEL

Chapter Eight

PROPHETIC PARABLES

THE PARABLE OF THE FIG TREE

Now learn a parable of the fig tree; When his branch is yet tender, and putteth forth leaves, ye know that summer is nigh: So likewise ye when ye shall see all these things, know that it is near, even at the doors. verily I say unto you, This generation shall not pass, till all these things be fulfilled (Matt. 24: 32-34).

The disciples of Jesus had just asked Him what would be the *signs* that the end of this hell-bent age is near (vs. 3). Then Jesus proceeded to give a *series* of events that would occur *simultaneously* prior to His second coming.

Jesus then gave an *outline* of future world conditions including, false prophets, wars, rumors of wars, famines, pestilences, earthquakes, persecution, lawlessness, the preaching of the gospel for a witness unto all nations, the Great Tribulation, the sun and moon darkened, stars falling from heaven and the earth shaken—then shall the end come! (verses 4-31).

The parable of *The Fig Tree* was then given as an *analogy*, to illustrate these SIGNS of the time. Just as a fig tree starts bearing leaves before summer—these signs would indicate that the return of Christ was imminent. Jesus further explained, **"So likewise ye,** when ye shall see *all* these things, know that it [Christ's return] is near, even at the doors" (vs. 33).**

Such *signs* will be the shock waves that will shake the very foundation of our human race! These fuse-lit time bombs will explode on the horizon like the Corona virus! Christians must always be ready for the return of our Savior, and not let His words merely rolling off us like water off a duck's back?

THE MARRIAGE SUPPER OF THE LAMB

> *Let us be glad and rejoice, and give honour to Him: for the marriage of the Lamb is come, and His wife hath made herself ready. And to her was granted that she should be arrayed in fine linen, clean and white: for the fine linen is the righteousness of saints. And He saith unto me, write, Blessed are they which are called unto the marriage supper of the Lamb...(Rev. 19:7-9).*

We have already established that the New Testament Church will comprise the Bride of Christ as well as the Old Covenant prophets. Where this marriage supper will take place and how long it will last is anyone's guess.

Perhaps there may even be two pre-nuptial suppers, one heavenly, and one earthly. One representing the *heavenly* Church and one for *earthly* Old Testament Israel.

This concept may sound like spiritual polygamy to some—but this is only speaking in *figurative* language. As already noted, two entities can apply to the same figure even as the Church is both Christ's Body and Wife.

Because the Bible is loaded with *duality*—is it not conceivable to think that there could be two marriage suppers expressing two different glories of God?

Could it be that the marriage supper of the Lamb in heaven would be for the New Testament Church while there could also be one on earth with the ancient prophets and apostles representing ancient Israel? Remember, the apostles will be ruling over each of the 12 tribes (Matt. 19:28). Christ said Himself that He would not drink of the fruit of the vine again until He drank it with the apostles in His Father's Kingdom (Matt. 26:29).

PROPHETIC PARABLES

Symbolically, the New Testament Church would represent Christ's heavenly Bride while Israel His earthly Bride. Both being purchased with His precious blood—but each being a special treasure with a different glory!

THE BRIDE BECOMES CHRIST'S ARMY

And I saw heaven opened, and behold a white horse; and he that sat upon him was called Faithful and true, and in righteousness he doth judge and make war. His eyes were as a flame of fire, and on his head were many crowns: and he had a name written, that no man knew, but He himself. And he was clothed with a vesture dipped in blood; and his name is called The Word of God, And the armies which were in heaven followed him upon white horses, clothed in fine linen, white and clean.

And out of his mouth goeth a sharp sword, that with it he should smite the nations: and he shall rule them with a rod of iron: and he treadeth the winepress of the fierceness and wrath of Almighty God. And he hath on his vesture and on his thigh a name written, KING OF KINGS, AND LORD OF LORDS (Rev. 19:11-16).

The next event to follow the marriage supper of the Lamb—will be the coming of the Lord to the earth with His Angels and Saints to smite the nations!

Obviously, the rider on the white horse is Jesus Christ who now comes as the champion of His people. The Prince of Peace now comes to RULE the world with a rod of iron, no longer a humble Lamb to be slaughtered. Now Jesus comes to take vengeance upon His enemies and to deliver His people from persecution. Faithful and True is His name—for He comes to execute righteous judgment of God's Word and to establish His Father's divine government on the earth.

The armies who follow Christ from heaven will comprise the holy angels (Mk. 8:38) and His wife Rev. 19:8,14).

All the kingdoms of the earth are to be His—the KING OF KINGS, AND LORD OF LORDS!

THE HARVEST OF SOULS

And I looked, and behold a white cloud, and upon the cloud one sat like unto the Son of man, having on his head a golden crown, and in his hand a sharp sickle (Rev. 14:14).

When the Son of Man [Christ] returns to this earth the second time—He will REAP the earth with a sharp sickle! But surprisingly, this reaping of souls on the earth is not for the Church!

This astounding truth is revealed in God's Word by several passages. But let's begin with the parable of the Sower, where Christ pictured the earth as His *field* to garner!

The *field* is not the *Church* as some believe in the parable of *The Sower,* but rather the *world* as interpreted by the Master story teller! Therefore, the *tares* are not as some suppose "Church members", but rather the "wicked" of the *earth* influenced by Satan (Matt. 13:38).

Both are to grow together in the world until the harvest when Christ will say to the reapers: **"Gather ye together *first* the tares, and bind them in bundles to burn them; but gather the wheat [Church] into my barn" (Matt. 13:30).**

The same sequence of end-time events is demonstrated through the parable of *"The Kingdom of Heaven likened unto a Net that was cast into the Sea,"* notice:

> **Again, the kingdom of heaven is like unto a net, that was cast into the sea, and gathered of every *kind*: which, when it was full, they drew to shore, and sat down, and gathered the good into vessels, but cast the bad away. So shall it be at the end of the world [age]: the angels shall come forth, and *sever* the wicked from among the just, and shall cast them into *the furnace of fire*: there shall be wailing and gnashing of teeth (Matt. 13:47-50).**

Notice this end-time scenario! The tares or wicked of the world are to be gathered to be burned!

At the end of the age, God's angels will gather the tares to be burned *before* He garners His people to inherit the Kingdom (Matt. 13:39-42). This will most likely occur during the 1290 and 1335 day period of time *after* Christ returns (Dan. 12). We will read this prophecy shortly.

The sequence of these end-time events also brings to mind the parable of **"One shall be *taken*, and the other left,"** which we will also cover shortly. So, notice again this end-time scenario, first, the tares will be taken to be BURNED—and the righteous shall be *left* to "shine forth as the sun in the kingdom of their Father..." (Matt. 13:43).

This end-time sequence is also illuminated by what occurred in the days of Noah! Concerning this *parallel* time, Christ said:

> **But the same day that Lot went out of Sodom it rained fire and brimstone from heaven and destroyed them *all*. Even thus shall it be in the day when the Son of man is revealed (Lk. 17:29:30).**

Realize, the lives of Noah and Lot are clearly *types* of what will happen in the last days! Here, Jesus expressly compared the destruction of mankind by the flood to the annihilation of the wicked in the end of the age.

Therefore, if this was a *type* of what is to come—ALL UNBELIEVERS will be wiped off the face of the earth! Could Jesus mean what He says? **"Even thus shall it be in the days when the Son of man is revealed."**

Can we take our Savior literally?

WHO WILL POPULATE THE MILLENNIUM?

Now we have a problem! If *all* the *wicked* are destroyed in the Great Tribulation—and if the righteous are changed into spiritual beings with eternal bodies upon Christ's return—who will be left to populate the Millennium?

Whoever this group is—they will have physical bodies! Why? Because those resurrected will be kings and priests over physical human beings!

During the Tribulation, multitudes will accept Jesus as their personal Savior and repent! However, these individuals will not be changed into spiritual beings at that time. Instead, they will inherit the Kingdom in their natural physical bodies!

The *Companion Bible* has an Appendix describing the period of time spoken of by Daniel as 1335 days and the *resurrection* of Israel *after* Christ returns (Dan. 12:11-12). This will be the gathering of the dispersed of Judah, which comes *after* the Tribulation at the end of the age—when the angels gather God's "elect" from the four corners of the earth (Isa. 11:12; Ezek. 5:10; Matt. 24:31). The *Companion Bible* states that the word "stand" in (Daniel 12:13), means "resurrection" (see margin on Dan. 12:13). This will be a great harvest of souls as *pictured* by the Feast of Tabernacles! Israel is called God's "elect" in (Isaiah 45:4 and 65:9).

According to this speculative scenario, this enmasse resurrection and *gathering* of the souls of Israel will begin prior to the glorious 1,000 year reign of Jesus Christ. Therefore, there may be a 75 day interval between Christ's return and the resurrection of Israel. This is calculated by adding 1260 + 75 = 1335 (see *Companion Bible,* Ap 89 & 90).

According to this concept, Christ's New Testament Bride is resurrected after the 1260 days, Israel 75 days later! Although this concept may be viewed as possible, we must realize that at best it is highly speculative, and we must proceed with due caution.

This gathering of God's "elect" [Israel] from the "four corners of the earth" will take place after Satan [Leviathan the piercing serpent] is bound and chained (Isa. 27:1; Rev. 20:1-3).

If only believers enter the Millennium, and all the incorrigible eradicated—someone is sure to ask, "what about the scripture in (Zechariah 14:16-19)?" This scripture reads:

> **And it shall come to pass, that every one that is left of all the nations which came against Jerusalem shall even go up from year to year to worship the King, the LORD of hosts, and to keep the feast of tabernacles. And it shall be, that whoso will not come up of all the families of the earth unto Jerusalem to worship the King, the LORD of hosts, even upon them shall be no rain. And if the family of Egypt go not up, and come not, that have no rain; there shall be the plague, wherewith *the LORD will smite the heathen that come not up to keep the feast of***

PROPHETIC PARABLES

> *tabernacles.* **This shall be the punishment of Egypt, and the punishment of all nations that come not up to keep the feast of tabernacles.**

How could this happen we might ask, if all were believers at the beginning of the Millennium? The answer is that although believers entered the Millennium as spirit beings—some of their physical children will become rebellious after a while as has always happened! Witness the nation of Israel in the wilderness.

The difference under God's perfect administration is that *rebellion* will not be tolerated and will be crushed immediately!

As we have just demonstrated, the *sickle* of the Lord is not for the righteous—but for the incorrigible of the earth! This sickle personifies a "cutting action" or *decision* making that will separate the righteous from the wicked—the Sheep from the Goats!

It is very possible that the separation of the Wheat from the Tares will take place *during* the 45 days (1290 + 45 = 1335) after Christ returns! Perhaps Satan will be bound and chained by the angel Gabriel 45 days after the 1290 days.

ONE SHALL BE TAKEN

> **I tell you, in that night there shall be two men in one bed;** *the one shall be taken, and the other left.* **Two women shall be grinding together;** *the one shall be taken*, **and** *the other left.* **Two men shall be in the field;** *the one shall be taken*, **and** *the other left.* **And they answered and said unto him, Where, Lord? And he said unto them, Wheresoever the body is, thither will** *the eagles be gathered together* **(Lk. 17:34-37).**

This parable has puzzled many—yet it is quite clear when viewing the entire context. Realize this! The taking of one and the leaving behind of one is in reference to *the days of Noah and Lot!* (see verses 26-33).

If we can understand what happened to Noah and Lot, we can understand the correct interpretation of this parable!

Both Noah and Lot are *types* of Tribulation Saints (Laodiceans) who will go through the Tribulation fires!

Noah's family is *typical* of the 144,000 physical Israelites of

Jacob's family who pass through the Tribulation under God's protection (Rev. 7).

Consider this!

If Noah's flood is a *type* of the Great Tribulation—"the flood took them ALL away!" Those that *remained* were saved, while those *taken* by the flood waters were destroyed!

As you will recall—*everyone* who was not aboard the Ark perished! Total annihilation of the wicked is *pictured* by this *duality* during the last days! This event is also a *foretaste* of Armageddon in which *all* the wicked will perish—rather than the Tribulation in which only partial destruction occurs!

Peter makes mention of the fact that Noah's flood was also a *type* of the "lake of fire" that will destroy the wicked at the Millennium's conclusion (2 Pet. 3). Both water and fire are *types* of cleansing agents! The old world of Noah was cleansed by water to prepare for a new world. Likewise, the earth will be cleansed by *fire* at the end of the Millennium before the new earth is made!

Lot's wife is a *type* of those individuals who neglect to "flee" during the Tribulation when the Abomination of desolation is set up!

Notice the wording in connection to "eagles" or vultures gathered together over dead bodies (vs. 37). This entire context is in reference to conditions of Noah's and Lot's day which were *types* of the Tribulation and Armageddon! Matthew gives the identical time setting as *prior* to the Tribulation (Matt. 24:28).

Matthew 24:27 places the chronology of the "eagles gathering" just *after* the Great Tribulation: **"For as the lightning cometh out of the east...so shall also the coming of the Son of man be."** This is the exact context of (Luke 17:24) which then proceeds to describe the days of Noah!

This should be clear as a bell! Luke 17 is in reference to the Tribulation and gathering of the wicked to be destroyed—but where? This is what the disciples asked Jesus! He explained: **"Wheresoever the body [corpse or carcass—Matt. 24:28] is, thither will the eagles [Gr. "vultures" or "birds of prey"], be gathered together" (vs. 37).** In other words, there are going to be a lot of vultures preying on the graveyard of dead bodies of the wicked or unrepentant of the earth.

The *King James Version* has the words *men* and *women* in italics which means it is not in the original Greek. Think about it—

why would two men be in one bed unless they were homosexuals? But it is dubious that Jesus was referring to homosexuals, as the apostle Paul stated, unless repentant! (1 Cor. 6:9-10).

This verse is referring to the *prepared* and *unprepared* who have "mingled together" in the closest intercourse of everyday life!

THE WINEPRESS

Quickly turn to (Revelation 14:19,20) for more substantial proof of the end-time sequence of events:

> **And the angel thrust in his *sickle* into the earth, and gathered the vine of the earth ["the one shall be taken, and the other left"] and cast it ["Where, Lord?"] into the great winepress of the wrath of God. And the winepress was trodden without the city [Jerusalem], and *blood came out of the winepress,* even unto the horse bridles, by the space of a thousand and six hundred furlongs (180 miles).**

Here we begin to get all of the pieces to this end-time puzzle together. The "woman" (converted Israelites) has escaped to a place of safety for 1260 days or 3 1/2 years (Rev.12). The 144,000 physical Israelites and possibly 144,000 Gentile Tribulation Saints are protected *during* the time of Satan's wrath (Rev.7;14)! Millions will be converted as a result of the Tribulation!

At the end of this dreaded time—Christ returns to separate the "wicked from the righteous", the "wheat from the tares", the "sheep from the goats"!

The righteous will stay to inherit the Kingdom—but the wicked will be *taken* to be squashed into *human wine* whose blood will run 180 miles long, reaching the bridles of a horse!

Where?

THE SUPPER OF THE GREAT GOD

Wherever the *eagles* [vultures] are gathered together! (Lk. 17:37). Now turn to (Revelation 19) to find the incredible answer:

He treadeth the winepress of the fierceness and wrath of Almighty God...And I saw an angel standing in the sun; and he cried with a loud voice, saying to *all the fowls that fly in the midst of heaven,* **Come and gather yourselves together unto the supper of the great God; that ye may eat the flesh of kings, and the flesh of captains, and the flesh of mighty men, and the flesh of horses, and of them that sit on them, and the flesh of all men, both free and bond, both small and great (Rev. 19:15-18).**

Now we come to the grand finale of God's feast—if you will, the dessert. This scene describes the destruction of the demonic led armies of the earth gathering for the final battle of Armageddon.

The "Beast" [Antichrist] and his religious cohort "False Prophet", scurry to combine the kings of the earth in one last desperate pursuit to destroy God's coming government. This will represent man's last effort to rule the earth before all unrighteousness is squelched.

However, these armies are completely smitten only to become food for the birds of prey.

Although this will be a gruesome sight—it will be filled with JUBILATION as God's ensuing utopia government will finally be ushered in—this will truly be "a feast fit for a king"!

According to (Zechariah 12:2,9) the location of the winepress will be just outside the city of Jerusalem. This will be where the armies of the earth will be gathered for the final battle of the earth.

THE VALLEY OF DECISION

I will also gather all nations, and bring them down into the valley of Jehoshaphat, and will plead with them there...Let the heathen be wakened, and come up to the valley of Jehoshaphat: for there will I sit to judge all the heathen round about. Put ye in the *sickle,* **for the harvest is ripe: come [tread], for the press is full, the [vats] overflow; for their wickedness is great. multitudes, multitudes in the valley of decision: for the day of the Lord is near in the valley of decision (Joel**

3:2, 12-14).

Realize this is all *symbolic* language used to illustrate the destruction of the wicked just after Christ's return—not the end of the Millennium!

The *sickle* the angel casts in is *symbolic* of the harvest of wicked souls—represented by the *vine!* The winepress is *symbolic* of Christ trampling on these human grapes to crush them or kill them!

But what about the 180 miles of blood that reaches the horses bridles—is this *symbolic* or real? If it is literal, this certainly would not entail just the armies of Armageddon—it would have to represent ALL of the wicked left on earth!

This prophecy will occur in the "Valley of Jehoshaphat" where the Lord will punish the wicked tares!

GOOD MIXED WITH BAD

There is a *definite* and *distinctive* DIVISION between "good" and "bad" people as outlined in many of the parables. These "bad" cannot therefore refer to those who are Christians—but rather those who are "professing" Christians as emphasized by the parable of the Sower!

The parables of the "Wheat and Tares"; "Good and Bad Fish"; "Good and Evil Servants"; "Wise and Foolish Virgins"; "Sheep and the Goats"; "Profitable and Unprofitable Servants"; the "Guest without a Wedding Garment"; and "One Shall be Taken, One Shall be Left"—all characterize this same theme!

Several of these parables show that God's angels will be the agency to SEPARATE the "just" from the "unjust" the "righteous" from the "wicked" the "good" from the "bad"!

Our Lord and Savior makes it very clear as to when this event transpires from several parables! The parables of the "Wheat and the Tares" the "Good and Bad fish" and the "Winepress" all give the vital time element of this separation. In the dynamic words of Jesus Christ, the division of the *wicked* and *righteous* is thundered loud and clear! Christ said dogmatically: **"So shall it be at the end of the age"!**

Under the Old Covenant, God made it abundantly clear that the Israelites were not to be "unequally yoked with unbelievers." The Almighty God gave vivid instructions concerning this in

Deuteronomy 22:9-11: **"Thou shall not sow thy vineyard with divers (different) seeds: lest the fruit of thy seed which thou hast sown, and the fruit of thy vineyard be defiled. Thou shall not plow with an ox and an ass together. Thou shalt not wear a garment of divers sorts, as of woolen and linen together."**

All these precepts refer to the *separation* of the *good* from the *bad* and therefore keeping the kind pure! The reason God instituted these laws, was to teach the Israelites a spiritual lesson from the physical things before them that they could understand. The lesson here was that the all-knowing God wanted to keep true worship pure, and therefore forbade the Israelites to marry other nations (Deut. 7:3).

Christians are also exhorted to keep unspotted from the world by not being *influenced* by them, or as Paul put it: **"Wherefore come out from among them, and be ye separate, saith the Lord, and touch not the unclean thing; and I will receive you" (11 Cor. 6:17).**

WHEN THE NEW COVENANT WILL BE MADE

Christians now form spiritually, the *true Israel* of the New Testament. A testament is a will that declares a person's will as to the disposal of his possessions after his death. Upon the death of Christ—He left a will, or testament in which Christians may become beneficiaries of His goods (Heb.9:14-18). These heirs of salvation are now being perfected to be Christ's spotless Bride upon His return (Eph. 4:12,13).

At the resurrection, when Christians are made immortal, they will enter into the New Testament. After 2520 years of Gentile rule, the living Jesus Christ is soon coming to *restore* the ecclesiastical government of His Father. He will be the mediator of the New Testament which is based upon better promises (Heb. 8:6-10, 9:15).

The New Testament will not be made with human mortals who fail to keep their word—but rather with individuals who have proven through *trial* and *test* that they desire to be faithful to the laws, authority and government of God! At the resurrection, the Church will become a perfect spiritual nation [a holy nation—1 Pet. 2:5,9] with a spiritual nature and power to keep God's way of life perfectly!

The Old Covenant was started by a marriage and the New

PROPHETIC PARABLES

Testament will also be started by a "marriage feast." So, if we can tell when the marriage feast takes place between Jesus and His Church—we will know when the New Testament begins! The "marriage feast" will take place only after the resurrection of the Church.

THE RESTORATION OF ISRAEL

Chapter Nine

JUDGMENT UPON FALSE RELIGION

In the 12th chapter of Exodus, while the children of Israel were still in Egypt—long before any of the "Law of Moses" had been given—prior to the time when God revealed to Moses and the Israelites He would make the Old Covenant with them—we find the annual FEAST DAYS He gave Israel being observed!

And in the 23rd chapter of Leviticus we find a summary of these annual feast days or set feasts. These feast days picture *the different dispensations in the Plan of God,* and can only be understood today because of the spiritual fulfillment of some already.

It should be pointed out also that these feast days are *not* called the "Feasts of the Jews" or "Holydays of the Israelites;" but rather the "Feasts of the Lord" (Lev. 23:2). In the early New Testament Church and throughout Church history, many Christians observed the Sabbaths of God, both weekly and annual.

The Feast Days God gave the nation of Israel present an outline of His great plan and purpose for the whole earth. They provide the *key* for fitting together the historical and prophetic scriptures, and they reveal to His people a *plan* which God initiated from the beginning of creation. God has given these days for the purpose of teaching His people *who* He is, and the work that He is doing here on earth.

God had given Israel the Feast days as a SIGN for the purpose of *identifying* the true God as we read in Ezekiel 20:12: **"Moreover I also gave them My Sabbaths, *to be a sign between them and Me,* that they might know that I am the LORD who sanctifies them."**

God established SEVEN *annual Sabbaths* in addition to the seventh-day Sabbath of each week. The seven annual Sabbaths are given in Leviticus 23 and are counted according to the religious calendar God gave Israel. The first annual Sabbath occurs on the day following Passover, on the fifteenth day of the first month, and is called **the First Day of Unleavened Bread.**

The second annual Sabbath is the seventh day in the week of Unleavened Bread, and is called **the Last Day of Unleavened Bread.**

The third annual Sabbath is **Pentecost,** which must be counted each year in order to be observed.

The remaining four annual Sabbaths occur in the seventh month in the fall of the year.

The fourth annual Sabbath is the first day of the seventh month, and is **the Feast of Trumpets.**

The fifth annual Sabbath of the seventh month, is **the Day of Atonement.** It is a day of fasting, and occurs on the tenth day of the month.

The sixth annual Sabbath is the fifteenth day of the seventh month, and is **the Feast of Tabernacles.**

The last annual Sabbath occurs on the eighth day following the Feast of Tabernacles, and is called **the Last Great Day.**

These feast days are a panorama in *type* of the entire time between the Passover or Christ's death to the Feast of Tabernacles, and Last Great Day representing the Millennium.

THE FUTURE PASSOVER

We normally think of the Passover as being only a *memorial* of Israel's deliverance from Egypt. Passover has a fulfillment in Jesus' death as God's Passover Lamb. However, Passover is *primarily* concerned with a future event, as the apostle Paul summed up very succinctly in Colossians 2:16-17: **"Let no man therefore judge you in meat, or in drink, or in respect of a feast day or a new moon, or a sabbath day: *which are a shadow of the things to come...*"**

The apostle says the feast days are *shadows* of things that are

JUDGMENT ON FALSE RELIGION

to come! God's *great future* Passover, of which the first one is a *type*, has not yet been fulfilled! But it will be fulfilled in the future when the Kingdom of God is brought in power to the earth by Jesus Christ Himself!

God used the Passover of A.D. 70 when He caused Jerusalem to be destroyed by the Romans, to make clear the real meaning of Passover. Jesus prophesied of this destruction in (Matthew 24), a few days before the Last Supper, when the Jews rejection of Him was complete.

According to Josephus, the Romans came suddenly upon the city and surrounded it during the Passover. From the known number of Passover lambs sacrificed that year [256,500], it is estimated about 1,250,000 people were trapped in Jerusalem since five people could eat one lamb. The vast majority was killed in the fighting or by sickness and starvation. God punished the nation of the Jews by using the Passover to trap a great number in one place.

The number trapped, corresponds closely to the number delivered over 1,500 years before during the first Passover in Egypt (*The Life and Works of Josephus,* Book V, Chapter III). The future *Passover* of which Egypt was a *type* and Jerusalem an example, is YET TO COME!

GOD'S JUDGEMENT UPON FALSE RELIGION

God is going to judge the whole earth in the future Passover which will have similarities to the first Passover in Egypt. The fall feasts of God *picture* this in detail and we will study them thoroughly. For the present, note the similarity between the first Passover and the one in the future:

> **After these things I saw another angel coming down out of heaven, having authority; and the earth was lightened with his glory. And he cried with a mighty voice, saying Fallen, fallen is Babylon the great, and is become a habitation of demons...And I heard another voice from heaven, saying,** *come forth, my people, out of her, that ye have no fellowship with her sins, and that ye receive not of her plagues:* **for her sins have reached even unto heaven, and God hath remembered her iniquities (Rev. 18:1-5).**

The reasons of God's wrath and destruction will be the same in the future, as they were when He delivered Israel from Egypt and judged the false gods of Egypt. He will judge the false religion spawned by ancient Babylon, which has deceived the whole world with her false doctrines through many daughter religions.

The people God will call out of Babylon will not be Christians, since true Christians have the true God revealed to them and cannot be worshippers of Babylonian gods and remain Christian. These called out of Babylon will be *the descendants of Jacob* as will be shown later.

This will be the fulfillment of Passover in the future, when God will again deliver His people Israel from slavery and will judge a great world-ruling system of government and religion just as He did Egypt. At that time Israel will literally be slaves to a system of government *symbolized* in Revelation as a "Beast."

This "Beast" is ridden by a woman called BABYLON, *symbolizing* a world-wide religious system. How it will come about will be discussed at length under the later feast days which come in the seventh month.

The woman riding the "Beast" is described as MYSTERY, BABYLON THE GREAT, THE MOTHER OF THE HARLOTS AND OF THE ABOMINATIONS OF THE EARTH (Rev. 17:5). In ancient Babylon built by Nimrod soon after the flood, a system of religion was instituted that was the mother of all the false religions [harlots], the filth and evil practices [abominations of the earth] in the world today.

Today, many holidays, doctrines and symbols that originated in the ancient Babylonian religion are called Christian. In the early centuries when Christianity grew popular, many people were converted from the pagan religions directly descended from the ancient Babylonian religion.

The pagan holidays were adapted for Christian use and the names were changed to honor Jesus Christ. When Christianity was adopted as the official religion of the decaying Roman Empire, the keeping of the former pagan holidays, now named in honor of Jesus Christ, was enforced by the authority of the Roman government.

The feast days that God gave the nation of Israel had been gradually eradicated by the early spurious Roman church. Soon after Christianity became the official Roman religion under Emperor Constantine, the feast days were completely discarded and ignored by Christianity for the most part.

JUDGMENT ON FALSE RELIGION

PASSOVER AND UNLEAVENED BREAD
PICTURE FUTURE EVENTS

We normally think of Passover as being only a memorial of Israel's supernatural deliverance from Egypt. However, Passover has a fulfillment in Jesus' death as God's Passover Lamb, and is primarily concerned with a FUTURE event, as are all of God's feast days. God's feast days are *shadows* of things that are yet to come!

Just before He instituted the memorial of His death on Passover night, Jesus Himself stated: "**...I have earnestly desired to eat this Passover with you before I suffer; for I say to you, I will no longer eat of it until it is *fulfilled* in the kingdom of God**" (Lk. 22:15-16).

Jesus Christ will eat the Passover again when it is *fulfilled!* God's great future Passover, of which the first one is a *type*, has not yet been fulfilled—but it will be fulfilled in the future when the Kingdom of God is brought in power to the earth by Jesus Christ Himself. We have a new memorial and a new mark upon our lives; which is the spiritual mark of the blood of our Passover Lamb, but the *future Passover* of which Jesus spoke has not yet occurred!

A Christian's present position is similar to ancient Israel's when they had killed the Passover lamb on Nisan 14, and had marked their homes and were remaining inside, waiting for God's wrath to be visited upon the Egyptians about them.

Christians have been "marked" with Jesus Christ's blood, and are like Israel, who were waiting in their homes, dressed and ready to leave Egypt. We are strangers and pilgrims in this world, and are also waiting for God's JUDGMENT on the world, and our orders to leave and be with Jesus Christ forevermore!

Christians are now going through their Passover individually as they live out their lives. However, the judgment upon Egypt [this world] and God's Passover remain for the future and will occur just before God's Kingdom comes to earth visibly. In the Passover deliverance, Christians meditate upon Christ's death until He comes.

The apostle Peter writes of the meaning of Christ's precious blood that redeems Christians:

> **For as much as ye know that ye were not redeemed with corruptible things, as silver and gold, from your vain conversation received by tradition from your fathers;** *But with the precious blood of Christ, as of a lamb without blemish and without spot"* (1 Pet. 1:18-19).

Christians have been REDEEMED by the precious blood of Jesus Christ which now identifies us—His life was given to redeem us from the *Egypt* of this world! But this does not mean that God's judgment has *passed over* us yet! Here we have a warning that we must live our lives as children of obedience, living a *new life* that is completely different from our former life before conversion, wherein we were controlled by the LUSTS of our flesh, and the ignorance of God's way which is righteous.

We have been made *holy by accepting* Jesus's blood, and living godly lives. If we do not, we will not escape His judgment any more than the Egyptians escaped God's judgment on their false religion and idol worship. We have been redeemed from the false religions of this world; we now become believers in the true God. We are adopted into Israel and become Abraham's children by *faith.*

The God of Abraham, Isaac and Jacob is now our God, and we are His people. We are separated from this world and its false religions, which God is going to judge in a future Passover. God judged the gods of Egypt on Passover night, and the great Passover of God yet to be fulfilled will be a judgment upon all false religion, when this world's false religions will be totally destroyed!

Because of God's love for us while we were yet sinners, Christ died for us, and we are, **."..now justified by his blood" (Rom. 5:8-9).**

Jesus Christ died for us while we were yet sinners, and His blood has JUSTIFIED us from our past guilt so that we can be saved from the wrath to come, through Him. The wrath of God speaks of the Passover in the future. God's judgment has not yet passed over the world and spared His own. His wrath is YET to be visited, from which we can escape through the mark of our *Passover Lamb!*

Let us heed the warnings contained in ancient Israel's Egyptian experience—and never again choose to go back to our Egypt—if we do, all we will be doing is building bricks made out

JUDGMENT ON FALSE RELIGION

of straw for our own grave!

THE YEAR OF JUBILEE

The number *fifty* denotes release from bondage of sin and to bring in everlasting righteousness. It also means "acceptance" and "unity."

Jesus began His public ministry in the year of Jubilee in the fall of A.D. 27-28. This was no accident! It was by God's algebraic design! The year of *Jubilee* is a very important part of God's plan in dealing with the nation of Israel.

One of the Messiah's principle responsibilities will be to lead His people back to their land out of *captivity* (Isa. 49:6). Jesus proclaimed this event as He read a prophecy in Isaiah:

> **And there was delivered unto him a book of the prophet Isaiah. And when he had opened the book, he found the place where it was written, the Spirit of the Lord is upon me, because he hath anointed me to preach the gospel to the poor; he hath sent me to heal the brokenhearted, to preach** *deliverance to the captives*, **and recovering of sight to the blind,** *to set at liberty* **them that are bruised, to preach** *the acceptable year of the Lord...*" **(Lk. 4:18-19).**

Notice, the **"acceptable year of the Lord"** or His return is connected with the **"deliverance"** and setting at **"liberty"** the *captives!*

Jesus read this prophecy during the *sabbath* [Heb. Day of Weeks] or Pentecost (Lk. 4:16). This was during the Jubilee year of A.D. 27-28! It is worth noting that both Pentecost and Jubilee are counted by numbering seven sabbaths and adding one—rather than a set date like the other Feast days!

THE ACCEPTABLE YEAR OF JUBILEE

In Israel, every 50th year was to be hailed as a year of Jubilee. All Israelites who were debtors were released from such bondage to any of their countrymen. All debts were cancelled, notice:

> And thou shalt number seven sabbaths of years unto thee, seven times seven years; and the space of the seven sabbaths of years shall be unto thee *forty and nine years*. Then shalt thou cause the trumpet of the jubilee to sound on the tenth day of the seventh month, in the day of atonement shall ye make the trumpet sound throughout all your land. And ye shall hallow the fiftieth year, and proclaim *liberty* throughout all the land unto all the inhabitants thereof: it shall be a jubilee unto you; and ye shall return every man unto his possession, and ye shall return every man unto his family. A jubilee shall that fiftieth year be unto you: ye shall not sow, neither reap that which groweth of itself in it, nor gather the grapes in it of thy vine undressed. For it is the jubilee; it shall be holy unto you: ye shall eat the increase thereof out of the field (Lev. 25:8-12).

The Jubilee year was the 50th year following the 7th Sabbatic year [actually 49 years apart]—(Lev. 25:8). The land was to rest even though it followed a Sabbatical rest the year before. This made for an unusual event, allowing the land to remain fallow two years in a row. The people were to live off the produce produced during the sixth year.

The Jubilee year began on the Day of Atonement, and both events *foreshadow* the time of Israel's REDEMPTION and return to their land! Each Jubilee year, the land that had been divided by lot to the families of Israel, was returned to their rightful birthright owners. In the year of Jubilee, the land was to be returned to the descendants of the family God had selected to own that particular piece of real estate under Joshua.

One commentator writes: "[The Jubilee year] did not teach either the socialistic economic theory...or the free-enterprise system that allows an unlimited expansion of private property. On the contrary, it established a fixed title to the property assigned by God" (*International Standard Bible Encyclopaedia,* volume II, page 1142).

The Jubilee year was to be proclaimed, not at the beginning of the civil calendar on the Feast of Trumpets, but on the Day of

JUDGMENT ON FALSE RELIGION

Atonement, 10 days later.

God wanted the nation of Israel freed from human oppression. But He desired much more. He wanted Israel to enjoy the same liberty Jesus Christ came to bring—freedom from sin! What is this liberating truth? Jesus explains: **"Most assuredly, I say to you, whoever commits sin is a slave of sin...If the Son makes you free, you shall be free indeed" (Jn. 8:34, 36).**

True liberty is freedom from bondage of sin. Christian liberty has its price. The apostle Paul explains:

> **Don't you know that when you offer yourselves to someone to obey him as slaves, you are slaves to the one whom you obey—whether you are slaves to sin, which leads to death, or to obedience, which leads to righteousness?...You have been set free from sin and have become slaves to righteousness (Romans 6:16-18, NIV).**

Paul continues his dissertation on Christian liberty:

> **[We] who have the firstfruits of the Spirit...[eagerly wait] for the adoption, the redemption of our body...The creation itself also will be delivered from the bondage of corruption into the glorious liberty of the children of God (Rom. 8:23, 21).**

The year of Jubilee was a *dress rehearsal* of the time that the nation of Israel will be "set free" from the bondage of their enemies as Christ returns to lead them out of captivity.

At this momentous time, *atonement* will be made for the sins of Israel, and they will begin to inherit the blessings God has promised them!

After our Lord had finished reading this passage from Isaiah, He closed the book and declared: **"This day is this scripture fulfilled in your ears."** But why did our Lord stop in the middle of this scripture instead of completing the remainder of the verse, **"And the day of vengeance of our Lord?"**

The answer is obvious! Our Lord Himself placed a comma in the middle of this sentence because He had only come to fulfill part of this prophecy at that time! The fulfillment of **"...the day of vengeance of our Lord"** will only transpire upon our Lord's second and final advent in which a parenthesis of nearly 2,000 years will have elapsed!

That is why the Bible says of the first century Church that, **"...when the Day of Pentecost had fully come [Pentecost was the 50th day after the spring wave-sheaf ceremony]—see (Leviticus 23:15-16) they were all of** *one accord in one place"* **(Acts 2:1).**

What a beautiful law to reunite families!

A DECADE OF JUBILEES

Now here is something very incredible but highly significant in the understanding of prophetic events. The "seventy weeks" prophecy of (Daniel 9), which prophesies **"...the coming of the Messiah to make an end of Israel's sins, and to bring in everlasting righteousness"** is *a decade of jubilees!*

In this verse, the Hebrew word *shabua,* meaning "seven" is translated "weeks" in the *King James Version* but is correct in the *Stuart's* translation! Thus, (Daniel 9:24) should read: **"Seventy *sevens* are determined upon thy people and upon thy holy city..."**

These "seventy sevens" technically are "seventy sabbatical cycles", and Ben Wacholder verifies this through his research of compelling evidence from Qumranic, rabbinic and epigraphic documents. He writes that the Hebrew word *shabua* clearly means "the sabbatical cycle" (*11 Q Melchizekek,* Ben Zion Wacholder, pp. 202-204).

In 1956 a fragmentary text, entitled (11Q Melchizedek) was discovered in Qumran Cave 11 and cross references the Jubilee from (Lev. 25:13; Deut. 15:2; Isa. 61:1) with Daniel's Seventy Weeks Prophecy. The description of the Messianic work of Melchizedek is described thusly:

> **He will restore (their patrimonies?) to them and proclaim freedom to them and make them abandon all their sins. This shall take place during the sabbatical cycle (*shabua*) of the first jubilee following the ni[ne] jubilees, and on the D[ay of Atone]ment f[alling] at the en[d of the ju]bilee, the tenth; to forgive on it (the day of atonement) for all of (the sins) of the children of**

JUDGMENT ON FALSE RELIGION

[God and] the men of the lot of Melchizedek (*11 Q Melchizekek*, translation by Ben Zion Wacholder, pp. 210-211).

But why prophesy seventy "sevens" instead of seventy "years"? The Hebrew word for years could have been used if only "seventy years" were God's intention concerning Israel's punishment!

Surely this is very important to God, and using His mathematical design we will now show its significance! Are there any other "sevens" of numbers mentioned in the Word of God that Daniel's people would understand? Indeed there were!

God gave His people a week of "seven" days—the Sabbath being the *seventh* day of the week. This seventh day of the physical *rest* was a *mirror* of God's Kingdom government of rest and peace upon the earth, in which the nation of Israel will be God's leading witness instrumentally!

In addition to the "seven of days" God instituted the "seven year" land rest every *seventh* year. The Israelites were to work their land the first six years, but were to let their land rest from sowing and tiling the seventh (Lev. 25:3-4). This also had similar connotation as did the seven days of the creation week!

It was upon this "seven sabbaths of years" that the foundation for counting the Jubilee year was formed! Every fiftieth year—all debts were cancelled and all real estate was returned to the rightful birthright landholders (Lev. 25:8-9).

The overwhelming evidence of the relationship of the tenth Jubilee and Daniel's Seventy Weeks is made clear from simple arithmetic. Ten Jubilee years ($10 \times 49 = 490$), and the seventy sabbatical cycles of Daniel 9:24 ($70 \times 7 = 490$).

Ben Wacholder adds: "when one reads in line 18 of our fragment: 'And the herald of good tidings' (Is. 52:7a) refers to the messiah, the Spirit concerning whom it was said by Dan[iel (9:25): 'Until the coming of the messiah, the prince seven sabbatical cycles.']...It is noteworthy that, as Daniel 9:24, the last year of jubilee involves atonement for iniquity: 'to forgive on it [the day of atonement] for all of' [the sins] (Ben Zion Walcholder, p. 211, Line 8, n. 87).

Another interesting point that many scholars have made in their assessment of Daniel 9, is that the Messiah or "anointed one" of (verse 25 and 26) and the "anointing" of "the most Holy" [Place or Holy of Holies] (Heb. *qodesh qodashim*) of (verse 24) may have reference to a place or a person or both.

Thus, after "seventy sabbatical cycles" the Messiah would come to cleanse the Holy of Holies [Jerusalem, the sanctuary and the holy people]. P. Grelot describes this final sabbatical cycle as "the Sabbath of Sabbaths for the tried people" (*Biblica 50*, 1969, p. 182). Andre Lacocque describes this time as "the Great Day of Forgiveness [Heb. *Yom hakippurim]*, (*The Book of Daniel*, p. 192).

This is the time that the Messiah will **"finish the transgression, and put an end to sin, and atone for iniquity, and bring in everlasting righteousness" (Dan. 9:24).** Jesus Christ is our true High Priest, but notice what the high priest of Israel was to do in *type* on the Day of Atonement:

> **And he shall make an atonement for the holy place, because of the uncleanness of the children of Israel, and because of their transgression in all their sins...and for the altar, and he shall make an atonement for the priests, and for all the people of the congregation (Lev. 16:16; 33).**

THE JUBILEE AND DANIEL 9:24

Daniel knew that these seventy "sevens" referred to seventy *prophetic years* in the desolations of Jerusalem (Dan. 9:2). As a youth, Daniel understood the impending captivity of His people by the Babylonian Empire under Nebuchadnezzar from the prophecies of Isaiah and Micah (Isa. 39:6; Micah 4:10). These prophets along with Jeremiah, had forecast Judah's destruction and forthcoming captivity for 70 years, almost 100 years before it happened! (Jer. 25:11,12; 29:10).

Daniel was also very familiar with God's penal code of justice for breaking His inexorable law of the Sabbatic year as stated in (11 Chron. 36:21; Lev. 26:34).

For every Sabbatic year Israel had violated—God was going to punish them one year in captivity! Because they had broken the land sabbath 70 times during the course of 490 years—God was going to punish them 70 years or seventy "sevens" of years!

How consistent this seems according to God's algebraic design! It is as though the angel of God were saying to Daniel, **"Because the captivity of your people had been 70 years for**

breaking the land Sabbath, the time between the captivity and the coming of the Messiah will be *seven times* as long!"

In the course of breaking seventy Sabbatical years [prophetic times], ten Jubilee years were also violated! Without this understanding, Daniel's seventy weeks prophecy is muddled! Because Israel broke seventy Sabbatical cycles afterwards, they were being punished *sevenfold* or seven times each Sabbatical year of violation. Simple arithmetic of (70 times 7) equals 490 years of punishment. The first 69 weeks of punishment as recorded in (Daniel 9) have since occurred—the 70th week [consisting of seven literal years] is still future!

In God's fury, He declared to this rebellious nation:

> **Ye have not hearkened unto me, in proclaiming liberty, every one to his brother, and every man to his neighbor: behold, I proclaim a liberty for you, saith the Lord, to the sword, to the pestilence, and to the famine; and I will make you to be removed into all the kingdoms of the earth (Jer. 34:8-17).**

This historic captivity of the nation of Judah by Nebuchadnezzar's Babylonian army began, **"...to fulfill the word of the Lord by the mouth of Jeremiah, until the land had enjoyed her sabbaths; for as long as she lay desolate she kept sabbath, to fulfill threescore and ten years" (11 Chron. 36:21).**

Because the Israel of Judah had failed to keep God's land Sabbath for seventy years, the Eternal was going to keep it for them for these seventy missing years—by sending them into captivity!

This seventy-year period of "desolations" began with the conquering of the land and besieging of Jerusalem by Nebuchadnezzar on the tenth day of the tenth month, in 589 B.C.; and ended seventy prophetic years later [360 day years] to the exact day in 520 B.C. when the foundation of the second Temple was laid (see Haggai 2:18).

The interval between these dates is exactly 70 biblical prophetic years, which equals 25,200 days (70 x 360 days equals 25,200 days).

This Jubilee Cycle of sabbatical years and Jubilee Years began when the Israelites crossed the Jordan River [presumably in

THE RESTORATION OF ISRAEL

1451 B.C., although this date varies from 1586-1446] (Joshua 4:19).

PENTECOST AND JUBILEE

Pentecost and Jubilee are both counted by numbering seven sabbaths and adding one, rather than a set date. Both add up to "50"! Pentecost is calculated by counting seven Sabbaths of days while Jubilee is calculated by counting seven Sabbaths of years!

Surely this must be a spiritual calculus equation that only God's Holy Spirit can unlock as our school teacher! The Day of Pentecost *symbolizes* the Church's acceptance to God as "firstfruits." Because Israel also observed the Feast of Pentecost—this understanding must also apply to her!

Now Pentecost pictures the *resurrection* of FIRSTFRUITS to be *acceptable* to God as they are released from the bondage of this world!

Could it be that there will be a *resurrection* of "firstfruits" to God on some future Day of Pentecost during a Jubilee year?

Could this also be a *dual* prophecy to Israel and the Church? It appears that 144,000 of the nation of Israel (Rev. 7) along with 144,000 *firstfruits* (Rev. 14:1,4) will be offered to God at some time prior to Christ's return!

The nation of Israel observed a Jubilee year in 1987-88 according to the first year Israel set foot in their land from the Exodus. This was also Israel's *seventieth* Jubilee year and may very well be the beginning of the time known as "Jacob's trouble." However, if we use the date they once again possessed the land of Palestine in 1948, their will be Jubilee years in 2048 and so on.

Thus we have the connecting link between Pentecost—Atonement—and Jubilee!

Chapter Ten

GOD'S "SEVEN TIMES" PUNISHMENT

There are *four* time cycles of 2,520 years indicated in the scriptures. Three of these periods find their fulfillment in the last days. We will now discuss the first of these 2,520 year time cycles.

God first pictured the succession of world-ruling governments from Nebuchadnezzar's time onward as a great imposing image of a man. This civilization was a product of *man's mind* and *heart* (intelligence and emotions). This image was described in (Daniel 2), as we have already read.

So proud was Nebuchadnezzar of the fact that he and his kingdom were its HEAD, he erected in Babylon in honor of himself an actual image of gold, and commanded all the people to worship it or face the penalty of a fiery death (Dan. 3).

God's servants Shadrach, Meshach, and Abednego would not bow down to the king's dictates and were thrown into the fiery furnace. However, these FAITHFUL servants of God were *miraculously saved,* and are a *type* of the trials that will face Christians in the last days, as the "Beast" power will impose it's *mark* on true Christians once again!

However, Nebuchadnezzar was not allowed to remain in his haughty grandeur for long. He was suddenly cut down by God, and given the mind of a *wild beast.*

Let's notice exactly what happened to King Nebuchadnezzar. The king had a second dream that troubled him greatly (Dan. 4:4-5). Nebuchadnezzar had a dream in which he saw a tree in the middle of the earth grow to a great height. The tree grew strong and tall until it reached unto heaven. The leaves of this prodigious

THE RESTORATION OF ISRAEL

tree produced much fruit—and all flesh was fed from it.

Then the king saw a watcher [angel] come down from heaven and said to cut the great tree down to a stump, cut off its branches, shake off his leaves, and scatter its fruit (vss. 11-15).

Then the frightened king called for his magicians and astrologers to interpret the dream, but they were unable to (vss. 6-7). Finally, the king called upon Daniel to interpret the dream. Daniel told the vaunted Nebuchadnezzar that the tree was *symbolic* of himself—whose empire had become strong and great in the dominion of the earth (vs. 22).

The dream *pictured* the king living with the beasts of the field and eating grass like an ox, if he didn't repent. This was to be for "seven times" (vs. 25).

The dream was given at first as a warning, with a chance for Nebuchadnezzar to repent and escape the dire punishment. God is always faithful to give man a chance to repent before He punishes!

"Seven Times," in prophetic language, means seven years. Therefore, Nebuchadnezzar was to live and act like a wild beast for seven literal years before his strange madness would pass.

Nebuchadnezzar, during his insanity, *symbolized* the real nature of the prophesied Gentile empires. No longer with any real understanding, cut off from God, ignorant of the *purpose* for man's being on earth, these empires, like *wild predatory beasts,* would fight and struggle, wage war, tear and devour, down through the centuries!

THE GENTILE'S SEVEN TIMES PUNISHMENT

Since much of Biblical prophecy is *dual*, the seven years of Nebuchadnezzar's personal punishment became a *type* of the duration of this world's human governments and their wild beast-like ways. But in the *antitypical fulfillment* in the succession of human empires, each one of the "seven times" becomes not a literal year, but a *symbolic* or prophetic year of 360 days. Each such "day" itself stands for a literal year, according to the well known Biblical principle given in (Numbers 4:34 and Ezekiel 4:4-6), which show that each *symbolic* day represents an actual year in fulfillment.

And so the "times" of God's punishment on the Gentiles, allowing them to go their own way and reap the natural consequences of sin—would last for a period of 2520 years (7 x

360). During this time the world's kingdoms would act like wild beasts—until they too finally learn, as Nebuchadnezzar did, that God Almighty rules in the affairs of men. The time when the great tree of Babylon fell was approximately 539 B.C.

Now here is something significant in determining *when* the "times of the Gentiles" would end. The *tree* is addressed to the *man* Nebuchadnezzar, as Daniel interpreted the tree as [you] O king—or the empire he personified (vss. 20-22). Babylon was Nebuchadnezzar, and Nebuchadnezzar was Babylon in *type*. The prophecy said 7 Times would pass over [you]—and Nebuchadnezzar was punished for 7 *literal years,* as the Gentile kingdoms in *antitype* would be punished for 7 *prophetic years*!

But what happened to Nebuchadnezzar after his 7 literal years of madness? Because he is a *type* of the Gentile world—whatever happened to him—would also happen to the Gentile world in the last days!

After 7 literal years of insanity—Nebuchadnezzar's mind was completely restored! Could this be a *duality* to what will happen to the last Gentile empire in the end-time? The 4th chapter of Daniel dealt with the person of Nebuchadnezzar, who is a *type* of the Babylonian system of this world. The very next chapter deals with the Babylonian system itself in the infamous "Handwriting on the Wall."

THE HANDWRITING ON THE WALL

One of the most fascinating revelations of the entire panorama of prophecy is found in the fifth chapter of Daniel. It also concerns the duration of the Gentile world empires which had been revealed previously.

Nebuchadnezzar had suffered a punishment for "seven times" (years). Yet his kingdom was kept safe while insane (Dan. 4:26, 36), after which he *resumed* his rule until his death. Following this, several other kings reigned and died (Jer. 27:6-7).

The time finally came for the first phase [Chaldean] of world government to end, and for the kingdom to be transferred to the Medes and Persians (Dan. 5:30 31).

That night, the unsuspecting king Belshazzar made a great feast for his lords and ladies (Dan. 5:1-4). Then the king "saw" some strange writing on the wall, notice:

THE RESTORATION OF ISRAEL

> **In the same hour came forth fingers of a man's hand, and wrote over against the candlestick upon the plaster of the wall of the kings' palace: and the king saw the part of the hand that wrote. Then the kings' countenance was changed, and his thoughts troubled him, so that the joints of his loins were loosed, and his knees smote one against another (vss. 5 6).**

The king's astrologers and wise men could not explain the strange writing (vs. 7), but Daniel could (vs. 17). God inspired Daniel to reveal that the strange writing, "mene, mene, tekel, upharsin" was a *sentence* that would add up to God's *judgment!*

But why was this so startling, that it made the king loose his bowels (the King James English is so colorful in describing what one goes through in fear)! But I think you get the picture!

While many are familiar with the feast he held in Babylon when the mysterious handwriting of doom appeared on the wall—they have failed to recognize, that this gathering was a *religious* gathering! The filthy and abominable practices on this occasion were part of the religious ceremonies of the Babylonian Mysteries!

Nimrod, the King and founder of Babylon, was its first priest-king, or its religious leader as well. Belshazzar was its priest-king at that time! Says the Bible about this religious festival: **"They drank wine, and praised the gods of wood, gold, silver, brass, iron, and stone" (Dan. 5:4).**

Adding to their blasphemy of the occasion, they drank their wine from the holy vessels of the Lord which had been taken from the House of God, when Judah was taken captive by Babylon, and the Temple ransacked! Such an attempt to combine that which was holy with that which was heathenism, brought about God's swift judgment!

"NUMBERED", "WEIGHED", AND "DIVIDED"

According to *Strong's Concordance* #4484, "mene" is a number, and it means "numbered" (5: 26). "Tekel" #8625 means "to balance or weigh" (5: 27). "Upharsin" or "parsin" means "divided" as does its root word *peres* (5: 28). So, Daniel interpreted these words to mean that Belshazzar's Chaldean Empire had received a divine sentence. God had *numbered* the days of the

GOD'S SEVEN TIMES PUNISHMENT

king's reign, as it had been *weighed* in God's balances, and it would soon be *divided* up among the Medes and Persians (Dan. 5:22-28).

What most Bible scholars have failed to realize about this intriguing prophecy is that it is *dual*, and not only refers to Belshazzar's kingdom and its impending doom, but it also refers to the entire Babylonish system and its final destruction upon Christ's return (Dan. 2:34,44). This fact is also concurred by the repetition of the words "mene, mene."

Now for the interpretation of these words "mene, mene, tekel upharsin" that can only be understood by unlocking its key. And its *key* is in the common denominator of Hebrew weights designating monetary values!

Mene is the Hebrew equivalent for the *minah* weight. *Tekel* is the Babylonian spelling for the Hebrew weight *shekel*, and *parsin* is equivalent to the *peres* weight. We are told to "halve" or "divide" these weights into their lowest common denominator (like dividing dollars into pennies).

The *minah* consists of 50 shekels according to *The Interpreter's Dictionary of the Bible* ("Weights"). The *shekel* can be subdivided into *geraphs*, 20 gerahs equaling one *shekel*. Strong's Concordance says that *peres* #6537 is a unit of weight. Hence, we have converted a number "mene", a verb "parsin" and a weight "tekel" to a common number.

Therefore, let's do as Daniel said, and divide everything into the smallest number—into gerahs:

one mene (minah)	= 50 shekels	= 1,000 gerahs
another mene (minah)	= 50 shekels	= 1,000 gerahs
a tekel (shekel)	= 1 shekel	= 20 gerahs
half a mene (peres)	= 25 shekels	= 500 gerahs
		Total 2,520

Adding up all the number of *gerahs* is 2520—the number of years of God's sentence on this Babylonian system! Ironically, this is the same number for Nebuchadnezzar's punishment of 7 x 360 days, or 2,520 days or seven years! This is also the same "seven times" punishment upon the nation of Israel!

Our Lord and Savior Jesus Christ said of the "times of the Gentiles", **"..Jerusalem shall be trodden down of the Gentiles, until the times of the Gentiles be fulfilled" (Lk. 21:24).** The

THE RESTORATION OF ISRAEL

"times of the Gentiles" began with the invasion and captivity of Jerusalem in 606 B.C. by king Nebuchadnezzar's Babylonian army, and Jesus plainly states they would end only upon His return!

The succession of the four world ruling Gentile governments from Nebuchadnezzar to Christ's second Advent are outlined in the prophecies of (Daniel 2 and 7). The final Gentile power will be cut down by Jesus Christ, the supernatural "stone made without hands" that will end the "times of the Gentile powers" (Dan. 2:34, 35, 44).

A RESTORATION TO SANITY

Nebuchadnezzar's insanity *symbolized* the beast-like nature of the Gentile kingdoms of the earth. He was punished for "seven Times" or (2520 days) after which his sanity was restored, as well as his rule! If Nebuchadnezzar is a *type* of what is to happen to the last Gentile kingdom upon this earth prior to Christ's return—then we can expect a *short lived* resurrection of sanity of these end-time nations after 2520 years!

It is as though Nebuchadnezzar and the Babylonian system [the tree] would fall for a period of "seven times", then the band would be removed from the stump and the Roman Empire would be restored as a great power! The implication is that 2520 years would elapse before the power would be restored, not end! Then a political power would emerge in Europe!

2520 YEARS TO WORLD PEACE

The number 2520 is highly significant prophetically, and has been mentioned several times already. It is used in describing the temporary worldwide insanity of Gentile governments—*symbolic* of king Nebuchadnezzar—and also the time that this Gentile insanity would end, by ushering in God's government as it is weighed in the balance!

But there is one more important prophecy regarding 2520 years—it has to do with the return of the nation of Israel, and their establishment to world PROMINENCE as a whole nation!

Ironically [by grand design] these dates coincide! At the very same time the powers of the Gentile kingdoms of this world end—the nation of Israel's power is to be RESTORED! At Mt. Sinai,

GOD'S SEVEN TIMES PUNISHMENT

God formed the nation of Israel into a theocratical model government. It was a combination of Church and State, regulated by God's 10 Commandments, statutes and judgments. This was the start of God's Church known as "The Church in the Wilderness" (Acts 7:38).

As we have read in chapter Two, the making of the Old Covenant, as recorded in the 24th chapter of Exodus was also a MARRIAGE COMPACT! It was this marriage ceremony that established the nation of Israel as God's chosen people over all other nations of the earth! As long as Israel was faithful to her husband [Christ] in keeping God's laws—He promised to provide and protect her.

At Mt. Sinai, the people of Israel accepted the terms of this agreement and promised never to commit adulterous relations with other nations [by worshiping their false gods] (Ex. 34:12-17). If Israel remained faithful to her husband—God promised to make them "a kingdom of *priests*, and an holy nation" (Ex. 19:5-6).

However, if they became disobedient and rebellious—God also stipulated a *seven* Times punishment: ."..**they that hate you shall REIGN OVER YOU...SEVEN TIMES" (Lev. 26:14-28; see also Lev. 23:24; 27:28).** A "Time" is God's "day for a year" principle (Ezek..4:4-6; Num. 14:34). In other words "one Time" would mean 360 years, each day representing a year—7 Times would be 7 x 360 or 2520 prophetic years!

Thus, God threatened to remove His government from Israel, and to allow the Gentile world to rule over them for a period of 2520 years—if Israel proved disobedient!

ISRAEL'S SEVEN TIMES PUNISHMENT.

Within a year after God made these explicit terms of the Old Covenant known to Israel, they began grossly violating the conditions of their marriage contract. At this point, the Eternal found it absolutely imperative to DIVORCE His wife and remove His government from them for 2520 long years (see Ezek. 20:13; Isa. 50:1; 59:1 2; Jer. 3:6,8).

Israel was now divorced and was taken captive by the Assyrians in 721 B.C. Soon afterward, the nation of Judah was also taken captive by the invading Gentile armies of king Nebuchadnezzar of Babylon in 606 B.C.

Both houses [Israel and Judah] were prophesied to be under

Gentile domination by Daniel and Ezekiel for a duration of 2520 years.

This Gentile rule over Israel is *pictured* very graphically by the great Gentile image Nebuchadnezzar saw in his dream, which we have already elaborated upon. The authority to rule was thus handed over to Nebuchadnezzar [the head of gold] and his successors [the Persian, Greecian and Roman empires] for 2520 years!

Finally, the government of God, *pictured* by a supernatural Stone [Jesus Christ] is to SMASH the feet of this last Gentile power [Roman] upon His second advent—and RESTORE *the government of God back to Israel* (Acts 3:21).

J. Dwight Pentecost explains the primary purpose for the Tribulation as it relates to restoring the nation of Israel:

> **God's purpose for Israel in the Tribulation is to bring about the conversion of a multitude of Jews, who will enter into the blessings of the kingdom and experience the fulfillment of all Israel's covenants. The good news that the King is about to return will be preached (Matt. 24:14) so that Israel may be turned to their deliverer. As John the Baptist preached such a message to prepare Israel for the first coming, [spiritual—emphasis mine] Elijah will preach to prepare Israel for the second advent...** (*Things to Come*, pp. 237).

Lewis Sperry Chafer adds these comments concerning the end-time prophecies relating to the nation that killed the prophets:

> **The address is to Jerusalem's children, which, in this instance is a representation of the nation of Israel...the entire discourse from Matthew 24:4 on,...immediately spoken to His disciples who are still classed as Jews and represented a people who will pass through the experiences described in this address, is directed toward the entire nation and especially to those who will endure the trials depicted therein. The phrase, 'I would have gathered thy children together,'**

> not only discloses that He speaks to Israel, but refers to the fulfillment of much prophecy respecting the final regathering of Israel into their own land (*Systematic Theology*, V, 116-117).

In his book, entitled, *The End*, pp. 231-33, Norman B. Harrison, makes these glaring comments regarding the parallel between the first century Church age and the last Church age:

> Speaking of the two ages, Church and Jewish: at its inception, 30 A.D., the Church paralled for 40 years the Jewish age, till the latter closed with the destruction of Jerusalem in 70 A.D. This argues for a similar overlapping at the close of the Church Age. If, for the moment, we think of the Church continuing up to the Tribulation, the time from which our Lord has promised to keep her, realizing that Israel will have been restored as a nation for three and one-half years prior to the Tribulation's setting in...we again have the same overlapping.

EZEKIEL'S LIVING LEGEND

The entire scenario of Israel's and Judah's iniquity and eventual *restoration* as a national power is graphically dramatized by an event God caused in Ezekiel's life. This event is a *type* of Israel's impending captivity. This prophecy is recorded in (Ezekiel 3:24; 4:1-8).

Essentially here's what happened. God told Ezekiel to lie on his left side for 390 days (*symbolic* of Israel's duration of iniquity) and to lie on his right side for 40 days (*symbolic* of Judah's duration of iniquity).

God spelled out His intent for Israel through this graphic illustration: **"I have laid upon thee *the years of their iniquity*, according to the number of days you laid on your side (vs. 5). "I have appointed each day for a year" (vs. 6).**

This entire *dramatization* had only one purpose—to show the length of time Israel (390 years) and Judah (40 years) were to be under Gentile domination till their *sins* would be *forgiven*! Here

THE RESTORATION OF ISRAEL

then is a total of 430 years of punishment that the entire house of Israel would endure until God granted them GRACE!

However, the iniquity and punishment of Israel and Judah did not end after 390 years, nor in 40 additional years! God had spoken to them previously of an additional SEVEN TIMES PUNISHMENT in Leviticus 26:18: **"If ye will not yet for all this hearken unto me, then I will punish you *seven times more* for your sins."**

It is a well established fact as recorded in (Jeremiah 29:10 and Daniel 9:2), that the duration of Judah's captivity in Babylon [representing the entire nation of Israel] would be for "seventy years." This is the captivity and partial return to their homeland in 536 B.C. recorded by Ezra and Nehemiah.

Because this was only a partial return of the Jews [described by Daniel's 70 weeks]—the remainder of the years of iniquity Ezekiel foretold still remain! This prophecy still remains for those in Israel who are still dispersed!

Realize also, that while Judah, the last remaining tribe of Israel was in captivity—the entire land of Canaan was resting, fulfilling the Jubilee rest and part of the "desolations" of Jerusalem.

By subtracting these 70 years of fulfilled captivity from the 430 years of prophesied iniquity we have a balance of sentence of 360 years. Multiplying these 360 years by 7 Times—we have 2520 years until Israel's land would be RESTORED in fulfillment of God's promise to Abraham.

But now we come to the crucial question. When do we start counting the 2520 years when Israel's punishment will end? This is a difficult question, since most historical dates are controversial. According to most Biblical and historical scholars, Israel's captivity began in 721 B.C. and Judah's in 606 B.C. Judah's captivity began in three stages and ended in 536 B.C. The first return of the Jews began seventy years later in 516 B.C.

As prophesied, at the end of the seventy years of captivity in Babylon, in the spring of 536 B.C.; in the month Nisan, under the decree of the Persian king Cyrus, a small remnant of the house of Judah returned to Jerusalem. This is the recorded historical date given by Flavius Josephus.

If we count 2520 prophetic biblical years of 360 days we get (2,520 X 360 = 907,200 days). Now we must convert these days into calendar years of 365.25 days by dividing 907,200 by 365.25 = (2,483.8). Therefore, counting from 536 B.C. we arrive at the

GOD'S SEVEN TIMES PUNISHMENT

very significant date of 1948, the rebirth of the nation of Israel!

70 SABBATICALS IN 430 YEARS

Now here is another amazing fact that few indeed realize—but once again demonstrates the *consistency* of God's master plan.

These 430 years of Israel's punishment were based upon the Jubilee cycle. During the course of 430 years, there are exactly 70 Sabbaticals or land rests. This is calculated by counting years 7,14,21,28,35,42,49,50 in one Jubilee cycle. In other words, there are 8 land rests in a 50 year period time.

I think you will agree that this is an astounding statistic and not merely coincidental that there are exactly 70 land rests during the course of 430 years!

The nation of Israel consistently profaned God's land Sabbaths. During the course of violating 70 Sabbaticals or land rests in 430 years—the Eternal punished the nation of Israel by removing them from their land and sending them into captivity. The nation of Israel had defiled the land Sabbath for 390 years, while Judah 40 years (Ezek. 4:1-6). Adding these totals together we obtain the sum of 430 years—the sum total of both houses' captivity. More importantly, is that Israel's punishment was for breaking God's Jubilee cycle!

The Day of Atonement *picturing* God's ultimate day of judgment was the most sacred day in Israel's history. This was the only day that the high priest of Israel was allowed to go behind the veil in the Tabernacle or Temple and into the Most Holy Place. This event has tremendous spiritual importance in regards to Israel's final cleansing and occurred on the TENTH day of the SEVENTH month.

Here again we see the consistency of God's marvelous plan of salvation in the month and day as $7 \times 10 = 70$. Seven, the number of *spiritual perfection* and Ten, the number of *ordinal perfection* equaling Seventy—the number of God's Judgment!

God's entire plan is a Sabbatical plan lasting approximately 7,000 years! In fact, man's allotted life span is 70 years, after which he will be judged!

THE RESTORATION OF ISRAEL

2520 PROPHETIC YEARS

Sabbatical	No. Years	Land Rests
1	49	8
2	49	8
3	49	8
4	49	8
5	49	8
6	49	8
7	49	8
8	49	8
9	38	6
Totals	430	70

3 is the number of *divine perfection.*
7 is the number of *spiritual perfection.*
10 is the number of *ordinal perfection.*
12 is the number of *governmental perfection.*

The summation of $3 \times 7 \times 10 \times 12 = 2520$. Is it merely coincidence or *design* that the product of these four *perfect* numbers, results in the prophetic time period of Israel's punishment and the times the Gentiles are given to rule? I think not! And I think you will agree that it is not merely coincidental that there are exactly 2520 biblical years from the ending of the Babylonian captivity in 536 B.C. to the rebirth of the nation of Israel in 1948!

Chapter Eleven

*And thou shalt observe **the feast of weeks, of the firstfruits** of wheat harvest, and the feast of ingathering at the years end.*
—Exodus 34:22.

PENTECOST AND "FIRSTFRUITS"

Pentecost is a *memorial* of an historical event, just as Passover and the Feast of Unleavened Bread. Most Christians know that Jesus Christ poured out the Holy Spirit on His Church on this day as recorded in (Acts 2:1). However, this was in fulfillment of an ancient occurrence of which very few people are aware. To understand exactly what Pentecost memorializes, one must carefully review the events that occurred at Mount Sinai after the exodus of the Israelites from Egypt.

God has arranged Pentecost so that it must be counted each year. Pentecost is the *memorial* of Israel entering into the covenant relationship with God as outlined in Exodus, chapters (21 through 23). Today, it is a memorial of Christians entering into the New Covenant relationship with God through Jesus Christ.

God is consistent in using His feast days for the same purpose. When the original work of that day was to be repeated, Jesus Christ, the Lamb of God for all men, was sacrificed during Passover. The meaning of His sacrifice can only be understood by knowing the original work God did on that day in Egypt.

The same is true of Pentecost. The meaning of the New Testament Pentecost, when Jesus poured out the Holy Spirit, can only be understood by knowing the meaning of the original Pentecost that God established when bringing Israel out of Egypt.

THE RESTORATION OF ISRAEL

Jesus Christ was the *Spokesman* who made the first covenant with Israel for God. It was He who received the long promised New Covenant from God the Father, and poured it out on His Church on the same day which memorialized the first covenant.

These Sabbaths are memorials of God's work in the *past*, and Passover and Pentecost would be repeated. **They will be repeated again in the future!**

Pentecost always falls on the same day of the week that Israel entered into the first covenant. Thus, God notes in scripture the day of the week Israel arrived at Mt Sinai, and the sequence of events leading to the entering of the agreement between Him and Israel.

In the latter days, God will bring Israel back out of captivity, and circumcise their heart so that they will truly love God and enter into His New Covenant. Then they will receive the blessings that God had promised to them under the first covenant, when He brought them out of Egypt.

The principal task God has given to the Messiah is to bring the descendants of Jacob back to the land and give them the New Covenant as He promised their forefathers. This task is yet for the future and will be done in the time described as the time of Jacob's trouble. Then God will pour out His spirit upon all of Israel (Jer. 31:31-34; Heb. 10:16; Joel 2:28; Acts 2:17).

GOD MAKES A COVENANT WITH ISRAEL

> **And Moses went up to God, and the LORD called to him from the mountain, saying, 'Thus you shall say to the house of Jacob, and tell the children of Israel: You have seen what I did to the Egyptians, and how** *I bore you on eagles' wings* **and brought you to Myself. Now therefore, if you will indeed obey my voice and keep My covenant, then you shall be a special treasure to Me above all people; for all the earth is Mine. And** *You shall be to Me a kingdom of priests and a holy nation...'* **(Ex. 19:3..6).**

Israel had come into the wilderness of Sin on the fifteenth day of the second month after leaving the land of Egypt (Ex. 16:1). It was at this time that God revealed the true Sabbath day

PENTECOST AND FIRSTFRUITS

to them—as it had been lost while in Egyptian bondage!

That evening, God gave them quails to eat, and rained manna from heaven upon them in the morning. This miracle continued for six days, and on the sixth day twice as much was given. Then on the seventh day, nothing was given as God would *test* Israel to see if they would be obedient to His Laws or not (vs. 6).

During the third month, after the children of Israel were gone out of Egypt, God proposed a covenant with them (Ex. 19:1-6). He called Moses up to the top of Mount Sinai and revealed the conditions of the covenant to him.

Upon his return from the mountain, God's servant Moses gave the terms of the contract to the nation of Israel. In essence, the agreement called for the obedience of God's laws, and in return, He would make them a chosen people above all the earth. Israel would become a *kingdom of priests* and a holy nation! Actually, the personage of Jesus Christ was the one who spoke these words to Moses. Under the New Covenant, Jesus makes these same promises to Christians today! (1 Pet. 2:9; Rev. 5:10). That's why Moses was a *type* of Christ!

THE RATIFICATION OF THE COVENANT

And the LORD said to Moses, 'Behold, I come to you in the thick cloud, that the people may hear when I speak with you, and believe you forever.' So Moses told the words of the people to the LORD. Then the LORD said to Moses, 'Go to the people and *sanctify* them today and tomorrow, and let them wash their clothes. And let them be ready for the third day. For on the third day the LORD will come down upon Mount Sinai in the sight of all the people' (Ex. 19:9-11).

The Israelite people eagerly accepted the terms of the covenant proposal, and Moses returned to the mountain top to give the Eternal their answer (Ex. 19:7-8). Then the Eternal told them to "sanctify" themselves by *washing* their clothes in anticipation of His glorious presence.

The Israelites were to abstain from *anything* that would

THE RESTORATION OF ISRAEL

make them "unclean" in God's eyes! Bounds were set around the mountain, so that no one could come near where God was to speak. On the third day, the people gathered at the foot of the mountain as God's *Spokesman* thundered the Ten Commandments! (Ex. 19:21-25; 20).

Like the sound of a mighty trumpet, the tremendous power of God's voice caused an unbelievable spectacle of thunder and lightnings that started the mountain smoking. When the people saw this, they were terrified, and asked Moses to intercede for them instead (Ex. 20:18-22).

Moses informed the startled Israelites that God performed this mighty feat so they would learn to FEAR Him, and not to transgress His Commandments!

THE CONDITIONS OF THE COVENANT

The terms and conditions of the covenant God made with Israel were written down by Moses in a book, and are recorded in chapters (21 through 23) of the book of Exodus.

Strict rules governing the Sabbath and Feast day observance, offerings, fornication, adultery, incest; etc., were mandatory upon Israel. In return for their faithfulness to the Eternal—God promised to fight their battles for them, heal them during sickness, bless their children with healthy bodies and minds, bless their animals and their land; etc.

However, this first covenant did not contain any provision for punishment if the entire nation became stiff-necked and disobedient. Later, judgments were made, known as "The Law Of Moses" for individual and national sins.

After hearing the conditions of this covenant, the people readily accepted it and Moses, along with seventy elders of Israel, made another journey to the mountain top to inform God of the people's decision (Ex. 24:1-3).

Moses wrote all the words of the Lord in the book of the Covenant, and ratified it by the sprinkling of blood (Ex. 24:4-8). Then the prophet Moses, the priests and seventy elders of Israel, representing the nation, appeared before God upon the mountain.

The Covenant between God and Israel was officially ratified!

PENTECOST AND FIRSTFRUITS

GOD GIVES THE TABLES OF STONE

Then the LORD said to Moses, 'Come up to Me on the mountain and be there; and I will give you tablets of stone, and the law and commandments which I have written, that you may teach them.' So Moses arose with his assistant Joshua, and Moses went up to the mountain of God. And he said to the elders, 'Wait here for us until we come back to you. Indeed Aaron and Hur are with you. If any man has a difficulty, let them go to them' (Ex. 24:12-14).

God requested Moses go up to the top of the mountain again to receive the Ten Commandments written upon two tables of stone. Moses remained upon the mountain top for a duration of forty days and forty nights, while he spoke with the Creator of the human race.

Meanwhile, Moses had made provision that his brother Aaron and Hur take charge of the camp in his absence. After God's *Spokesman* had finished His discourse with Moses, He gave him the two tables of stone which God Himself had penned with His finger! (Ex. 31:18).

Later, while coming down the mountain, and seeing the nation of Israel committing idolatry—in a fit of rage, Moses broke these two tables of stone, and had to fashion two additional ones, which God again wrote the Commandments upon.

ISRAEL COMMITS IDOLATRY

So all the people broke off the golden earrings which were in their ears, and brought them to Aaron. And he received the gold from their hand, and he fashioned it with an engraving tool, and made a molded calf. Then they said, 'This is you god, O Israel, that brought you out of the land of Egypt!.'..Then they rose on the next day, offered burnt offerings, and brought peace offerings; and the people sat down to eat and drink, and rose up to play (Ex. 32:3-6).

THE RESTORATION OF ISRAEL

Israel was a physical nation that looked to a man [Moses] as their *deliverer* instead of the invisible powerful God! It was the visible Moses that performed mighty miracles in Egypt before the Pharaoh, and who was in the vanguard leading them through the Red Sea! But now their hero had been out of touch for over a month. They perceived he had been killed by an enemy or wild animal.

These ungrateful knuckleheads wanted a visible image representing God before them—so Aaron told the people to break off their gold jewelry and they fashioned a golden calf out of them!

What an abomination!

Notice what these perverted minds said of this golden image: **"These are thy gods, O Israel, which brought thee up out of the land of Egypt."**

Can you believe that?

When Aaron saw that the people accepted the idol as their god, he proclaimed the following day to be a feast day in honor to the Lord—after he saw what the people desired!

Here is another interesting parallel to the time of the first Exodus. Following the feasting, the Israelites rose up to *play*! The original Hebrew word here indicates this playing was an *orgy!* This same Greek epicurean philosophy of "live for today" is prevalent in our world today!

GOD'S PROMISE OF FUTURE RETRIBUTION

Then Moses returned to the LORD and said, 'Oh, these people have sinned a great sin, and have made for themselves a god of gold! Yet now, if You will forgive their sin—but if not, I pray, blot me out of Your book which You have written.' And the LORD said to Moses, 'Whoever has sinned against Me, I will blot him out of My book. Now therefore, go, lead the people to the place of which I have spoken to you. *Nevertheless, in the day when I visit for punishment, I will visit punishment upon them for their sin.'* So the LORD plagued the people because of what they did with the calf which Aaron made (Ex. 32:31-

PENTECOST AND FIRSTFRUITS

35).

God's wrath was kindled when He saw the idolatrous and orgiastic feast the Israelites were engaged in at the very same time He was speaking to Moses! God was appalled, and His wrath waxed so hot, He threatened to kill every idol worshiping Israelite and start a new nation out of Moses (Ex. 32:7-10).

But Moses pleaded for God not to destroy His people, and to remember the promise He made to Abraham, Isaac and Jacob (Ex. 32:11-14). Moses acknowledged Israel's sins, and asked God to forgive them and have mercy!

The all-loving and forgiving God heard the plea of Moses and repented of destroying the entire nation of Israel. Instead, He told Moses He would only punish those who actually sinned against Him—but in the *latter days He would visit them!* Remember these words, and *why* God said them, for they are vital in understanding the fall feast days!

As a result of being obedient to His Covenant—God had promised Israel to be a *kingdom of priests and a holy nation.* These plans were now changed and the prophecies henceforth are concerned with how God was going to bring these people into a new covenant relationship with Him.

God refused to go in the midst of the nation of Israel lest He should consume them for their evil (Ex. 33:1-6). At this time, God revised His plans and sent an angel to guide them.

Before God makes the New Covenant with Israel, He will do *a terrible thing* to them in the sight of all the other nations. Israel will be a CAPTIVE people at this time, and God will make the other nations stand in amazement (Ex. 34:9-10). Eventually, every one of the descendants of Jacob will become a part of this New Covenant relationship (Deut. 29:14-18).

JESUS TO LEAD ISRAEL OUT OF CAPTIVITY

And the LORD *will scatter you among the peoples,* and you will be left few in number among the nations where the LORD will drive you. And there you will serve gods, the work of men's hands, wood and stone, which neither see nor hear nor eat nor smell. But from there you will seek the LORD your God, and you will find

THE RESTORATION OF ISRAEL

> **Him if you seek Him with all your heart and with all your soul. When you are in distress, and all these things come upon you *in the latter days,* when you turn to the LORD your God and obey His voice (for the LORD your God is a merciful God), He will not forsake you nor destroy you, nor forget the covenant of your fathers which He swore to them (Deut. 23:27-31). See also (Lk. 21:36).**

God made this covenant with the ancient Israelites, but He will hold their modern-day descendants accountable in the *last days!* Like the nation of Israel, they have been WARNED not to turn to the worship of the heathen nations around them! (Deut. 4:23-26).

Todays golden calves take on many forms that masquerade as the true teachings of Christianity! However, God hates this as much as molten golden calves and promises *grave consequences* for those who practice such abominations! This national disobedience will result in destruction and captivity!

Strong curses and plagues are to come upon the disobedient, including famine, pestilence and captivity! But once modern-day Israel starts to repent, and truly seeks to return to the Eternal—with great compassion on them, Jesus will gather them, and bring them back to the land their ancient ancestors possessed. This sequence of Israel's forthcoming retribution and re-gathering is described very vividly by Moses in Deuteronomy 30:1-5:

> **Now it shall come to pass, when all these things come upon you, the blessing and the curse which I have set before you, and you call them to mind among all the nations where the LORD your God drives you...and you return to the LORD your God and obey His voice, according to all that I command you today, you and your children, with all your heart and with all your soul...that the LORD** *Your God will bring you back from captivity, and have compassion on you, and gather you again from all the nations where the LORD your God has scattered you.*

GOD TO CIRCUMCISE ISRAEL'S HEART

Then the LORD your God will bring you to the land which your fathers possessed, and you shall possess it. He will prosper you and multiply you more than your fathers. *And the LORD Your God will circumcise your heart* **and the heart of your descendants, to love the LORD your God with all your heart and with all your soul, that you may live (Deut. 30:5-6).**

The Eternal promised to *circumcise* the hearts of Israel at Mount Horeb, after He brings them back to their land out of captivity *in the last days!*

This will be done so that Israel will be able to worship their Creator with all their heart and soul! The fault of the first covenant was with the hardened hearts of the people—not the covenant itself! These people had carnal minds that only were satisfied by worshiping the idols of Egypt! They were without God's Holy Spirit! The Holy Spirit was not promised under the Old Covenant, and only a few of God's prophets received it (Jn. 7:38-39).

Israel's modern-day descendants are no different! Today, they are blinded to true religious worship and have forsaken God! These people do not understand *who* God is, and *what* His plan is for them on planet earth!

The false gods of religion today are prodigious homes with inground swimming pools, fancy cars, designer clothes, luxurious vacations, famous sports celebrities, movie stars and rock stars, occultism, money; etc. etc.

But the day is fast approaching when God will again allow Israel to be taken captive by a foreign power! Then He will bring Israel back to the land He promised them—just as He brought them out of Egyptian slavery centuries ago! Only then will God circumcise their heart!

This is the very same circumcision of the heart that was made available to the New Testament Church [beginning God's holy nation] on the Day of Pentecost in A.D. 31. Paul wrote of this fantastic miracle: ."..**for in him ye are made full, who is the head of all principality and power:** *in whom ye were also circumcised with a circumcision not made with hands, in*

THE RESTORATION OF ISRAEL

*putting off of the body of the flesh in circumcision of Christ..."*4 (Col. 2:9-11).

Continuing this dissertation on circumcision of the mind, Paul said in Philippians 3:3: **"..for *we are the circumcision,* who worship by the Spirit of God, and glory in Christ Jesus, and have no confidence in the flesh..."**

This circumcision of the heart was offered to the Jews by Jesus Christ, before their national rejection and dispersion in A.D. 70. Previously, the nation of Israel was sent into captivity in 721 B.C. and the nation of Judah in 606 B.C. Judah was later regathered out of Babylonian captivity and allowed to return to Palestine under Ezra and Nehemiah.

Jesus Christ, God's *Spokesman* at Mount Sinai brought the promised New Covenant for Israel [and all nations] to have opportunity to enter into—*if they would worship Him and glorify Him by the way of life Jesus set as an example!*

Jesus Christ, God's *Messenger,* brought the Covenant that was promised to the descendants of the nation of Israel—but they rejected Him! God then allowed Gentiles and all nations the opportunity to enter the New Covenant through *faith* in Jesus Christ today!

Circumcision of the heart is the gift of God's Holy Spirit that cuts away our old carnal fleshly nature! Now our minds can be renewed to conquer our fleshly lusts and desires by receiving the spirit and mind of Christ!

In the *latter days,* God [Jesus Christ] will bring Israel out of TRUBULATION, and circumcise their heart so they will truly love God with all their heart and soul! At this time, they will enter into the New Covenant and be a blessed and leading nation of the earth! Then Israel will receive the blessings God promised them upon their land, cattle, and children—along with God's protection from their enemies!

PENTECOST AND THE START OF THE NEW TESTAMENT CHURCH

Now when the Day of Pentecost had fully come, they were all with one accord in one place. And suddenly there came a sound from heaven, as of a rushing mighty wind, and it filled the whole house where they were sitting. Then there

PENTECOST AND FIRSTFRUITS

> **appeared to them divided tongues, as of fire, and one sat upon each of them. And they were all filled with the Holy Spirit and began to speak with other tongues, as the Spirit gave them utterance (Acts 2:1-4).**

On the Day of Pentecost A.D. 31, God poured out His Holy Spirit starting the New Testament Church. It was appropriately given on the same day Israel had entered into the Old Covenant approximately 1500 years previously—and was the *partial fulfillment* of the promise of the New Testament!

At Mount Sinai when God first entered into a covenant [a marriage] relationship with the nation of Israel, it seems possible, and Jewish tradition affirms, that Israel was gathered around Mount Sinai to receive the Ten Commandments and other laws *on the Day of Pentecost*—the Day of Firstfruits [Beginnings] (Edersheim, *The Temple,* p. 227). This is the time when the Old Testament church came into existence (Acts 7:38). Remarkably, the church which Christ raised up right after His resurrection was also born *on the very same day!* (Acts 2:1). These were not mere accidental occurrences!

The purpose of the New Covenant was for correcting the *weakness* of the peoples heart—now God was going to CIRCUMCISE their heart with His Holy Spirit! God's Holy Spirit would enable them to OBEY Him as their minds would be cleansed spiritually!

This momentous event, like the entering of the first covenant, was filled with a startling array of miraculous signs. There occurred the sound of a rushing mighty wind, followed by the appearance of cloven tongues like fire, that sat upon each of them. As the Holy Spirit filled the apostles, they began to speak in foreign languages so the Jews from other countries could understand (Acts 2:5-13).

This was not speaking in an emotional gibberish as many in the "tongues movement" claim. True, the speaking in tongues was a gift of God's Holy Spirit (Acts 19:6). However, Paul makes it crystal clear that speaking in a language that nobody understands is not profitable (1 Cor. 14).

Then the apostle Peter gave an inspired speech explaining the strange phenomena they had just witnessed. He quoted the prophecy from the prophet Joel—that God would pour out His

THE RESTORATION OF ISRAEL

Spirit upon Israel in the latter days (Acts 2:14-21). However, Peter perceived that this was only *a partial fulfillment* of the promise that God would make in the last days—when He would pour out His Holy Spirit upon the entire nation of Israel just prior to His Son's return!

Peter further explained that the Holy Spirit was only made available to start the New Covenant because Jesus had given His very life, and was resurrected to fulfill the prophecies. Only after Jesus ascended into Heaven to be *accepted* by His Father as a *perfect* sacrifice for mankind—could the gift of the Holy Spirit be given (Acts 2:32-36). That very day 3,000 repentant Jewish souls were baptized into the faith (Acts 2:41).

Today, God's Holy Spirit is made available to all [including Israel] who will turn from their evil ways (Acts 2:38). However, God's prophets made it very clear that the majority of Israel would remain scattered and be taken out of captivity in the *last days* before their hearts are circumcised!

The principal task of the Messiah will be to bring the descendants of ancient Israel back to the Promised Land, and give them the New Covenant He promised their forefathers Abraham, Isaac and Jacob. This prophecy is yet to be fulfilled in the *latter days*. But in the meantime, God has allowed salvation to come to the Gentiles as well as all those in Israel—who will readily accept the conditions of the New Covenant.

THE NEW COVENANT WITH ISRAEL

> **Behold, the days are coming, says the LORD, when I will make a new covenant with the house of Israel and with the house of Judah...not according to the covenant that I made with their fathers in the day that I took them by the hand to bring them out of the land of Egypt, My covenant which they broke, though I was a husband to them," says the LORD. But this is the covenant that I will make with the house of Israel: After those days, says the LORD, *I will put My law in their minds, and write it on their hearts;* and I will be their God, and they shall be My people (Jer. 31:31-33).**

Again we read in Ezekiel 11:19:

And I will give them one heart, and I will put a new spirit within you; and I will take the stony heart out of their flesh, and will give them an heart of flesh.

This same promise is repeated in (Hebrews 10:16) as applying to New Testament Christians. After Israel rejected God's first covenant—He sent them into national captivity, only to restore them to their land in the *latter days!*

When God brings them out of bondage from their new Egyptian taskmasters—modern-day Israel will gladly accept the conditions of the New Covenant. It will be at this time God will put His laws into their *inward parts!* God will write them upon their heart or mind, so they will be able to keep His divine laws!

The Eternal has not cast off His people—and He will yet choose Israel as His model nation to start His Kingdom upon His regturn! At this time, the Great God of Heaven will make them prosperous in their land and they will once again be reconciled to Him! During the 1,000 year reign of Jesus Christ, Israel will once again possess the **"city of peace set on a hill"** [Jerusalem] to be a shining light to the Gentile world (Matt. 5:14).

Here is what Isaiah prophesied of the Messiah's chief commission:

And now the LORD says, who formed me from the womb to be His servant *to bring Jacob back to Him,* So that Israel is gathered to Him...to raise up the tribes of Jacob, and to restore the preserved ones of Israel: I will also give you as a *light to the Gentiles,* that you should be My salvation to the ends of the earth (Isa. 49:5-6). See also (Zech. 8:20; Isa. 60).

Remember, it was God's Spokesman [Jesus Christ] who spoke at Mount Sinai, and gave the Old Covenant to Israel. It will be this same personage who will make the New Covenant with modern-day Israel, and who is now writing God's laws into the hearts and minds of Christians.

The Israelites were told by God to circumcise their children

THE RESTORATION OF ISRAEL

upon the eighth day after birth (Gen. 17:12; 21:4; Lk. 2:21). This event is what made them an Israelite and is *symbolic* of the Christians's initiation of *baptism*. Throwing away of the foreskin was *symbolic* of discarding the "old sinful man." This event or initiation started a "new life" for both Israelite and Christian alike.

When Christ brings Israel out of captivity, He will not circumcise their foreskin—but rather their hearts, as He writes His laws upon their hearts!

THE NEW COVENANT FOR GENTILES

Therefore remember that you, once Gentiles in the flesh...who are called Uncircumcision by what is called the Circumcision made in the flesh by hands ...that at that time you were without Christ, being aliens from the commonwealth of Israel and strangers from the covenants of promise, having no hope and without God in the world. But now in Christ Jesus you who once were far off have been made near by the blood of Christ. *For He Himself is our peace, who has made both one, and has broken down the middle wall of division between us...For through Him we both have access by one Spirit to the Father...* **Now therefore, you are no longer strangers and foreigners, but fellow citizens with the saints and members of the household of God (Eph. 2:11-22).**

Because of His resurrection and acceptance upon His ascension, Jesus can now offer the Holy Spirit to His disciples! Once an individual has God's Spirit they will be producing the *fruit* of Jesus as a way of life (Jn. 15:5).

Once a Christian accepts the sacrifice of Jesus Christ, and *repents* of His sins—God stands ready to give him His Holy Spirit as a free gift.

Then a Christian's mind will begin to be renewed, and a spiritual nature will dominate his life! Jesus will literally live His life over in him! The brotherly love of Jesus will shine through in his heart for his fellow man! Compassion, empathy, mercy, kindness, gentleness, faith, joy, peace, meekness and patience—will replace lust, greed, vanity, jealousy, pride, hatred, etc. (Gal.

5:16-23).

Should a Christian break the New Covenant [and he will until changed through the resurrection], the precious blood of Jesus will cover his transgressions as long as his attitude remains repentant!

Paul tells us that Gentiles, who were considered uncircumcised by God, and as a foreigner—can now be accepted as fellow-citizens with the Saints! These Gentiles were considered as *outsiders* in which no part of the covenant or promises given to Israel applied—but through Israel's rejection and Christ's sacrifice—it was now possible for them to enter into Israel's covenant relationship with God!

Israel had rejected the covenant and promises of God Almighty. Christ then became head of a new nation of people which God Himself is selecting. That's why Christians are called an "elect" race, a royal priesthood, a holy nation (1 Pet. 2:1-10).

REPOTING THE NATION OF ISRAEL

The nation of Israel was the first theocratic [Church and State] government upon the earth. They were chosen by God to be an example to the other nations—they were God's kingdom on earth! This was the start of God's Church, known as "The Church in the Wilderness" (Acts 7:38) and was also a marriage compact!

However, when Israel failed to be *faithful* to God, He divorced her according to the marriage law! Later, when Jesus came in the flesh, He came to His disobedient wife to restore again the kingdom of God on earth. The apostles were well aware of this (Acts 1:6) as Jesus came to the Jews first (Jn. 1:11; Matt. 10:5; 15:24). That's why the early Church was composed solely of Jews (Acts 2:5; 3:25,26; 13:36).

Through the parable of the Vineyard in (Matthew 21), our Master Gardener graphically explains the transfer of the Kingdom to another nation (the Church—composed also of kings and priests).

In the eleventh chapter of Romans, Paul through the inspiration of the Master Horticulturist explains that Gentiles could now be adopted into His garden (family) through the analogy of wild olive trees (Gentiles) being grafted into branches that were broken off (Israelites). Paul explains further that these branches that were cut off (Israelites) can also be grafted back into God's Vineyard! Thus, all of Israel shall one day be saved (Rom. 11:26).

There is going to come a time that God will pour out His Holy Spirit upon the nation of Israel through a modern-day Elijah! He will begin turning the hearts of Israel back to their Father in heaven (Mal. 4:6).

This coming conversion of the nation of Israel will be similar to what occurred on the Day of Pentecost nearly 2,000 years ago. Then, Peter, full of God's Holy Spirit, proclaimed God's truth to the devout of Israel, accompanied by spectacular miracles, and 3,000 Jews were baptized into the faith (Acts 2:41).

That event was merely a *type* of what will transpire in these last days, as Peter said himself that God will pour out His Spirit upon the house of Israel prior to the heavenly signs (Acts 2:17-21). This will be the start of a "Jewish Church" in Jerusalem! Truly, ."..the **vineyard of the LORD of hosts is the house of Israel, and the men of Judah his pleasant plant..."** (Isa. 5:7). This grafting back of the nation of Israel, will be undoubtedly just as hard for Christians to accept as it was for the nation of Israel to accept Gentiles into God's Church!

Concerning the fulfillment of Joel's *dual* prophecy, Gerhard F. Hasel writes on page 289 of *70 Weeks, Leviticus, Nature of Prophecy:*

> **Joel 2:28-32 may be cited also as an OT prophecy intended to have two fulfillments. God promised to cause the early and latter rains to fall upon the devestated lands of a penitent Israel (Joel 2:11-12, 23-27). As a spiritual counterpart to the rains, an outpouring of the Holy Spirit also was promised at some point in the future (1:28-32). The apostle Peter recognized the great Pentecostal operation of the Holy Spirit as fulfilling Joel's prediction (Acts 2:16). However, the data in the original prophecy refering to certain celestial wonders that would occur before "the great and terrible day of the Lord" as well as the biblical concept of the *latter rain* and the close of the harvest clearly indicate a future, more complete fulfillment of the original prophecy (Joel 2:30-31; Acts 2:19-20).**

PENTECOST AND FIRSTFRUITS

God, the Master Gardener, is harvesting His Church as **"a kind of firstfruits" (Jas. 1:18),** during this present age as pictured by the Feast of Pentecost. It was on Pentecost that the Old Covenant with Israel was *ratified* and when the Holy Spirit came to start the New Testament Church who are the *firstfruits* of the Holy Spirit (Rom. 8:23).

The "wave sheaf" ritual the high priest of Israel performed on Pentecost envisioned the firstfruits of the Church, and multitudes of first century Jews who were obedient to the faith were converted (Acts 6:7).

The early grain harvest of Pentecost *pictures* the first harvest of people into God's Kingdom—the great fall harvest of Tabernacles *pictures* the saving of the majority of humanity!

What a beautiful plan—cultivated by the Master Gardener!

SPIRITUAL MEANING OF ANNUAL HARVESTS

...when ye become into the land which I give unto you, and shall reap the harvests thereof, then ye shall bring a sheaf of the *firstfruits* of your harvest unto the priest (Lev. 23:10).

In Palestine there are two main annual harvests that God uses to depict His spiritual plan. Pentecost, or "Feast of Weeks" or "Feast of Firstfruits" *pictures* God's Church or the ones He is CALLING during this present age to become His begotten children.

Passover *symbolized* **Christ's sacrifice** for the remission of our sins, and the days of Unleavened Bread the **putting away of sin.** Pentecost *pictures* the first part of the Spiritual harvest—**the calling out of the Church**—the dispensation or period of time for the Church.

THE WAVE SHEAF OFFERING

The Wheat Harvest in (Leviticus 23:11-17, and Numbers 28:16), God told the Israelites to count "50" days from the morrow after the Sabbath that they waved the first wave sheaf (*symbolic* of Jesus Christ), and wave *two loaves* of bread.

They must have been very large loaves, for each contained 1/2 gallon or about 4 pounds of flour raised with leaven (vs. 17).

According to the *Mishna* (the writings of the oral law), the length of a loaf was 7 handbreadths (about 28 inches), the width 4 handbreadths (about 16 inches), and the depth equal to 7 fingers' width (about 6 or 7 inches). These loaves were probably made out of wheat, since this was the next harvest (Ruth 2:23).

They were to count seven Sabbaths [weeks] (Lev. 23:15). So here is a period of 50 days after the *acceptance* of Christ that something representing "two loaves" [in which preparation leaven had a part] became eligible to also be lifted up and waved toward the heavens to be accepted.

God Himself interprets the meaning of the wave-loaves in Leviticus 23:17: **"they are the *firstfruits* unto the Lord."** Here we find that the two leavened loaves offered on Pentecost correspond to the two covenant *firstfruits*, or the two major groups of people God is working with—Old Testament Israel and the New Testament Church.

There is a prophecy in (Luke 4:16) that was fulfilled when Jesus went into the Temple on the Sabbath day (the Greek says "day of weeks"). Jesus read the prophecy in (Isaiah 61:1-2), about the Messiah coming with the Spirit of God upon him to preach the gospel. Christ fulfilled this prophecy by sending the Holy Spirit on the Day of Pentecost (Acts 2:1-17). Jewish religious history show this portion of scripture was to be always read on the Feast of Weeks.

It is no mere accident that multitudes of first century Jews, knowing as they did the facts about "wave sheaf" ritual were converted, as **"a great company of priests were obedient to the faith" (Acts 6:7).**

Anyone acquainted with the Bible is aware that a grain harvest is used in the Scriptures as a *symbol* of the conversion and salvation of human beings. Reaping the harvest *pictures* bringing people into God's Kingdom (Matt. 13:18-30). The first grain harvest was celebrated by the Feast of Firstfruits or Pentecost. It pictured the FEW who are now called to salvation.

The **great grain harvest** took place in the autumn. It is appropriately celebrated at that time by the autumn Festival of Ingathering or Tabernacles. This GREAT fall harvest portrays the saving of the majority of humanity—including all the billions who ever lived and died without understanding about salvation. They will all have an opportunity to be saved following Christ's return to earth when God sets His hand to save mankind.

PENTECOST AND FIRSTFRUITS

But what does this have to do with what most Christians believe today? Here is revealed in this ancient ceremony, God is apparently only calling, a *small* number of people—the *firstfruits*!

The New Testament Church began on the Day of Firstfruits or Pentecost (Acts 2). This festive season *pictures* the whole age of the New Testament Church from its beginning in A.D. 31 to the time of Jesus' return to earth.

THE WAVE SHEAF OFFERING

Chapter Twelve

THE FALL FEASTS AND JACOB'S TROUBLE

We have seen how the spring and early summer Festivals of Passover, Unleavened Bread and Pentecost are *shadows* of events that will come in the *latter days*. They portray God's blueprints of the modern nations which will be involved in the endtime prophecies.

These feast days also pertain to Christians today, who have now become a part of the New Covenant promises. They do not, however, have any *significance* to the outside world at this time. The feast days of the Feast of Trumpets, Day of Atonement, and Feast of Tabernacles and The Last Great Day, although observed by the nation of Israel are mostly prophetic of *future* events!

Both Old and New Testaments are filled with prophecies that deal with the nation of Israel and their influence upon the entire world. They contain God's grand design of how He will convert the global earth, and bring them under the New Covenant. The world is blind to God's marvelous plan today because of their lack of understanding God's feast days!

The number *seven* in God's plan signifies *completion* and *perfection*. The seventh month of God's calendar contains the final four festivals, picturing the completion of God's great master plan for mankind!

The previous spring and early summer feast days have been *memorials* of past events—and are also prophetic. They are applicable to both Israelite and Christian alike. The fall feast days begin the time when God will *actively* begin to save the remainder

THE RESTORATION OF ISRAEL

of Israel and bring them to repentance!

> *Then the LORD spoke to Moses, saying, Speak to the children of Israel, saying: 'In the seventh month, on the first day of the month, you shall have a sabbath-rest,* **a memorial of blowing of trumpets,** *a holy convocation. You shall do no customary work on it; and you shall offer an offering made by fire to the LORD.' —Lev. 23:23-25.*

TRUMPETS

The Feast of Trumpets begins the fall feast days and it is called *Rosh hashanah* by the Jews. This feast day comes on the first day of the seventh month and starts the Jewish civil new year. Because God's feast day calendar is based upon the phases of the moon, the Feast of Trumpets is the only feast day that lands on a *new moon!*

To the Jew, this day marks the beginning of ten days of repentance and prayer, concluding with the Day of Atonement or *Yom Kippur*. The Feast of Trumpets is a *picture* of the time when God is going to call on all men, particularly Israel to repent and turn to obey Him!

God will begin His conversion or "circumcision of the hearts" of Israel—by sending a man with the spirit and power of the prophet Elijah! He will preach the good news of God's soon coming Kingdom to them—and many of them will be converted!

This miraculous event will be similar to the experience that occurred on the Day of Pentecost, when the apostle Peter began preaching! This modern-day Elijah will turn the hearts of the children of Israel to their spiritual Father! (Mal. 4:6).

Those who will refuse to repent will suffer the Great Tribulation, and the impending plagues. Unlike the time their forefathers were protected and "set apart" by the Passover lamb's blood in Egypt—these plagues will be poured out on Israel undiluted! This will be a time that the Eternal *will visit them in the*

JACOB'S TROUBLE

last days!

THE TRUMPET SIGNAL OF JACOB'S TROUBLE

> **O my soul, my soul! I am pained in my heart! My heart makes a noise in me; I cannot hold my peace, Because you have heard, O my soul, *the sound of the trumpet, The alarm of war.* Destruction upon destruction is cried, for the whole land is plundered...How long will I see the standard, And hear the sound of the trumpet? For My people are foolish, they have not known Me, They are silly children, And they have no understanding, They are wise to do evil, But to do good they have no knowledge (Jer. 4:19-22).**

Many prophets of old have prophesied the impending famine, pestilence and captivity of modern-day Israel in the *latter days.* These curses and plagues are outlined in the 26th chapter of Leviticus.

On the Day of Trumpets, a trumpet (Heb. *shofar)* was blown throughout the land of Israel. It was a signal for religious as well as secular ceremonies. The *shofar* was a ram's horn that signaled impending *war,* and a time to gather the people for WARFARE! Revelation 6 describes the time when peace will be taken from the earth as the second Seal. This will be a time of war and the beginning of Jacob's trouble!

The prophet Jeremiah revealed God's plan for the modern-day descendants of Jacob in the latter days! God gave him visions of how He would *destroy* the nation of Israel, and then *restore* them back into their land, and rebuild them as His leading nation.

Jeremiah was a prophet who prophesied the forthcoming destruction and captivity of the Jewish nation in 606 B.C. His prophecies are *dual* in nature and also declare the terrible judgments that will come upon Israel in the last days!

However, these curses will be much more severe than those that occurred in Jeremiah's time. Jeremiah lamented a great deal for Judah, as this prophecy gave him much anguish and pain. He knew the *trumpet* was an alarm for war, and his country would be laid desolate during Jacob's trouble!

The second, third and fourth Seals of Revelation 6, describe

THE RESTORATION OF ISRAEL

the same period of war, famine and pestilence that Jeremiah saw in vision (Jer. 4:23-29). This is a time that the entire earth will suffer the plagues of God along with those in Israel!

The Eternal has sworn with an oath that He is going to *punish* His people before He becomes King over them. During Jacob's trouble, the nation will even turn to her enemies for help—but God will allow her enemies to despise and destroy her! (Jer. 4:30-31).

Israel is compared to a harlot who sells herself to men [her enemies], who will cause her to have great tribulation! She is also compared to a woman in travail ready to give birth—but wholesome children will only come out of her seed after a great deal of *pain* and *suffering* as in natural child birth!

ASSYRIA TO PUNISH ISRAEL AGAIN

> **Thus says the LORD: 'Behold, a people comes from the *north country*, And a great nation will be raised from the farthest parts of the earth. They will lay hold on bow and spear; They are cruel and have no mercy; Their voice roars like the sea; And they ride on horses, As men of war set in array against you, O daughter of Zion...' We have heard the report of it; Our hands grow feeble. Anguish has taken hold of us, *Pain as of a woman in labor*...O daughter of my people, Clothe yourself with sackcloth, and roll about in ashes! ...For the plunderer will suddenly come upon us (Jer. 6:22-26).**

Under King Tiglath Pileser, ancient Assyria destroyed and took captive the nation of Israel in 721 B.C. In the *last days*, God is again going to use the modern-day descendants of the ancient Assyrian Empire—to once again plunder and pillage and conquer modern-day Israel!

History is once again to repeat itself, notice:

> ...I will bring thy seed from the east, and gather thee from the west; I will say to the north, Give up; and to the south, Keep not back: bring my sons from afar, and my daughters from the ends of the earth; even every one that is called by my

name (Isa. 43:5-7).

> ...I will bring them again to this land (Jer. 24:6). And ye shall know that I am the Lord, when I shall bring you into the land of Israel, into the country for the which I lifted up mine hand to give it to your fathers (Ezek. 20:42).

> For behold, in those days, and in that time, when I shall bring again the captivity of Judah and Jerusalem (Joel 3:1).

> And I will bring again the captivity of my people Israel, and they shall build waste cities, and inhabit them...(Amos 9:14-15).

> I will bring them again also out of the land of Egypt, and gather them out of Assyria; and I will bring them into the land of Gilead and Lebanon; and place shall not be found for them (Zech. 10:10).

The peoples of the ancient Assyrian Empire eventually migrated into Europe, and many believe they will unify into a modern "Holy Roman Empire."

ASSYRIA—THE ROD OF GOD'S ANGER

> Woe to Assyria, *the rod of MY anger* and the staff in whose hand is My indignation. I will send him against an ungodly nation, And against the people of My wrath I will give him charge, To seize the spoil, to take the prey, And to tread them down like the mire of the streets. Yet he does not mean so, Nor does his heart think so; But it is in his heart to destroy, And cut off not a few nations (Isa. 10:5-7).

THE RESTORATION OF ISRAEL

ISRAEL'S ENEMIES TO BE PUNISHED

A great political figure known as the "Beast" and a miracle working religious leader, identified as the "False-Prophet" will dominate this theocratic system. These deceived and demon controlled human pawns of Satan, will befuddle the inhabitants of the earth into believing they are doing God's service bringing in a millennium of peace!

False teachings, and economic policies will be forced upon all peoples—and all those who refuse to accept the "Mark of the Beast" will be martyred! This *Beast power* will try to force God's people to obey these spurious regulations while they are in Assyrian bondage. Fortunately, through the preaching of the "Two Witnesses", many of God's people will finally have their eyes opened, and cry out for God's help!

This entire scenario will be *dual* to Israel's Egyptian captivity, when Moses and Aaron [*prototypes* of the "Two Witnesses"] pleaded with Pharaoh to "let God's people go"!

We have shown the destruction of the Egyptians during the first Passover, demonstrating God's great power and vengeance. Consequently, there will be a *future Passover* when the Eternal will deliver His people from slavery in a second exodus. He will do this as He did in Egypt, by devastating *plagues* to Israel's enemies!

This second Passover will be so magnificent, that from thenceforth, God will be hailed as the God who brought His people out of captivity from the north country, instead of Egypt!

Once the Assyrian rod will have accomplished God's wrath upon Israel, and after they have glorified themselves in their heart—God's anger will wax hot upon them, and His wrath will be loosed upon them!

A SYMBOL OF WAR

With great excitement and anticipation of our Savior's intervention in the course of human affairs, Paul writes that Christ will return in clouds, with a SHOUT, with the voice of the archangel, and with the TRUMP of God (1 Thess. 4:14-17). It shall be, "**...at the last *trumpet* for the *trumpet* shall sound, and the dead shall be raised incorruptible, and we shall be changed**" (**1 Cor. 15:52**). Christ directly intervenes in world affairs at the seventh or last trumpet of the 7th Seal (Rev. 11:15-19).

A TRUMPET is a *symbol* of WAR—when the nations of the world are angry! God's Word tells us in (Jeremiah 4:19; Ezekiel 33:1-3, 30; Numbers 10:9; Amos 3:6 and Isaiah 58:1) that a *trumpet* is an alarm for war!

Jesus returns to the earth with His Saints (Gr. *hagios*, "most holy ones," angels) to FIGHT in the battle of Armageddon (Jude 14; Rev. 19:14). This will occur immediately after the Tribulation when a great sound of a *trumpet* [the 7th trumpet of the 7th Seal] is blown (Matt. 24:30-31). This will be the time to recover the remnant of the children of Israel.

Read Isaiah 11:11, **"..and He shall set his hand again the *second time* to recover the remnant of His people" (Israel).** Notice exactly when this event takes place: **"And it shall come to pass in that day, that the great TRUMPET shall be blown, and they [Israel] shall come which were ready to perish...and shall worship the Eternal in the holy mount at Jerusalem" (Isa. 27:13).** This is when God will once again set up the tabernacle of David (Acts 15:16).

The "Feast of Firstfruits" pictured the *gathering* of the Church. The "Feast of Trumpets" pictures the *coming* of Jesus Christ with His Bride—to set up the tabernacle of David or to RESTORE again the Kingdom to Israel (Acts 1:6; 3:21).

God instructed the ancient Israelites to keep the Feast of Trumpets in (Leviticus 23:24 and Numbers 29:1)—but He never revealed to them *why* they were keeping it! When Christ returns, Israel will understand the meaning of Trumpets!

THE ATONEMENT MONEY

Silver, as used in the Bible, *symbolizes* the redeeming character for the atonement of sin! Both Joseph and Jesus' lives were bartered for a mere pittance of silver!

This astounding truth is enunciated by the "atonement money" that was used in construction of the Tabernacle:

> **And thou shalt take the *atonement money* of the children of Israel, and shalt appoint it for the service of the tabernacle of the congregation; that it may be a memorial unto the children of Israel before the Lord to make *atonement* for**

THE RESTORATION OF ISRAEL

your souls (Ex. 30:11-16).

The sockets of the Tabernacle and Vail were all made out of the *silver* from the atonement money collected from the children of Israel (Ex. 26:18-25, 38:25-28).

Throughout Israel's history, *type* is crowned upon *type* expressing *atonement* by *substitution!* This was made manifest by the Cross our Savior hung upon as our reconciliation for sin. The various verbs such as ransom, atonement, redemption, covering, propitiation, forgiveness, pardon, reconciliation, cleansing, etc, all express this important truth!

The blood of the Passover lamb in Egypt was *substituted* for the life of each family in Israel. After God destroyed the first-born children of the Egyptians, God claimed Israel's first-born as His by *substitution!*

Every Sin-offering that the priests laid their hands upon as substitution for the individuals sins perpetrated this same truth! Likewise, the *atonement money* used for the sockets of the Tabernacle related this same meaning!

These silver foundations held up the entire tent as a beautiful *figure* of the imminent government of God! The price that had been paid for this strong foundation was the precious blood of the Lamb of God!

Ironically, multiples of the number 12 are found to characterize the dimensions of the Tabernacle boards and sockets. There were 48 boards that were placed in 96 sockets, gathered from the atonement money of 12,000 Israelites!

Twelve is the number that symbolizes *Church government,* and Christ, our Rock of Ages, laid the strong foundation for that government by giving His very life as a ransom for many!

The Tabernacle had no floor to support a foundation—the earth was its foundation! But Christ, our High Priest, has entered into the heavenly Temple whose sure foundation was laid upon His death!

THE SILVER TRUMPETS AND REDEMPTION

Our High Tribunal of the universe instructed Moses to make *two silver trumpets* from the atonement money, to be used to call the assembling of Israel:

The Lord spake unto Moses, saying, make thee *two trumpets of silver*; of a whole piece shalt thou make them; that thou mayest use them *for the calling* of the assembly, and for the journeying of the camp (Num. 10:1-10).

These silver trumpets were blown in Israel's camp to *assemble* the tribes for journeying, war and feast days! The magnificent sound from these glaring trumpets in unison rang out loud and clear of REDEMPTION in the Israelites ears! They recollected how the *atonement* money had fashioned those trumpets, and they were *redeemed* out of Egyptian bondage for a price!

Every sacrifice, every feast day, all the furniture of the Tabernacle, every sound of the silver trumpet pointed to Israel's REDEMPTION! The killing of the Lamb during Passover, the bread that was broken during the days of Unleavened Bread, the blood that was sprinkled during the Day of Atonement, the waving of the wave-sheaf during Pentecost, the sound of the trumpet on the Day of Atonement, dwelling in booths during the Feast of Tabernacles—all echoed REDEMPTION through the stripes our Savior took!

The silver trumpets were to assemble Israel in times of war and for holy convocations (Num. 31:6; 2 Chron. 13:12). We are reminded of the Christian exhortation in Hebrews 10:25: **"Not forsaking the *assembling* of ourselves together, as the manner of some..."**

Today, Christians are commanded to *assemble* in the house of God around their High Priest Jesus Christ!

But we may ask—why were *two* dueling trumpets sounded instead of one in Israel's camp? In view of the *double symbolism* rampant throughout God's Word for Old Testament Israel and the Church—perhaps these two trumpets *picture* the *assembling* of Old and New Testament Israel prior to Christ's return!

This assembling would correspond to the trumpet blast occurring to gather the "elect" of Israel who are gathered from the four corners of the earth out of captivity (Isa. 11:12; Ezek. 5:10; Zech. 9:14; Matt. 24:31). The New Testament Saints would have been previously gathered at the sound of the *last trumpet* prior to Christ's second advent! (1 Cor. 15:52).

Both "Israels" have been redeemed by the redemption money of Christ's blood! Both "Israels", like the two silver trumpets will compliment each other in unison working together in God's Kingdom in the future!

> *And the LORD spoke to Moses saying: "Also the tenth day of this seventh month shall be the Day of Atonement. It shall be a holy convocation for you;* ***you shall afflict your souls*** *and offer an offering made by fire to the LORD. And you shall do no work on that same day, for* ***it is the Day of Atonement****, to make atonement for you before the LORD your God. For any person who is not afflicted of soul on that same day, he shall be cut off from his people."*
> —Lev. 23:26-29.

THE DAY OF ATONEMENT

The Day of Atonement, called *Yom Kippur* by the Jews, is the most solemn holy day of God's feast days—and *foreshadows* the time when *all* of Israel's sins will be forgiven!

The Feast of Trumpets *pictures* the start of Jacob's tribulation. This will be the time God will bring Israel to its knees so He can be their soon ruling King! In the depths of their captivity, Israel will repent before their God—and in His loving mercy, He will forgive their sins!

On this most solemn day, God's people are to "afflict their soul" or *fast* without food or water! The reason for this self affliction will be explained shortly.

Yom Kippur is derived from the Hebrew words *yom*, meaning [day], and *kippur*, meaning [atonement, covering], and is reminiscent of the time the Eternal will *cover* the sins of Israel! Recall how the nation Israel began a national period of repentance and prayer on the Feast of Trumpets. This time of national repentance culminates 10 days later in the Day of Atonement, or Day of Covering!

To "afflict one's soul" or fasting is a way of showing *repentance* and *sorrow* for one's sins. This is a day that

JACOB'S TROUBLE

represents the FORGIVENESS of *all* Israel's sins—as they are placed upon their true perpetrator! Those who refused to fast in Israel were to be cut off from being God's people! The Eternal has promised to destroy anyone who will not rest or afflict his soul among His people!

There is a very important meaning to the ceremony performed by the high priest on this most sacred day of Israel's calendar. But first, in order to better understand, we must explain the Tabernacles relationship to the heavenly.

THE SPIRITUAL MEANING OF
THE DAY OF ATONEMENT

And he shall take two goats, and present them before the Lord at the door of the tabernacle of the congregation. And Aaron shall cast lots upon the two goats; the one lot for the LORD, and the other lot for the scapegoat (margin, Heb. AZAZEL). The word AZAZEL means "the Devil" (see *The Comprehensive Commentary*) (Lev. 16:7-8).

The ceremony that the high priest performed on the Day of Atonement has a very profound spiritual significance. The two goats to be sacrificed were *symbolic* of Christ and Satan!

These two goats were, of course, *types* to represent a deeper spiritual meaning. Notice, it was necessary to be decided by lot, which one was qualified to represent Christ, and which AZAZEL. God was to decide this doubtful decision by lot for these men—"One lot for the Eternal, and the other lot for AZAZEL." One lot was for the Lord—this goat *typified* Christ—but the other lot was not for the Lord, did not typify Christ, but AZAZEL (Satan).

Now the goat which God selected, through lot, to represent Christ, was *slain*—as Christ, its *antitype* was slain. But the other goat selected by God to represent Azazel was not slain—but was driven alive, into an uninhabited wilderness. This *pictured* Satan going out to deceive the world [wilderness] rather than dying.

After God designated which goat represented Christ and which Azazel; the high priest killed the bullock for a Sin-offering for himself. Then he took the burning coals of fire and the sweet incense into the Holy of Holies, also sprinkling the blood of the

THE RESTORATION OF ISRAEL

bullock before the *Mercy Seat*, typical of the throne of God, covering the tables of testimony (the Law).

This, the high priest was required to do in order to *purify himself* to officiate, and to represent Christ as High Priest. In the *antitype,* this was not done, for Christ, our High Priest, had no need of this purification as the typical substitutionary priests did (Lev. 16:11).

Next, the goat which God selected by lot to represent Christ, as the *Sin-offering of the people*, was killed (vs. 15). Thus, the sins of the people were borne by this goat, even as Christ, finally, once for all bore our sins on the cross. After the goat was killed, the high priest would go behind the Veil into the Holy of Holies. He would then sprinkle the blood of the goat on the MERCY SEAT (vs. 15), and make ATONEMENT for the holy place. He would place blood round about the horns (vs. 16), *symbolic* of Christs' blood covering the sins of the WORLD!

It was the high priest taking the blood within the Veil [which represented God's Throne] to the Mercy Seat, that *typified* the risen Christ *figuratively* taking HIS blood, once for all, within the Veil to the very throne of God in heaven. There He would intercede for us as our High Priest. This ceremony is explained by the apostle Paul in (Hebrews 9:6-11) in greater detail.

THE AZAZEL GOAT
NOT OUR SIN BEARER

And when he hath made an end of reconciling the holy place, and the tabernacle of the congregation, and the altar, he shall bring the LIVE goat; and Aaron shall lay both his hands upon the head of the live goat, and confess over him ALL THE INIQUITIES of the children of Israel, and ALL their transgressions in ALL their sins, PUTTING THEM UPON THE HEAD OF THE GOAT, and shall send him by the hand of a FIT MAN into the wilderness: and the goat shall bear upon him all their iniquities unto a LAND NOT INHABITED: and he shall let go the goat IN THE WILDERNESS. And Aaron shall...wash his flesh with water...and he that let go the goat for the scapegoat (Azazel)

> **shall wash his clothes, and bathe his flesh in water, and AFTERWARD come into the camp (Lev. 16:20-26).**

This ceremony *pictures* very graphically justice done by laying Satan's guilt in our sins upon his own head, removing him and chaining him in the "symbolic pit." The English word "scapegoat" signifies "one who bears blame or guilt FOR OTHERS." But *scapegoat* is not an English word, and is NOT a translation of the Hebrew word Azazel. Satan is no SCAPEGOAT who is taking the blame for someone elses guilt—the guilt is his and his alone!

The analogy of a "fit man" taking the goat into the wilderness is describing the actual event in which a strong man (Matt. 12:28-29), will bind Satan for 1,000 years in uninhabited wilderness (Rev. 20:2). Most likely, this "fit man" will be the archangel Michael who fights for the nation of Israel!

The reason Aaron and the "fit man" had to wash themselves after coming in contact with the AZAZEL goat is that it represented an "unclean" spirit or demon.

Passover and Atonement are very similar in that both require the BLOOD of Christ, and *forgiveness* of sin. However, Passover is for Christians NOW—Atonement is for Israel and the world LATER!

"TO MAKE RECONCILIATION FOR INIQUITY"

Hebrew scholar Pierre Winandy explains that the meaning of the root word *Kipper* in the expression **."..to make reconciliation for iniquity"** in fulfillment of Daniel's Seventy Weeks Prophecy (Dan. 9:24), does not mean "to cover" as its verb form *kapor* (as used in describing the pitch of Noah's Ark). Winandy elaborates:

> **...its cultic or religious usage *kipper* means to expiate or to wipe away through sacrifice. It does not carry the idea of covering up something. Thus, the focus of the central phrase in 9:24 is on the greatest of all sacrifices, the death of the Lamb of God, that accomplished a full expiation, a complete wiping away of sin...Therefore, if these premises are accepted, the third expression of Daniel 9:24 ("to atone**

for wickedness") would involve much more than a vague ethical aspect. It would definitely imply an act of sacrifice when the expiation manner would take place. As Christians we believe that Calvary was that precise act which became the basis of the Savior's priestly ministry (*70 Weeks, Leviticus, Nature of Prophecy*, p. 120, 127).

THE CLEANSING OF THE SANCTUARY

Throughout this book we have consistently viewed the *typological* application between the physical and spiritual—and God's earthly sanctuary is no exception.

Whenever an Israelite sinned throughout the year, he would take his offering to the priest [an ordinary priest, not the high priest], who made *atonement* for him.

The confessed sins of the repentant in *type* were transferred to the earthly sanctuary—and on the Day of Atonement the sanctuary itself was cleansed by transferring all of its accumulated sins of Israel to their true perpetrator. The whole of this ceremony is a *picture* of New Testament salvation.

However, this is not to say that the sinners sins were only forgiven on the Day of Atonement—for the Bible clearly states: **"..the priest shall make atonement for him for the sin which he has committed and he shall be forgiven" (Lev. 5:10).**

Here then, is established the relationship between the book of Leviticus [which elaborates the sacrificial system and sanctuary] and the book of Daniel, which speaks of it's final cleansing!

To the casual observer, these two books appear to have nothing in common at first glance. However, upon closer scrutiny, we begin to see that the book of Leviticus is a treasure house of truth concerning the Levitical system, including the sanctuary—and that it is a *type* of New Testament salvation!

Chapters one through sixteen of Leviticus describe the various aspects of the sacrificial system, finally culminating in the Day of Atonement as the capstone of cleansing the sanctuary.

We read of a most interesting scripture concerning the cleansing of the Most Holy Place on the Day of Atonement in Leviticus 16:16:

> **And he shall make an atonement for the holy place, because of the uncleanness of the children of Israel, and because of their transgression in all their sins: and so shall he do for the tabernacle of the congregation, that remaineth among them in the midst of their uncleanness.**

Now we might ask, "why was the cleansing of the earthly sanctuary necessary, if the repentants' sins were previously forgiven?" Let's continue reading God's answer:

> **And he shall sprinkle of the blood upon it with his finger seven times, and cleanse it, and hallow it from *the uncleanness of the children of Israel* (vs. 19).**

Notice it! God says the reason for cleansing the Most Holy Place where the Mercy Seat was located, was to hallow [sanctify] it from the "uncleanness of the children of Israel."

Again, we might ask, "what was the purpose of this annual ceremony and how does it apply to the people of God today, if the peoples sins were already forgiven?" Clearly, there must have been a legal code of God's law that yet needed to be satisfied!

TRANSFERENCE TO THE SANCTUARY

The Mercy Seat overlaid with gold was the literal seat or cover for the Ark of the Covenant that housed the 10 Commandments. On the Day of Atonement, the high priest of Israel entered into the second compartment of the Tabernacle [the Most Holy Place] through the curtain [Veil] and sprinkled the blood over the Mercy Seat.

In effect, he was sprinkling the blood on the 10 Commandments, thus *foreshadowing* the satisfying of the Law through the shed blood of our Savior Jesus Christ!

Now realize! The entire SANCTUARY consisted of the holy place, Most Holy Place, as well as the ground inside the "court of the gentiles." More specifically, it was God's earthly "dwelling place." The word is used particularly in describing the Most Holy Place or Holy of Holies, whether of the Tabernacle or the Temple.

THE RESTORATION OF ISRAEL

God Himself is the ultimate SANCTUARY for His people (Isa. 8:14; Ezek. 11:19).

Therefore, it was God's "dwelling place" that needed to be *cleansed!* A curtain [Veil] separated the holy place from the Most Holy Place in the very heart of the sanctuary. The whole was a *type* of God's Heavenly throne and represented God's government on earth.

Thus, on the Day of Atonement, the high priest of Israel [representing Jesus Christ] made atonement for the entire sanctuary. This in effect, cleansed the sanctuary from the confessed sins of the people that had been transferred to it throughout the year.

Whenever an Israelite sinned, he took his offering to the priest, who laid his hand upon the victim, thus *transferring* the sin of the offerer to the victim. Then upon sacrificing the victim, the priest took the blood and sprinkled it before the Veil in the holy place [but never entering the Most Holy Place] through the curtain during the year.

Thus, the sin of the offender was *transferred* to the sanctuary via the blood. In sprinkling the blood, even the pure or holy objects it touched became contaminated and therefore needed cleansing. This is an interesting paradox to "the blood of sanctification", for it served a twofold function, 1) it purified the sinner, while 2) it contaminated that which was holy.

THE SPIRITUAL FULFILLMENT

On a spiritual plane, the Day of Atonement was a *picture* of the time when all of the sins of mankind will ultimately be *transferred* to their originator—Satan the devil—as God's sanctuary is finally cleansed forever!

This future fulfillment is similar to the satisfying of God's legal code of justice as prevalent in the kinds of sanctuary defilement. Whenever the sanctuary was DEFILED because of rebellion, idol worship, neglect of ceremonial purification or an unclean person [ceremonially not physically—one who was unauthorized to worship in the sanctuary] only complete destruction of the individual satisfied the law.

In these instances, sanctification could not be satisfied by a cleansing ceremony, and the same is true of Satan's defilement of the human race! Any individual coming to visit God's sanctuary in an impure state—contaminated it! Their lives were required! (see Num. 19:13; 20; Lev. 20:2-3; Ezek. 23:38-39; 8:18; 5:11; Jer. 7:32-34).

In *type*, on the Day of Atonement the high priest of Israel legally removed the sins from the "contaminated sanctuary"— after being *transferred* there from the sinning Israelites throughout the year.

Though our sins be forgiven now, in this sense Jesus became the *antitype* or literal SANCTUARY for our sins—as He bare them on the cross at Calgary—only to have them finally removed when they are placed upon Satan in a future fulfillment of the Day of Atonement!

Proving the relationship between the high priest [a *type* of Christ] and the earthly sanctuary [also a *type* of Christ] we read in Leviticus 8:10-12:

> **And Moses took the anointing oil, and anointed the tabernacle and all that was therein, and sanctified them. And he sprinkled thereof upon the altar seven times, and anointed the altar and all his vessels, both the laver and his foot, to sanctify them. And he poured of the anointing oil upon Aaron's head, and anointed him, to sanctify him. See also (Lev. 21:12).**

As the Eternal inspired Moses to write of the Levitical priesthood: **"And the LORD said unto Aaron, Thou and thy sons and thy father's house shall bear the iniquity of the sanctuary..." (Num. 18:1).** Throughout the year when the priest ate of the peoples sacrifices—he was in *type* transferring their sins to him—just as our ultimate High Priest did for us!

These sins were in turn transferred to the sanctuary by the sprinkling of blood in the holy place seven times—finally to be removed on the Day of Atonement. During this time, a complete cleansing of the Most Holy Place, holy place and outer altar were sprinkled with blood—thus cleansing the entire sanctuary! (Lev. 16:15-20).

With this ancient custom in mind, perhaps we can better understand the New Testament cleansing process as outlined in the book of Hebrews. After making reconciliation for our sins by His sacrifice (Heb. 8:9; 9:15), our Heavenly High Priest has torn down the curtain [Veil] and now resides in God's Heavenly Sanctuary! (Heb. 1:3; 8:1-2; 10:12).

Now we have a High Priest in Jesus who is seated at the right hand of the Father, who is our Mediator (Heb. 8:1). Soon Jesus will return to the earth and carry out the corresponding earthly phase of cleansing the sanctuary as He opens up His sanctuary to all those who wait outside its courtyard (Heb. 9:28).

JACOB'S CLEANSING

> **Therefore say to the house of Israel, 'Thus says the LORD GOD: I do not do this for your sake, which you have profaned among the nations wherever you went. And I will sanctify My great name, which has been profaned among the nations, which you have profaned in their midst; and the nations shall know that I am the LORD,' says the Lord GOD, 'when I am hallowed in you before their eyes. For I will take you from among the nations, gather you out of all countries, and bring you into your own land.** *Then I will sprinkle clean water on you, and you shall be clean; I will cleanse you from your filthiness and from all your idols. I will give you a new heart and put a new spirit within you;* **I will take the heart of stone out of your flesh and give you a heart of flesh. I will put My Spirit within you and cause you to walk in My statutes, and you will keep My judgments and do them'** **(Ezek. 36:22-27).**

Here are additional scriptures on this prophetic theme, of Israel's future cleansing:

> **...he that remaineth in Jerusalem, shall be called holy...When the Lord shall have** *washed away the filth* **of the daughter of Zion, and shall have purged the blood of Jerusalem (Isa. 4:3-4).**

> **And I will give them an heart to know me, that I am the Lord: and they shall be my people, and**

> I will be their God: for they shall return unto me with their whole hearts (Jer. 24:7).

> Who is a God like unto thee, that pardoneth iniquity, and passeth by the transgression of the remnant of his heritage? he retaineth not his anger for ever, because he delighteth in mercy. He will turn again, he will have compassion upon us; he will subdue our iniquities; and thou wilt cast all their sins into the depths of the sea (Micah. 7:18-19).

> And I will bring the third part through the fire, and will refine them as silver is refined, and will try them as gold is tried: they shall call on my name, and I will hear them: I will say, It is my people: and they shall say, The Lord is my God (Zech. 13:9).

As already demonstrated, there are many prophecies that declare the national captivity of the descendants of Jacob—followed by a time of sorrow and repentance. God will punish them for their insubordination, then there will come a time when God will hear their cries—and FORGIVE them of all their iniquities! The apostle Peter was well aware that Jesus was sent to grant **"...repentance to Israel, and forgiveness of sins" (Acts 5:31).**

Israel will then be gathered *one by one* out of all the nations where they have been held captive—and be brought back into their own land. The prophet Isaiah declares of this joyous time:

> And it shall come to pass in that day that the LORD will thresh, from the channel of the River to the Brook of Egypt; *And you will be gathered one by one, O you children of Israel.* So it shall be in that day. That *the great trumpet will be blown;* They will come, who are about to perish in the land of Assyria, And they who are outcasts in the land of Egypt, And shall worship the LORD in the holy mount at Jerusalem (Isa. 27:12-13).

THE RESTORATION OF ISRAEL

Jesus Christ's primary responsibility will be to gather the Israelites held in bondage *one by one*. A *trumpet blast* will be blown signaling this glorious event. This was *foreshadowed* by the ceremony on the Day of Atonement, in the year of Jubilee!

At that time Israel will be a captive people, but God will FORGIVE them of their sins and bring them back into the Promised Land. Upon their return to Jerusalem, all of Israel will begin worshiping their Savior [Jesus Christ] with a new heart! Their sins will have been forgiven, and the defilement of their land removed!

God will then give them the New Covenant as He begins writing His laws in their hearts and minds! Israel will be *washed clean* of their past sins, and those surviving Jacob's trouble will be given a new Spirit to walk in all of God's statutes, judgments and laws!

ISRAEL'S LAND TO BLOSSOM AGAIN

> **Then you shall dwell in the land that I gave to your fathers; you shall be My people, and I will be your God. I will deliver you from all your uncleanness. I will call for the grain and multiply it, and bring no famine upon you. And I will multiply the fruit of your trees and the increase of your fields, so that you need never again bear the reproach of famine among the nations. Then you will remember your evil ways and your deeds that were not good; and you will loathe yourselves in your own sight, for your iniquities and your abominations (Ezek. 36:28-31).**

After Israel is brought back into their land, and made clean in God's sight—God will then bless and RESTORE their land to a bountiful state of productivity.

Israel will be blessed above all the nations of the earth, as she becomes abundant and fruitful. Her sins will have been *covered,* and the sins that have defiled the land, will be removed! This is the basic meaning of the Day of Atonement!

Never again will the nation of Israel suffer the ravages of war, and the plagues of famine and pestilence! Those in Israel who survive the next holocaust, will be returned to rebuild the old waste places, and the land laid desolate for generations! Notice Isaiah 61:4: **"And they shall rebuild the old ruins, They shall raise up the former desolations, And they shall repair the ruined cities, The** *desolations* **of many generations."**

The cities that had become barren from the Great Tribulation and World War III will be refurbished, and the land will blossom like the garden of Eden:

> **...O house of Israel! Thus says the LORD GOD: 'On the day that I cleanse you from all your iniquities, I will also enable you to dwell in the cities, and the ruins shall be rebuilt'...So they will say, 'This land that was desolate has become** *like the garden of Eden*; **and the wasted, desolate, and ruined cities are now fortified and inhabited' (Ezek. 36:32-35).**

This is the time Jesus spoke of in regards to deliverance of the prisoners in the prophecy He read in the year of Jubilee!

ATONEMENT—FUTURE

God's plan of salvation for the world is revealed in the mysterious ceremony the high priest of Israel performed on the Day of Atonement. Of course, everything he did upon that day, *typified* what our real High Priest of God, Jesus Christ was to do!

Jesus was the only being allowed to enter beyond the Veil into heaven. There, He appeared on behalf of His house [the Church] to RECONCILE them back to the Father, and then He appeared to reconcile the nation of Israel back to the Father as their long awaited Messiah!

Jesus will first reconcile the Church, then the nation of Israel back to the Father—later through them, He will reconcile the entire earth back to the Father!

The future Day of Atonement will find its complete Kingdom-wide fulfillment during the 1,000 year reign of Christ with His Bride as He restores back to the Father what Satan has stolen! The Millennial Jubilee will be the restoration of all possessions to their rightful inheritors!

The future Day of Atonement will be the act of uniting the Bride and Bridegroom, while the Feast of Tabernacles will be the Kingdom-wide fulfillment of that courtship—consummating in marriage as "New Jerusalem" is presented to the Bridegroom!

Chapter Thirteen

> *Then the LORD spoke to Moses, saying, Speak to the children of Israel, saying: 'The fifteenth day of this seventh month shall be* **the Feast of Tabernacles** *for seven days to the LORD. On the first day there shall be a holy convocation. You shall do no customary work on it. For seven days you shall offer an offering made by fire to the LORD...and You shall rejoice before the LORD Your God for seven days..*
> — *Lev. 23:33-44.*

THE FEAST OF TABERNACLES

All of God's feast days are designed to teach His people *who* He is and His *purpose* for the human race!

For those who observe it, the Feast of Tabernacles begins an eight day festival of rejoicing with food and drink! Actually, the Feast of Tabernacles only lasts seven days, and the eighth day, called the Last Great Day is separate, and the last feast day in God's plan.

To the Israelites, the Feast of Tabernacles is a *memorial* of the time they left Egypt and dwelt in *tents* or booths on their journey to the Promised Land. These transportable homes were TEMPORARY DWELLINGS till they would settle down in their permanent residence.

This delightful festival has a deep spiritual meaning to the Christian and is prophetic to the nation of Israel as well. We shall now read several prophecies concerning Israel's future deliverance

THE RESTORATION OF ISRAEL

and second dwelling in booths.

ISRAEL TO DWELL IN TENTS AGAIN

God had commanded His people to dwell in booths [*tepmorary dwellings*] during the seven days of the Feast of Tabernacles. This was to remind them and us that God caused Israel to dwell in tents when He brought them out of the land of Egypt. This feast is an identification of God, His purposes and His work. It *reminded* Israel of their *deliverance* from Egypt, and today it reminds us of a future deliverance of Israel.

The clearest connection between the Feast of Tabernacles that God has commanded to be kept, and a prophetic event yet in the future for Israel is recorded in Hosea 12:9-10:

> **And I am the LORD thy God from the land of Egypt,** *I will yet make thee to dwell in tabernacles* **(tents), as in the days of the solemn feast. I have also spoken by the prophets, and I have multiplied visions, and used similitudes, by the ministry of the prophets.**

The Feast of Tabernacles is for the purpose of reminding God's people that He once saved Israel from Egypt, and it is also a testimony to them that He will do a similar work in the future. At the end of (Leviticus 23), the chapter in which God gave Israel His commanded Feast days, He revealed to them the reason *why* they were dwelling in booths (tents):

> **Ye shall dwell in booths seven days; all that are Israelites born shall dwell in booths: That your generations may know that I made the children of Israel to dwell in booths, when I brought them out of the land of Egypt: I am the LORD your God.**

Once again God will make Israel dwell in tents as in the days of the solemn feast, the Feast of Tabernacles. God will again save them from captivity and time of trouble. They will be told to return to their land and they will make the journey in the same way as their fathers when they came out of Egypt. Modern-day Israel will dwell in *tents* on their journey to the land God set aside for His people. At this time, Israel will be a nation of happy campers!

God has spoken of this event through all of His prophets, and has multiplied many visions, using many similitudes setting forth this event. The Word of God is full of prophetic visions of the events which the fall feasts foreshadow. These give God's people who obey Him a clear picture of His dealings with Israel in the latter times!

GOD TO HAVE A NEW FAME

Because of Israel's sins, God sent them away from their land. But since God's promises stand sure, He will once again bring them into their land as He did their forefathers from Egypt. The deliverance of the children of Israel in the *latter days* will be such a great event, that thereafter, God will be known as the God who saved Israel from the land of the north, and from all the countries where He had driven them, rather than the God who brought them out of the land of Egypt. Notice this astounding truth in the book of Jeremiah:

> **Therefore, behold, the days come, saith the LORD, that it shall no more be said, The LORD liveth, that brought up the children of Israel out of the land of Egypt; But, The LORD liveth, that brought up the children of Israel from the land of the north, and from all the lands whither he had driven them: and *I will bring them again into their land* that I gave unto their fathers (Jer. 16:14-15).**

God is going to set His hand again the *second time* to recover His people "one by one." God will deliver them in the same manner as He delivered their fathers out of Egypt, by the use of PLAGUES and *judgments* upon their captors.

After this event, He will be known as the God who saved His people from the north country, not as the God who saved Israel from Egypt! God will regather His people individually from the various countries where they will have been in captivity, and will re-unite the outcasts of Israel and the dispersed of Judah.

The remnant of God's people who will return from their

THE RESTORATION OF ISRAEL

captives, will return in the same manner as they did in the day when Israel came out of the land of Egypt. God is going to prepare a *highway* for them so that they will again march dry-shod through rivers! They will again dwell in *tents* as in the Feast of Tabernacles. During their journey from the north to their ancestral home, they will dwell in tents and will be led in MIRACULOUS crossings of water bodies in the same manner as when their fathers came out of Egypt!

A REMNANT OF ISRAEL RETURNS

And it shall come to pass in that day that the remnant of Israel, And such as have escaped of the house of Jacob, will never again depend on him who defeated them, But will depend on the LORD, the Holy One of Israel, in truth. The remnant will return, the remnant of Jacob, To the Mighty God. *For though your people, O Israel, be as the sand of the sea, yet a remnant of them will return;* **The destruction decreed shall overflow with righteousness. For the Lord God of hosts will make a determined end In the midst of all the land (Isa. 10:20-23).**

In that day that will live in infamy—Israel will be a multitude of people before their obliteration. After Jacob's trouble is over, and they are led out of captivity, only a *remnant* (perhaps 10%) will be left.

Prior to their overthrow, Israel will be a numerous people, as the sand of the sea—but only a handful will return to the Promised Land after the destruction to begin the reign of Christ on earth!

Upon their return, Israel will have learned some very bitter lessons. Among them will be to *trust* in their great God, rather than enter into political alliances with other nations.

After God's anger is accomplished upon Israel, He will unleash His wrath upon their oppressors. It is indeed a *fearful* thing to fall into the hands of the living God! Israel's yoke will be removed from her neck in the same manner God delivered their forefathers out of Egypt.

God's prophet Isaiah described the similarities to ancient Israel's burden in Egypt, to their new captors in the last days in

THE FEAST OF TABERNACLES

(Isaiah 10:15-19). God will again *deliver* His people by strong plagues upon Israel's new taskmasters!

THE DAY OF THE LORD

Wail, for the day of the LORD is at hand! It will come as destruction from the Almighty...Behold, the day of the LORD comes, Cruel, with both wrath and fierce anger, To lay the land desolate; And He will destroy its sinners from it. For the stars *of heaven and their constellations will not give their light; The sun will be darkened in its going forth,* And the moon will not cause it to shine. 'I will punish the world for its evil, And the wicked for their iniquity; ...Therefore *I will shake the heavens, And the earth will move out of her place,* In the wrath of the LORD of hosts, And in the day of His fierce anger' (Isa. 13:6-13).

Israel's deliverance in the *latter days* is graphically portrayed by Isaiah's prophecy, describing the vengeance upon Israel's captors. This is the time known as "The Day of The Lord"—and will be characterized by devastating plagues!

Prior to the wrath of God, the sun is to be *blackened,* and the *moon* shall not give its *light.* These same *signs* are given in other prophecies such as (Joel, Matthew and Revelation).

Revelation 6:12 describes the time sequence of this frightful event as the sixth Seal. This precedes the seventh Seal, or the return of Jesus Christ to smite the nations. The seventh Seal consists of seven trumpet plagues—to be poured out by God's holy angels upon the disobedient of the earth!

But before these terrible plagues are poured out—144,000 of the nation of Israel are *sealed* or supernaturally protected by God! These 144,000 physical Israelites consists of 12,000 men from each of the 12 tribes of Israel! Although the world has lost track of where these tribes have since migrated—God certainly has not! He knows exactly where each descendant of each tribe has scattered! (Rev. 7:1-8).

The *supernatural* protection granted these 144,000 Israelites will be similar to the *divine* protection received in Egypt prior to the plagues poured out on the Egyptians! These "firstfruits" will be the nucleus of *rebuilding* a new nation of Israel and the start to save all of Israel!

ARMAGEDDON

And in that day His feet will stand on the Mount of Olives, Which faces Jerusalem on the east. And the Mount of Olives shall be split in two, From east to west, and their shall be a very large valley; Half of the mountain shall move toward the north, And half of it toward the south. Then you shall flee through the mountain valley, For the mountain valley shall reach to Azal. Yes, You shall flee as you fled from the earthquake in the days of Uzziah king of Judah. Thus the LORD my God will come, And all the saints with you (Zech. 14:4-8).

The *seventh Seal* constitutes *seven trumpets,* and the seventh trumpet consists of *seven* last plagues to be poured out to complete God's wrath. The battle of Armageddon occurs prior to these seven last plagues, and is a time when the Messiah will *personally* intervene and fight for His people!

As the seventh trumpet is blown, Jesus Christ will descend to the Mount of Olives on earth, accompanied by the host of heaven, and His newly *resurrected* Bride. Together, God's army will FIGHT in the final battle for the earth called "Armageddon."

Recall how the angel declared Jesus' return to the very spot He ascended into heaven (Acts 1:10-11). Simultaneously, a gigantic earthquake will take place that will cause the Mount of Olives to divide in an east-west direction. As the mountain splits in two, half will fall to the north, and half to the south. This dreadful spectacle will cause Jerusalem's inhabitants to flee in horror!

This unprecedented earthquake will send the Richter scale toppling, as the entire land of Israel will be physically *elevated* above all other nations! In that day, Jesus Christ will be *exalted* King over Israel and the entire earth!

Prodigious hail stones weighing nearly one hundred pounds will destroy the armies gathered for battle at Armageddon—then

THE FEAST OF TABERNACLES

Jesus will be hailed as King of Kings and Lords of Lords (Rev. 19:11-16).

ISRAEL'S 2nd EXODUS

It shall come to pass in that day that the LORD shall set His hand again the second time to recover the remnant of His people who are left, From Assyria and Egypt, From Pathros and Cush, From Elam and Shinar, From Hamath and the islands of the sea. He will set up a banner for the nations, And will assemble the outcasts of Israel, And gather together the dispersed of Judah *from the four corners of the earth* (see Matt. 24:31)...The LORD will utterly destroy the tongue of the Sea of Egypt; With His mighty wind He will shake His fist over *the River, And strike it in the seven streams,* And make them cross over dryshod. There will be *a highway for the remnant of His people who will be left from Assyria, as it was for Israel in the day that he came up from the land of Egypt* (Isa.11:11- 16).

Those Israelites who are fortunate to survive the Beast power's invasion, the captivity, the famine and the pestilence—will return to the Promised Land in a similar manner as when they left Egypt.

There shall be a *highway* that will lead the captive remnant of Israel from Assyria to Palestine. Once again Israel will march through the Red Sea dry-shod and dwell in *tents!* This is the basic meaning of the Feast of Tabernacles [tents] for the nation of Israel!

ISRAEL TO RULE OVER THEIR OPPRESSORS

For the LORD will have mercy on Jacob, and will still choose Israel, and settle them in their own land. The strangers will be joined with them, and they will cling to the house of Jacob. Then people will take them and bring them to their place, and the house of Israel will possess

THE RESTORATION OF ISRAEL

them for servants and maids in the land of the LORD; *then will take them captives whose captives they were, and rule over their oppressors.* **It shall come to pass in the day the LORD gives you rest from your sorrow, and from your fear and the hard bondage in which you were made to serve (Isa. 14:1-3).**

The Eternal will have *compassion* on His chosen people, and will yet CHOOSE Israel, and set them in their own land. These prophecies may seem redundant because they are continually repeated over and over by God's prophets. However, they are emphasized to show the importance of them—and that they are yet to be fulfilled!

Isaiah describes the same theme as the other prophets—that Israel and Judah will be bond-servants again like their ancestors were in Assyria and Babylon. Then the All-Merciful God will lead them out of captivity of these heathen nations, only to have *vengeance* on Israel's oppressors!

Finally, in Israel's deepest period of darkness, they will abhor themselves for the grief they have caused their Great God—and *repent* in sackcloth and ashes! God will lead them into the land He promised their forefathers, and make them His leading nation over the entire earth. At that time, Israel will be a blessed people—eventually RULING over their very oppressors!

Jesus will be exonerated as Israel's *Redeemer*, as the prophet Isaiah declares: **"And a Redeemer will come to Zion, and unto them that turn from transgression in Jacob, saith the Lord. And as for me this is my covenant with them saith the Lord..." (Isa. 59:19-21).**

All the prophecies of Israel's *deliverance* and *forgiveness* will be fulfilled at this time—as God sets out to save ALL of Israel (Rom. 11:26). Israel will begin to keep the New Covenant with a new heart or spirit! They will be *faithful* and loyal to the terms of the Covenant, unlike their ancient ancestors!

The glory of Jesus Christ's REDEMPTION of Israel will eventually stir all the nations to repent and turn to the Lord of mercy and compassion. Surrounding nations will see Israel's blessings, and begin to keep the Feast of Tabernacles (Zech. 14:16). This is why the Feast of Tabernacles is a *merry* occasion filled with JOY in food and drink! It expresses the joy of the earth

THE FEAST OF TABERNACLES

when Israel will be in their land of milk and honey, as a blessed and chosen people!

God will eventually bless all nations, and the entire earth will be showered with abundance by the magnanimous Creator! This most marvelous time is envisioned throughout the prophecies—and the *key* to understanding them is in God's feast days!

PICTURES THE MILLENNIUM

To portray His plan, God took the yearly material harvest seasons in Palestine as the picture of the *spiritual harvest of souls*. In Palestine there are two main annual harvests. The first, produced by the *early rain,* is the spring grain harvest. The second, produced by the *latter rain,* comes the main harvest—the much greater fall harvest.

Now notice when the "Festival of Tabernacles" is to be held: **"at the years end" (Ex. 34:22).** In this verse the Festival of Tabernacles or "Booths" is specifically called the **"Feast of Ingathering."** The harvest year ended at the beginning of autumn. Just as Pentecost pictures the *early* harvest—this Church age, so the Festival of Ingathering or Tabernacles pictures the fall harvest—the—GREAT HARVEST of souls of Israel and the world!

The Kingdom of God or government of God composed of resurrected Christians, will *rule* the nations which are composed of mortal men on the earth (Rev. 5:10; Matt. 6:10). This will last for 1,000 glorious years (Rev. 20:4). The billions of mortals alive during the Millennium will still be heirs to the Kingdom of God. They will not yet have *inherited* it as long as they remain mortal flesh, for, **"...flesh and blood cannot inherit the kingdom of God" (1 Cor. 15:50).**

Recall that Abraham, Isaac and Jacob were merely *heirs* when they dwelled on the earth (Heb. 11:9). While heirs they dwelled in *tabernacles or booths,* sojourning in the land of promise. Booths or temporary dwellings *pictured* that they were not yet inheritors. Thus, we read that, **"Ye shall dwell in booths seven days...that your generation may know that I made the children of Israel to dwell in booths when I brought them out of the land of Egypt" (Lev. 23:43).**

Ancient Israel was a *type* of God's Kingdom in the flesh. Israel dwelled in booths in the wilderness *before* they entered the

THE RESTORATION OF ISRAEL

Promised Land. Those booths *pictured* that they were only heirs. Even during the Millennium, when the Kingdom of God is ruling over mortal nations, the people will be only *heirs* to the Kingdom.

They must OVERCOME their carnal nature and grow in knowledge and wisdom to inherit God's spiritual promises, just as ancient Israel had to in order to inherit the promised physical land. Israel, in the wilderness, was a *type* of all people who must go through trials and tribulations to inherit the promises of salvation. They were wanderers, *waiting to inherit* the promises of salvation (physically).

Abraham, Isaac and Jacob dwelled in a strange country, in tabernacles, heirs of the same promise (Heb. 11:9). Abraham looked for the city whose builder and maker is God (Heb. 11:10).

Today, traditional Jewish communities practice an interesting custom during this Feast. Families build small booths on their porches or in their yards. These booths *symbolize* the temporary abodes that their forefathers built during the 40 years of wandering in the wilderness.

This temporary dwelling is called a *sukkah*, which means "booth" or "tabernacle." It represents God's protection, since similar temporary dwellings protected the ancient Israelites from the sun, wind and rain in the wilderness.

ISRAEL—A TYPE OF GOD'S FAMILY

We have read how Israel was a *type* of God's Kingdom, and we shall now see that Israel was also a *type* of God's FAMILY!

Israel was a *family* of the children of Jacob whose name was changed to *Israel*. Thus, the 12 children of Jacob became the 12 *children of Israel*.

As the children of Israel [Jacob] began to multiply, they became known as "the 12 tribes of Israel." And so, the tribes of Israel, started with a typical marriage relationship of husband and wife, that produced children.

Then, a father and son relationship was established. Abraham is called "the father of the faithful" spiritually, and was the grandfather of Jacob. Isaac was Jacob's father, and his wife Rebekah is a *type* of the Church, even as Isaac is a *type* of Christ. Here we see the family relationship established in ancient Israel typical of God's Kingdom!

Currently, even God the Father resides in a tabernacle [temporary dwelling], but after the Millennium, the Father will dwell with His

THE FEAST OF TABERNACLES

family forever, notice: ."..**Behold, the tabernacle of God is with men, and he will dwell with them, and they shall be his people [family], and God [the Father] himself shall be with them, and be their God"** (Rev. 22:3).

A TYPE OF EARTHLY DWELLING

The Feast of Tabernacles *pictures* Christians dwelling in temporary physical dwellings (our bodies and homes). The apostle Paul talked about this in 11 Corinthians 5:1: **"For we know that if *our earthly house* of this tabernacle were dissolved [destroyed], we have a building [again he speaks of a place in which you dwell] of God, an house not made with hands, eternal in the heavens."**

In (verse 2) we read, "For in this [in this temporary physical body—this instrument in which we can function and operate to gain experience and to learn] we groan, earnestly desiring to be clothed upon with our house which is from heaven (the body of spirit, which is to be given to each of us at the resurrection)." All we are doing in this body of flesh is *temporarily* residing in it—waiting until made immortal at the resurrection to inherit the Kingdom of God!

The apostle Peter also referred to the *temporary* bodies we are residing in as a [tent] *tabernacle:* **"Yea, I think it meet [fit], as long as I am in this tabernacle, to stir you up by putting you in remembrance; Knowing that shortly I must put off this my tabernacle, even as our Lord Jesus Christ hath shewed me? (11 Pet. 1:13-14).**

The *temporary dwellings* ancient Israel built were depicting our temporary dwelling of the earth—before we as ancient Israel enter the promised land. The Promised Land we will inherit will not be *temporary* or physical, but rather ETERNAL and spiritual!

The Feast of Tabernacles is held in the 7th month for 7 days. The number 7 pictures *completion*, and as the Feast of Tabernacles comes to completion under Christ's rule—God's plan will be coming closer to PERFECTION!

The Feast of Tabernacles is held on the 15th day of the 7th month (Lev. 23:34). Using God's day for a year principle, it may very well be 15 years before the Millennium actually starts—since not all the nations will willingly accept Christ (Zech. 14:16).

Paul, being both an Israelite and Christian kept the Feast of

Tabernacles. He said: **"By all means must I keep this Feast that comes in Jerusalem" (Acts 18:21).**

> *Then the LORD spoke to Moses, saying, "Speak to the children of Israel, saying: On* **the eighth day You shall have a holy convocation,** *and you shall offer an offering made by fire to the LORD. It is a sacred assembly and you shall do no customary work on it."*
> —*Lev23:33-36.*

THE LAST GREAT DAY

The eighth day following the seven-day Feast of Tabernacles does not have a name given in the Old Covenant—but is the *final* festival in God's plan and called the Last Great Day.

The *eighth day* is a separate feast from, but immediately follows, the Feast of Tabernacles. We learn the name of this feast from the New Testament: "Now the Jews feast of tabernacles was at hand" (Jn. 7:2)...(Vs. 37) **"In the last day, that GREAT DAY of the feast, Jesus stood and cried, saying, if any man thirst, let him come unto me and drink"** [emphasis mine].

This was the last Feast of Tabernacles that Jesus was to keep here on earth. He knew leaders of the Jews were seeking for an excuse to have Him put to death as a false teacher, and He did not go up to the feast openly at first. Later, during the feast, He stood up openly and taught in the Temple.

At the end of the feast, on the last day, the Great Day of the feast, Jesus stood up and made a long speech. This day was the *eighth day* of the feast, and it is here called The Last Day. It is the last annual feast day of the year, and it is also called The Last Great Day. The outline of the things Jesus spoke on this feast day is recorded.

The Jews rejected what He had to say and took up stones to stone Him, but He hid Himself and went out of the Temple. He healed a blind man, and the authorities accused Him of breaking the law for doing this act of mercy: **"Now it was the sabbath on the day when Jesus made the clay, and opened his eyes " (Jn. 9:14).**

THE FEAST OF TABERNACLES

It was the Sabbath on the day that Jesus made the clay. This occurred in the fall of A.D. 30, the year preceding Jesus' crucifixion. The Last Great Day of that year occurred on a weekly Sabbath. The sequence of events on this Last Day has been distorted because of an addition in the gospel of John. The verses from (John 7:53 to 8:11) comprise an addition that does not belong in the events of this day.

The account of the woman taken in adultery may be an actual occurrence, but it does not belong in this place in John's narrative. The events from (John 7:37 to John 9:12) all occurred on the *Last Great Day,* the eighth day after the Feast of Tabernacles.

The eighth-day closing festival is described with two words: LAST and GREAT. God's feast days are *shadows* of coming events, and the two words *last* and *great* refer to a RESURRECTION of the dead. On several occasions Jesus referred to a resurrection as occurring at the Last Day. This will be the second resurrection and it will be GREAT!

RESURRECTION ON LAST DAY

Jesus stated that the will of His Father is that everyone who would behold the Son and believe on Him would be given the gift of *eternal life.* Jesus further promised that He will raise him up at the Last Day:

> **This is the will of the Father who sent Me, that of all He has given Me I should lose nothing, but should raise it up at *the last day*. And this is the will of Him who sent Me, that everyone who sees the Son and believes in Him may have everlasting life; and I will raise Him up at *the last day*...Whosoever eats My flesh and drinks My blood has eternal life, and I will raise him up at *the last day* (Jn. 6:39,40,54).**

The Jews to whom Jesus was speaking did not understand or approve the things they were hearing. Jesus further explained they had to feed upon Him in order to have eternal life, and that He would raise them up at the Last Day. When Lazarus died, Jesus came to Bethany and spoke with Mary and Martha, his sisters:

THE RESTORATION OF ISRAEL

Then Martha said to Jesus, 'Lord, if You had been here, my brother would not have died. But even now I know that whatever You ask of God, God will give You.' Jesus said to her, 'Your brother will rise again.' Martha said to Him, 'I know that he will rise again *in the resurrection at the last day.*' Jesus said to her, 'I am the resurrection and the life. He who believes in Me, though he may die, he shall live' (Jn. 11:21-25).

The belief of the resurrection occurring at the time known as "The Last Day" was known to Martha. Jesus said that He is the resurrection. The first resurrection occurs at Christ's return, when He calls forth His Saints—others will be resurrected after the millennial reign of Jesus Christ and His Saints. This is known as the Great White Throne Judgment or *The Last Great Day!*

CREATION DAY NO. 7
AND THE LAST GREAT DAY

You will recall it was on the 7th day that the family of God rested. Sabbath means "to rest." Jesus said in Matthew 11:28, **"Come to me...and I will give you rest."**

On the Last Great Day, Jesus said, **"If any man thirst, let him come unto me and drink. He that believeth on me, as the scripture hath said, out of his belly shall flow rivers of living water" (Jn. 7:37).**

It is highly significant that only after the Sabbath was created, were the rivers named as recorded in Genesis! These rivers represent the *flowing of God's Holy Spirit to the earth*!

The 7th day of creation is related to the Last Great Day in that ALL the family of God will finally rest *after* ALL His work is completed! God's work will be completed on earth AFTER the Millennium when everyone has had the opportunity to drink of the river of life!

GOD TO POUR OUT HIS SPIRIT ON ISRAEL

Perhaps it is not coincidental that the Last Great Day in which Jesus healed the blind man, and offered God's Holy Spirit was a weekly Sabbath! Furthermore, it is not accidental that the Last

THE FEAST OF TABERNACLES

Great Day is the *7th annual Sabbath*, even as the weekly Sabbath is the *7th day of the creation* week picturing the Millennium!

Possibly, probably and I think most likely—*both* days *picture* the time when God will pour out His Holy Spirit to all people including Israel! Perhaps the Feast of Tabernacles pictures Israel's *re-gathering* and *rebirth* as a nation prior to the Millennium (Ezek. 37), while the Last Great Day *envisions* the actual 1,000 year *courtship* of Christ and His Bride?

As scripture records in 11 Peter 3:8: ."**..one day is with the Lord as a thousand years, and a thousand years as one day.**" If the Last Great Day does in fact represent the Millennium, we would have the relationship of God's 1,000 year *Millennial Sabbath day* established as a *type* of the *Last Great day!* Although this concept may be viewed as probable, it must be held with due caution.

The actual time at which Israel will receive the pouring out of God's Holy Spirit is difficult to discern. However, it will occur sometime after the battle of Armageddon and after Christ leads Israel out of captivity to her enemies. Ezekiel presents this commentary in chapter (39, verses 25-29) of his book:

> **Therefore thus saith the Lord GOD; Now will I bring again the captivity of Jacob, and have mercy upon the whole house of Israel, and will be jealous for my holy name; After that they have borne their shame, and all their trespasses whereby they have trespassed against me, when they dwelt safely in their land, and none made them afraid.** *When I have brought them again from the people, and gathered them out* **of their enemies lands, and am sanctified in them in the sight of many nations; Then shall they know that I am the LORD their God, which caused them to be led into captivity among the heathen: but I have gathered them unto their own land, and have left none of them any more there. Neither will I hide my face any more from them:** *for I have poured out my spirit upon the house of Israel,* **saith the Lord GOD.**

The entire context of this verse appears to be the same time element that the whole house of Israel is *resurrected,* as God's *breath* [Holy Spirit] is breathed into "dry bones" (Ezek. 37).

Undoubtedly this chapter has a *dual* meaning to the nation of Israel's *spiritual* rebirth and resurrection as a nation to world prominence, and also has reference to her *literal* resurrection!

This is a time when Christ raises up "flesh" (vs. 6) and reunites the entire house of Israel (vs. 11). It is a time when Christ brings Israel out of the captivity of heathen nations (vss. 12,14,21) and when King David rules over them (vs. 24).

The great "in-gathering" or harvest of the nation of Israel pictured by the Feast of Tabernacles will occur immediately after Christ returns. This is when Abraham, Isaac, Jacob, David, Daniel [all of the prophets] and speculatively the whole house of Israel will be resurrected and given God's Holy Spirit (Dan. 12:12-13; Ezek. 37).

Just as the New Testament Church began on Pentecost Day when the Holy Spirit was poured out, the Last Great Day will begin the time that the whole house of Israel, all the living descendants of Jacob, will have opportunity to receive the Holy Spirit and enter into their New Covenant with God. Every living descendant of Jacob will receive the Holy Spirit on this day!

The Church began receiving the Holy Spirit upon the Pentecost day, and all Israel will begin receiving it upon the coming fulfillment of the "Last Great Day", when they come to Jesus Christ in repentance.

As pictured by the Millennium, the "Last Great Day" may be a one-thousand year day, "a marriage feast", pictured by the parable of the King who gave his son a "Great Feast"—a time of great things supplied by the Father to celebrate all Israel having put on white garments—becoming HOLY!

The descendants of Jacob will be the principle participants in that feast, but all other nations will participate also and be greatly blessed. It will be a time of great rejoicing for the whole earth!

SALVATION—PAST—PRESENT—FUTURE

It may surprise many to learn that this is not the only day of salvation, and the millions in countries who have not heard the name Jesus Christ are not yet eternally damned!

The door of salvation has not been shut in the face of these Gentiles as the apostle to the Gentiles writes:

> **Being in times past Gentiles...at that time ye were without Christ, being aliens...and strangers from the covenants of promise, having no *hope*, and without God in the world (Eph. 2:11-12).**

But these Gentiles are not without *hope* for the day is coming that: **"God our Savior, who will have *all men to be saved*, and to come unto the knowledge of the truth" (1 Tim. 2:3-4).** The apostle Peter writes in 2 Peter 3:9: **"The Eternal is longsuffering to usward, *not willing that any should perish*, but that all should come to repentance."**

God definitely wants every being on this planet to come to the KNOWLEDGE of the truth so they would repent of sin and be SAVED by His mercy—the only question is when?

Would a just and loving God *condemn* all those who lived in ignorance of His truth of salvation in Old Testament times? Is everyone lost since the Church age began who has not come to repentance because they did not hear the gospel preached? Or has God in fact purposely *blinded* the minds of the majority of the world to salvation, only to show them the way at a later time?

ISRAEL BLINDED

Believe it or not, ancient Israel was purposely BLINDED by God to teach them vital lessons. Moses said to the ancient Israelites shortly after leaving Egypt:

> **Ye have seen all that the Eternal did before your eyes in the land of Egypt...those miracles: yet the Eternal (not Satan) *hath not given you an heart to perceive, eyes to see, and ears to hear, unto this day* (Duet. 29:2-4).**

Realize this—God Himself blinded Israel and Ezekiel explains why:

> **And I gave them my statutes, and shewed them my judgments, which if a man do, he shall even live in them. Moreover also I gave them my Sabbaths (Ezek. 20:11-12).**

THE RESTORATION OF ISRAEL

Ezekiel continues to explain what God did when Israel refused to keep His divine laws:

> **Because they had not executed my judgments...had polluted my Sabbaths...wherefore** *I gave them also* **(over to)** *statutes that were not good***, and judgments whereby they should not live (Ezek. 20:24-25).**

When an individual or nation rejects God's knowledge—He punishes them through hard and bitter experiences, so, "**...that they may know that I am the Eternal**" (Ezek. 20-26).

However, the fact that God blinded Israel does not mean they are lost forever! Paul said concerning God's mercy: "For God hath concluded them all in unbelief, **that He might have mercy upon all**" (Rom. 11:32).

BLINDNESS—THE CAUSE OF DECEPTION

God, the Creator of the human body and mind, fully realizes man naturally desires to go contrary to His laws as the apostle Paul wrote:

> **The carnal mind [without God's Holy Spirit] is enmity against God: for it is not subject [or will not submit] to the law of God, neither indeed can be (Rom. 8:7).**

Israel, like the majority of the world today is without God's Holy Spirit, and is INFLUENCED by Satan to rebel against God's way of life. Understanding this, a merciful God blinds man to His truths, instead of destroying him.

God has allowed man to grope in the dark as it were, seeking what is right in his own eyes (Prov. 21:2), without realizing: **"There is a way that seemeth right to a man, but the way thereof leads to death" (Prov. 14:12).**

God did not give Israel a perfect heart to keep His laws (Deut. 5:29), but instead let them *choose* their own form of government, as He does today, after they *rejected* Him.

THE FEAST OF TABERNACLES

PARABLES—NOT FOR EVERYONE

Jesus said to His disciples as to why He spoke in parables:

Unto you it is given to know the mystery of the Kingdom of God: but unto them [the vast majority] that are without, all these things are done in parables: that seeing they may see, and not perceive, and hearing they may hear, and not understand (Mk. 4:11-12).

Clearly, Jesus did not speak in parables to make the truth of God easier to understand, but rather *to muddle the truth*! Why did Jesus do this? Simply because God is only calling His Church—a small nucleus to the full understanding of His way of life NOW—others will learn when He sets up His Kingdom!

Only after mankind has exercised his own free will, and realized it has been utterly futile, will he be ready to *listen* to and be *ruled* by the all Omnipotent God.

Speaking of Gentile nations of old, Paul says:

As they did not like to retain God in their knowledge. God gave them over to a *reprobate mind*, to do those things which are not convenient; being filled with all unrighteousness, fornication, wickedness...full of envy (Rom. 1:28-29).

Paul concludes his dissertation of Gentile blindness: **"For God hath concluded them all in unbelief [all mankind],** *that He might have mercy upon all***" (Rom. 11:32).** The Gentiles were blinded then, and they are blinded today!

A DAY OF SALVATION

Some have been misled into thinking that this is the only day of salvation for *everyone*, based on 11 Corinthians 6:2: **."..behold, now is the day of salvation."** Actually, this is a quote from (Isaiah 49:8) and the *Knox* translation reads as follows:

I have answered thy prayer, He says, in a [not the only one] time of pardon, I have brought

THE RESTORATION OF ISRAEL

thee help in a [not the only one] day of salvation (Isa. 49:8).

Truly, this is the day [time] of salvation for those who have been called to understand God's truths, but the day [time] for the vast MAJORITY is yet future!

The Bible tells us that the majority of this present age has been *blinded* to the truths of God by Satan, who DECEIVES the whole world (Rev. 17:2,5; 18:4). The *first chance* for these people to know and understand God's truths will come when Satan is bound and God's Kingdom ushers in His truths for 1,000 glorious years (Rev. 20:14).

Only then will the veil that is spread over the eyes of all nations be lifted (Isa. 25:7). At this time Christ will pour out His Holy Spirit on *all* flesh (Acts 2:17), and the earth shall be *full of the knowledge* of the Eternal (Isa. 11:9).

Those Gentiles who will be alive at the return of Christ to live into the Millennium—will be relatively few in number compared to the billions that will be *resurrected* to life *after* the one thousand year reign of Jesus Christ. Let's read more of this time element:

The rest of the dead lived not again until the thousand years were finished (This is the *great white throne judgment* spoken of in verses 11-12). And I saw a great white throne, and him that sat on it, from whose face the earth and the heaven fled away: and there was found no place for them. And I saw the dead, small and great, stand (a resurrection) before God; and the books were opened, and another book was opened, which is the book of life (there is still a chance of obtaining eternal life): and the dead were judged out of those things which were written in the books, according to their works (Rev. 20:15).

These people are to be judged by the Word of God—the books of the Bible—in accordance with what they have done in this life, and what they will do after they are resurrected to mortal life.

The scene in (Revelation 20) pictures the climax of God's

THE FEAST OF TABERNACLES

marvelous plan—the **Great White Throne Judgment.** This is when the vast number of unsaved people will be resurrected and be given their first chance for salvation. All those millions and millions who have lived and died since the time of Adam up through our age, and have not known the truth about *eternal life*, will be resurrected.

This will not be a *second chance* but rather a FIRST OPPORTUNITY—because these people *were blinded to the knowledge of salvation.* The world today is BLINDED to this wonderful truth, but will someday realize it was a loving and just God that gave everyone a chance to choose to accept His way—and receive the gift of eternal life (Duet. 30:19).

THE SEVENTH PERIOD AND JUDGMENT

The Feast of Tabernacles is, strictly speaking, seven days long and pictures the entire Millennium. SEVEN is God's number of completeness. Therefore, there must also be SEVEN festivals! The Feast of Tabernacles was the sixth Festival. In (Leviticus 23:34,36) we read of the SEVENTH festival:

> **On the fifteenth day of this seventh month is the Feast of Tabernacles for seven days unto the Lord...on the EIGHTH day shall be a Holy convocation unto you...it is a day of solemn assembly; ye shall do no manner of servile work.**

This eighth day, technically, is a separate feast, and is called the LAST GREAT DAY of the feast (Jn. 7:37).

Jesus explained the meaning of this day as He preached on this day: **"If any thirst, let him come unto me, and drink... out of his innermost being shall flow rivers of living water. [But this spoke He of the Spirit, which they that believe on Him should receive...]" (Jn. 7:37-39).**

Revelation 20 tells us dogmatically that there is to be a resurrection of the dead, after the 1,000 year period known as the Millennium. These couldn't be the Christians of today as they will be ruling with Christ when He returns.

They couldn't be those converted during the Millennium as they will have already inherited the Kingdom during the

THE RESTORATION OF ISRAEL

Millennium, after living out a normal life span. Those in this resurrection must be those who died in ignorance in PAST AGES! They are not brought to life until AFTER the Millennium (Rev. 20:5).

THREE PERIODS OF JUDGMENT

There are 3 periods of judgment or times to qualify for God's Kingdom as mentioned in the Bible.

1) Christians who have qualified to rule with Christ during the Millennium are being judged now. They will comprise the Church age *pictured* by the Feast of Pentecost. This resurrection will occur at Christ's return.

2) The Millennium, when Christ separates the sheep from the goats (Matt. 25:31). This will be taking place all during the Millennium. Those who repent will be changed to spirit beings *immediately* upon their death to inherit the Kingdom of God.

The *great* "in-gathering" or harvest of the nation of Israel *pictured* by the Feast of Tabernacles will occur after Christ's return. This is when Abraham, Isaac, Jacob, David, Daniel (all the prophets) and perhaps the house of Israel will be resurrected (Dan. 12:12-13; Ezek. 37).

3) The Great White Throne Judgment after the Millennium (Rev. 20:5). This is spoken of as "a day of judgment" in (Matt. 10:15). Gentiles who died in ignorance will be resurrected (Ezek. 16:53-55), along with those in Israel who were ignorant of God's truth.

The Gentiles of Nineveh and the queen of the south will be resurrected at this time (Matt. 12:41-42). It will most likely be for a 100 year period of time (Isa. 65:20).

In (John 9:1-41), Jesus performed a very unusual miracle of a man who was blind from birth. Jesus spit on the ground and made clay [of the earth] and anointed the blind man's eyes. The blind man's eyes were then healed. This *healing* is representative of the healing of the people on the earth—whose eyes will be opened to truth as man is now *spiritually blinded*.

Jesus performed this miracle to show this analogy to people who are blind [spiritually] and they which see, might be made

THE FEAST OF TABERNACLES

blind (vs. 39).

ALL ISRAEL SAVED

God's Word records an interesting, but mysterious, sacrificial system that God told Moses to have instituted during the Feast of Tabernacles and the Last Great Day (Num. 29:12-35). These sacrifices were not originally instituted when the Feast days were given, but added later.

Starting in (verse 13) we read that on the 1st day beginning the Feast of Tabernacles, 13 bullocks were to be offered. The number 13 is representative of rebellion in the Bible. On the 2nd day, 12 bullocks were to be offered (vs. 13), 11 on the 3rd day (vs. 20), 10 on the 4th day (vs. 23), 9 on the 5th day (vs. 26), 8 on the 6th day (vs. 29), 7 on the last day (vs. 32), and one on the last Great Day (vs. 35).

What spiritual meaning could these sacrifices possibly represent? Perhaps these numbers represent the gradual change and CONVERSION of Israel throughout the Millennium, until less and less sacrifice for sin is required. The number 13 picturing rebellion, and the number 7 representative of perfection!

Finally, all of Israel will be saved as represented by the one sacrifice on the Last Great Day!

A RESURRECTION OF THE JUST AND THE UNJUST

The apostle Paul declared: **."..there shall be a resurrection of the dead, both of the *just* and *unjust*" (Acts 24:15).** However, many people have erred in thinking that both the just and the unjust will rise at the same time.

According to this thinking, both wicked and righteous will be resurrected at the same time to be either rewarded or punished. This concept is confirmed in the *World Book Encyclopedia,* 1972 edition: Most Christians believe that on the last day of the world all the dead will come to life. They call this Judgment Day, because God will judge everyone."

True, the Bible states dogmatically that there will be a resurrection of the *just* and the *unjust*—but nowhere does the Bible say this will occur at the identical time!

Jesus, said Himself:

THE RESTORATION OF ISRAEL

> ...for the hour is coming, in the which *all* that are in the *graves* shall hear his voice, and shall *come forth*; they that have done *good* unto the resurrection of *life* [eternal]; and they that have done *evil* unto the resurrection of *damnation* [Gr. judgment] (Jn. 5:28,29 R.S.V.).

We know from several scriptures that the RIGHTEOUS Saints will be resurrected and shine forth as the sun when Christ returns (1 Cor. 15:53; Dan. 12:3; Matt. 13:43; 1 Thess. 4:13-18). But what happens to the WICKED or "unjust"—are they merely left in their graves to rot eternally?

When Jesus said, ."..they that have *done evil* will be resurrected unto the resurrection of judgment" (Jn. 5:29)— what did He mean? Are all of these *unjust* to be burned up in the Lake of Fire? Have those who Paul described as *unjust* in (Acts 24:15), who have died in sin—lost out on eternal life?

Believe it or not, the Bible teaches that the majority of mankind has not yet received their "first chance" to receive eternal life—and will be resurrected to mortal life in the future.

Countless billions are yet to be given the knowledge of Jesus Christ and how to attain eternal life through Him. Those who have died in ignorance to God's truths will not be held accountable by a just and loving God!

Untold billions who have never heard of the name Jesus Christ, or have never seen a Bible in their lifetimes—are not doomed forever—but will be given a "first chance" opportunity to receive salvation!

JUDGMENT VERSUS DAMNATION

The Word of God makes a very clear distinction between *judgment* and *damnation*. Virtually all modern translations interpret the words of Jesus in John 5:29, **"the resurrection of damnation" as "the resurrection of judgment."**

Most people make the mistake of assuming a resurrection to judgment means damnation—this is erroneous! Peter made this abundantly evident when he wrote: **"For the time is come that *judgment* must begin at the house of God..." (1 Pet. 4:17).**

This scripture is in reference to starting the New Testament

THE FEAST OF TABERNACLES

Church of God nearly 2,000 years ago. Surely this *judgment* did not necessarily mean CONDEMNATION! Those who willingly accept Jesus Christ as their personal Savior—will be given eternal life upon the returning Jesus Christ. This is the *first resurrection*! True, those who willingly reject the Word of God will *perish,* as Peter warned (11 Pet. 2:20-22; Heb. 6:4-6).

Christians are *now* being *judged* under the dispensation of grace—and are *accountable* for their actions! Paul therefore warns: **"How shall we escape, if we neglect so great salvation...? (Heb. 2:3).** See also (Hebrews 10:26-29).

God is now judging Christians—but the vast majority of the world has been *blinded* to God's precious truth! Think about it! Would a just and merciful God hold people accountable for their actions who have been deceived by Satan? (Rev. 12:9).

God is not willing that any should perish (11 Pet. 3:9)—and the day of *judgment* is coming when all those who died in ignorance through deception, will be resurrected to have their first opportunity to walk in God's truths. This time period may last 100 years (Isa. 65:20), or whatever length of time God feels necessary to render a verdict based upon the way they live with this new knowledge!

The Christian world has a dilemma. How then can Christ make the statement that **"...all that are in the graves shall hear his voice, And shall come forth; they that have done good, unto the resurrection of life; and they that have done evil, unto the resurrection of damnation"?**

If there is a resurrection to life and a resurrection to damnation, how then can there be a "single event" for the righteous and the wicked"?

The answer to that question lies in understanding that the word '*damnation*' is a bad translation of the Greek word, '*krisis*', and in understanding that those who are resurrected to life are judged in this life.

So if 'damnation' is a bad translation of the Greek word, 'krisis' what is the proper translation? Just showing how it is normally translated will answer that question.

The Greek word 'krisis' appears in the New Testament 48 times, and of those 48 it is translated 'judgment' 39 times. Only three times is it translated 'damnation', and in those instances it would better be translated as 'judgment'.

Matthew 23:33, should read: "Ye serpents, ye generation of

THE RESTORATION OF ISRAEL

vipers, how can ye escape the damnation [Greek: *krisis*—judgment] of hell? [Greek, *Gehenna*, a type of the lake of fire].

Perhaps John 5:24-30 is the best example of how the changing of this Greek word 'krisis' from 'condemnation' to 'judgement' changes the entire meaning, notice:

Verily, verily, I say unto you, He that heareth my word, and believeth on him that sent me, hath everlasting life, and shall not come into *condemnation;* but is passed from death unto life.

Verily, verily, I say unto you, The hour is coming, and now is, when the dead shall hear the voice of the Son of God: and they that hear shall live.

For as the Father hath life in himself; so hath he given to the Son to have life in himself;

And hath given him authority to execute judgment also, because he is the Son of man.

Marvel not at this: for the hour is coming, in the which all that are in the graves shall hear his voice,

And shall come forth; they that have done good, unto the resurrection of life; and they that have done evil, unto the resurrection of damnation.

I can of mine own self do nothing: as I hear, I judge: and my judgment is just; because I seek not mine own will, but the will of the Father which hath sent me.

JUDGMENT DAY FOR GENTILE CITIES

Jesus had performed countless miracles in the Jewish city of Capernaum—yet His people failed to believe on Him! Jesus reprimanded these inhabitants and said if such mighty miracles had been performed in Sodom—they would have believed Him! Then Jesus gave this strong warning to these faithless wonders: **"But I say unto you, that it shall be more tolerable for the land of Sodom in *the day of judgment* than for thee" (Matt. 11:24).**

The Israelite cities of Bethsaida and Chorazin also saw the mighty works of Jesus—yet they would not heed His messages. To them Jesus prophesied: **"But I say unto you, it shall be more tolerable for Tyre and Sidon [Gentile cities] at *the day of judgment* than for you" (Matt. 11:21,22).**

Regarding the fate of the Gentile city of Nineveh, Jesus pronounced: **"The men of Nineveh *shall rise in judgment with***

THE FEAST OF TABERNACLES

this generation. **and shall condemn it: Because they repented at the preaching of Jonas, and behold, a greater than Jonas is here" (Matt. 12:41).**

Furthermore, Jesus made a similar prophecy about the Gentile city of Sheba: **"The Queen of the south [Queen of Sheba] shall *rise up in judgment with this generation,* and shall condemn it; for she came from the uttermost parts of the earth to hear the wisdom of Solomon; and behold, a greater than Solomon is here" (vs. 42).**

What *judgment Day* was Jesus referring to in these remarkable scriptures? When will the Gentile cities of Sodom and Gomorrah, Tyre and Sidon, Nineveh, and the Queen of Sheba rise up in Judgment? Whenever this day comes—it will be more tolerable for them, than the Israelite cities that *rejected* the gospel message of Christ!

In His loving mercy, God will resurrect these Gentile cities, and provide an opportunity to understand the GOOD NEWS of His Kingdom. These people never heard the message of Christ, or saw His miracles—that's why it will be more tolerable for them, than those who were eye witnesses of Christ's gospel message!

God's prophet Ezekiel also prophesied of the time when the peoples of ancient Sodom, Samaria and Jerusalem would be resurrected. He stated they will, **."..return to their *former estate"* (Ezek. 16:55).**

These Gentiles, like the ancient Israelites—will be resurrected and restored in their native land. Ezekiel described the imminent resurrection of the entire house of Israel, as coming up out of their graves as *fleshly beings* in the "valley of dry bones" chapter (Ezek. 37:1-10). At this precise time, God will put them in their own land and give them His Holy Spirit so they can attain eternal life (vs. 14).

THE GREAT WHITE THRONE JUDGMENT

Granted, the resurrection of the Saints will transpire upon the return of Jesus Christ. Granted, the physical nation of Israel will be resurrected and restored in their land, along with Gentile nations. Granted, their will be a resurrection of the *just* to eternal life, and a resurrection of the *unjust* to judgment—but when does this occur?

Our all loving and merciful Father is not willing that any

should perish—and desires every human being to come to repentance! God in His wisdom, has not ordained that the eyes of this evil world, influenced by Satan, would have its eyes opened to truth in this age. Instead, our great God has destined the vast majority of mankind to understand His truth in a world that is not under the devil's influence. That is why the majority of mankind will be given a "first chance" opportunity in the *second resurrection!*

This resurrection to mortal substance is described in the 20th chapter of the book of Revelation, notice: **"And I saw *a great white throne* and him that sat on it...And I saw the *dead,* small and great, *stand* [be resurrected] before God..."** (Rev. 20:11,12).

Here we find the small [small frys] and great [those of world prominence], being resurrected to stand before God's judgment. Then what does God do? **"...and the books [Gr. *biblos*—books or Bible] were opened, which is the book of life: and the dead were judged out of those things which were written in the books [Bible]** *according to their works* **(vs. 12).**

The billions of individuals resurrected during this period of time will be given their *first* real chance to understand God's plan of salvation. God will open the Bible to their understanding for the first time—and they will be given the opportunity to *repent* and ACCEPT Jesus as their personal Savior! God will then give them His Holy Spirit, and write their names in the book of life!

These people will be judged "according to their works" in the sense of mercy, not condemnation! God will judge these "unjust" dead, who will be raised to life by the standards of the Holy Bible.

Thus, the unjust dead, who will be the vast billions who have ever lived, will have an opportunity for salvation according to God's master plan!

SUMMARY

The Feast days given to the nation of Israel present to God's people an outline of His great master plan and purpose for saving the whole earth. They provide the missing key for understanding future prophecies. God has given His people Israel these days for the purpose of teaching them who He is, and the work He is doing.

The New Testament Church is called "the Israel of God" (Gal. 6:16), and the Feast days God gave to Israel, will help Christians better understand God's plan for them and the world.

THE FEAST OF TABERNACLES

God gave the nation of Israel *seven* annual feast days listed in Leviticus 23. The first three have had a fulfillment in Jesus Christ already, and four remain to be fulfilled. The last four are prophetic. It is not possible to understand the last four, without a good perception of the first three, for there is a parallel, a similarity, a repetition of the first three, in the last four feast days!

The Passover parallels the Day of Atonement in that both require sacrifice and blood for atonement of sin! The 7 days of Unleavened Bread parallel the 7 days of the Feast of Tabernacles in that both *picture* a time of removing sin from our lives!

Closely connected with the days of Unleavened Bread was Pentecost, *picturing* the pouring out of God's Holy Spirit to the Church. This *parallels* the Feast of Tabernacles and its inclusion of the Last Great Day, in which God's Spirit will be poured out upon all flesh!

The Feast of Unleavened Bread celebrated two deliverances, and began a time of dwelling in tents. The first was a celebration for being set free from slavery through the Passover, and the second was a celebration for being protected from re-capture by Pharaoh through a destruction of his army in the Red Sea. Certainly, we can see similar events described in prophecy about the ending of this age and *pictured* by the Feast of Tabernacles.

There will come an initial setting free of Israelites from slavery in their enemies' land and a return, dwelling in tents, just as there was in Egypt. Then afterward, there is to come the Day of the Lord, which will bring a destruction upon their enemies, similar to the destruction of Pharaoh's army. All peoples are to be judged upon the basis of how they treated God's people when they were in their time of trouble.

One such description is in (Matthew 24:31-46) where Jesus described how the nations were to be separated into goats and sheep according to how they had treated His followers. If they had shown kindness to His followers when they were hungry, thirsty, strangers, naked, sick and in prison— then they will be treated as sheep and allowed to enter into the glories of His Kingdom. Those who showed them no kindness during their difficulty will be sent into destruction! They will not be allowed to live into the time of Jesus Christ's righteous reign on the earth!

The feast days hold the key to many past and future prophecies—and many Christians observe them today. As clearly seen from the future aspect of the feast days, there are yet many prophetic events to occur that will affect both Israel and Christians alike!.

Chapter Fourteen

THE TEMPLE TO BE REBUILT?

There are many scriptures which seem to suggest that another Temple or Tabernacle will have to be built in Jerusalem—before the second Coming of our Savior, in order to fulfill prophecy as we have already demonstrated.

Bible prophecies indicate that a religious center, Tabernacle or Temple will have to be built in Jerusalem before the return of Jesus Christ.

Of this time, Irenaeus (130-202 A.D.), bishop of Lyons France, formally Lugdunum in Gaul, disciple of Polycarp of Smyrna, disciple of the apostle Paul, gives a well developed eschatology when he writes:

> **But when this Antichrist shall devastate all things in this world, he will reign for three years and six months, and sit in the temple at Jerusalem; and then the Lord will come from heaven in the clouds, in the glory of the Father, sending this man and those who follow him into the lake of fire; but bringing in for the righteousness the times of the kingdom, that is, the rest, the hallowed seventh day; and restoring to Abraham the promised inheritance, in which kingdom the Lord declared, that "many coming from the east and from the west should sit down**

THE RESTORATION OF ISRAEL

with Abraham, Isaac, and Jacob, (Charles C., Ryrie, *The Basis of the Premillennial Faith*, **(p. 22-23).**

Notice how he relates the seventh day of the creation week to the Kingdom that Jesus will bring of peace and rest. The Israeli victory in 1967 gave them complete control of the city of Jerusalem—including the original site of Solomon's Temple.

The stage is now set for the construction of the "Temple" as indicated by (11 Thessalonians 2:4, Revelation 11:1,2 and Daniel 8:13; 11:31).

To build a Temple is the hope and dream of religious Jews all over the world. One of the primary reasons Jews haven't yet started *sacrificing,* is because they don't have a Temple—but *sacrifices* must start again before the return of Christ as indicated from many other prophecies.

Many Jews have said, **"It was one generation from David till Solomon when a Temple was built and so it will be with us."** The Jews gained control of Jerusalem in 1967. A generation is approximately 30 years.

Some have thought that the end-time prophecies referring to a "Temple" are speaking of the Church in "spiritual terms." Undoubtedly, there are parallels between the accounts of Zechariah and John where they saw visions.

According to Zechariah's account, a man [angel] measured the city of Jerusalem, whereas John was told to measure the Temple of God (Zech. 2:1,2; Rev. 11:1,2).

Because the Church is referred to as "New Jerusalem" and God's "Temple", many have felt these scriptures express its spiritual measurement in preparation for its end-time protection.

Ezekiel's account of the "writer's inkhorn" in which an angel sets a "mark" on the *forehead* of the faithful men who cry out for their holy city, also parallels the protection the 144,000 will receive, as they are sealed by a "mark" upon their foreheads by an angel (Ezek. 9:4; Rev. 7:3).

True, these scriptures could have a *dual* meaning to the physical Temple and spiritual Temple (the Church). John was told not to measure the "court of the Gentiles", who in a spiritual sense could also refer to those who like the physical Temple, could not enter its gates and therefore receive its protection!

THE TEMPLE OF DOOM!

There are many scriptures which seem to indicate that another Temple or Tabernacle will have to be built before the second Coming of Christ, in order to fulfill prophecy. In order to prove that a *literal* building or tent must be built before Christ's Coming, it is necessary to connect several interrelated prophecies.

As we dovetail these prophecies, we shall list the points they have in common.

By using deductive chronological reasoning, we shall see it seems imminent that a *literal* Temple must yet be built in Jerusalem before the second Advent of Jesus Christ!

THE ABOMINATION OF DESOLATION—(Matt. 24:15)

Jesus gave this stern warning when asked by His apostles concerning His second Coming:

> **When ye see the Abomination of desolation** *spoke of by Daniel the prophet* **stand in the holy place** *...then will be great Tribulation,* **such as was not since the beginning of the world to this time, nor ever shall be again (Matt. 24:15:21).**

Notice these several significant points from this verse:

- The **Abomination** had not yet occurred when Jesus spoke these words in A.D. 31.
- Once it did occur, **The Great Tribulation** would also occur.
- It would be something that **could be seen.**
- It was **spoken of by Daniel** the prophet.
- It would occur at **the end-time,** or just before Christ's

THE RESTORATION OF ISRAEL

return.

GENTILES TROD DOWN JERUSALEM

In Luke's account of the Great Tribulation, he calls this "the days of vengeance", that all things which are written may be fulfilled:

> **And when *ye shall see Jerusalem compassed with armies*, then know that the desolation thereof is nigh. Then let them which are in Judaea flee to the mountains; and let them which are in the midst of it depart out; and let not them that are in the countries enter thereinto. For these be the *days of vengeance, that all things which are written be fulfilled.* But woe unto them that are with child, and to them that give suck, in those days! For there shall be great distress in the land, and wrath upon this people. And they shall fall by the edge of the sword, and SHALL BE LED AWAY CAPTIVE INTO ALL NATIONS: and *Jerusalem shall be trodden down of the Gentiles*, until the times of the Gentiles be fulfilled (Lk. 21:20-24). [emphasis mine].**

Revelation says this of the holy city which shall be trodden down of the Gentiles:

> **But the court which is without the temple leave out, and measure it not: *for it is given unto the Gentiles: and the holy city shall they tread under foot forty and two months.* And I will give power unto *My two witnesses*, and they shall prophesy a thousand two hundred and threescore days, clothed in sackcloth...And when they shall have finished their testimony, *the beast* that ascendeth out of the bottomless pit shall make war against them, and *shall***

> *overcome them, and kill them.* **And their dead bodies shall lie in the street of the great city, which spiritually is called Sodom and Egypt, where also our Lord was crucified...And after three days and an half the spirit of life from God entered into them, and they stood upon their feet; and great fear fell upon them which saw them. And they heard a great voice from heaven saying unto them, Come up hither.**
>
> **And** *they ascended up to heaven* **in a cloud; and their enemies beheld them.** *And the same hour* **was there a great earthquake, and the tenth part of the city fell, and in the earthquake were slain of men seven thousand; and the remnant were affrighted, and gave glory to the God of heaven.** *The second woe is past;* **and behold** *the third woe cometh quickly.* **And the seventh angel sounded; and there were great voices in heaven, saying,** *The kingdoms of this world are become the kingdoms of our Lord,* **and of his Christ; and he shall reign for ever and ever (Rev. 11:2,3,7,8, 11-15).**

Daniel the prophet, provides more information concerning this "time of the Gentiles."

> **And out of one of them came forth** *a little horn***, which waxed exceeding great, toward the south, and toward the east, and toward the pleasant land. And it waxed great, even to the host of heaven; and it cast down some of the host and of the stars to the ground, and stamped upon them. Yea he magnified himself even to the prince of the host, and** *by him the daily sacrifice was taken away and the place of his sanctuary was cast down.*

> **And an host was given him against the daily sacrifice by reason of transgression, and it cast down the truth to the ground; and it practiced and prospered. Then I heard one saint speaking, and another saint said unto that certain saint which spake, How long shall be the vision concerning the daily sacrifice, and the transgression of desolation to give both the sanctuary and the host to be *trodden under foot?* And he said unto me, *Unto two thousand and three hundred days*; then shall the sanctuary be cleansed (Dan. 8:9-14).**

We now find several additional significant points that must occur along with *the time of the Gentiles* which occurs during *The Great Tribulation*, which occurs when *the Two Witnesses* are preaching from Jerusalem, just prior to Christ's second and final Coming:

- The daily sacrifice will be taken away by the little horn 2300 days.
- The sanctuary will be polluted at the same time.
- The "Two Witnesses" will be killed by the "Beast Power", only to be *resurrected* by the returning Christ.

THE DAILY SACRIFICE TAKEN AWAY

The last "King of the North" is pictured as occupying "the glorious land" Palestine (Dan. 11:41). This is the same region that the "little horn" of (Daniel 8) is yet to control in the end time.

In Palestine the final King of the North "shall come to his end, and none shall help him" (Dan. 11:45). The "little horn" of (Daniel 8) also comes to his end in Palestine when he stands up against the "Prince of princes" (Dan. 8:25). Both of these prophecies refer to the same event!

The "little horn"—the final "King of the North"—is going to manifest himself on the world scene one day, and take away the daily sacrifice of the Jews for 2300 evenings and mornings!

THE 2300 LITERAL DAYS

This amazing prophecy of the 2300 evenings and mornings is yet to be fulfilled in these last days. A great crisis is yet to occur in Palestine, which began when the Jews captured Old Jerusalem in June, 1967. After 1900 years, a part of the tribe of Judah—the Jews, have returned to Palestine.

In their war of independence in 1948, Israel gained control of the new part of Jerusalem, but the Arabs still held the old part. The Jews took complete possession of Jerusalem during the 1967 war. Now, the next step of the prophecy has been fulfilled—the Jews are in Jerusalem and in possession of the Temple site. Not only Jerusalem, but the whole Near East is an armed camp, likely to explode at any moment.

Daniel 8 indicated that in the last days we shall see literally fulfilled the mysterious prophecy of the "daily sacrifice" with the "sanctuary" restored.

Both the Arabs and the Jews claim Old Jerusalem. To build a Temple there is the hope and dream of religious Jews the world over. When you see the first stone laid for the Temple—you will know there is not much time left! Many interpret the 2300 days of (Daniel 8:13 and 14) falsely, but let us clarify its meaning:

Then I heard one saint speaking, and another saint said unto that certain saint which spake, 'How long shall be the vision concerning the daily sacrifice, and the transgression of desolation, to give both the sanctuary and the host to be trodden under foot?' And he said unto me, '*unto two thousand and three hundred days; then shall the sanctuary be cleansed.*'

Turn in your Bibles to (verse 14) of Daniel (chapter 8). In most Bibles you will find a marginal note for the word "days." This reveals that the original Hebrew for the word "days" is "evening morning." This prophecy is not referring to 24-hour days, but to evenings and mornings—the evening and morning sacrifice in the Temple! According to (verse 11), the "little

THE RESTORATION OF ISRAEL

horn" takes away the daily sacrifice. The *daily sacrifice* was offered in the evening and in the morning (see Lev. 6:9 and 12).

Daniel 8:14 is a mistranslation in the text of the *King James Version*, though it is correct in the margin. The *Revised Standard Version* reads, "for two thousand three hundred evenings and mornings."

In other words, here is a prophecy that *two thousand three hundred evening and morning sacrifices* would cease to be offered. Since the daily sacrifice was offered twice a day, this prophecy is actually speaking of one thousand one hundred fifty (1150) days. In 1150 days there would be exactly two thousand three hundred sacrifices offered at evening and morning.

There is no direct indication of how long sacrifices will be offered, but they are to be abolished for exactly 1150 days by a great False Prophet spoken of in Daniel 8:11:

> **...he magnified himself even against the Prince of Host, and by him *the daily sacrifice was taken away* and the place of his sanctuary was cast down.**

Then this same "False Prophet" will sit on a throne hailing himself to be very God (2 Thess. 2:3-5). We may be very close to the fulfillment of these momentous end-time prophecies which will usher in Christ's Coming in all power and glory!

These things are a warning to us, because Jesus said:

> **When ye therefore shall *see* the abomination of desolation, spoken of by Daniel the prophet, stand in the holy place...then let them which be in Judea flee into the mountains...pray ye that your flight be not in the winter, neither on the sabbath day: *For then shall be great tribulation,* such as was not since the beginning of the world to this time, no, nor ever shall. And except those days be shortened, there should no flesh be saved [alive]...(Matt. 24:15-22).**

Daniel 12 speaks of the same prophecies we have just read and the same events. Notice, "A time never since there was a nation" (Dan. 12:1). "It shall be for a time, times, an half" [3 1/2 yrs], (Dan. 12:7). The end-time prophecies will be for 3 1/2 yrs (Dan. 7:25; Rev. 13:5, 11:2, 12:14).

There is yet another end-time prophecy that revolves around the termination of the sacrifices. It has to do with the mysterious 1290 day and 1335 day prophecies. Notice, **"And from the time that the continual burnt offering is taken away and *the abomination that makes desolate* is set up will be 1290 days (Dan. 12:11).**

Another prophecy in Daniel that relates to these same events is "the king of the North" in Daniel 11. This prophecy occurs at the end-time, Daniel 11:40: ."..**and they shall pollute the sanctuary of strength *and shall take away the daily sacrifice*, and they shall place the Abomination that makes desolate" (Dan. 11:31).**

These sacrifices shall stop for 1150 days as we have shown previously. So, in addition, we now know that the sacrifices will stop 1150 days and the abomination that makes desolate will be set up.

Now we have the following points to occur just before the Great Tribulation would begin:

- The **Abomination of desolation** had not yet occurred when Jesus spoke these words in 31 A.D.
- Once it did occur, **The Great Tribulation** would also occur.
- It would be something that **could be seen.**
- It was **spoken of by Daniel** the prophet.
- It would occur at **the end-time,** or just before Christ's return.
- The **sacrifices would start** and then stop for 1150 days.
- The Abomination of desolation **would occur simultaneously** with the termination of the sacrifices.
- The **counting of the 1290 and 1335 days** begins from the Abomination of Desolation or when the sacrifices are stopped.

THE RESTORATION OF ISRAEL

ANCIENT FULFILLMENT

Anciently, in *type* the prophecy of the 2300 evening and morning sacrifices were fulfilled, as Professor Dewey M. Beegle informs us:

> **The "Prince" was probably the high priest Onias III, who was ordered slain in 171 B.C. by Menelaus the wicked priest appointed by Antiochus. The "host" was the Jews, the people of God. On the 15th of Kislev (about Dec. 1) 168 B.C., burnt offerings were stopped and the temple desecrated by an altar of Zeus, the Greek God worshipped by Antiochus, erected over the Jewish altar. When a "holy one" inquired as to the duration of the desecration, Daniel heard "another holy one" reply, "For 2,300 evenings and mornings; then the sanctuary shall be restored to its rightful state" (8:13-14)...But burnt offerings were not stopped until 168; therefore the liberals have contended that the reference is to the evening and morning sacrifices which used to be offered in the temple. Accordingly, the answer to the question, "How long will the desecration last?" was 2,300 sacrifices, that is, 1,150 days (*Prophecy and Prediction*, p. 101).**

2300 PROPHETIC DAYS

As with most of God's prophecies, there is a *dual* meaning, and most likely there is a *spiritual* significance to the "2300" evening and morning sacrifices. In his famous *Commentary* on this scripture, Adam Clarke, provides his interpretation as to the spiritual interpretation of the 2300 days:

> **Though literally it be two thousand three hundred evenings and mornings, yet I think the prophetic day should be understood here,**

> as in other parts of this prophecy, and must signify so many years. If we date these years from the vision of the he-goat (Alexander's invading Asia,) this was B.C. 334; and two thousand three hundred years from that time will reach to A.D. 1966, or one hundred and forty-one years from the present A.D. 1825.

Some have concluded that Adam Clarke was correct in his assessment of this prophecy, but that there was one small detail that Adam Clarke failed to understand. Adherents to this interpretation say, since there is no year zero, we must add one year when going from B.C. to A.D. Therefore, we would arrive at the significant year of 1967 when counting 2300 years from the invasion of Alexander in 334 B.C.

As already mentioned, a very significant event occurred in 1967, when the Jews recaptured the old part of Jerusalem, including the Temple Mount!

However, fascinating this scenario of prophecy may seem, there are some serious questions we must ask. Firstly, "Why did Adam Clarke begin the counting of the prophecy from 334 B.C. when in fact Antiochus, the *type*, invaded Israel in June 168 B.C. and sacrificed a pig on the Temple altar in defiance of the Jews!"

Secondly, "Why use ordinary calendar years of 365 days when in fact God uses a 360 day prophetic year?"

According to ancient history and the book of Maccabees, we can piece together a most fascinating scenario. The ancient Temple was desecrated for three years from 168-165 B.C. by Antiochus Epiphanes (*New Commentary on the whole Bible*, by Tyndale). It was finally cleansed exactly 1,080 days later [exactly three prophetic 360 day years] from the day the vision was given in the fall of 168 B.C., on the twenty-fourth day of the ninth month during Antiochus' revolt.

Unfortunately for us, this is one prophetic number that has been translated three different ways in the old manuscripts. The Greek Septuagint, as used by the Jews during the first century uses 2400 days, while Jerome used a third set of manuscripts that recorded this prophecy as 2200 days. Bishop Thomas

Newton confirms these discrepancies as provided in his book *"Dissertations on the Prophecies"*, written in 1754.

If we use 2200 days for our prophetic fulfillment, and convert them to 360 prophetic years of 360 days each, we would have 2200 x 360 = 792,000 prophetic days. Converting these days to calendar years by dividing by 365.25 equals 2,168.4 calendar years.

Subtracting 168 [the year the prophecy commenced under Antiochus] brings us to the year A.D. 2000. Now consider, in order for the *sanctuary to be cleansed* by Jesus Christ, as this prophecy indicates—the Jews would have to be in control of the Temple Mount! It is difficult to discern what God considers as "the sanctuary" in this verse, whether it is a rebuilt Temple or Jerusalem itself. However, the event that occurred in 1967 must be highly significant!

TRIGGERS THE GREAT TRIBULATION

Thus far we have seen that the *Abomination of desolation* will trigger the Great Tribulation, but we have not speculated as to what it could be. From (Matthew 24:14), we can conclude that the Abomination of desolation did not occur in 168 B.C. when Antiochus Epiphanes desecrated the Holy of Holies with swine's blood, took away the sacrifices, and therefore polluted the sanctuary as some believe. Jesus Christ spoke in around A.D. 31 and He said it did not yet occur!

We can also conclude from what we have just proven in the scriptures—that Titus could not have fulfilled this event in A.D. 70 when he invaded Jerusalem. Obviously, Christ has not returned, the "Two Witnesses" did not come on the world scene, and the Great Tribulation has never occurred!

In Jesus' own words He tells us that just after the Great Tribulation, He would return. The Great Tribulation would be one of the things that would occur just before His Coming. Let's read this account:

> **And as he sat upon the mount of Olives, the disciples came unto him privately, saying, tell us, when shall these things be? and what shall**

> be the sign of thy coming, and of the end of the world? (Greek—age Matt. 24:3). *When ye therefore shall see the abomination, spoken of by Daniel the prophet stand in the holy place*, (whoso readeth, let him understand). Immediately after the tribulation of those days shall the sun be darkened, and the moon shall not give her light, and the stars shall fall from heaven, and the powers of the heavens shall be shaken: *And then shall appear the sign of the Son of man in heaven:* and then shall all the tribes of the earth mourn, *and they shall see the Son of man coming* in the clouds of heaven with power and great glory (Matt. 24:15,29,30).

Since Christ returns to *resurrect* the "Two Witnesses" (Rev. 11:15), who will have been killed by the "Beast" power (Rev. 11:17), which brings about the Great Tribulation—we can safely conclude that the Great Tribulation has not yet occurred!

Continuing this fascinating scenario, let's notice what the "False Prophet" does. He exalts himself above all that is called God. The "little horn" does the same thing (Dan. 8:11, 23-25), as does the "king of the North" (Dan. 11:36).

The "king of the North" comes to his end in Palestine in the last days and none shall help him (Dan. 11:45). The "little horn" comes to his end in Palestine when he stands up to the Prince of princes [Christ] (Dan. 8:25). The "False Prophet" comes to his end when he makes war with Christ (Rev. 13:5-17; Dan. 7:26; 8:17,19; 9:26; 11:40; 12:4,9,13).

And so, we see that the "little horn", "king of the North" and "False Prophet" are one and the same beings! He will perform false miracles (11 Thess. 2:9; Dan. 11:28).

This charlatan will take away the sacrifices and then set up the Abomination that makes desolate (Dan. 12:11). But this "great pretender" certainly could not do this if the "Two Witnesses" were in power in Jerusalem—for they would strike him dead (Rev. 11:5). The "Two Witnesses" may therefore only be killed in Jerusalem, not that they preached there the entire 3

THE RESTORATION OF ISRAEL

1/2 years of their ministry.

THE "HOLY PLACE"

The Greek word used for "holy" in (Matthew 24:15) is "hagios" which means sacred, pure, blameless, or religious. The Greek word used for "place" is "topos" from which our modern word "topography" is derived. It simply means locality. When Christ said, **"when ye therefore see the Abomination stand in the "holy place"**, He was simply referring to a "religious locality."

By comparing Luke's account with Matthew's, we see that the Abomination will be the city of Jerusalem [the religious locality] surrounded by Gentile armies ready to make it a desolation (Lk. 21:20-24). Jerusalem will be trodden down of the Gentiles for 3 1/2 years as already noted. Such idol-worshipping Gentile armies will certainly be something that can be *seen*, and loathsome or an *abomination!*

Notice that the "king of the North", who takes away the daily sacrifice during the time of the end and pollutes the sanctuary—places the abomination that makes desolate [with arms—or armies] (Dan. 11:31).

Many have thought that the Abomination would be a statue, or even the "False Prophet" standing in the Temple or "holy place" in the Temple from this context. This is concluded from the belief that a "False Prophet" will someday *sit* in the Temple of God (11 Thess. 2:4). Although this may indeed happen, one cannot receive this revelation from the Greek in which we have just examined!

THE GREEK WORD "NAOS"

If Matthew wanted to refer to a *literal* Temple in describing the "holy place"—he could have used the Greek word "Naos" which he did use in describing the literal Temple, then in existence in (Matthew 26:61; 27:40,51). But Matthew chose to use the words "hagios topos"; meaning "religious locality" instead.

Matthew could also have used the Greek word "hagion",

in which the apostle Paul used in describing the literal "Holy Place" of the Temple in (Hebrews 9:12,24,25,39). This is the only place this particular Greek word is used in the New Testament!

The apostle Paul used the Greek word "Naos" in (11 Thessalonians 2:4) to describe *where* the "False Prophet" would sit. Notice: **"And he shall sit in the Temple [Gr. *Naos*] of God shewing himself that he is God."**

We have already seen where Matthew uses this word in describing a *literal* Temple, but the apostle Paul uses this same word in a *spiritual* sense in referring to Christians as the temple [Gr. *Naos*] of God in (1 Cor. 3:16-17). The apostle John also used this Greek word in a *spiritual* sense in (John 2:19-21). John used the Greek word "hieron" in describing the *literal* Temple in (John 2:14,14; 7:14).

If the apostle Paul wanted to describe the Temple the False Prophet sits in as a *literal* Temple in (11 Thess. 2:4), he could have used the Greek word "hieron" which is used 71 times in the New Testament in referring to a *literal* Temple. Paul could have used the Greek word "hagion" as he did in (Hebrews 9), instead of the Greek word "Naos" which can have either a *physical* or *spiritual* meaning.

How then can we know if Paul was referring to a *literal* or *spiritual* Temple? (11 Thess. 2:4).

To complicate matters further, the Greek word for "sits" in (11 Thess. 2:4) is "kathizo" which means "a seat" or perhaps "office." This same word is used in (Matt. 19:28; 20:21; 23:2; and 25:31), in a *spiritual* sense.

Paul could be describing the "man of sin" as sitting in a "seat of authority" in a Temple or Church—the false church!

Thus far, we have attempted to show that you cannot prove conclusively, that a *literal* Temple has to be built in Jerusalem—before the second coming of Jesus Christ by the Greek word "Naos." Although many may be correct in their assessment, they have done it erroneously using this Greek word.

THE RESTORATION OF ISRAEL

THE GREEK WORD "SKENE"

Now focus your eyes on (Revelation 13:6) where the False Prophet *blasphemes* against God's tabernacle, notice:

And he opened his mouth in blasphemy against God, to blaspheme his name, and his tabernacle (Gr. *skene*).

The Greek word used in this verse for Tabernacle is *skene* and means a tent, or cloth hut, habitation or tabernacle—and is used solely in the New Testament in referring to a *literal* Tabernacle. See (Acts 7:44; Heb. 8:5; 9:6,8,21), where this same Greek word is used.

If the apostle John wanted to refer to a *spiritual* Tabernacle he could have used the Greek word *Skenos* as did the apostle Paul in (11 Cor. 5:1,4).

From this, it seems that a *literal* Tabernacle could be built, but *not* necessarily a Temple.

Therefore, the Greek word "Naos" could refer to a *literal* Tabernacle or Temple in (11 Thess. 2:4 and also in Rev. 11:1,2).

We cannot even conclude that a *literal* Temple is implied from (Daniel 11:45), in speaking of the "king of the North" setting up his palace in Jerusalem in the last days. The Hebrew word used for "Palace" is "Appenden" which means a pavilion, palace, or tent, not necessarily a Temple.

Conclusively, a *literal* Temple is not needed in order for the sacrifices to be started and taken away for 1150 days, and the Abomination of desolation [Armies surrounding Jerusalem] be set up. The Jews were sacrificing once before without a Temple (Ezra 3:1-6), when there was only a Tabernacle!

THE SANCTUARY

Daniel 8:13 and 11:31 speak of the time sequence after the sacrifices are taken away. This is when the Abomination of desolation set up—the *sanctuary* is polluted and then is cleansed.

The Hebrew word used for *sanctuary* in this verse is "miqdash"—which has the same meaning as the Greek word Paul used in (Hebrews 9) as "hagion." This word refers almost exclusively to the *literal* Tabernacle or Temple. The word is particularly used in describing the "Holy of Holies", whether of the Tabernacle or Temple, and can mean a "holy place", "hallowed place", or "sanctuary." This Hebrew word is used throughout the Old Testament in reference to the holy sanctuary of God (Ex. 25:8, 36:1-6; 16:33).

This word is used in (Daniel 8:11; 11:31, and Leviticus 4:12). The other Hebrew word used for *sanctuary* is "qodesh" and has the same connotation as "miqdash." It is used in (Daniel 8:13,14 and Exodus 36:1).

We have just given the prophecies (Dan. 11:31; 8:13) that deal with the end-time, in which the sacrifices are taken away by the "False Prophet." When this occurs, the Abomination of desolation is set up, and the Sanctuary is polluted. But could this be a *spiritual* Sanctuary?

NOT A SPIRITUAL SANCTUARY

Turn to (Daniel 8:11) where we read more about the sanctuary the "little horn" will cast down:

Yea, he [the little horn] magnified himself even to the prince of the host, and by him the daily sacrifice was taken away, and the place of his *sanctuary* was cast down.

The margin in the *King James Version* provides an alternative rendering of this verse. Instead of "by him" meaning the "little horn"—it has "from him"—meaning the Prince of the host or Christ. The original inspired Hebrew can be translated both ways into English. Either translation is correct.

But notice what this scripture says! The daily sacrifice is to be cast down! Now consider: If the daily sacrifice is, as some believe, the daily work of Jesus Christ in heaven, then a mortal man—the "little horn"—would have power to intervene in heaven and stop the work of Jesus Christ!

Further, if the "sanctuary" were a spiritual one in heaven, he would have the power to "cast down" the sanctuary—the very throne of God in heaven! This would be absurd!

No man can stop the work of the living God in heaven or earth! No human being or even Satan himself can cast down the throne of God and profane His Holy Sanctuary!

Since this cannot be referring to God's Sanctuary in heaven, the only other *spiritual* explanation is that it is referring to Jerusalem itself as God's Holy Place, or dwelling place. But if this were true, "why does Daniel distinguish the City of Jerusalem from the *Sanctuary* as two separate entities?" (Daniel 9:26).

Furthermore, "how could a sanctuary be cast down unless it first exists?" Another question we must ask is, "If what Antiochus did was a *type* of the coming Beast, then he must do similar things—otherwise, what is the significance of the *types?* For Antiochus to be a true *type*, it would seem apparent that a literal Temple must be built with a sanctuary and sacrificial system.

A PROPHETIC ROSEBUD UNFOLDED

The prophecies we have just examined will occur just prior to Jesus Christ's second Coming. Since Jesus has not yet returned—they have not yet occurred! The sacrifices will have to start, and then stop for 1150 days, then the Abomination of desolation [Jerusalem surrounded by invading hostile armies will occur].

A *Sanctuary* will have to exist other than in a spiritual sense to be polluted! It is true that a temporary Tabernacle would suffice to fulfill this prophecy—but it is hardly probable that the Jews would settle for anything less than a permanent structure. They were not satisfied with a temporary Tabernacle when they finally settled in their promised land—and they would not be satisfied with a Tabernacle now!

The Jews have regained the promised land, and have said, **"as it was one generation from David to Solomon in building the Temple, so it will be with us."** Only time will tell!

JEWS HAVE HOPE

Ask any Jew today why they have not started sacrificing, and he will tell you because there is no Temple! Someday more than likely, a Jewish Rabbi will pick up the book of Haggai and read, **"The time has come, the time that the Lord's house should be built" (Hagg. 1:2).** They will believe the reason the nation of Israel hasn't been blessed by God is because they have not built Him a Temple (Hagg. 1:5-15).

Thus far we could say that all the prophecies could be fulfilled with the construction of a *literal* Tabernacle. Just before Christ's second Advent, the sacrifices could start and stop for 1150 days without a Temple. The *Abomination of desolation* could be set up triggering the Great Tribulation. The sanctuary could be polluted in a Tabernacle and *cleansed* upon the return of Jesus Christ.

We read in (Malachi 3:1) that Jesus, **"..shall suddenly come to His temple..."** The Hebrew word here is "heykal" and refers to a large public building, such as a palace or temple according to *Strong's Concordance*. This could also have a *dual* meaning in that Jesus will come for His *spiritual* Temple (the Church). The Jews understood this in a literal sense to refer to a Temple!

Whether Christ comes to a Tabernacle or Temple, only God knows for sure, but it does seem logical that He will return to a *literal physical structure*. While in the flesh, Jesus cleansed the Temple twice. He did it at the beginning of His ministry (Jn. 2:16) and at the conclusion (Mk. 11:15). It makes a lot of sense that Jesus would do it for one *final* time upon His return!

Now here is an amazing statistic!

The date of the destruction of both Solomon's Temple and the second Temple was 656 years apart on the tenth day of Ab, in the Jewish calendar!

Could it be that a future Temple existent during the Great Tribulation will be *cleansed* on the same date in the future?

This Temple may in fact be destroyed by the returning Jesus Christ to the mount of Olives. The mount of Olives stands just east of the Temple site and could destroy the Temple from its imminent earthquake (Zech. 14:3-4).

Who would have guessed 100 years ago that the Jews would be back in their homeland? And who now would believe

THE RESTORATION OF ISRAEL

that a Temple will be built in Jerusalem? On the surface, it may look bleak—but then, if it's God's will—it will be done!

THE MILLENNIAL TEMPLE

The description of the Millennial Temple is described in the book of Ezekiel in (chapters 40-48). There are many who think this vision was of something *spiritual*—not of something *physical* that would someday *literally* happen. However, there is more reason to believe this vision represented what is to become REALITY as we shall see.

It is noteworthy that in all the description of this Millennial Temple, there is no mention of an Ark, Mercy Seat, Veil, Cherubim above the Mercy Seat, or Tables of Stone. The only article of furniture described is the table or altar of wood (41:22). This table corresponds to the table of Shewbread, which envisions communion or fellowship with God.

Undoubtedly, the reason for a lack of Temple furniture has repercussions of Israel's repentance, as divine grace has been exercised in restoring the *prodigal nation* to God.

This Millennial Temple is roughly the general plan of Solomon's Temple with its furnishings, courts, and arrangements—but much, much larger in size!

THE RESTORATION OF ALL THINGS

The fact that this Temple and the city would be as large as the whole of present day Judea, west of the Jordan—makes most Bible scholars believe this proves the vision therefore represented a spiritual Temple, rather than have a literal interpretation. Some claim that the Millennium is the "restoration of all things", and this is not the right proportions for restoring the old Temple of Solomon!

It is true the Millennium is the restoration of all things (Acts 3:21). However, what these advocates fail to realize in their assessment of this Temple—is that God is *not* restoring this Temple to characterize Solomon's Temple—rather what Solomon's Temple represented! The Temple was *patterned* after the Tabernacle (which the garden of Eden was a *prototype).*

THE LEVITICAL SYSTEM RESTORED

One of the problems accompanying the *literal* interpretation of the Old Covenant presentation of the Millennium is the interpretation of (Ezekiel 20: 40-41; 43:18; 46:24; Zechariah 14:15; Isaiah 56:6-8; 66:21; and Jeremiah 33:15-18)—which all speak of the restoration of a Levitical priesthood and sacrificial system during the Millennium.

In (chapter 48:22-34) of Ezekiel, we read where the Levitical priesthood and the sacrifices, will once again be RESTORED during Christ's *rulership* on earth (Ezek. 43:18-27; 45:18-25). In (Ezekiel 43:19), we read of the re-institution of the Levitical order of the sons of Zadok who are set aside for a priestly ministry.

Concerning the line of Zadok, Grant informs us:

> **Zadok fills a prominent place in the history of Israel, being high priest in David's and Solomon's reigns. He remained faithful to David during Absalom's rebellion, and with Nathan the prophet espoused the cause of Solomon when Adonijah sought to secure the throne. David being of one mind with them instructed Zadok to anoint Bathsheba's son (1 Kings 1:26, 32-45). Zadok thus stands as representative of the priesthood in association with the king of God's choice, and with the kingdom as established by Him in David's seed—type of Christ (F.W. Grant, *The Numerical Bible*, IV; 270).**

West keenly observes of the Temple furniture in the Millennial Temple:

> **There is no Ark of the Covenant, no Pot of Manna, no Aaron's rod to bud, no Tables of the Law, no Cherubim, no Mercy-Seat, no**

THE RESTORATION OF ISRAEL

> Golden Candlestick, no Shew-bread, no Veil, no unapproachable Holy of Holies where the High Priest alone might enter, nor is there any High-Priest to offer atonement to take away sin, or to make intercession for the people. None of this. The Levites have passed away as a sacred order. The priesthood is confined to the sons of Zadok, and only for a special purpose. There is no evening sacrifice. The measures of the Altar of Burnt-Offerings differ from those of the Mosaic altar, and the offerings themselves are barely named. The preparation for the Singers is different from what it was. The social, moral and civil prescriptions enforced by Moses with such emphasis, are all wanting (Nathaniel West, *The Thousand Years in Both Testaments*, p. 493).

The very center of the whole Levitical system revolved around the Day of Atonement, with its ritual of the high priest sprinkling the blood of the goat on the Mercy Seat in the Holy of Holies. However, it is highly significant, that the Temple furniture [Ark and Mercy Seat] including the high-priest himself, which made this important ceremony possible—are omitted in the future house of God!

This only goes to prove that the very absence of these necessary parts that made this a very special day in Israel's history—[including sacrifices] will not be the re-establishment of Judaism.

These sacrifices will be done not looking forward to Christ's sacrifice—but rather *commemorating* it. These sacrifices will be as "gifts" being offered to a King—even as presents are given to dignitaries today!

SACRIFICES REINSTITUTED

Concerning the millennial sacrifices as they parallel the Lord's Supper, as a *memorial* of Christ's death, Adolph Saphir

writes:
> ...may we not suppose that what was typical before the first coming of Christ, pointing to the great salvation which was to come, may in the kingdom be commemorative of the redemption accomplished? In the Lord's Supper we commemorate Christ's death; we altogether repudiate the Popish doctrine of a repetition of the offering of Christ; we do not believe in any such renewal of the sacrifice, but we gratefully obey the command of Christ to commemorate His death in such a way that both an external memorial is presented to the world, and an outward and visible sign and seal given to the believing partaker (*Christ and Israel*, p. 182).

Burlington B. Wale helps us to better understand the meaning of these *symbolic* symbols:

> ...the bread and wine of the Lord's supper are, to the believer, physical and material symbols and memorials of a redemption already accomplished on his behalf. And this will be the case with the reinstituted sacrifices at Jerusalem, they will be *commemorative*, as the sacrifices of old were anticipative. And why should they not be? Was there any virtue in the legal sacrifices which prefigured the sacrifices of Christ? None whatever. Their only value and meaning was derived from the fact that they pointed to Him. And such will be the value and meaning of those future sacrifices which God has declared shall yet be offered in that future temple. Whatever the difficulty the reader may imagine in the way of the accomplishment of the prediction, it is sufficient for us that GOD HAS SAID IT (*The Closing Days of Christendom*, p. 485).

Finally, many reject this interpretation of the millennial sacrifices believing that such a "bloody" system would be in retrogression. However, let us simply say that if God planned such a *memorial* system of our Savior Jesus Christ—it can no more be a retrogression to the "weak and beggarly elements" than the Passover *symbols* of the bread and wine *picturing* the shed blood and broken body of our Lord.

The Levitical system is to teach people the difference between the *holy* and the *profane* (Ezek. 44:15-24). Jesus will tabernacle [dwell] in the midst of His people during this time (Lev. 26:11; Zech. 8:3-8; Ezek. 43:7).

These "millennial sacrifices" could be performed to teach people DEATH! They will learn why they need a Savior!

The nations will also be taught the meaning of God's Sabbath (Ezek. 46:1), Feast Days (Zech. 14:16-19), and unclean (Ezek. 44:23,24). If any of the families of the earth fail to keep God's Feast days, they will not receive God's blessing of rain (Zech. 14:17).

The nation of Egypt will quickly learn this vital lesson (Zech. 14:18), and build God an *altar* to offer up sacrifices, notice:

> **In that day shall there be an *altar* to the Lord in the midst of the land of Egypt, and a pillar at the border thereof to the Lord...And the Lord shall be known to Egypt, and the Egyptians shall know the Lord in that day, and shall do *sacrifice* and oblation; yea they shall vow a vow unto the LORD, and perform it (Isa. 19:19-21).**

Remember, God's plan originally was that the nation of Israel be the "Light of the World." But Israel failed! God is now *restoring* that responsibility upon Christians, who will eventually teach the nations on earth! The same government that Lucifer failed to enact!

The Millennial Temple, like all of God's *physical patterns*—will represent something yet to come. And that is

JEWS HAVE HOPE

God's *final* completed spiritual Temple, "New Jerusalem" where a physical Temple is no longer needed!

BACK TO EDEN

As previously noted, the Millennium will be the RESTORATION of all things! It is only fitting that in the place where mankind sinned, and went away from their God and Creator—God and mankind should be *reconciled* together once again!

The Garden of Eden was probably located in present day Jerusalem, according to the Jewish historian Josephus (Josephus, *Antiquities,* I,i,3). Therefore, the restoration of Jerusalem during the Millennium may be like the Garden of Eden! Here is further evidence of this from scripture: **"For the Lord shall comfort Zion, He will make her wilderness like *Eden*, and her desert like the *Garden of the Lord*..." (Isa. 51:3).**

More *analogies* to Eden are found in the book of Ezekiel. Starting in (verse 35) of chapter 36, he declares: **"And they shall say, this land that was desolate is become like the *Garden of Eden*; and the waste and desolate and ruined cities are become fenced, and are inhabited."** Observe, this is when Israel gets a "new heart" (Ezek. 36:26-28). Eden was "the Garden of God" (Ezek. 28:13).

That's why the Millennial Temple will be prodigious compared to Solomon's Temple—for Solomon's Temple was *patterned* after the Tabernacle, which the Garden of Eden was the physical *archetype.* Here, God is *restoring* all things back to where they were from Creation—not since Solomon!

THE GLORY OF GOD TO REAPPEAR

The Millennial Temple is described in the last nine chapters of Ezekiel and is to be built and engineered by Jesus: **"Behold the man whose name is *The Branch;* and he shall grow up out of his place, *and he shall build the temple of the Lord*...and *he shall bear the glory*, and shall sit and rule upon his throne; and he shall be a priest upon his throne" (Zech.**

6:12,13).

Once again as during Solomon's Temple—the GLORY of the Lord will be present! Here is what the Bible records of the glory of God in Solomon's Temple after it was dedicated:

> **The fire came down from heaven, and consumed the burnt-offering and the sacrifices; and *the glory of the Lord* filled the house. And the priests could not enter into the house of the Lord, because *the glory of the Lord* had filled the Lord's house (2 Chron. 7:1,2).**

Note the striking parallel to the Millennial Temple as Ezekiel was allowed to see it through a vision:

> **Behold, *the glory of the God of Israel* came from the way of the east: and his voice was like a noise of many waters: and the earth shined with his glory....And the *glory of the Lord* came into the house by the way of the gate whose prospect is toward the east. So the spirit took me up, and brought me into the inner court; and behold, *the glory of the Lord* filled the house (Ezek. 43:2-5).**

The Jews called the *glory* that filled Solomon's Temple, the *Shekinah* whose root word means "to dwell" or "to tabernacle." This *glory* was manifested as a "supernatural light" that *symbolized* our Lord's presence! This divine light became visible as it shown between the Cheribim over the Mercy Seat and the Ark.

There is a remarkable prophecy in the New Testament that uses the Greek equivalent of *Shekinah* to show the *symbolic* meaning to Christ as *dwelling* among His people. This prophecy is found in John 1:14: **"And the Word was made flesh, and *dwelt* [Gr. shekinize] among us, (and we beheld his glory)."**

The "Seventy Weeks" prophecy of (Daniel 9:24-27), promises these blessings to the nation of Israel: 1) to finish the transgression (of Israel's punishment for violating God's land Sabbaths), 2) to make an end of (Israel's) sins, 3) to make reconciliation for iniquity, 4) to bring in everlasting righteousness, 5) to seal up the vision and prophecy, and 6) to *anoint the most holy*.

The "everlasting righteousness" can only refer to the millennial Kingdom promised the nation of Israel. This was the goal and expectation of all the covenants and promises given to Israel, and will be fulfilled upon the King's arrival. This Kingdom can only be established when the Holy One or the Holy Place in the Millennial Temple is anointed. The Millennium will witness the reception of the Messiah by the nation of Israel, and will also witness the return of the *Shekinah* to the Holy of Holies!

Although there are many similarities to Solomon's Temple—there are also vast differences in the Millennial Temple. For example, there is no reference to, or need for the Ark of the Covenant—for the TRUE ARK will be in their midst! The same holds true for the high priest—for Jesus Himself will hold this esteemed office!

Of this glorious time, when the Eternal will *dwell* with the nation of Israel, Ezekiel records:

> **And they shall dwell in the land that I have given unto Jacob my servant, wherein your fathers have dwelt; and they shall dwell therein, even they, and their children, and their children's children for ever: and my servant David shall be their prince for ever. Moreover I will make a covenant of peace with them [the New Covenant]; it shall be an everlasting covenant with them: and I will place them, and multiply them, and *will set my sanctuary in the midst of them for evermore*. My tabernacle also shall be with them: yea, I will be their God, and they shall be my people. And the heathen shall know that I the LORD do sanctify Israel *when my sanctuary shall be in the midst of them for*

THE RESTORATION OF ISRAEL

evermore **(Ezek. 37:25-28).**

The regenerated nation of Israel will be a priestly nation, administering to the needs of the surrounding nations. Chapter 48 of Ezekiel describes the location of the twelve tribes as they surround the Millennial Temple, and Jesus [the Prince] will have His parsal of property (vs. 21).

Healing of the nations will take place from the trees (Ezek. 47:12; Rev. 22:2), as **"the name of the city from that day shall be THE LORD (*Jehovah-Shammah*) IS THERE" (Ezek. 48:35).** The Hebrew name *Jehovah-Shammah* implies, THE LORD IS THERE!

Chapter Fifteen

JEWS HAVE HOPE

Rebuilding the Temple at the present time has been a real possibility to some Jewish Rabbis. On August 2, 1968, Rabbi Sinai Halberstram, wrote the following excerpt in *The Jewish Press:*

> **When Jerusalem was in foreign hands the question always arose, 'When can we rebuild our beloved Temple?' Even more so does this question arise today when, with the blessing of the Almighty, Jerusalem has been returned to the caretaking of Jewish hands. The Temple grounds are again under the control of the descendants of those who stood upon Mount Sinai. When will the Temple be rebuilt?**

After the 1967 Six-Day war, *Time* magazine published an article entitled, "Should the Temple be Rebuilt?" Historian Israel Eldad commented in the *Time* article:

> **We are at the stage where David was when he liberated Jerusalem. From that time until the construction of the Temple by Solomon, only one generation passes. So will it be with us.**

The question of considering to build the Temple is now being discussed in Rabbinical circles as a recent quotation from an Israeli press indicates:

> In the Ministry of Religion a document concerning this was put forward, in which proposals from all over the world were collected. Religious activist, such as the military Chief Rabbi Schlomo Goren, are for the erection of the temple as soon as possible. There is some opposition, but everything urges towards the building of the temple.

The *Time* article continues to elaborate on the hope of the Jews to rebuild their Temple:

> Since the destruction of Jerusalem by the Romans in A.D. 70, Conservative and Orthodox Jews have beseeched God four times a week to `renew our days as they once were'—a plea for the restoration of the Temple. Although Zionism was largely a secular movement, one of its sources was the prayers of the Jews for a return to Palestine so that they could build a new Temple ...some Jews see plausible theological grounds for discussing reconstruction. They base their argument on the contention that Israel has already entered its 'Messianic era'. In 1948, they note, Israel's chief rabbis ruled that with the establishment of the Jewish state and the 'ingathering of the exiles' the age of redemption had begun (*Time*. June 30, 1967, p. 56).

As a result of the war with Iraq, fundamentalist Jews are interpreting the recent Gulf War as the catalyst that will speed up the building of the Temple according to a *Newsweek* article:

> Rabbi Leon Ashkenazi, a Jerusalem-based scholar, points to the war between Iraq and the allies as the fulfillment of many texts that speak of a conflict between Babylonia and Rome and Greece, and now this has happened. Equally important, says Ashkenazi, is the immigration of Soviet Jews, which is seen as a fulfillment of

> the 'ingathering' of the exiles prophesied in Hebrew scriptures. In this view, preparation for the Messiah began with the Balfour Declaration in 1917, followed by the 'unification' of Israel in 1967, *it will be completed in 1992 with the rebuilding of the Temple* (March 18, 1991, *"The Final Days Are Here Again," p. 55).*

JEWISH COMPLICATIONS

Although most Jews would like to build another Temple, very few are now contemplating it. One reason of course is that the Moslem shrine, the Dome of the Rock stands on the very location of the supposed ancient Temple site. It is a law of Israel that Jews will not destroy any sacred site of any religion. But, then again, as Israel Eldad said in the *Time* article: "it is of course an open question. Who knows? Perhaps there will be an earthquake."

The second complication to religious Jews, is that their law does not permit Jews on the Mount since the exact location of the Holy of Holies is not known. Only the high priest was permitted in the Holy of Holies, so Jews do not wish to even accidentally enter that location.

Presently, rabbinical law forbids Jews to even touch the Temple site. The reason for this is that Jewish Rabbis feel that the Messiah is the only one who can rebuild the Temple. This understanding is based on Old Testament scriptures that point to Israel's deliverance and regathering by the Messiah. Jews feel this is the Messianic age for this prophetic fulfillment.

Another obstacle in the way of reconstruction of the Temple, even if the Dome of the Rock were removed—is a viable and active priesthood. Since the days of the second Temple, the Levitical Priesthood has dissolved.

Still another problem in restoring Temple worship, is the Temple furniture. During the siege of Nebuchadnezzar in 606 B.C., some of the Temple articles were carried into the land of Shinar to the house of his god (Dan. 1:2). After seventy years of captivity, King Cyrus of Persia allowed the Jews to return to Jerusalem to rebuild their Temple in 536 B.C.

Cyrus strengthened their hands with vessels of silver and gold and precious things, including the vessels of the house of God which Nebuchadnezzar had brought forth out of Jerusalem and put

THE RESTORATION OF ISRAEL

in the house of his gods (Ezra 1:6-9). But notice, nothing is said of the most notable artifacts including the Ark of the Covenant! Where did they disappear?

More flack in the immediate reconstruction of a Temple is the thought of reestablishing the Old Testament sacrificial system. A Temple would mean sacrifice (11 Chron. 7:12) and many 20th century Jews are opposed to what they refer to as "primitive slaughterhouse religion."

WHAT COULD HAPPEN

What about it? Are these obstacles enough to stop the construction of another Temple? Let's ponder this question and use God's Word as our guide to consider what might happen!

First of all, let's find out what will happen! Despite Jewish objection—sacrifices will start in Jerusalem once again as already proven from the prophecies! This absolutely *must* happen in order to fulfill prophecy!

But where would the Jews get a Temple priesthood from to officiate during animal sacrifices? Only the Levites could officiate in the Temple! Are there any known descendants of Aaron today?

According to the *Jewish Encyclopedia,* article "Cohen", it states that Jews named Cohen [Heb. priests] as well as Levy, Levine, etc. [Levites] are direct descendants of the priestly line. They are the ones chosen to read scripture in the synagogues and officiate at Jewish functions today!

For a number of years now, certain Jews have been undergoing preparation and education for Temple Mount service, should that become a reality. A training program of priests at Yeshivah Ateret Hacohanim is preparing priests for temple service. The Temple Institute has been doing research on ninety-three of the sacred vessels and garments described in the Bible.

Other groups are studying priestly ritual and the manufacturing of priestly garments. The "Jerusalem Temple Foundation", headquartered in Jerusalem, explains in their brochure of their continual commitment to archaeological expiditions, preservation of the Holy Places in Israel, and their restoration in connection to the Temple Mount.

So sincere are the efforts of some orthodox Jewish organizatioins, that efforts to instill the "Ashes of the Red Heffer" are already in place. According to the Talmud, the "Ashes of the Red Heifer" are

JEWS HAVE HOPE

needed to cleanse the Temple Mount and priesthood from sin. According to the Mishneh, there have been only seven occurences throughout Israel's history in which the "Ashes of the Red Heifer" have ever been burned.

The Red Heifer is a very rare animal, and that makes it a "pure" sacrifice without "blemish" symbolizing our Savior Jesus Christ! However, most cattle have some coloring, and therefore are imperfect for this particular sacrifice. On October 16, 1989, *Time Magazine* stated that the chief Rabbi of Israel sent a team of scientists to Europe to obtain frozen embryos of a pure breed of Red Heifers, to raise on an Israeli cattle ranch in hope of obtaining a pure Red Heifer!

Should animal sacrificing start once again as prophecy says it must—conceivably the priestly garments of the Levitical system could be worn by contemporary descendants of Aaron known as Cohen's and Levy's!

Granted that sacrifices will start and a Levitical officiating system through the Cohen and Levy families will be formed—what would precipitate a change in Jewish thinking to start the so-called "primitive slaughterhouse sacrifices" without a Levitical priesthood once again?

THE ENSIGN OF THE ARK

The HEBREW word *nes* as translated into our authorized Version, means *Ensign, Banner, Standard* and *Pole*. It can mean a flag or object *symbol* of God's presence. This word *nes* is used symbolically to describe Christ as an ENSIGN in (Isaiah 11:10-12).

It is used to describe the *crucifixion* and *resurrection* of Christ *symbolically*, as the "pole" on which Moses raised the fiery serpent in the wilderness.

The Ark is a *nes* and is a *symbol* of Christ's atoning sacrifice for mankind's sins—even as the blood was sprinkled on the Mercy Seat by the high priest once a year on the Day of Atonement.

There is yet to arise a *nes* or ensign in Jerusalem in these last days that will again perform mighty miracles that accompanied the Ark. Undoubtedly, this would trigger many of the end-time prophecies!

THE RESTORATION OF ISRAEL

IN SEARCH OF THE LOST ARK

Most readers have seen the exciting movie entitled, *Raiders Of The Lost Ark*. Although highly fictional—it did raise the question, "What has happened to the holy Ark"?

Is the Ark lost, or has God preserved and protected it to fulfill many end-time prophecies? Does the Bible make mention of the Ark in prophecy?

Indeed!

There is a prophecy in the book of Jeremiah that speaks of the Ark in the near future:

> **And it shall come to pass, when ye be multiplied and increased in the land, in those days, saith the Lord, they shall say no more, The *ark of the Covenant* of the Lord: neither shall it come to mind: neither shall they remember it; neither shall they visit it; neither shall that be done anymore (Jer. 3:16).**

Now notice the time setting of this prophecy:

> **At that time they shall call Jerusalem the throne of the Lord: and all the nations shall be gathered unto it, to the name of the Lord, to Jerusalem; neither shall they walk any more after the imagination of their evil heart. *In those days the house of Judah shall walk with the house of Israel*, and they shall come together out of the land of the north to the land that I have given for an inheritance unto your fathers (Jer. 3:17,18).**

The only time the houses of Israel and Judah will be reunited is *after* Christ's intervention in world affairs! (Ezek. 37). This is a time when Jerusalem is called "the throne of the Lord."

The Ark may be in Jerusalem at this time—but may only be *visited* as a memorial! It will only be a memorial because the real Ark [Christ] will be present and RULING from Jerusalem! The Ark symbolizes the *mercy, power and authority* of Jesus Christ as pictured by the 10 Commandments and Aaron's rod that budded which it contained. It was used by Israel in battle to destroy their enemies! It had miraculous power!

But prior to Christ's return, it seems evident that the Ark would reappear or an *ensign* of the Ark in Jerusalem. God only does away with the *type* when the *antitype* appears!

After the Crucifixion, the *Veil* in the Temple was "rent in two" and the Holy of Holies no longer had any prophetic significance. But the Ark was not there! In the days of Christ, the Ark was not in the Temple that Herod had refurbished. In its place, **"a heavy double veil concealed the entrance to the most Holy Place, which in the second Temple was empty, nothing being there but the piece of rock called** *the foundation stone"* **(J.F.B; Eldersheim).**

Christ fulfilled many of the Temple *types* and symbols at His first Coming—but the Ark was not one of them!

THE ARK TO REAPPEAR?

The Mercy Seat on the Ark pointed to the atoning sacrifice of Christ's first Coming. This has erroneously led many to assume it's prophetic import has been fulfilled! But the Ark was a *type* of *many* symbols!

Besides a *shadow* of the redeeming sacrifice of Christ's blood, it was also a *symbol* of THE THRONE OF GOD, representative of Christ's *rule* upon the earth! This has not yet happened! Therefore, there *remains* a spiritual significance to the Ark in prophecy!

Would God Almighty take such painstaking care to preserve the Ark all through Israel's dismal history—then allow it to be lost before it's *symbolic* purpose was fulfilled by the reality?

In the eleventh chapter of the book of Revelation, we read concerning the true Ark:

> **And the seventh angel sounded; and there were great voices in heaven, saying, The kingdoms of this world are become the kingdoms of our Lord, and of his Christ, and he shall reign for ever and ever. And** *the temple of God was opened in heaven, and there was seen in his temple the ark of his testament* **(covenant): and there were lightnings, and voices, and thunderings, and a earthquake, and great hail (Rev. 11:15-19).**

Observe, this is the *true* Ark that the earthly was patterned after! However, this scripture shows that the *symbolism* of the Ark will only be fulfilled when Christ returns to set up His Kingdom upon the earth. Then will the throne of David and God's heavenly throne be restored to the earth!

It will be at this time that the houses of Israel and Judah will be re-united! This is when Jeremiah's prophecy will be fulfilled, as the Ark of the Covenant will no longer be needed—as Christ, the *antitype* will take it's place!

The Ark is the earthly manifestation of Christ leading His people into the *spiritual* Promised Land. Then, they will possess the land *forever* fulfilling the Covenant. Then, will the Kingdom be everlasting! The fulfillment of these prophecies is still future!

Because the Ark *symbolizes* Christ's *first Coming* and *second Advent* to set up God's throne on earth—it seems evident that the Ark will be in Jerusalem before the return of Christ!

Sacrifices are to start once again in Jerusalem before the end of this age. A Tabernacle or Temple will have to be built. During this time the Jews will have a "nes" or *object of some kind* that will help them unite as a people and awaken their consciences. The Ark may be in Jerusalem upon Christ's return as a *memorial* according to Jeremiah's prophecy. Could it be that the Ark will be the *nes* that brings about this end-time rallying of the Jews? Here is more scriptural proof that some kind of *nes* will be a SIGN for the conspiring nations against Jerusalem:

> **And he shall set up an *ensign* for the nations, and shall assemble the outcasts of Israel and gather together the dispersed of Judah from the four corners of the earth... But they shall fly upon the shoulders of the Philistines toward the west; they shall spoil them of the east together...And the Lord shall utterly destroy the tongue of the Egyptian sea; and with his mighty wind shall he shake his hand over the river...and make men go over dryshod (Isa. 11:12,14,15).**

Continuing in Isaiah 31:8,9:

JEWS HAVE HOPE

> Then shall the Assyrian fall with the sword...and he shall pass over to his strong hold for fear, and his princes shall be afraid of the *ensign* saith the Lord, whose fire is in Zion. Go through, go through the gates; prepare ye the way of the people; cast up, cast up the highway; gather out the stones; lift up a standard [Heb. *nes,* ensign] for the people. Behold, the Lord hath proclaimed unto the end of the world. Say ye to the daughter of Zion, Behold, thy salvation cometh; behold, his reward is with him, and his work before him. And they shall call them, The holy people, The redeemed of the Lord: and thou shalt be called, Sought out, A city not forsaken (Isa. 62:10-12).

Isaiah concludes:

> Thus saith the Lord God, Behold I will lift up mine hand to the Gentiles, and set up my standard [*nes*] to the people: and they shall bring thy sons in their arms, and thy daughters shall be carried upon their shoulders (Isa. 49:22).

As the nations of the earth gather to do battle against Jerusalem (Zech. 14:2), God's *ensign* will ward off the ensuing vultures of Antichrist temporarily. God tells His people: **"Set up the standard [ensign] toward Zion: retire, stay not: for I will bring evil from the north, and a great destruction"** (Jer. 4:6).

THE ETHIOPIAN CONNECTION

There is a *prophetic* reference to the nation of Ethiopia, that may indicate *where* the *ensign* of the Eternal may first arise. The eighteenth chapter of Isaiah contains this prophecy, verse three in particular: **"All ye inhabitants of the *world* and dwellers on the *earth*, see ye, where he lifteth an *ensign* on the mountains: and when he bloweth a trumpet, hear ye."**

Could an *ensign* or object be found in Ethiopia that would be so precious that it would be brought to Mount Zion in Jerusalem? If it were the Ark—surely the Jews would desire to build a Temple

THE RESTORATION OF ISRAEL

to house it!

The Ethiopian dynasty is the oldest known in history. It dates back to the Biblical days of King Solomon and the Queen of Sheba who was from Ethiopia! Jews have reigned in this country since that time.

Before his coup and exile, Emperor Haile Selassie had claimed the title as "The Lion of Judah." Why did Haile Selassie claimed this covetus title? Because he is an Ethiopian Jew! There are many Jews in Ethiopia today called *Falashas,* as distinguished from African Ethiopians.

Ethiopia definitely seems to have a role in future prophecies concerning an "ensign." Could this ensign be the Ark? It is very interesting that so many authoritative references on Ethiopia mention its connection with the Ark.

Here is what the *Encyclopedia Britannica* has to say:

It (Aksum) contains the ancient church where according to tradition the Tobot, or Ark of the Covenant, brought from Jerusalem by the son of Solomon and Queen of Sheba, was deposited and is still supposed to rest.

MORE EVIDENCE

Think about it! How could anyone have *stolen,* or *taken* the Ark when anyone who was not authorized to touch it died? Recall how Uzzah died when he tried to help steady the Ark when it was falling. And when 50,000 men of Bethshemesh looked into the Ark, and died instantly (1 Chron. 13:9-10).

This only proves that not just anyone could handle or carry the Ark!

Then how could it disappear?

According to the Bible, the Queen of Sheba heard of the fame of King Solomon and came to visit him (1 Kings 10:1).

Josephus, the Jewish historian, preserves an account of this famous visitor, "There was then a woman, queen of Egypt and Ethiopia...she came to Jerusalem with great splendor..." (*Antiquities,* book VIII, chapter vi, part 5).

Josephus preserves the name of the Queen of Sheba. He quotes from Herodotus and calls her "Nicaule" (*Antiquities,* book VIII, chapter vi, part 2).

JEWS HAVE HOPE

Any philologist would immediately recognize in the name Nicaule [Nikaule in Greek], a dilalectic form of the Egyptian Maekaure, the *prenomen* of Hashepsowe.

Perhaps the most striking proof that Hashepsowe visited Palestine may be found in the temple at Deir el Bahari. The walls of this temple enshrine the visit of the Queen to "God's Land."

The event occurred in her ninth year (988-987), the year Solomon completed his great palace. A complete listing of the Ethiopian Chronicles, entitled, *In the Country of the Blue Nile*, by C. F. Rey, London, 1927, lists Menelik I as Hashepsowe's successor (975-950).

THE REIGN OF MENELIK 1

The dynasty begins with the death of Hashepsowe in 975 B.C. and lists Menelik, the first ruler, who was the son of Solomon and an Egyptian princess.

As the mother of the Egyptian princess whom Solomon married is unrecorded, it is presently impossible to determine from history whether Hashepsowe was Solomon's mother-in-law or step-mother-in-law.

According to tradition, Hathshepsowe, who was also known as Makeda, adopted Menelik as her heir, since she had no son of her own.

Menelik thus was of the line of Sheba, which explains the racial intermixture of the Ethiopian royalty.

Author Grant Jeffrey writes on page 115 of his book, *Appointment With Destiny*, how the true Ark found a new home in Ethiopia:

> **The Ethiopian official national epic known as the *Glory of the Kings (Kebra-Nagast)* contains an amazing story which offers an explanation of what happened to the Ark of the Covenant. In addition of what happened to the Ark of murals which tell how the Ark and the tablets of the Law were taken to Ethiopia for safekeeping by Prince Menelik 1. The Queen of Sheba, his mother, had died and the prince prepared to leave Jerusalem to return twenty-five hundred miles to his native country to become its king.**

THE RESTORATION OF ISRAEL

Prince Menelik bore an uncanny resemblance in beauty and regal bearing to his father. King Solomon wanted to give him *a replica of the Ark* to take with him to Ethiopia because the long distance would prevent him from ever again worshiping at the Temple in Jerusalem.

According to the Ethiopian Chronicles, at the age of nineteen, Menelik's mother died, and being educated by the priests in the Temple, he became a strong believer in Jehovah.

Being a righteous Jew, Prince Menelik saw his father [Solomon] going back into apostasy, bringing in pagan practices into the house of God from marrying pagan wives.

Solomon desired that his son return to Ethiopia, 2,000 miles to the south, and be its Emperor. He told his son that he would make him a replica of the Ark to take with him so he would always be reminded of the faith in Jerusalem.

Solomon had a replica Ark made by his craftsman, that consisted of the identical materials and dimensions of the real Ark, as a going away present for his son. The only difference in the two Arks was that one contained the "glory of God", and the other one did not!

The following morning Menelik 1 and many of the faithful righteous priests, who despised the abominations of Solomon—switched Arks. They put the replica Ark in the Holy of Holies, and took the real Ark for safe keeping to Ethiopia, until the nation of Israel would repent, and turn to God once again!

Unfortunately, that never materialized, and the nation of Israel went further and further into idolatry, until they were finally taken captive by the Assyrians in 721 B.C.

THE UNDERGROUND TEMPLE

In a television interview in June of 1989, Grant Jeffrey stated his personal relationship with Crown Prince Steven Mengesha, the great-grandson of Emperor Halie Selassie, who lives in Toronto Canada.

According to Prince Mengesha, the Ethiopians took the Ark down to Ethiopia 3,000 years ago and built an underground Temple with 7 concentric rings. In the Holy of Holies, way underground beneath the ancient Church of Zion in northern Ethiopia—through a

JEWS HAVE HOPE

myriad of secret passages that are highly guarded, they claim to have the Ark of the Covenant.

Only "the guardian of the Ark" is allowed to enter the room where the Ark of the Covenant has been safely guarded for three thousand years. The "guardian of the Ark" is chosen at the age of seven from the priestly family, and remains in the seventh ring for the remainder of his life, never seeing the light of day! He is fed daily by the high priest, who can only enter the sixth concentric ring.

The Ark, according to Prince Mengesha is not on public display, but has been guarded by faithful black Ethiopian Jews in a kind of secret vatican in the historic Church of Zion of Mary in Aksum, northern Ethiopia.

In 1935, when Mussolini was about to invade Ethiopia, it is reported that a French underwriters insurance company in Paris wrote a contract to insure the Ark against war damage, as they moved the Ark for safe keeping.

The *B'nai B'rith Messenger*, a Jewish magazine stated in 1936 that the Ark was moved to prevent capture by Mussolini:

> **The Tablets of the Law received by Moses on Mount Sinai and the Ark of the Covenant, both said to have been brought to Ethiopia from Jerusalem by Menelik, the son of King Solomon and the Queen of Sheba, who was the founder of the present Abyssinian dynasty, have been removed to the mountain strongholds of Abyssinia for safekeeping because of the impending Italian invasion, according to word received here from Addis Ababa, the capital of Ethiopia.**

According to tradition, once Mussolini's army retreated from Ethiopia, the Ark was safely returned to the Holy of Holies in the underground Temple in Aksum. Approximately 10% of Ethiopia consists of black Jews called "Falashas," which means "exiles," who have their own Hebrew language.

In 1948, when the state of Israel was being created, 10,000 of these exiled Jews came to the capital, and asked if they could return to Israel to rebuild the Temple with the Ark of the Covenant!

In 1965, the father of Prince Mengesha went on national television, and stated publically that the Ark is in Ethiopia. He showed pictures of taking the royal family, including Queen Elizabeth II and Prince Philip to visit the church in Aksum in a three hour ceremony.

RECENT DEVELOPMENTS

In 1985, "60 Minutes" reported that rabbinical students at Yeshiva, or theological college, were being trained in the ancient priestly sacrificial system. Rabbi Goren, the head Rabbi at Yeshiva, stated in an interview with *Newsweek* in 1981 that "the secret of the location of the Ark will be revealed just prior to building the Third Temple."

Remember, the primary reason for building the tabernacle in the wilderness, and the Temple in Jerusalem— was to house the Ark of the Covenant (Ex. 25:22).

The Ark was what made Israel invincible in battle. When the army of Israel escorted the Ark of the Covenant around the city of Jericho seven times, the power of God caused the walls of the city to come crumbling down like a house of cards.

That's the reason why Mussolini and Hitler wanted it!

Another Jewish tradition believes that the Temple objects are buried under the Temple Mount where they were placed prior to Nebuchadnezzar's siege by king Josiah (*Mishnah Shekalim 6:1*).

Could it be that in the last days, when Jerusalem is surrounded by the hostile armies of Antichrist—that the Jews of Ethiopia will take the holy Ark to the mountain of Zion to fight for Israel? (Isa. 18). Only time will tell—but watch for an *ensign* out of Ethiopia to give inspiration to Israel in these last days!

Perhaps it will be the discovery of the lost Ark that will trigger the consciences of the Jewish people to want to house it in a rebuilt Temple?

Should this happen—sacrificing would definitely start! Faithful Jews the world over, as well as Christians would contribute to its building fund! Certainly the building of the Temple would be a political act of great significance. Jews the world over would identify with it—making Israel stronger, and the annexation of Jerusalem permanent!

According to a prophecy in the book of Maccabees, the physical Ark will one day reappear as Jeremiah prophesied. Prior to the destruction of the Temple by the Babylonians in the sixth century B.C.; according to Jewish tradition, Jeremiah prophesied that just before the end of the age, the Ark would be found and put in the Millennial Temple. Here is what 11 Maccabees 2:4 says:

> **It was also contained in the same writing, how the prophet, being warned by God, commanded that the tabernacle and the ark should accompany him, till he came forth to the mountain where Moses went up and saw the inheritance of God. And when Jeremias came thither he found a hollow cave: and he carried in thither the tabernacle, and the ark, and the altar of incense, and so stopped the door. Then some of them that followed him came up to mark the place: but they could not find it.**

Jeremiah's prophecy continues:

> **And when Jeremias perceived it, he blamed them, saying: The place shall be unknown *till God gather the congregation of the people and receive them to mercy.* And then the Lord will show these things, and the majesty of the Lord shall appear, and there shall be a cloud as it was also showed Moses, and he showed it when Solomon prayed that the place might be sanctified to the great God...and like a wise man, he offered the sacrifice of the dedication, *and the finishing of the temple* (11 Macc. 2:4-9).**

Will the Ark one day be found prior to our Lord's return and placed in an existing Temple? Watch for an *ensign* in Jerusalem!

A NEW ARCHAEOLOGICAL DISCOVERY

While many have wondered *how* a new Temple could be built in Jerusalem while the current Moslem Dome of the Rock occupies the traditional site of Solomon's Temple—new archaeological evidence may solve this dilemma!

Many Biblical scholars have speculated that a new Temple could only be built if an earthquake, bomb or war would destroy the most sacred Moslem shrine. However, recent evidence

THE RESTORATION OF ISRAEL

suggests that the original Temple site of Solomon's Temple may have been situated approximately 330 feet north of the Dome of the Rock! If this is so, there no longer would be a logistical problem to building a new Temple in Jerusalem!

Until recently, the most difficult problem facing archaeologists attempting to locate Solomon's Temple, was the lack of material artifacts such as walls, gates, and furniture. This was mainly due to a shortage of material evidence, as the renowned British archaeologist, Kathleen Kenyon put it: "Absolutely nothing survived of the temple built by Herod" (*The Bible and Recent Archaeology*, 1978).

The Moslem Dome of the Rock, constructed in A.D. 691 is the highest point of elevation on Mount Moriah. It is where Mohammed ascended directly into the heavens according to Moslem tradition. Until now, theologians and archaeologists had assumed the Temple had once been constructed on the site beneath the Dome of the Rock. Because of it's elevation, this was believed to be the most logical place to erect the Temple.

However, recent investigations by Professor Kaufman of the Hebrew University show evidence that the original Temple site may have been approximately 330 feet north of the Dome of the Rock. And interestingly, the new site is only three feet lower in elevation than the highest point of the bedrock beneath the Dome.

Perhaps the most significant find to date, was discovered in 1969 by a young archaeologist named James Fleming by a freak accident. It seems young Fleming was browsing around the Golden Gate, which is the most important and spectacular gate in Jerusalem. It is the only entrance to the city of Jerusalem from the East.

The night before, there had been a terrific down-pour, and suddenly, Fleming found himself falling into a deep hole beneath his feet. Further investigation revealed this hole to contain "five wedge-shaped stones neatly set in a massive arch spanning the turret wall" (BAR. Jan./Feb. 1983, p. 30).

Fleming realized, here were the remains of an earlier gate to Jerusalem, below the Golden Gate. But what could this possibly be?

Professor Kaufman believes this gate to be the original gate of Solomon's Temple—for Josephus states the eastern Temple enclosure wall was the only one that Herod did not rebuild (*War* V, 184-189).

If this is true, the present Golden Gate is in the right position for Temple entrance of the newly theorized site. According to Kaufman, the mid point of the Golden Gate is about 348 feet north of the East-West centerline of the Dome of the Rock. This would make for a more logical entrance into the Temple, as it would be directly in front of you, rather than facing you in a southwesterly direction.

This makes a lot of sense, when realizing the Temple was the focal point of Judeo life and is unlikely that God would inspire it's location off to the side of it's entrance. Assuming the old entrance to be correct [the Golden Gate] and the newly proposed Temple site correct, the entrance of the Golden Gate would line up perfectly with the new Temple location.

HEROD THE PHILANTHROPIST

Lawrence D. Sporty wrote an article in the December 1990 *Biblical Archaeologist,* supporting Professor Kaufman's find. According to Sporty, the first century Jewish historian Josephus wrote that Herod's Temple was adjacent to the Antonia Fortress, built on a rock 50 cubits high and dominated the Temple *(Wars of the Jews, bk.5,5,8)*.

The Antonia Fortress was located on the northwestern corner of the Temple Mount and housed troops that guarded the Temple. The Fortress had towers at its four corners, the largest at the southeast corner, 70 cubits [approximately 100 feet] from which the entire Temple could be seen (Bk. 5,5,8).

The purpose of the tower was to control the crowds from rioting as there was always a Roman legion stationed there with arms on the Jewish festivals.

King Herod not only rebuilt the Temple and Antonia Fortress, but he also built a public marketplace southward of the Temple in an effort to Hellenize the Jews. Herod's intended purpose of this commercial center was to bring the Jews under his control through Gentile mercantilism, trade and social activities.

Sporty writes of Herod's lavish expenditures:

> **Together with the many porticoes, the royal stoa, and other nearby administrative buildings, shops, palaces, and monuments built just outside the esplanade, the general area of the city became the**

> kind of civic center characteristic of a Greek agora or a Roman forum...This conflicted with the more traditional view of the sacred, unapproachable mountain in Jewish thought...Previously isolated, the Temple Mount was now surrounded by public structures and secular activities. The area became a public gathering place...a focus of conflict between the conservative elements of the Jewish population and Greco-Roman culture. Religious riots broke out repeatedly in this area (*Biblical Archaeologist*, Dec. 1990, p. 200-202).

Now exactly what is the significance of all this to the Temple location and current Dome of the Rock? Simply this! The Dome of the Rock is in the vicinity of Herod's expanded "marketplace" and not within the boundaries of the original Temple Mount!

It was this very commercialized area that insensitized our Savior when He drove the money changers out of the Temple area, who made His Father's house a market (Jn. 2:13-16).

A fascinating passage in the Mishneh Torah by Rambam quotes Jewish Talmudic writings from the time before the burning of the Temple in A.D. 70. These eyewitness sources declare that the Temple was not built dead center on the Temple Mount, the location now occupied by the Muslim Dome of the Rock. Rambam states that:

> ...the Temple Courtyard was not situated directly in the centre of the Temple Mount. Rather, it was set off farther from the southern [wall] of the Temple Mount than from [the wall of] any other direction. The reason is that worshippers usually entered and exited through the southern Hulda gates. They needed adequate room to congregate in that area. Rambam continued to quote sources that declare that the Temple itself was situated directly opposite the Eastern Gate in the northern part of the Temple Mount. 'These five gates were placed in a straight line from the Eastern Gate into the entrance hall of the Holy of Holies. These gates were the Eastern Gate [now sealed], the gate of the Chayl, the gate to the Women's Courtyard, the gate

> of Nicanor, and the gate of the entrance hall. Thus had the Temple been built on flat ground, one would have been able to see through all the gates at once' (*Mishneh Torah, Commentary Halachah 5 and 6*).

Considering this new theory, there still remains a problem for the New Temple to be built. True, it could be constructed 330 feet north of the Dome of the Rock—but many feel Arabs would hardly stand for two magnificent edifices standing adjacent to one another! However, researcher Grant Jeffrey does not agree:

> Many question the plausibility of the Jewish Temple being rebuilt side-by-side with the Muslim Dome of the Rock. While it certainly seems odd for us to contemplate this outcome, it would not be that unusual in the crowded, complicated religious architecture of Israel. The Tomb of Abraham in Hebron, for example, includes worship sites for both Muslims and Jews in the same building because both value the site. The Church of the Holy Sepulchre in Jerusalem has been shared by five antagonistic religious groups of Armenians, Ethiopians, Coptics, Catholics and Greek Orthodox priests and their competing services for almost seventeen hundred years. In addition, Jews now worship at the Western Wall while Muslims worship above them on the Temple Mount, less than a hundred yards away *Messiah, p. 176-177*).

How then will this issue be resolved and the Jews be allowed to rebuild their Temple on a new Temple site? How could a solution to this dilemma be solved in such a manner to satisfy both Jews and Arabs alike?

Perhaps a clue is found in a prophecy in the book of Daniel. There are prophecies that speak of a "False Prophet" who will one day enter into Jerusalem through peaceful means (Dan. 11:21); and with craftiness and deceit (Dan. 8:5), obtain the kingdom by flatteries (Dan. 11:21).

Could this "False Prophet" perform the most colossal human

achievement of the ages and accomplish what no-one else has been able to accomplish since A.D. 70? If such a miracle worker could persuade the Jews, Arabs and Christian world to allow the Temple's construction—He would be hailed as the all-time peace maker and given the Nobel peace prize!

We need to keep our eyes focused on the city of Jerusalem!

Chapter Sixteen

And he shall send his angels with a great sound of a trumpet, and they shall gather together his elect from the four winds, from one end of heaven to the other
—Matt. 24:31.

THE GATHERING OF "THE ELECT"

The expression "four corners of the earth" is used in several scriptures to describe the universal nature of this event (see Isa. 11:12; Ezek. 7:2; Rev. 7:1). It has the same connotation as "the four winds" (Matt. 24:31).

However, contrary to popular opinion, the verse in (Matthew 24:31) is not speaking solely of "a gathering into the air of the Church" as many suppose—but also of a *regathering* of the nation of Israel from captivity, who are about to perish in their land! God's prophet Isaiah marshals in impressive evidence of this event in Isaiah 27:12-13:

> **And it shall come to pass in that day, that the LORD shall beat off from the channel of the river unto the stream of Egypt, and *ye shall be gathered one by one, O ye children of Israel.* And it shall come to pass in that day, that the *great trumpet shall be blown*, and they shall come which were ready to perish in the land of**

THE RESTORATION OF ISRAEL

Assyria, and the outcasts in the land of Egypt, and shall worship the LORD in the holy mount at Jerusalem (see also Zech. 9:14).

Undoubtedly, the *trumpet* in this verse has a *dual* meaning to "physical Israelites" and "spiritual Israelites" (the Church)! In other words there will be *two* gatherings—one for physical Israel in captivity, and one for the Church! This seems to be indicative of the *two silver trumpets* our Lord instructed Moses to make for the *assembling* of the people (Num. 10:1-10).

Recall how the Feast of Trumpets is a *shadow* of the time when God is going to call on all men, particularly Israelites, to repent and to turn to *obey* Him.

The fall feast days *picture* how Jesus Christ will save all Israel! There will come a time when Jesus Christ will finish His passive work of purchasing many people unto God, and will begin a "new work" that will bring the remnant of Israel to repentance.

Leviticus 26 describes the curses for transgression of God's Law. Israel's trouble will begin with *famine* and *pestilence* and end with *captivity!* The second Seal, described in Revelation 6, initiates a time when peace will be taken from the earth and a great *sword* will be given. The trumpet blown through the land of Israel was a signal of impending war, a time to "gather the people" together for warfare. The Feast of Trumpets *pictures* warfare, the beginning of Jacob's trouble! (see also Zeph. 1:14-16; Zech. 1:16; Joel 2:1).

THE POURING OUT OF GOD'S HOLY SPIRIT UPON JERUSALEM

When the Day of Pentecost came starting the New Testament Church, the Holy Spirit was *poured* out upon many devout Jews dwelling in Jerusalem from every nation (Acts 2:1-5).

Many who observed the miracle of them speaking in their native tongues thought they were drunk, but the apostle Peter proclaimed:

...these are not drunken as ye suppose, seeing it is but the third hour of the day. But this is that which was spoken by the prophet Joel: And it shall come to pass in the last days, saith God, I

> **will pour out My Spirit upon all flesh and *your sons* and *your daughters* shall prophesy, and *your young men* shall see visions, and *your old men* shall dream dreams (Acts 2:15-17).**

Now realize, what happened on the Day of Pentecost A.D. 31, was merely a *type* of what will occur on a grander magnitude prior to Christ's return. Let's read a bit further to get the right time setting:

> **And I will shew wonders in heaven above, and signs in the earth beneath; blood, and fire, and vapour of smoke: The sun shall be turned into darkness, and the moon into blood, before that great and notable day of the Lord come (Acts 2:19,20).**

Realize also, that this speech of Peter's was a direct quotation from Joel's prophecy (Joel 2:28-32).

When was Joel's prophecy to occur? Just before Christ's return, after the 6th Seal as the sun is turned to darkness (Joel 2:10,11; 19,20; 3:15,16). It is the "Day of the Lord", which John depicts in Revelation as the pouring out of the final plagues.

Now to *whom* was Peter and Joel addressing? Let's read further of Peter's comments in the book of Acts, **"Ye *men of Israel*, hear these words..." (Acts 2:22)**. Peter continued his message declaring of the nation of Israel:

> **Ye are the children of the prophets, and of the covenant which God made with our fathers, saying unto Abraham, And in thy seed shall all the kindreds of the earth be blessed. Unto you first God having raised up his Son Jesus, sent him to bless you in turning away every one of you from his iniquities (Acts 3:25-26).**

Let's read more of Joel's prophecy to understand *who* God was speaking to, and *where* these end-time events will occur and *why!*

> **And it shall come to pass, that whosoever shall call on the name of the LORD shall be delivered:**

> for in mount Zion and in *Jerusalem* shall be deliverance, and in the *remnant* whom the Lord shall call. For behold, in those days, and in that time, when I shall bring again the captivity of *Judah* and *Jerusalem* (Joel 2:32; 3:1).

This is the time period known as "Jacob's trouble" when God will bring *again* the captivity of His people. It is a time when thousands of Israelites will fall by the *sword,* and be led away captive into all nations (Lk. 21:24). It is a time when God will gather all nations, and bring them down into the valley of Jehoshaphat for the battle of Armageddon (Joel 3:2).

Prior to that time, *sacrifices* will start in Jerusalem, but will then be cut off *from the house of the LORD* [a Temple] and the priests will mourn (Joel 1:9). But it is a time when God's Spirit will be poured out upon Jerusalem, and a remnant will be saved! The apostle Paul was well aware of God's intentions to save a remnant from Israel as he asked:

> **I say then, Hath God cast away his people? God forbid. For I also am an Israelite, of the seed of Abraham...God hath not cast away his people which he foreknew...even so then at this present time also there is a *remnant* according to the election of grace (Rom. 11:1-5).**

Paul then quoted (Isaiah 10:22,23) concerning salvation to a *remnant* of Israel: **"Esaias (Isaiah) also crieth concerning Israel, though the number of the children of Israel be as the sand of the sea, a *remnant* shall be saved" (Rom. 9:27).** This event of Isaiah's occurs prior to the 6th Seal (Isa. 12:10). Of this event Isaiah wrote:

> **Yet now hear, O Jacob my servant; and Israel, whom I have chosen: Thus saith the LORD that made thee, and formed thee from the womb, which will help thee; Fear not, O Jacob, My servant; and thou, Jesurun, [Jacob] whom I have chosen. For I will pour water upon him that is thirsty, and floods upon the dry ground:** *I will pour my spirit upon thy seed, and My*

THE GATHERING OF THE ELECT

blessing upon thine offspring.

Most definitely, all eyes will be focused upon Jerusalem and the many spectacular things God will do to it's inhabitants in the last days, as He pours out His Spirit upon the nation of Israel!

THE "REMNANT" "ELECT" "WOMAN" "144,000"

As we have finely divided the Word of God through progressive revelation, it has become apparent that God's plan is indeed far more intricate than we have imagined. And it should be apparent that the end-time scenario of events may indeed be quite different than we had first envisioned.

We have realized that God's mind is indeed higher than ours, and that every number, symbol, type, feast-day and name has deep spiritual significance.

We have learned that God's plan began with the Old Testament Church in the wilderness, and that when Israel *rebelled* against her husband, she was divorced!

God then began working with a new nation of people—*a holy nation* [the Church], consisting of both Jew and Gentile, when Christ came to the earth in human form. God gave over the right to rule in this age to the Gentile powers for 2520 years—the same time period that Israel would be punished for her sins!

Through the feast days, God revealed that He will make Israel a captive people because of her sins, and then *forgive* them and bring back a *remnant* (perhaps 10%) out of captivity! Then God will once again *restore the kingdom to Israel*!

The prophetic parables of Israel's history have revealed that God will once again *repot* or *restore* the nation of Israel, as He begins to graft them back into His Vineyard. God will *pour* out His Holy Spirit upon them just prior to Christ's return!

In the *types*, we have seen how a Levitical priesthood, sacrificial system, and most likely a Temple will once again be restored!

Clearly, *everything* points to, and focuses on the nation of Israel in the last days! It is where the sacrifices will begin, the Gentile armies will invade, the "Two Witnesses" will preach and die, the faithful will flee, the "False Prophet" will establish his headquarters, where Armageddon will occur and Christ will return!

THE RESTORATION OF ISRAEL

Perhaps we can now begin to clarify some of the terminology as to *who* represent the "remnant"; "elect"; "woman"; and the "144,000" as mentioned in end-time prophetic events.

Obviously, the *remnant* cannot represent the *woman* who is taken to a place of safety for 3 1/2 years, since the "remnant" are taken out of captivity. The remnant will consist of Israelite exiles being brought back "one by one", from the four corners of the earth to the promised land by Jesus Christ.

The conversion of the "remnant" will take place just prior to Christ's return, as He delivers them from their final captivity. Then Israel's Messiah will fulfill Daniel's seventieth week by "finishing their transgression", "make an end of their sins", "make reconciliation for their iniquity", "and bring in everlasting righteousness" (Dan. 9:24-26).

The "woman" cannot represent the 144,000, because she is protected for 3 1/2 years from the Tribulation, while the 144,000 go through the Tribulation, but are protected only from the seven last plagues. The 144,000 are *supernaturally* protected just after the 6th Seal, prior to the 7th Seal. The Tribulation begins on the 5th Seal.

AN "ELECTION" OF ISRAEL

What about the "Elect" Paul spoke of in (Romans 11), who were also a "remnant" of physical Israelites to receive salvation through grace?

What category of Israelites can they possibly represent? The entire chapters of (Romans 10 and 11) emphasize God's relationship with Israel, and how He wishes they would *repent* (10:21).

Paul is clearly speaking to flesh and blood descendants of Abraham's stock! Then Paul writes in Romans 11:5: "**..at this present time [Paul thought he was living in the end-time] also there is a *remnant according to the election of grace* that shall be saved!**

In (verse 7 of Romans 11), Paul calls this small group of *physical* Israelites that shall obtain salvation in the end-time an "election."

This "election" will go through the Tribulation, but will not bow down to the *image of the Beast*!

Notice the *duality* to what Paul describes, as happened in the day when seven thousand Israelites would not bow down to the "image of the Beast" (vs. 4).

Paul further elaborates as to *who* these "elect" are by saying the rest of them were blinded (vs. 7).

The apostle to the Gentiles is most certainly addressing the *blindness* of the majority of Israelites at this present time, except for a *remnant* that will have their eyes opened to God's truth!

In (verse 12), Paul declares *why* salvation was then offered to the Gentiles, and that God will once again graft Israel back into His Olive Tree once they believe (vs. 23).

Could it be that in these verses, God is *differentiating* "different groups" of physical Israelites that will eventually comprise His repoting and *rebirth* of the nation of Israel?

Most definitely the *remnant* returning from captivity and exile will be *physical* Israelites. And most definitely, Paul referred to the conversion of *physical* Israelites as "an elect" or remnant of grace during the start of the New Testament Church (Romans 11).

Now, *who* can these *sealed* 144,000 of Revelation 7 possibly represent?

The 144,000 have been clearly identified by the Bible as being from the tribes of Israel. Since Israel is *literal* here and the tribes are *literal,* it would also seem that the numbers would also be taken *literally.*

In his rebuttal to the Seventh-Day Adventists and other sects who interpret the 144,000 as representative of their faithful, H.A. Ironside writes:

> **All of these, however, overlook a very simple fact, which, if observed, would save them from their folly. That is, the hundred and forty-four thousand are composed of twelve thousand from each tribe of the children of Israel. There is not a Gentile among them, nor is there confusion as to tribe (*Lectures on the Revelation,* p. 124).**

The question arises as to whether the 144,000 of Revelation seven, is the same group as mentioned in Revelation fourteen. The 144,000 of Revelation seven appear to be *sealed* prior to the plagues of the 7th Seal as Christ returns, but go through the Great Tribulation. The 144,000 of Revelation fourteen, appear to be *sealed* at the "end" of the Tribulation, just before God's Kingdom is restored to the earth. They are called **"the first-fruits unto God and to the Lamb" (Rev. 14:4),** indicating that they are the "first harvest" of the Tribulation period that will populate the millennial earth.

From this, we can only make the observation that God is converting the world and the nation of Israel in stages.

ARE THE 144,000 OF REVELATION 7 AND 14 THE SAME?

Many believe the 144,000 of Revelation **7** are the same as the 144,000 of Revelation 14. They appear to be described in a similar way. Both appear to be sealed for protection just prior to the judgment of the seventh seal as Christ returns to the earth with plagues on those who worship the Beast and his Image.

The 144,00 of Revelation 14, *are not defiled with women for they are virgins,* meaning they have kept themselves pure from the defilements of sin as they keep the commandments of God (14:12).

The apostle Paul believed he was living in the end time and described a small group of *physical* Israelites that shall obtain salvation in the end-time as an "election" (Rom. 11:7).

Similarly, Paul further described a historical event that happened to the nation of Israel as he compared this "election" who will go through the Tribulation, but will not bow down to the *image of the Beast*!

Notice the *duality* to what Paul describes, as happened in the day when seven thousand Israelites would not bow down to the "image of the Beast" (vs. 4).

Ezekiel's account of the "writer's inkhorn" in which an angel sets a "mark" on the *forehead* of the faithful men who cry out for their holy city, also parallels the protection the 144,000 will receive, as they are sealed by a "mark" upon their foreheads by an angel (Ezek. 9:4; Rev. 7:3).

Paul further elaborates as to *who* these "elect" are by saying the rest of them were blinded (vs. 7).

The argument can be made that the 144,000 does not represent a literal number as the apostle saw a "great multitude, which no man can number" out of every nation. These people were redeemed individuals who had been made white in the Lamb's blood (vs. 14). Here again we find significance in the reference of the "Lamb" mentioned 4 times in Revelation 7 in association with the nation of Israel.

THE GATHERING OF THE ELECT

We have previously studied the meaning of the grain harvest of Pentecost (p. 194) as a *symbol* of the salvation process in God's plan. Reaping the harvest *pictures* bringing people into God's Kingdom (Matt. 13:24-30, 36-43; 24:3, 29-31; 1 Thess. 4:13-17).The first grain harvest was celebrated by the Feast of *Firstfruits* or Pentecost

The nation of Israel was to count seven Sabbaths [weeks] (Lev. 23:15) of 50 days after the *acceptance* of Christ (as the firstfruit of the grain harvest) that "two loaves" [in which preparation leaven had a part] became eligible to be lifted up and waved toward the heavens to be accepted at the end of the harvest.

After new grain was lifted up at the beginning of the harvest (representing Jesus as Savior) to be accepted by God, these loaves were also accepted at the end of the 50 days. But what could they possibly represent?

God Himself interprets the meaning of the wave-loaves in Leviticus 23:17: **"...they are the *firstfruits* unto the Lord."** Some find the two leavened loaves offered on Pentecost correspond to the two covenant *firstfruits*, or the two major groups of people God is working with—Old Testament Israel and the New Testament Church composed of Jew and Gentile.

The prophet Jeremiah symbolically referred to ancient Israel as "the firstfruits of his harvest" (Jeremiah 2:3). New Testament writers also referred to *Firstfruit*s for Christians in the New Testament. James says we are "a kind of firstfruits" (James 1:17-18). The 144,000 of Revelation 14 are those "redeemed from mankind as *firstfruits* unto God and to theLamb" (Rev.14:1-4). The apostle Paul also calls those first converted where he preached *firstfruits* (Rom.8:23,16:5; 1 Cor.16).

THE WOMAN AND THE MANCHILD

The exact identity of the "woman" of Revelation twelve is of paramount importance to the understanding of prophecy. But once again we have a bone of contention among several schools of thought.

One proclaims this "woman" to represent Old Testament Israel, while others believe her to be the New Testament Church. Some believe her to represent a system of teaching. The Catholics have seen the virgin Mary in her, and suppose this to represent her ascension into heaven. However, we might ask, other than motherhood, when did Mary ever fulfill the rest of this prophecy?

When was she persecuted, or flee into the wilderness for 1260 days?

Others, however, believe the parallel reference in (Revelation 12) is primarily to *spiritual Israel* (Gal. 4:26). Here we find that the New Testament Church is described as a woman. During the middle ages, God's Church literally went underground for 1,260 years from A.D. 554 to 1814 during the Roman persecution. Thus, the 1260 day persecution of (Revelation 12:6) is calculated as years, using God's day for a year principle.

Who then is right?

Let's read this very important prophecy, that promises protection during the Great Tribulation to those fortunate to be classified as "the woman." Starting in verse one of Revelation twelve we read:

> **And there appeared a great wonder in heaven; a *woman clothed with the sun, and the moon under her feet, and upon her head a crown of twelve stars:* And she being with child, travailing in birth, and pained to be delivered... and the dragon stood before the woman which was ready to be delivered, for to devour her child as soon as it was born. And she brought forth a man child, who was to rule all nations with a rod of iron: and her child was caught up unto God, and to his throne.**

At this point, most prophetic scholars believe the "woman" ready to deliver the manchild and crowned with 12 stars—represents ancient Israel whose seed produced Jesus Christ—the child to eventually rule all nations with a rod of iron. The dragon of course is Satan, who did try to devour [kill] Christ as soon as He was born—through Herod when he ordered all males under two years of age killed (Matt. 2:16).

Most dispensational writers believe that the woman in this passage represents the nation of Israel. There are a number of considerations which support this view. Gaebelein writes why this passage reveals that John is dealing with the physical nation of Israel:

THE GATHERING OF THE ELECT

> Revelation, chapters eleven to fourteen, leads us prophetically to Israel, Israel's land and Israel's final tribulation, the time of Jacob's trouble and the salvation of the godly remnant. The scene of the eleventh chapter is 'the great city, which spiritually is called Sodom and Egypt, where our Lord was crucified.' That city is not Rome but Jerusalem. The twelfth chapter begins a connected prophecy, ending with the fourteenth (*The Annotated Bible*).

F.W. Grant comments on Revelation 11:19: "The ark, then, seen in the temple in heaven is the sign of God's unforgotten grace toward Israel" (*The Revelation of Christ*, p. 126). Here then is revealed by context, that God is once again dealing with His chosen nation.

J. Dwight Pentecost summarizes the points of Israel's identity:

> **The use of the term *woman*.** Eight times the term *woman* is used in this chapter, and eight additional times the pronoun *she* or *her* is used in reference to the woman. We find this term used frequently in the Old Testament to refer to the nation Israel. It is used in Isaiah 47:7-9; 54:5-6; Jeremiah 4:31; Micah 4:9-10; 5:3; Isaiah 66:7-8. While the church is called a *bride*, or a *chaste virgin*, we never find the church referred to as a *woman*.
>
> **The name of the adversary.** The name *dragon* is used throughout the Old Testament to describe some particular adversary of the nation Israel. Inasmuch as this name is applied to Satan in this chapter, it must be because all those persecutors, who bore the name dragon, were only foreshadows of this great persecution that is to come through the instrumentality of Satan. The use of the name *dragon* in reference to the persecutor would identify the persecuted one as Israel from its past usages in the Word of God

303

(*Things to Come*, p. 288).

This prophecy then skips to the *resurrection* of Jesus Christ, and His bodily ascension to the throne of God in heaven.

That *the woman clothed with the sun, and having the moon under her feet and a crown of 12 stars upon her head* represents ancient Israel [Christ's mother] is made plain by the dream given to Joseph in (Genesis 37:9). Let's read it:

> **And he dreamed yet another dream, and told it his brethren, and said, Behold, I have dreamed a dream more; and, behold,** *the sun and the moon and the eleven stars* **made obeisance to me.**

In this dream and the previous dream (verses 5-8), Joseph saw that he would be the *ruler* over the other eleven *stars* or tribes; he himself being the twelfth star. Even his father Jacob agreed with the interpretation of this dream (verses 10-11).

H.A. Ironside gives his viewpoint concerning Joseph's dream:

> **But who, then, is this star-crowned, sun-robed woman, who has the moon beneath her feet? First, let me ask, 'Is there any other place in Scripture where we have the sun, moon and twelve stars brought together in a similar way? You will at once recall Joseph's dream. He beheld the sun, moon and elven stars making obeisance to him. He himself was the twelfth star. His father rightly saw in this a picture of all Israel with its twelve tribes...For immediately after this, Satan, again acting through the Roman Empire which is to be revived in the last days, turns upon the woman Israel and seeks to vent his wrath and indignation against her. But God prepares a place for her, and she is hidden in the wilderness'** (*Lectures on the Revelation*, **pp. 210, 212).**

Over and over again, God's Word describes the nation of Israel symbolically as a *woman* in travail-pain waiting to be delivered [by the Messiah]—see (Micah 5:2 and Isa. 66:7,8).

THE GATHERING OF THE ELECT

Israel is the "mother woman" that delivered Jesus, her Son. Israel's Son [Jesus], gave birth to the Church—not visa versa!

THE "CONVERTED WOMAN"

Clearly, the nation of Israel stands identified as *the woman clothed with the sun and having the moon under her feet and a crown of 12 stars upon her head.*

However, the Bible also describes God's unspotted Church as "spiritual Israel" or Zion and "the mother" of all Christians (Gal. 4:26; 6:16; Eph. 5:23-24; 30-32; Heb. 12:22).

Undoubtedly, (Revelation 12) is a *parallel* account of the happenings to both *physical* and *spiritual* Israel. Revelation 12 describes the beginning of Christ's Church and it's battle with it's adversary—Satan the devil down through the ages!

Who then is this "woman" that will be *protected* by God during the impending world catastrophe called the Great Tribulation? Is it Old Testament Israel who gave birth to Jesus Christ [the man child] through the seed of Abraham? Or is it the New Testament Church that has *now* been grafted into Israel?

We have already proven that God started to build His Church with an *ekklesia* [called out ones] of ancient Israelites. This was also a typical marriage of a husband and wife relationship. When Israel failed to keep their part of this marriage agreement—God divorced her and started to build an *ekklesia* composed of Jews and Gentiles.

Anyone who becomes a Christian [Jew or Gentile] can become a part of this New Covenant. This will also be a marriage relationship. Only when the ancient Israelites become Christians will they become part of this new contract!

God is starting His *New Covenant* with a *New Israel* or a *New Wife* or a New WOMAN! The New Testament Church is NOW God's espoused wife and the New Israel to be protected from the wrath to come (Rev. 3:10). However, the New Testament Church is composed of many different entities as we shall see, including converted Jews and Israelites in Jerusalem!

THE GRAFTING BACK OF ISRAEL

Sound Biblical exhortation tells us that in order to understand prophecy—we must let the Bible interpret itself! (11 Pet. 1:20).

THE RESTORATION OF ISRAEL

We must also realize that another *key* of understanding prophecy is the *duality* between Israel and the Church!

Now back to putting line upon line (Isa. 28:10-13) and allowing the Bible to interpret the identity of the "woman" in Revelation 12:

> **And there was war in heaven: Michael and his angels fought against the dragon; and the dragon fought and his angels [demons], and prevailed not; neither was their place found any more in heaven...And when the dragon saw that he was cast unto the earth, he persecuted the woman who brought forth the man-child (Israel). And the woman [who brought forth the man child] were given two wings of a great eagle, that she might fly into the wilderness, into her place, where she is nourished for a time, and times, and half times, from the face of the serpent (Rev. 12:12-14).**

By rightly dividing God's Word of truth (11 Tim. 2:15)—we have our answer. Physical Israelites will be led to a place of safety for a period of 3 1/2 years during the Great Tribulation!

But who can these Israelites be? They cannot represent the entire nation of Israel, for many prophecies speak of her punishment in tribulation as "Jacob's trouble." On the other hand, we know there is going to be 144,000 physical Israelites *protected* from the seven last plagues of God, who go through the Tribulation (Rev. 7). Clearly, these Israelites cannot represent the "woman" who escapes the Tribulation completely for a 3 1/2 year duration.

There can only be one remaining possibility—these are converted Israelites prior to the Great Tribulation! There is going to come a time as the apostle Peter declared, that God will pour out His Spirit upon the nation of Israel through a modern-day Elijah! Speculatively, this individual could represent one of the "Two Witnesses"—and he would begin "turning the hearts of Israel to their Father in heaven" (Mal. 4:6).

Perhaps this event will be a similar feat as occurred on the Day of Pentecost, when Peter proclaimed God's truth and 3,000 Jews were baptized into the faith (Acts 2:41). Historically, this miraculous event was only a *type* of what will happen in Jerusalem in the last days! Peter said that God will pour out His Spirit upon

THE GATHERING OF THE ELECT

Israel prior to the heavenly signs (Acts 2:17-21).

This will be the start of a "Jewish Church" in Jerusalem. Undoubtedly, many of these converts will "flee to the mountains" in observation of (Matthew 24:15,16), when they see Jerusalem compassed with armies (Lk. 21:20,21). However, many of these Jewish believers will be martyred by the invading "Beast" power in fulfillment of (Daniel 12:10; 11:35).

Because the "Two Witnesses" are killed in Jerusalem (Rev. 11:8), it makes a great deal of sense that this would be their prime area of responsibility. Prophecy demands that they will begin their preaching three days before the Tribulation—since they are killed after the second Woe is past (vs. 11), and before Christ returns (Rev. 11:14).

Because they prophesy for 1260 days (Rev. 11:3); and the time from the Abomination of desolation till Christ returns is 1260 days—they would have to start their commission three days prior to the Abomination of desolation.

Witnesses are just that—and the "Two Witnesses" will be instrumental in the conversion of many end-time Jewish *witnesses* for God! This end-time *witnessing* Jewish remnant will be the "first ones" God will bring back into His Church!

They will testify to the Messiah's imminent Coming and kingdom by having visions and dreams (Acts 2:17). Great signs and wonders in the heavens, accompanied by the prophesying of this Jewish remnant (Acts 2:18-20), will cause many to repent in Israel for having pierced their Savior (Zech. 12:10-14).

Several of the parables tell us that God will once again plant His Vineyard in Jerusalem! Israel will once again be a "fruitful bough" and produce luscious spiritual fruit! The start to *repot* God's Vineyard began in 1948 when Israel regained possession of the holy land. Today, massive migration and exodus from well over one hundred countries is being done continuously, as God *replants* His Jewish Vineyard in Jerusalem!

Arno C. Gaebelein, comments on this viewpoint in his *The Annotated Bible*, p. 28:

> **...there is yet to be a Jewish remnant, a strong and mighty witness that God hath not cast away His people. This future remnant of believing Hebrews will be called as soon as the church is complete and removed from the earth. This**

remnant to be called through Grace corresponds to the remnant at the beginning of this age.

However, not all of this Hebrew Vineyard will produce fruit at this time. A Jewish Church and remnant will be formed. Some of them will escape the Great Tribulation and flee to the mountains. Some of them will go through the Tribulation and be martyred, while 144,000 will be protected during the Tribulation! These groups are not the same as those who will be captives during the Tribulation forming the returning "remnant."

Reporting from Jerusalem on January 6, 1980, *United Press International* Correspondent, Howard Arenstein reported that three aged Rabbis had each independently recounted dreams of the Messiah's imminent return. Many Rabbis feel the Messiah must come soon to save the nation of Israel from invading forces. That's why they will readily accept a peace proposal by the "False Prophet."

ISRAEL—GOD'S "FIRSTBORN"

We must remember that originally God started His plan with the nation of Israel—His Church in the wilderness! Israel was God's *ekklesia* of "called out ones" and also God's "firstborn." God's prophet Moses wrote of God's "firstborn" in Exodus 4:22: **"And thou shalt say unto Pharaoh, Thus saith the Lord,** *Israel is my son, even my first born."*

There were three very special blessings belonging to the firstborn of Israelite households and are a *type* of spiritual blessings:

1) the first born was *sanctified* [set apart] for the Lord, notice God's words, **"Sanctify unto me all the firstborn, whatsoever openeth the womb among the children of Israel, both of man and of beast: it is mine" (Ex. 13:2),**

2) the first born was a *special treasure* to the parents, particularly the father, ."**..and they shall mourn for him, as one mourneth for his only son, and shall be in bitterness for him, as one that is in bitterness for his firstborn" (Zech. 12:10),** and

3) the first born received a *double portion* or inheritance of all his father's goods, **"But he shall acknowledge the ...firstborn, by giving him a double portion of all that he hath: for he is the beginning of his strength; the right of the firstborn is his" (Deut. 21:17).**

Positively, Israel as God's "firstborn" will receive God's three-fold blessings of special "firstborn privileges"! But Gentiles, who were *afar off* can also receive these same privileges!

Luke writes Peter's words in the book of Acts: **"For the promise is unto you [Israelites], and to your children, and to all that are *afar off,* even as many as the Lord our God shall call" (Acts 2:39).** As a result of Peter's preaching, **"Then they [Jews] that gladly received his word were baptized: and the same day there were added unto them about three thousand [Jewish] souls" (Acts 2:41).**

Remember, Christ came to His own first—the first converts of the New Testament Church were Jews! Only afterwards were those added to it who were *afar off,* (Gentiles). Plainly, the Church is added to Israel—not Israel to the Church!

The apostle Paul makes clear the transition of Gentiles to the Church in Ephesians 2:11-13:

> **Wherefore remember, that ye being in time past Gentiles in the flesh, who are called Uncircumcision by that which is called Circumcision in the flesh made by hands; that at that time ye were without Christ, being aliens from the commonwealth of Israel,** *and strangers from the covenants of promise, having no hope,* **and without God in the world: but now in Christ Jesus ye who sometimes were *afar off* are made nigh by the blood of Christ.**

Paul continues his dissertation on the "grafting in" of Gentiles into the Jewish vine: **"Now therefore ye [Gentiles] are no more strangers and foreigners,** *but fellowcitizens with the saints, and of the household of God"* **(Eph. 2:19).**

The Church of Jesus Christ was born in Israel, even as Jesus was born of a literal Jewish woman in Bethlehem. Therefore, if Mary is representative of "Israel"—she also *symbolizes* the New Testament Church! Recall how Mary was one of the very first converts of the New Testament Church!

It is as though God first used the nation of Israel as His *witness* upon the earth, then, after they rejected Him—God used Gentiles to carry on with His witnessing. Therefore, regardless of which interpretation we choose to agree with, one thing is for certain—the "woman" who flees into the wilderness will be representative of New Testament *spiritual Israel*! Now in these last days, God is once again using His "firstborn" son as His witnesses to the world!

Since 1948, the nation of Israel has once again been "sanctified" by God for His holy use—as His end-time witness to the nations. All nations will eventually be gathered against the nation of Israel, for they will hate her even as they did Jesus (Zech. 14:2)—God's "firstborn" spiritual Son!

Israel has been miraculously restored to her land, and the city of Jerusalem has become the possession of Israel once again! This has not happened by chance—but rather by divine design!

Soon God will start pouring out His Holy Spirit on this nation, as they begin to be "grafted back" into the covenant He made with their forefathers. God has not forgotten, nor forsaken His "firstborn" son—and they will yet receive their "double portion" of blessing!

As God pours out His Holy Spirit upon the nation of Israel through a modern-day Elijah—their consciences will once again be re-awakened toward *repentance.* They will desire to start sacrificing and build a Temple to honor God. Two end-time "Witnesses" [most likely two converted Jewish Rabbis], will start to turn the hearts of Israel to their spiritual Father as they prophesy from Jerusalem.

Tremendous miracles will be performed by them as they witness to the nation of Israel, and as the nation of Israel witnesses to a startled world. They, like Moses and Aaron, will plead God's words to the world, **"Let My People Go"**!

THE START OF THE NEW TESTAMENT "JEWISH CHURCH"

God made a covenant with the nation of Israel at Mt. Sinai, that they would be His chosen people or "ekklesia" to be a *witness* of His laws and government to the people on earth.

The nation of Judah [Jews] was to have a special role in carrying out this witness. It would be this nation that would gender the Messiah, as well as being an end-time witness to the world.

When Israel rebelled against God's government, He took away their right to be His witness on the earth for 2520 years, and gave over this right to a "holy nation"—the Church!

THE GATHERING OF THE ELECT

But in these last days, God is once again RESTORING His chosen people back to their land, and will soon pour out His Holy Spirit upon them.

Many of the parables picture *Israel's restoration* as God replants them back into His Vineyard. The feast days [Atonement and Tabernacles] picture Israel's *forgiveness* and *restoration* prior to Christ's return. Pentecost pictures the pouring out of the Holy Spirit similarly to the beginning of the New Testament Church.

Over and over again, the emphasis throughout the Bible is on the *restoration of the kingdom of God to Israel* upon her repentance.

The conversion of the nation of Israel will begin when a "Jewish Church" is formed in Jerusalem. It will be in Jerusalem that this repentance will first take place, as "Two Witnesses" of Levitical extraction will inspire that nation to begin sacrificing in a newly built Temple! It will be in Jerusalem that these "Two Witnesses" will be killed, as well as where the "Abomination of desolation" will be set up.

Jerusalem is where a remnant of converted Israelites will flee from, prior to the Tribulation, as well as where 144,000 will be protected during the Tribulation.

It will be Daniel's flesh and blood people [Jews] that Michael the archangel will help during the Tribulation. These will be the "firstfruits" of Israel offered to God in His restoration of the Kingdom to Israel!

The Greek word "diaspora" [disperse, spread out, that which is sown] was the name given to the Jews living outside of Palestine and maintaining their religious faith among the Gentiles.

God had warned the Jews through Moses that dispersion among other nations would be their fate if they departed from the Mosaic Law (Deut. 4:27; 28:64-68).

These prophecies were largely fulfilled in the two captivities, by Assyria and Babylonia. However, the book of Ezra continues the narrative and tells the story of the return from Babylon and the rebuilding of the temple.

Ezra shows how God fulfilled His promise given through His prophets, to restore His exiled people to their own land through heathen monarchs, and raised up such great men as Zerubbabel, Haggai, Zechariah, and Ezra—to rebuild the Temple, re-establish the old forms of worship, and put a stop to compromise with heathenism.

THE RESTORATION OF ISRAEL

In 538 B.C. the LORD stirred up the spirit of Cyrus, king of Persia, to allow the Jews to return and build the house of the Lord in Jerusalem (Ezra 1:1-2).

At this time approximately 50,000 Jews returned, but from the time of Alexander the Great, (331 B.C.) many thousands of Jews emigrated for purposes of trade and commerce into the neighboring cities of Alexandria, Ephesus, Smyrna, Corinth, Athens, Philadelphia, etc.

By the time of Christ, the diaspora must have been several times the population of Palestine. The synagogues in every part of the known world helped in the spread of Christianity, for Paul invariably visited them preaching the gospel (Acts 17:1,10).

Here we see how the Eternal prepared for the preaching of the gospel several hundred years in advance. In these last days, we may find a *duality* to what happened to the early church in Jerusalem!

God is once again restoring His chosen people back to their land, and will soon pour out His Holy Spirit as He did on the early Church on the Day of Pentecost (Acts 2:17-20). That is why there were Jews from many different nations on the Day of Pentecost assembled in Jerusalem (Acts 2:5-11). These Diaspora Jews were able to be "witnesses" of their new religious experience to many different countries. If this were to occur again, it will pave the way for many of the end-time prophecies!

Undoubtedly, this would open the door for the gospel to be preached, and the fulfillment of the scripture: **"..for verily I say unto you, Ye shall not have gone over the cities of Israel, till the Son of man be come" (Matt. 10:23).**

Chapter Seventeen

Because thou hast kept the word of my patience, I also will keep thee from the hour of temptation, which shall come upon all the world, to try them that dwell upon the earth.
—Rev. 3:10.

END-TIME PROTECTION

Exactly what did Jesus mean by His promise to the Philadelphia Church: ."..I will *keep* thee *from* the hour of temptation...? A dynamic controversy has developed between fundamentalists as to the rendering of the Greek word "keep" in this verse.

One exegesis maintains the Greek word *(tereo)* "keep" refers to protection *during* the Tribulation or while *in* the Tribulation. The Greek preposition *ek* translated "from" in this verse, should be translated "out of" according to these Post-tribulationists.

This belief implies protection *while in the Tribulation,* based on several scriptures that use these same words elsewhere. The same Greek preposition *ek* is used in (Revelation 7:14) as "out of", notice: **"These are they which came *out of* great tribulation."** These identical words are used in (John 17:15) where Jesus prayed to the Father: **"I pray not that thou shouldest take them out of the world, but that thou shouldest *keep* [Gr. tereo] them *from* [Gr. ek] the evil."**

Clearly, these scriptures use the same Greek word and preposition in (Revelation 3:10) to mean *protection while still in the world!*

Continuing the logic or irrational [which ever you prefer] of this concept, Post-tribulationists contend that this "keeping" implies a continual *keeping* or protection while in the world throughout the Tribulation.

The Greek scholar Gundry believes the preposition *ek* in this passage emphasizes *emergence* (Gundry, *The Church and the Tribulation,* pp. 57,58). However, Post-tribulationists ask, "If the emphasis is on "emergence" why not use the Greek word (*hruomai),* meaning "deliver" or "save from."

As a counter question, Pre-tribulationists ask, "If God wanted to protect His people during the Tribulation, why not use the words "keep in" instead of "keep from"? Furthermore, why did God use the words "to try" those who dwell upon the earth, if the Church was still around? Supposedly, the Philadelphia Church is no longer on trial at this point—Laodiceans are! The Philadelphia Church has already proven their faithfulness and no longer need to be tried!

On pages 85 and 86 of his book entitled, *The Blessed Hope,* Ladd adds this in harmony with Gundry's exegeses:

> **The language of this verse, taken by itself, could be interpreted to teach complete escape from the coming hour of Tribulation. The language is, 'I will keep thee *out of* the hour of trial' *(tereso ek).* This language, however, neither asserts nor demands the idea of bodily removal from the midst of the coming trial. This is proven by the fact that precisely the same words are used by our Lord in His prayer that God would keep His disciples 'out of the evil' *tereses ek tou ponerou,* (Jn. 17:1). In our Lord's prayer, there is no idea of bodily removal of the disciples from the evil world but of preservation from the power of evil even when they are in its very presence. A similar thought occurs in Galatians 1:4, where we read that Christ gave Himself for our sins to deliver us from (literally, 'out of', *ek)* this present evil age. This does not refer to a physical removal from the age but to deliverance from its power and control. 'This age' will not pass away until the return of Christ. In the same way, the promise of Revelation 3:10 of being**

> kept *ek* the hour of trial need not be a promise of a removal from the very physical presence of tribulation. It is a promise of preservation and deliverance in and through it.

Thayer says that when this verb is used with *en* it means "to cause one to persevere or stand firm in a thing"; while when used with *ek* it means "by guarding to cause one to escape in safety out of" (*A Greek-English Lexicon of the New Testament* p. 622).

Since *ek* is used here, it would indicate that John is promising a removal from the sphere of testing, not a preservation through it. This is not only guarding from the trials, but from the "very hour" itself when these trials will come.

Henry C. Thiessen, comments on this verse in his book *Will the Church Pass Through the Tribulation*, p. 22-24:

> ...we want to know what is the meaning of the verb "will keep" (tereo) and of the preposition 'from' *(ek)*. Alford says on the preposition *ek*, that it means 'out of the midst of: but whether by immunity from, or by being brought safe through, the preposition does not clearly define..'..Thus he points out that grammatically the two terms can have the same meaning, so that Rev. 3:10 may mean, not 'passing unscathed through the evil,' but 'perfect immunity from it..'..the grammar permits the interpretation of absolute immunity from the period. Other scholars say the same thing as to the preposition *ek (out of, from)*. Buttmann-Thayer says that *ek* and *apo* 'often serve to denote one and the same relation,' referring to John 17:15; Acts 15:29; Rev. 3:10 as examples of this usage. Abbott doubts 'if in the LXX and John, *ek* always implies previous existence in the evils from which one is delivered when used with *sozo* and *tereso*' (i.e. with the verbs to *save* and *to keep*). Westcott says regarding *ek sozo* (to save from) that it 'does not necessarily imply that that is actually realized out of which deliverance is granted (cf. 2 Cor. 1:10), though it does so commonly (John 12:27). Similarly we read in 1 Thess. 1:10 that Jesus delivers us from

> (ek) the wrath to come.' This can hardly mean protection *in* it; it must mean exemption *from* it.
>
> **It would seem, then, to be perfectly clear that the preposition 'from" may be taken to mean complete exemption from that which is predicted. It is clear that the context and other statements in Scriptures require that this be the interpretation. As for the context, note that the promise is not merely to be kept from the temptation, but from the *hour* of temptation, i.e. from the period of trial as such, not only from the trial during the period. And, again, why should the Apostle write *ek tes horas (from the hour)*, as he did, when he might easily have written *en te hora (in the hour)*, if that is what he meant to say? Surely the Spirit of God guided him in the very language he employed.'**

Assuming the "woman" represents a converted "Jewish Church" escaping to the mountains prior to the Tribulation, what happens to the Philadelphia Church era, assuming they are "kept from" or "out of" the Tribulation?

Good question—but one thing is certain, whether she *escapes from* the Tribulation, or *passes through* the Tribulation—she is *protected!* Assuming she escapes *from* the Tribulation completely, where does she go? One would have to believe if the "Jewish Church" escapes the Tribulation completely—so would the Philadelphia era!

While argument from *analogy* is a weak argument in itself, yet if a teaching is contrary to all *typology,* it cannot be a true interpretation. Scripture abounds in *types* which teach that those who walked by FAITH were *delivered* from the visitations of judgment which overtook the unbelieving. Such *types* are seen in the experience of Noah and Rahab, but perhaps the clearest illustration is that of Lot.

In (2 Peter 2:6-9) Lot is called a righteous man. This divine commentary will shed light on (Genesis 19:22), where the angel sought to hasten the departure of Lot with the words, **"Haste thee, escape thither; for I cannot do anything till thou be come thither."** If the presence of one righteous man prevented the outpouring of deserved judgment on the city of Sodom, how much more will the presence of the Church on earth prevent the outpouring of divine wrath until after her removal?

As a final and conclusive point on this subject, we have the comforting words of Jesus Christ to those who are blessed to escape all these things recorded in Luke 21:36: **"Watch ye therefore, and pray always, that ye may be accounted worthy to escape all these things that shall come to pass, and to stand before the Son of man."**

Here, Jesus mentions at the beginning of the chapter what things we could escape (vs. 11—earthquakes, famines, pestilences, etc). Yes, it is possible to escape all the calamities of the Great Tribulation—but only if we are *overcomers* and granted God's mercy!

THE PETRA CONTROVERSY

One of the most controversial theological concepts to emerge during the past decade, has been the idea of the red rose city of Petra as an end-time haven for God's Philadelphia Church.

This belief has been promoted by several religious groups, with emphasis on *their* particular denomination being blessed to be taken to an earthly place of protection and final training prior to the return of Jesus Christ!

Petra advocates link certain end-time prophetic events described in Daniel, Isaiah, and Revelation with "a place of Safety" for Christians from the Tribulation. Petra has been selected as the place of safety based on passages in Psalms and Isaiah, as it's Greek name Sela, was a city of ancient Edom, and Edom is one of the places mentioned escaping the "Beast" power (Dan. 11:41).

Prophetic writer, Howard Estep, one of the prime promotors of the Petra belief, writes on page 45 of his booklet, *Petra, the Rose Red City:*

> **There is positive Bible evidence that the rock city of Petra is located in one of the three countries which are to escape the tyranny of the Antichrist when he appears on the world scene and heads up the one-world government!...Petra is located in Biblical Edom, whose history goes back to the Genesis record that declares Esau to be Edom.**

THE RESTORATION OF ISRAEL

Petra lies in the midst of a desert in the nation of Jordan. It is a popular Middle East tourist attraction with many steep rocks and caves.

Because Moses, Israel and Paul were all trained in the wilderness in preparation of their calling—Petra has been believed to be the final training place for Christians.

However, before we jump to any hasty conclusions on this subject, let's take an in depth look at some hard facts. First of all, the two most important scriptures advocating a place of protection for the Philadelphia Church are (Revelation 3:10 and 12:7-17).

Being open minded, we must realize from the foregoing explanations on these particular scriptures, that other interpretations are possible and nothing is set in concrete.

In fact, if we take the many clear biblical principles as well as specific scriptures on the place of safety—we may realize that God may have other plans for His Church!

First of all, Christ said...**"he who seeks to save his life shall lose it" (Lk. 17:33).** In fact, those who **"..hide themselves in dens and in the *rocks of the mountains...*" (Rev. 6:15-17)** during the Tribulation from the wrath of the Lamb will lose their lives!

Another point we must consider is that Jesus said Himself: **"No man can know the day of his return" (Matt. 24:36).** Rather, His return would be *unexpectedly,* like a thief in the night (Matt. 24:42-44; 1 Thess. 5:2).

Based on this understanding, *how* will the Church be notified *when* to flee from the Tribulation, and *who* will notify them? Some believe an angel will be sent or that the physical leader of the Philadelphia era will be inspired to know.

Furthermore, some even claim that the Church will have a 30 day and 45 day grace period to flee to Petra from Jerusalem. Yet our Lord cautioned anyone living in the end-time to stay clear from Jerusalem and its surrounding area (Lk. 21:21).

And didn't Jesus specifically pray to His Father not to take His Church *out of* the world, but rather that they be *kept in* the world (Jn. 17:15,18).

Another interesting, yet contradictory point for Petra advocates is that Jesus warned His disciples not to flee to the *desert* to meet or await His return in secret chambers (Matt. 24:26).

Guess where Petra is?

In summary, let me say that it is not my purpose to condemn

anyone advocating Petra as a place of safety. My purpose is to only point out all the possibilities. We should realize however, at worse, this is a highly speculative teaching, and at best it could be a *petrafying* experience!

DOUBLE INDEMNITY

There are some who believe that a remnant (144,000) of the modern-day nation of Israel, are the only ones who will be granted protection during the Great Tribulation. Adherents of this *faith* arrive at this conclusion based upon the identity of the "woman" of Revelation twelve. Such proponents believe this "woman" to represent the 144,000 physical Israelites who will receive *supernatural* protection as God "seals" them *after* the Great Tribulation (Rev. 7).

But, we may ask—how does this concept square with a *taking* to a place of safety for 3 1/2 years (Rev. 12:14). A *sealing after* the Tribulation isn't a taking to a place prepared for safety *prior* to the Tribulation! Furthermore, why would God have to "seal" or protect anyone in a place no-one knows about anyway?

Contrariwise, most modern-day Christians believe God will take the Philadelphia era of the Church to a place of final training and safety for 3 1/2 years *during* the Tribulation (Rev. 3:10), fulfilling (Revelation 12).

Those who disagree with this understanding maintain that the promise granted this era is not protection *from* the Great Tribulation, but *during* the Tribulation! This school believes a mistranslation has caused this confusion and is correctly rendered in other translations.

We have just studied this teaching in which they say (Revelation 3:10) should read: **"Because thou hast kept the word of my patience, I also will protect thee *during* [not from] the hour of temptation, which shall come upon all the world, to try them that dwell upon the earth."**

Another argument that anti-Philadelphia protectionists have, is that Jesus spoke of those in Judea fleeing to the mountains for protection, and this could not be referring to the Church!

Well, what about it? Who is right? Are only 144,000 *physical* Israelites forming an end-time "Jewish Church", going to be protected as they flee Judea into the mountains of Petra as a place of safety? Or are only Christians comprising the Philadelphia era going to be granted protection?

Perhaps this question can be best answered from our understanding of the *types* and their *antitypes*! It appears that everything that happens to the nation of Israel, also happens to the Gentile Church! Could it be that God will provide "double indemnity" for both His Church and a few observant Israelites who have been converted by the "Two Witnesses"?

If the days of Noah are a *type* of the coming Tribulation, it appears there will be *three classes of individuals* as follows:

1) Most of the world will be destroyed as a result of the Tribulation and *winepress* as they were destroyed by the flood. This event is described by the "Harvest of Souls" as Christ reaps the earth with a *sharp sickle,* and the parable of "The Winepress" (see chapter 8).

2) Some of God's people will go through the Tribulation—the 144,000 Israelite firstfruits (Rev. 7) and the 144,000 of (Rev. 14), who may be Gentile firstfruits, but be protected from the plagues. This is *pictured* by Noah and his family passing through the flood unharmed, even as those inside the Ark were *sealed* with pitch. The 144,00 are *sealed* or protected by God, as He *seals* or protects these people by an identifying mark on their forehead (symbolic of their attitude or mind). The Laodicean Church era will go through the Tribulation unprotected and be martyred because of their wrong attitude toward God's laws!

3) The "woman" comprising converted Israelites in Jerusalem will be taken to a place of safety to escape the Tribulation! This is *dual* to Enoch's miraculous delivery prior to the flood and also *represents* the Philadelphia Church era!

There can be no nation of Israel taken to a place of safety—for all nations will be gathered against her (Zech. 14:2). The nation of Israel will be hated by all nations (Matt. 24:9) and many **"shall be led away captive into all nations, and Jerusalem shall be trodden down of the Gentiles, until the times of the Gentiles be fulfilled" (Lk. 21:24).** It will be these *elect* that God's angels's will gather from the four winds [corners of the earth] prior to Christ's return (Ezek. 5:10; Isa. 27:12-13; Matt. 24:31).

GOD'S END-TIME PROTECTION

However, many of the converts of the Elijah to come will escape to the mountains as they did during the first century. Here is what Josephus wrote concerning this well documented event:

> **The Christians of Jerusalem [Jewish Christians], remembering the Lord's admonition, forsook the doomed city in good time and fled to the town of Pella in the Decapolis, beyond the Jordan...An old tradition says that a divine voice or angel revealed to their leaders the duty of flight (Josephus, *Antiquities of the Jews*, 15.11.5).**

Here is what the *Encyclopedia Britannica* says of this same event:

> **Nazarenes, an obscure Jewish-Christian sect dated their settlement in Pella from the time of the flight of the Jewish Christians from Jerusalem, immediately before the siege in A.D. 70. The Church there escaped the horrors of the siege by following the instruction of Christ in Matthew 24, and fleeing to the mountains beyond the Jordan. This timely retreat was made to the small town of Pella (Hugh Smith's, *History*, also pg. 41, 42 Hurlbuts' *Story of the Christian Church*).**

Now one final quote from the Roman historian Gibbon:

> **The Jewish converts, or as they were afterwards called, the Nazarenes, retired from the ruins of A.D. 80 Jerusalem to the little town of Pella beyond the Jordan where that ancient church languished above sixty years in solitude and obscurity *(Decline and Fall*, chp. 15).**

Israelites will once again flee to the mountains in *duality* of what occurred in A.D. 70, and what also happened in the Old Testament, notice: **"And ye shall flee to the valley of the mountains; for the valley of the mountains shall reach unto Azal: yea, ye shall flee,** *like as ye fled from before the earthquake* *in the days of Uzziah king of Judah:* **and the LORD my God shall come, and all the saints with thee" (Zech. 14:5)**.

Conclusively, if the 144,000 remnant of (Revelation 7) are protected *from* the impending plagues *after* the Tribulation—they certainly do not represent the "woman" taken to a place of safety for 3 1/2 years!

The fact that God will once again be dealing with the nation of Israel on a national plane, *sanctifying* them by national identities, and sending them as witnesses to the world, indicates that the Church is no longer around.

By analogy of the *types* and progressive revelation—we have our answer!

There will be a "remnant" of physical Israelites converted by the preaching of the "Two Witnesses," that will be protected for 1260 days in a place of safety in the wilderness (Rev. 12:6). Michael the archangel will fight on her behalf (Rev. 12:7). This must be speaking of physical Jews, since they are the children of Daniel's people, notice:

> **And at that time shall *Michael stand up*, the great prince which standeth for *the children of thy people* [Jews]: and there shall be a time of trouble, such as never was since there was a nation even to that same time: and at that time thy people shall be delivered every one that shall be delivered, every one that shall be found written in the book (Dan. 12:1).**

See (Revelation 12:7) for the exact time element of this prophecy when the archangel Michael will help God's people.

Should Christ return on Trumpets, then this event would have to occur 3 1/2 years earlier, around Passover, being a "second exodus." Israel was delivered by the "wings of an eagle" once before, and this will occur once more (Deut. 32:11; Ex. 19:4; Rev. 12:14).

One final point on this subject is worth pondering about, where on earth would God put 400 million Protestants and 600 million Catholics, if they supposedly comprise the faithful?

GOD'S END-TIME PROTECTION

THE MYSTERIOUS "EAGLE"

The fifth chapter of the book of Ezekiel contains an abstruse prophecy concerning those of the nation of Israel that will go through the Great Tribulation. Let's read it:

> **And thou, son of man, take thee a sharp knife, take thee a barber's razor, and cause it to pass upon thine head and upon thy beard: then take thee balances to weigh, and divide the hair. Thou shalt burn with fire a third part in the midst of the city, when the days of the siege are fulfilled: and thou shalt take a third part, and smite about it with a knife: and a third part thou shalt scatter in the wind; and I will draw out a sword after them. Thou shalt also take thereof *a few in number*, and bind them in thy skirts. Then take of them again, and cast them into the midst of the fire, and burn them in the fire; for thereof shall a fire come forth into all the house of Israel (Ezek. 5:1-4).**

Here then is a prophecy that is to occur to the nation of Israel in the last days, that God's prophet Ezekiel *literally* fulfilled! Ezekiel cut off all his hair, weighed it and divided it into thirds. Each third represented a group of people from Israel and their fate during the last days as follows: 1) one third would be "burned with fire" (these will die through famine and disease), 2) one third will be "cut with a knife" (these will be killed through war), and 3) one third will be "scattered in the wind" [these will go through the Great Tribulation).

The explanation of this prophecy is made vivid in verse 12: **"A third part of thee shall die with *pestilence*, and with *famine* shall they be consumed in the midst of thee: and a third part shall fall by the *sword* round about thee; and I will scatter a third part into all the winds, and I will draw out a sword after them."**

Perhaps only 10'% of the remaining 1/3 of the nation of Israel who goes into captivity, will live to begin the Millennium as indicated from (Ezekiel 20:37-38; Amos 5:3).

FLYING ON EAGLE'S WINGS

Now here's something interesting!

Of this third group that is to be scattered, "a few in number" was to be bound in Ezekiel's skirts [margin *wings*]. The rest were then to be put into the fire [Tribulation] (vs. 4). This final group will comprise *many* who will form the Laodicean era of God's Church.

Those that were bound in Ezekiel's skirt [wings] represent the "woman" who are to escape via *a great Eagle* to a place of safety.

But what could this great Eagle possible represent? There are two passages in the Bible that refer to "eagle's wings" that might give us more insight. The first one is found in (Exodus 19:4) where the Children of Israel were delivered from the hands of the Egyptians on "eagle's wings." The second passage is found in (Deuteronomy 32:11) in reference to God *protecting* Israel during their wilderness experience.

Both passages make reference to *God Himself* as being the "Great Eagle." Notice Exodus 19:4, **"Ye have seen *what I did unto the Egyptians, and how I bare You on eagle's wings*, and brought you unto myself."** And in Deuteronomy 32:11-12, **"As an eagle stirreth up her nest, fluttereth over her young, spreadeth abroad her wings, taketh them, beareth them on her wings: so *the LORD alone lead him*, and there was no strange god with him."**

Here are some interesting facts. There is a particular type of eagle in the Middle East that has a most unusual way of teaching it's young to fly. They will fly with their young on their wings into the air—then they will drop them and catch them until the little eaglets learn to fly. Their parents know exactly when they are ready.

God was *"the Eagle"* that led Israel out of Egyptian bondage and provided food for them in the wilderness. He did this through specific miracles—but Israel had to do their part as well. They had to *walk* out of Egypt and gather the manna in the wilderness themselves. This may be *analogous* to God's end-time Church during the last days!

Because the apostle John said the "woman" will "fly" on eagle's wings—why not believe him? If I told you I was going to fly to Florida, you wouldn't ask me how I was going to get there would you? Most likely, God will use some sort of *supernatural* means to "fly" His Church into a place He has prepared.

Jesus gives us more details of this time setting in the seventeenth chapter of Luke. Jesus said this time would be like the days of Noah (vs. 26).

Now, what happened in the days of Noah?

As already noted, the flood that came in the days of Noah was a *type* of the Great Tribulation that is to come in the last days. Three types of people existed at this time: 1) the majority of *rebellious* mankind that perished in the flood, 2) Noah and his family who went through the flood but were saved, and 3) Enoch, a *type* of the Church who was "translated" and escaped the peril to come. God may indeed "fly" His Church to a place of safety via "translation", "airplane", or "UFO's" monitored by angels.

Noah and his family represent those Israelites going through the Tribulation, but will be saved. The 144,000 physical Israelites and the multitude fulfill this event during the Tribulation (Rev. 7).

But why was Enoch "translated" before the flood came? Could he be a *type* of what will happen to the Church? Was this a *type* of Rapture or supernatural protection?

TO BE ON EARTH

And the *earth* helped the woman, and the *earth* opened her mouth and swallowed up the flood which the dragon cast out of his mouth (Rev. 12:16).

Before any destruction, God has always warned the inhabitants in advance, and His people had very little time to escape. Witness Noah and the flood, Lot in Sodom and Gomorrah, Israel in Egypt and the nation of Judah during the destruction of Jerusalem in A.D. 70.

Since the Church will live in a *type* of Sodom and Gomorrah, like Lot, it will probably experience some of the evils before the time to flee—and like Lot, God will allow the righteous to escape.

For those wondering if they will be able to take their non-believing mates, family, neighbors or friends with them—the question might be asked of them, "could you leave without them"?

During the Noation flood, Noah was the only one called righteous, yet he took some of his family with him. Noah's wife, sons and their wives were able to come with him (Gen. 6:9,12).

But what about the rest of Noah's family? Noah was 900 years old and must have had a lot of relatives that would not listen to his message. Jesus said, **"But as the days of Noah were, so shall the coming of the Son of man be" (Matt. 24:37).**

God told Abraham to leave the country in which he lived, and go to a foreign land (Gen. 12). Abraham had to leave his father and relatives, a nice home, peace, safety, etc. and go in *faith* to a new land of which he knew nothing!

The account of Abraham's nephew Lot in (Genesis 19) tells a similar story. Abraham pleaded with God not to destroy Sodom and Gomorrah if there were any righteous individuals. Lot was a *righteous* man who lived in a perverted society. Lot's in-laws and daughters were made righteous or "clean" in God's sight because of him (Gen. 7:14). But Lot's family only mocked him (Gen. 19:14). Lot's wife wanted to go back because she didn't have enough *faith* and instead turned into a pillar of salt!

Jesus said of this parallel time in Luke 17:28-32, **"Likewise also as it was in the days of Lot; they did eat, they drank, they bought, they sold, they planted, they built; (in other words it was business as usual). But the same day that Lot went out of Sodom it rained fire and brimstone from heaven, and destroyed them all."** Jesus said to remember Lot's wife!

Recall also how God warned the Pharaoh of Egypt through Moses, how He would destroy their firstborn if they would not repent. When the plagues were poured out on Egypt, the Israelites suffered some of them as well!

God provides us with the answer as to whether we will be able to take our children and non-believing family members with us in Ezekiel 14:14-23:

> **Even if these three men, Noah, Daniel, and Job, were in it, they would deliver their own lives by** *their righteousness,* **says the Lord God. If I cause wild beasts to pass through the land, and they ravage it, and it be made desolate, so that no man may pass through because of the beasts; even if these men were in it, as I live says the Lord God, they would deliver neither sons nor daughters;** *they alone would be delivered,* **but the land would be desolate.**

> Or if I bring a sword upon that land, and say, Let a sword go through the land; and I cut off from it man and beast; though these three men were in it, as I live, says the Lord God, they would deliver neither sons nor daughters, but *they alone would be delivered.* Or if I send a pestilence into that land, and pour out my wrath upon it with blood, to cut off from it man and beast; even if Noah, Daniel, and Job were in it, as I live, says the Lord God, they would deliver neither son nor daughter; *they would deliver but their own lives by their righteousness.* For thus says the Lord God: How much more when I send upon Jerusalem my four sore acts of judgment, sword, famine, evil beasts, and pestilence, to cut off from it man and beast!
>
> Yet, if there should be left in it any survivors to lead out sons and daughters, when they come forth to you, and you see their ways and their doings, you will be consoled for the evil that I have brought upon Jerusalem, for all that I have brought upon it. They will console you, when you see their ways and their doings; and you shall know that I have not done without cause all that I have done in it, says the Lord God (R.S.V.).

Notice, God says that sons and daughters [of accountable age] will have to stand on their own two [spiritual] feet! They cannot come into God's Kingdom or place of safety on the spiritual coattail of their converted parents!

Many accounts of *faith* are recorded in (Hebrews 11) of individuals who had to leave their habitations by faith:

> By *faith* (Enoch) was taken up [to a place of safety]—vs. 5). Noah by *faith*, left the world and went to a place of safety from the flood (vs. 7). Abraham went to a place [of safety] where he should receive an inheritance by *faith* without knowing where he was going (vs. 8). Jacob left

THE RESTORATION OF ISRAEL

this world as he was dying by *faith* (vs. 21). Moses left Egypt by *faith* with the children of Israel to a place of safety in the promised land (vs. 21). Rehab, the harlot left Jericho by *faith* to go to a place of safety (vs. 31).

Jesus said we must be ready to forsake our houses, or brothers or sisters, or father, or mother, or wife, or children, or lands for His sake (Matt. 19:29). We must be always ready to leave EVERYTHING in this world by *faith* and follow Jesus!

To answer the question then, "How will you be notified to leave for a place of safety and where will it be?"—have FAITH!

Many organizations teach that Christians will be *raptured* off of the earth during this troublous time; but the Bible tells us the *earth* [not heaven] helped the "woman" (Rev. 12:16). Why did Christ tell those in Jerusalem to pray that their *flight* would not be in the *winter,* if they were going to be raptured away to heaven?

Whoever the "woman" is, and *wherever* the "woman" goes, one thing is for sure—it will be on earth and will already have been prepared by God (Rev. 12:6).

MANY PLACES OF SAFETY?

There has been much speculation over the years as to where the place of safety will be. Some have thought it to be the red rose city of Petra, while others have said it could be in your home.

Can there be many places of safety?

True, God could protect you wherever you are during the Tribulation—but is that what the Bible indicates?

When Noah and his family were protected during the tribulation of the ancient world—God made him build an ark for a haven of safety. Certainly God could have miraculously protected Noah's family by other means, but He didn't! God could have told them to go to a certain location where the flood waters would not reach—or God could have had an isolated flood! But this was not in God's plan!

Lot and his family were emphatically warned to "come out" of the sin filled city of Sodom—instead of remaining there to receive divine protection. God could have protected Lot's family in their houses, as He did the Israelites when the death angel passed over the Egyptians—but this was not the will of God!

GOD'S END-TIME PROTECTION

FOUR TYPES OF THE CHURCH

By understanding past *types* of the Church—we can have a greater comprehension of its deliverance in the last days. There are *four types* of the Church mentioned in the Bible, and there will be several *different groups* of people comprising God's Church in the last days.

The "Two Witnesses" will begin their preaching in Jerusalem approximately 3 days prior to the Great Tribulation—as God pours out His Holy Spirit upon that nation. As a result, a "Jewish Church" will be formed, but it will be formed in stages throughout the Great Tribulation.

It will be comprised of:

- Some observant Jews who will flee [Gr. literally run or escape] to the mountains when they see the "Abomination of desolation" set up, or Jerusalem encompassed with armies in observance of (Luke 21:21).

- A remnant or "election" of Israelites that will be captured by the "Beast" power and comprise the Jewish exiles taken out of captivity by the returning Jesus Christ (Matt. 24:31). Many of them will not bow down to the "Beast" power and will be martyred. They will comprise the Laodicean era, as well as any Gentiles converted previously who remained "lukewarm."

- The "woman" who will escape the entire Tribulation and be protected on earth in a place of safety provided by Jesus Christ (Rev. 12). The Philadelphia Church era also is protected in like manner.

- 144,000 faithful Israelites and Gentiles who will go through the Tribulation, but be protected from the seven last plagues (Rev. 7, 14).

Now notice the parallels of these future events to what happened previously in Church history.

The 1*st type* of what will happen to the Church in the end-time occurred in A.D. 70. Jesus had warned the early New Testament

THE RESTORATION OF ISRAEL

Church to *depart* to a place of safety in the mountains, from the invading Roman armies (Lk. 21:20,21; Matt. 24:15-22).

According to early church historian Eusebius who lived in A.D. 260-340—the Church escaped to Pella beyond the Jordan River around A.D. 66-70. Here is what Eusebius wrote concerning the Church's departure as the advancing Roman armies of Titus drew near:

> **But the members of the Church in Jerusalem were instructed by a prophecy, revealed to the leaders, to abandon the city before the war and to take up residence in one of the cities of Perea which was named Pella. From Jerusalem the followings of Christ migrated to Pella (Eusibius,** ***Ecclesiastical History,*** **111,5).**

Had the Church left any sooner, it would have been captured or killed by Vespasians's advancing army in northern Palestine. But notice, Jesus instructed them to *flee* into the mountains when they saw Jerusalem encompassed by armies (Matt. 24:16-21)—not pray for protection in their home!

The *second type* of the Church's deliverance happened to ancient Israel. The Eternal brought Israel [the Church in the Wilderness—Acts 7:38], out of Egypt by supernatural power. God said to His people: **"..how I bare you on eagles' wings, and brought you unto myself" (Ex. 19:4).**

Notice how this parallels the "woman" [Church] of the end-time. The Church is to be **"..given two wings of a great eagle, that she might *fly* into the wilderness into her place..." (Rev. 12:14).**

Although God Himself led Israel via a pillar of fire to her place of safety—this most likely will not occur to the end-time Church. But this scripture definitely shows God will provide a place of protection for the Church, and deliver it supernaturally!

How you ask? We don't know! Where you ask? We don't know that either! Surely if we don't know *where* or *how* we're going—we don't know *when* we're going! But God will reveal this vital knowledge when the time is right!

The *third type* of the end-time Church revolves around the prophesied Church during the middle ages. This prophecy is written in Revelation 12:6: **"And the woman *fled* into the**

GOD'S END-TIME PROTECTION

wilderness, where she hath a place prepared of God, that they should feed her there a thousand two hundred and threescore days." This prophecy occurs after Christ's ascension (vs. 5), but prior to the end-time climatic battle in heaven (vs. 7).

This woman [Church] *fled* into a place for 1,260 prophetic days or years during the middle ages from A.D. 325-1585. This is the time when the Church was persecuted by the Roman Empire under Constantine. They fled to the valleys and mountains of Europe and went underground spiritually until the Protestant Reformation in 1585. Once again, the Church was removed from the general society to a place of refuge!

Noah and his family represent the *4th type* of the Church and they were protected from the turbulent flood waters which were *symbolic* of the Great Tribulation. Three kinds of people went through this experience as representative of the last days.

Except for Noah's family, all of the old world *perished* by the flood waters as will 90% of mankind in the last days! Noah and his family are *figures* of those who will go through the Tribulation but be *protected*. The 144,000 physical Israelites who receive special protection through the Tribulation represent the family of Noah. They will be *sealed* (Rev. 7:2-4)—just as Noah's Ark was *sealed* with pitch—a *type* of God's Holy Spirit which "sealed" the inhabitants inside the Ark (Gen. 6:14).

The only individual who escaped the Tribulation completely, was Enoch who was "translated." Many believe this to represent a "rapture" of the Church. His son Methuselah is also a *type* of the Church—and his death signaled the flood. Methuselah's very name means "when he dies, the end will come."

Likewise, when the "woman" and the Philadelphia Church era leave for a place of safety—the end of this age will come! Only when Methuselah was born did his father Enoch begin to "walk with God." This event changed his very life and as a *type* of the Church—Enoch was granted *supernatural* deliverance to a place of safety!

ONE PLACE OF SAFETY

Using the previous *types* of the Church as examples for the end-time—it definitely appears that the "woman" and Philadelphia Church era will leave for a place of safety supernaturally. However, this will not be a "fleeing" or "departing" as other

THE RESTORATION OF ISRAEL

examples—rather a "flying" (Gr. literally fly like a bird). Realize also this woman *flies* to a *place* [not *places*] of safety! This place may very well be Petra which is located near Ammon, one of the three areas that are protected from the "Beast" power (Dan. 11:41).

One word of caution to those who are *blessed* to make it to this haven of protection. If this event parallels the wilderness experience of ancient Israel—it may not be very pleasant. In fact, there may not be abundance of food or water there, and a great deal of *faith* will have to be exercised. The place of *safety* may in fact turn out to be the very place where some lose out on salvation because of bad attitudes and sin!

The Philadelphia era of God's Church is given this end-time promise: **"Because thou hast kept the word of my patience, I also will keep thee from the *hour* of temptation, which shall come upon all the world, to try them that dwell upon the earth" (Rev. 3:10).** This prophecy must be referring to the second last Church era prior to Christ's advent, for the literal Church of Philadelphia was destroyed in A.D. 70, and John wrote this in A.D. 90.

Compare this *trial* [tribulation] that takes place for an "hour" with the "hour" the 10 kings who receive power with the "Beast" (Rev. 17:12). This "hour" can only refer to the Great Tribulation!

Pray always, as Jesus said, to be worthy to escape all of these things!

THE MODEL FOR END-TIME PROPHECIES

Now we get down to brass-tacks. As already demonstrated time and time again—God has given us physical entities to understand spiritual truths. He has given us countless *dualities* in the physical realm to help us comprehend future prophecies.

The events which happened to ancient Israel will help us to better understand many prophecies about the conclusion of this age (1 Cor. 10:11).

Israel's deliverance from Egyptian bondage and the wilderness experience portrays the Christian experience of salvation. It is a *model* to help us comprehend our deliverance from sin and bondage to Satan's cruel taskmasters. It helps us to perceive that we will *only* be delivered from this evil world *if* we have deep abiding FAITH in our loving God!

The "sprinkling of the blood" of lambs on the doorposts of

GOD'S END-TIME PROTECTION

Israelite houses in ancient Egypt, as a protection from God's plagues upon the Egyptians, was a *type* of the "sealing" of the 144,000 in (Revelation 7).

Israel's walking through the Red Sea, was a *type* of baptism by the Holy Spirit—after they ate the Passover, *symbolic* of Jesus Christ, our Passover lamb and deliverer!

All of these physical experiences and trials of Israel were done to help Christians better understand this Christian experience on a spiritual level.

Did the Eternal give us all of these physical experiences of Israel, and not give a *model* or figure for the conclusion of this present evil age?

Has God left us to grope in the dark concerning the fate of end-time Christians? Most assuredly not!

In fact, our merciful Dad has given us a great deal of information using Israel as our *model* for end-time events.

The model design of the Temple is no exception, and from it we can piece together many end-time prophecies. The destruction of Solomon's Temple, the Babylonian captivity, the return and the re-building of the Temple by Zerubbabel-Joshua, are all model *pictures* of the consummation of this age!

THE MODEL—SOLOMON'S TEMPLE

The destruction of Solomon's Temple and the Babylon captivity, serve as model events in which Israel is a *type* of what will befall Christians [Jew and Gentile] during the Tribulation.

Today, Christians are called the "Temple of God." The attack on, and destruction of Solomon's Temple portrays the end-time attack upon God's Church.

When the Babylonian attack came upon Solomon's Temple—all the *holy vessels,* valuables and *precious things* were removed *before* the building was burned! (11 Chron. 36:18).

Like Solomon's Temple, the Church will not be totally destroyed during the Great Tribulation. However, like Solomon's Temple, some of the *holy vessels* [Laodiceans] will be carried away into captivity.

Christians, whose faith is likened unto gold, silver and precious stones (holy vessels), will escape the wrath to come. But those whose faith is as wood or stone will be put into the *fiery trial* (1 Cor. 3:12-13).

THE RESTORATION OF ISRAEL

A WARNING TO LUKEWARM CHRISTIANS

The apostle Paul gave this stern warning to lukewarm Christians:

> **For if God spared not the natural branches [Israel], take heed lest He also spare not thee. Behold therefore the goodness and severity of God: on them which fell, severity; but toward thee, goodness,** *if* **thou continue in His goodness:** *otherwise thou also shalt be cut off* **(Rom. 11:21-22).**

The audacious apostle Paul warned Christians to take earnest heed of this strong admonition. Paul was referring to when God destroyed the Temple and sent the Jews into Babylonian captivity!

Lukewarm Saints, whether converted Jew or Gentile, like the *holy vessels* in Solomon's Temple, will be carried away by the invading "Beast" power into captivity!

MORE PARALLELS

There are yet more parallels of the Babylonian captivity of God's *holy vessels* to that of end-time *lukewarm* Christians.

The golden *image* which King Nebuchadnezzar's subjects were required to worship (Dan. 3), is also a *type* of the *image* the "Beast" will require everyone to worship in the last days (Rev. 13:14-15).

Refusal to do so will mean certain death!

Daniel in the lion's den, Shadrach, Meshach and Abednego in the "fiery furnace" are also *figures* of what end-time Laodiceans will have to endure during the Great Tribulation!

Indeed, there is coming a time of *purification* of lukewarm Christians by the Tribulation (Dan. 11:32-35). But after this will also come *the restoration of the Kingdom of God!*

The saving of the remnant of Jacob to return and rebuild God's second Temple is also characteristic of what will happen to God's end-time *holy vessels*. God will rebuild a literal Temple that will be far more glorious than even Solomon's. It will be a holy Temple lasting 1,000 years and be followed by a more glorious spiritual Temple in "New Jerusalem."

In each case, the physical and spiritual—three entities exist. Jerusalem, a Temple and a sacrificial system.

Solomon's Temple was destroyed in Jerusalem, only to be rebuilt to start sacrifices once again. The same pattern will exist prior to our Lord's return. The same pattern will also transpire in the spiritual Temple—the Church! Holy Jerusalem, [God's spiritual Temple] with a system of sacrifices will also exist again in a spiritual sense during the Millennium!

THE RESTORATION OF ISRAEL

Chapter Eighteen

THE RESTORATION OF THE KINGDOM

The apostles were well aware that some day the restoration of Israel would be imminent as they curiously asked Jesus in Acts 1:6: **"...Lord, will thou at this time restore again the kingdom of Israel?"**

We read more of the restoration of Israel in Acts 3:20-21:

> **And he shall send Jesus Christ, which before was preached unto you. Whom the heaven must receive until the time of restitution [RESTORATION] OF ALL THINGS which God hath spoken by the mouth of all his holy prophets since the world began.**

The apostles were cognizant of Israel's restoration because of the many prophecies in the Old Testament. The start to RESTORE Israel as a nation will begin soon after the return of Jesus Christ to the earth. At this time, He will personally lead His chosen people out of the captivity of heathen nations and into the "promised land." Notice the abundant proof of this memorable event from the following biblical scriptures:

Isa. 27:12-13 "And it shall come to pass in that day, that the LORD shall beat off from the channel of the river unto the stream of Egypt, and *ye shall be gathered one by one, O ye children of Israel.* And it shall come to pass in that day, that the great trumpet [the 7th trumpet] shall be blown, and they shall come which were ready to perish in the land of Assyria, and the outcasts in the land of Egypt, *and shall worship the LORD in the holy mount at Jerusalem."*

Isa. 11:10-13 "And in that day there shall be *a root of Jesse*, which shall stand for an ensign of the people [Christ]; to it shall the Gentiles seek: and *his rest shall be glorious*. And it shall come to pass in that day, that *the Lord shall set his hand again the second time to recover the remnant of his people*, which shall be left, from Assyria, and from Egypt, and from Pathros, and from Cush, and from Elam, and from Shinar, and from Hamath, and from the islands of the sea. *And he shall set up an ensign for the nations, and shall assemble the outcasts of Israel,* and gather together the dispersed of Judah from *the four corners of the earth* (see Matt. 24:31). The envy also of Ephraim shall depart, and the adversaries of Judah shall be cut off. Ephraim shall not envy Judah, and Judah shall not vex Ephraim. (Vs. 15) And the LORD shall utterly destroy the tongue of the Egyptian sea...(Vs. 16) And there shall be an highway for the remnant of his people, which shall be left, from Assyria: like as it was to Israel in the day that he came up out of the land of Egypt."

Isa. 14:1-3: *"For the LORD will have mercy on Jacob, and will Yet choose Israel, and set them in their own land:* and the strangers shall be joined with them, and they shall cleave to the house of Jacob. And the people shall take them, and bring them to their place: and the house of Israel shall possess them in the land of the LORD for servants and handmaids: *and they shall rule over their oppressors.* And it shall come to pass in that day that the LORD shall give thee rest from thy sorrow, and from thy fear, and from the hard bondage wherein thou wast made to serve."

THE KINGDOM RESTORED

Ezek. 39:25-29   "Therefore thus saith the LORD GOD: Now will *I bring again the captivity of Jacob*, and have mercy upon *the whole house of Israel*, and will be Jealous for my holy name: After that they have borne their shame, and all their trespasses whereby they have trespassed against me, when they dwelt safely in their land, and none made them afraid. *When I have brought them again from the people, and gathered them out of their enemies lands,* and am sanctified in them in the sight of many nations; Then shall they know that I am the LORD their God, which caused them to be led into captivity among the heathen: *but I have gathered them unto their own land,* and have left none of them any more there. Neither will I hide My face any more from them: *for I have poured out my spirit upon the house of Israel,* saith the Lord GOD."

See also   (Jer.31:8;23:3-8;3:18;-;16:15;50:4,5,19,20 Ezek.36:24-28;11:17-19;20:33-2;28:25,26; 38:8; 39:9,21,23; Zech. 2; 8:22,23; 14:1-21).

If the nation of Israel had repented when Christ came to them, there would have been no need to start the New Testament Church and the "first resurrection" to restore Israel would most likely have occurred!

Perhaps now we can better understand the mysterious 1290 and 1335 days mentioned in the book of Daniel.

THE 1290 AND 1335 DAY CONTROVERSY

And *from* the time that the daily sacrifice shall be taken away, and the abomination that maketh desolate set up, there shall be a thousand two hundred and ninety days. Blessed is he that waiteth, and cometh to the thousand three hundred and five and thirty days. But go thou thy way (Daniel) till the end be: for thou shalt rest, and stand in thy lot at the end of the days (Dan. 12:11-13).

Several theories exist as to the interpretation of the 1290 and 1335 days—but the most critical point in understanding their meaning is determined by where to start counting them.

There are two possible ways to count these days *from* the Abomination of desolation. One concept is to put the extra days *before* the Abomination of desolation by counting backwards from the 1260 days. According to this belief, 45 additional days are needed for the Church to flee the impending Great Tribulation.

The other more popular concept is to place the extra days *after* the return of Christ. This concept is outlined with charts and explained in the Companion Bible index. Allen Beechick expresses this viewpoint on page 23 of his book, *The Pre-Tribulation Rapture:*

> **The important thing to remember about these dates is that they are all counted *from* the abomination. Daniel 12:11 makes the abomination the beginning point for the 1290 days. This implies that the other two dates share the same beginning point. They begin at this same point, but they end at different points. On day 1260, Christ returns. On day 1290 something else happens. On day 1335 something else happens. What happens? Scripture doesn't spell it out, but we can make some good guesses.**

Perhaps the *Companion Bible* provides us with a clue. It suggests that this verse refers to a resurrection, and could therefore read as follows: "An angel appeared unto Daniel and told him: 'But go thou thy way till the end be: for thou shalt *rest* [in the grave], and *stand* [stand up in a resurrection] in thy lot at the end of the days' (verse 13). The word "resurrect" literally means "to stand again from below"—*re* [again]; *sur* [below]; *rect* [to stand]."

Those who advocate counting forwards claim, a simple reading of the prophecy itself seems to clearly imply that we count in the normal method—that is forwards, not backwards. They further state, that those who tell us to count backwards have also suggested that the "sign" that the Church is to flee, which occurs 45 days before the Great Tribulation, is the presence of the "abomination of desolation" in the Temple Mount in Jerusalem, or armies surrounding Jerusalem.

Yet, Daniel actually says this abominable "presence" will actually occur at the beginning of the 1260 day period, not 45 days prior to it. Jesus said when we *see* the abomination of desolation established in the holy place, we are to *immediately* flee—not even go back to get a coat out of the house. This warning and instruction by Jesus was for something that would be immediate—not something that would occur 45 days previously, that would give someone the opportunity to rationalize over. Jesus emphasizes the *urgency* of fleeing when these signs occur, He gave no indication of an apparent 45 day lapse of grace!

Beechick continues to enlighten us on page 88 of his book:

> **Did you find the answer? The answer is in the last verse, 'For thou shalt rest, and stand in thy lot at the end of the days' (Daniel 12:13). Daniel's resurrection is at *the end of the days*. When is that? Daniel gives three sets of days in this chapter. Verse 7 gives 1260 days (a time, times, and an half) which is the day that Christ returns...Verse 11 gives 1290 days. Verse 12 gives 1335 days. Three sets of days.**
>
> **When is Daniel's resurrection? Daniel's resurrection is at the *end of the days*. Which day is that? The 1335th day! Day 1260 is the return of Christ and day 1335 is the resurrection of Daniel. Therefore, Daniel's resurrection comes *75 days* after Christ's return. Yes, the difference between Paul's resurrection and Daniel's resurrection is very real. In Paul's resurrection (1 Cor. 15:52; 1 Thess. 4:16), the dead are raised *first*, the moment Christ descends in the clouds. In Daniel's resurrection, the dead are raised *later*, 75 days after Christ returns. These two men are talking about *two different resurrections*, different resurrections at *different times*.**

But there is more to this 75 day gap after Christ returns according to Allen Beechick. He writes on page 199: "What, then, is the gathering? (Matt. 24:31; Mark 13:27). It is a gathering of Israel to Jerusalem, not a gathering of the church in the air. Israel is called the "elect" in Isaiah 45:4 and 65:9. Now let's go to the next question. How soon after Christ's return will the gathering of Israel take place? Daniel indicates a 75 day gap between the return of Christ and the beginning of the millennium."

Prophetic writer Beechick, who holds a Master of Divinity degree from Western Conservative Baptist Seminary, gives further details of this end-time 75 day gap scenario. With pure speculation, he writes on page 200 of his book:

> **Scripture does not spell it out, but let me share with you my guesses which I think are based on Scripture. You be the judge. The first 30 days allows time for the rooting out of the tares...These 30 days of destroying the wicked may be concluded on day 1290 by the chaining of Satan (Revelation 20:1-3). Then—according to the proper order of Matthew 13, tares first, wheat second—begins the gathering of the elect from the four corners of the earth. Then on day 1335 the gathering is completed to the uttermost part of heaven as the believing souls join new bodies in the resurrection. Thus this 75-day "time of harvest" allows 30 days for the destruction of the wicked and 45 days for the gathering of the righteous, and it is all according to the proper order of Matthew 13.**

THE 1290 DAYS

The theme of (Daniel 12) is the "resurrection", notice verses 2,3:

> **And many of them that *sleep* in the dust of the earth *shall awake*, [be resurrected] some to everlasting life, and some to shame and everlasting contempt. And they that be wise shall shine as the brightness of the firmament; and they that turn many to righteousness as the stars for ever and ever.**

THE KINGDOM RESTORED

Continuing the concept of "the resurrection of the just and the unjust", we read in verse 10:

Many shall be purified, and made white, and tried; but the wicked shall do wickedly: and none of the wicked shall understand; but the wise shall understand. (Vs. 11) And from the time that the daily sacrifice shall be taken away, and the abomination that maketh desolate set up (inclusive), there shall be a thousand two hundred and ninety days (to a resurrection).

In other words, a *resurrection* could take place 1290 days after the sacrifices are taken away and at the same time the Abomination of desolation set up. The first phase for RESTORING ISRAEL could begin with the resurrection of the 144,000 first-fruit Israelites (Rev. 7, 14). They will be the first Israelites to be converted, primarily through the preaching of the "Two Witnesses." See also (Dan. 12:1,10; Matt. 24:9). This resurrection could occur 30 days *after* Christ returns.

THE 1335 DAYS

Another *resurrection* of Israel could occur 45 days later for those waiting for the 1335 days, as Daniel 12:12 states:

Blessed is he that waiteth, and cometh to the thousand three hundred and five and thirty days [to be resurrected]. But go thou thy way [Daniel] till the end be: for thou shalt rest [in the grave], and stand [be resurrected] in thy lot at the end of the days.

This was a continuation of thought about the *resurrection*! Daniel was to be a part of this one—notice, "...you shall rest [sleep in the ground] and stand" [be resurrected]—see the *Companion Bible* for a more accurate translation. This *resurrection* would be for RESTORING THE NATION OF ISRAEL, in which King David and the prophets of Israel, including Daniel, who technically were not "in Christ" will be *resurrected!*

This concept also ties in with the "first resurrection" of

Revelation 20:6: **"*Blessed* and holy is he that hath part in the first resurrection..."** Notice the similar wording to those who wait for the 1335 days in Daniel 12:12: **"*Blessed* is he that waiteth and cometh to the thousand three hundred and five and thirty days" [to be resurrected].** If there were only one resurrection, why would anyone be "blessed" if they waited? One would only wait if they had a choice!

THE KINGDOM RESTORED

THE 1335 DAY CONTROVERSY

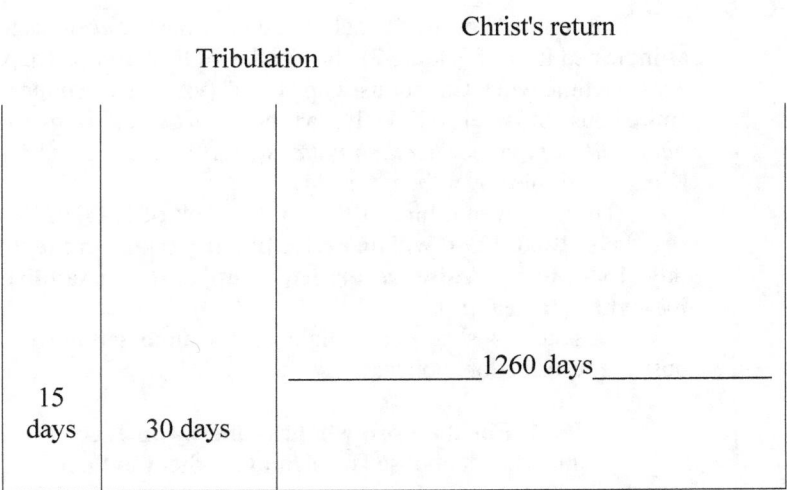

Pre Tribulation Theory

Post Tribulation Theory

THE RESTORATION OF ISRAEL

THE VALLEY OF DRY BONES AND ISRAEL'S RESURRECTION

The entire "house of Israel" could be *resurrected* at this time as indicated from (Ezekiel 37), the "Valley of Dry Bones" chapter. This is a time when Christ raises up "flesh" (vs. 6) and reunites the entire house of Israel (vs. 11). It is a time *when Christ brings Israel out of the captivity of heathen nations* (vss. 12,14,21), and when King David rules over them (vs. 24).

There is even a hint of this in the book of Hosea: **"After two days (1260, 1290) will he revive [resurrect] us; in the third day (1335) he will raise [resurrect] us up, and we shall live in his sight" (Hosea 6:2).**

Isaiah 14 sheds more light on the time setting of this possible resurrection, notice:

(Vs. 1) For the Lord will have mercy on Jacob, and will yet choose Israel, and set them in their own land: and the strangers shall be joined with them, and they shall cleave to the house of Jacob. (Vs.3) And it shall come to pass in *the day that the LORD shall give thee rest* **[the Millennium] from thy sorrow, and from thy fear, and from the hard bondage wherein thou wast made to serve. (Vs. 7)** *The whole earth is at rest* **[the Millennium], and is quiet: they break forth into singing. (Vs. 9) Hell from beneath is moved for thee to** *meet thee at thy coming* **[resurrection]:** *It stirred up the dead* **from thee [resurrection], even all the chief ones of the earth; it hath raised up [resurrected] from their thrones all the kings of the nations.**

This *resurrection* to restore Israel appears to be premillennial, for it is in the very same context when Gog and Magog come to take the spoil from the peace dwelling and prosperous Israel (Ezekiel 38 and 39). This event happens shortly into the Millennium, and is a continuation of thought of (Ezekiel 37).

If this coup of Gog and Magog were the same as the one in (Revelation 20:7-8); it would occur after the 1,000 year reign of Christ's Kingdom. But this coup occurs shortly after Israel is brought back from captivity [in the latter years], prior to, or shortly into the beginning of the Millennium!

SUMMARY

The 1260 day *resurrection* of the 7 Church eras comprising the New Testament Church, the *resurrection* of the 144,000 firstfruits of Israel, and Gentile Tribulation Saints after 1290 days, and the *resurrection* of the prophets and entire "House of Israel" after 1335 days, could technically all be part of the "first resurrection."

Prior to Christ's return, we know that Christ, the "Two Witnesses", Lazerus and Dorcas rose from the dead—yet (Revelation 20:5) mentions "the first resurrection" as coming *after* these. This only goes to prove that other resurrections after (1260, 1290, 1335) could technically be classified as part of the first resurrection.

But why call this the "first resurrection" if other resurrections occur before this? Obviously, there must be an explanation. Could it be that the "first resurrection" entails all the preceding resurrections, including Old Testament, New Testament and Tribulation Saints?

The key to understanding the significance of the 1290 days and 1335 days is realizing they are both counted from the "Abomination of desolation"! Both begin at the same starting point, but end at different points.

We might also ask one final question. Because the 144,000 are *sealed* from the seven last plagues as Christ returns with His resurrected Bride—when are they resurrected? The Bible says they are *sealed* not *resurrected* at a time the Bride is already resurrected with her husband.

The 144,000 physical Israelites of (Revelation 7) will be the *firstfruits* or first converted of Israel during the Tribulation! They will go through the Tribulation and be converted through the efforts of the "Two Witnesses"!

The 144,000 of Revelation 14 may very well be a *different firstfruits*—these could be converts of Gentiles during the Tribulation from all nations (Rev. 7:9). Both of these groups could comprise the Tribulation Saints and be resurrected 1290 days after the Abomination of desolation is set up. This momentous event could take place 30 days after Christ returns with His Bride! This resurrection along with the Church is pictured by the harvest of

THE RESTORATION OF ISRAEL

Pentecost!

If these groups comprise *firstfruits*—there must also be *secondfruits* or the great harvest of souls! The great harvest of souls is pictured by the Feast of Tabernacles—could begin with the resurrection of the Old Testament Saints and houses of Israel 1335 days after the Abomination of desolation is set up! This most awe-inspiring miracle could transpire 45 days after the return of Christ with His Bride!

The New Testament Church and "the woman" will be resurrected fulfilling the 1260 day resurrection, and will return with Jesus Christ to witness the battle of Armageddon.

Thirty days later, a resurrection of "firstfruits" of Israel comprising the 144,000 physical Israelites could occur. Also 144,000 Tribulation "firstfruits" of Gentiles from all nations could be resurrected at this time! Then 45 days later, the remainder of the whole house of Israel could be restored along with the Old Testament prophets!

Upon restoring the nation of Israel to prominence—Christ will cleanse Israel of her sins fulfilling the "Day of Atonement." The Day of Atonement, *picturing* the redemption of Israel's sins, and then placing them upon their true perpetrator [Satan] could transpire!

The 1290 day and 1335 day resurrections could occur *after* Christ returns, and after Satan is bound so the Millennium can begin! Notice the time sequence of the "first resurrection" of Revelation 20! Only after the Devil is chained (vs.2) does the "first resurrection" occur (vs. 4).

THE WISE SHALL UNDERSTAND

The angel of the Lord told Daniel the wise would understand the mystery of the 1260, 1290, and 1335 day intervals in the end-time. Daniel did not understand them then—but we can understand them today!

If we are correct in our understanding of these days—we have a dilemma! If we know the time from when the "Abomination of desolation" is set up to the return of Christ is 1260 days—why did Jesus say: **"But of that day and hour knoweth no man, no, not the angels of heaven, but my Father only" (Matt. 24:36).**

Let's ask for a moment!

THE KINGDOM RESTORED

Didn't the angel of the Lord tell Daniel these things? It certainly sounded like he knew the meaning of these days! And what about the angels who blow the 7 last trumpets culminating in the return of Jesus Christ in the book of Revelation? Surely, they would know when Jesus was about to return to the earth as they blow their trumpets!

What about this?

Do we have a biblical contradiction here? No, I think not, but let me give you my undogmatic opinion.

When Jesus spoke these words—it was in the *present* tense! Even He didn't know at that time when He would return, because He had forgotten God's plan. Jesus was like a man suffering from amnesia, until His mind gradually began to be restored while in the flesh!

Finally, when He was resurrected, this temporary amnesia subsided and He recalled all that He and His Father had discussed in deified form. To say that Jesus does not *now* know when He will return—could be stretching the truth!

My answer to this biblical enigma for what its worth is this: no man knew the day or hour of Christ's return when Jesus spoke these words—however, the wise shall understand them in the last days! The wicked nonbelievers will not know or understand, and therefore will fulfill this prophecy in part!

ISRAEL'S FOUR RETURNS

Not only does the Bible prophesy that the nation of Israel would be in their land when Christ returns—but that they would be taken from their land *four* different times before Christ returns!

1) The first dispersion from Palestine began in the days of Joseph, when God said Israel would **"...be a stranger in a land that is not theirs, and shall serve them: and they shall afflict them four hundred years"** (Gen. 15:13).

This prophecy occurred when Jacob's sons went down to Egypt during a famine in the land of Canaan where their brother Joseph had become Pharaoh's right-hand-man.

The Israelites remained in Egypt only to become slaves to the Egyptians who feared their great numbers. But Israel was finally

THE RESTORATION OF ISRAEL

led out of this bondage as God raised up Moses to lead them into the promised land. God said, **"That nation, whom they serve, will I judge: and afterward shall they come out with great substance" (Gen. 15:14).**

2) The second occasion in which the nation of Israel was removed out of their land began in 721 B.C. in which the divided Kingdom of Israel and Judah were taken captive. The 10 tribes forming the nation of Israel went into captivity to the Assyrians in 721 B.C., and the nation of Judah composed of the tribes of Judah and Benjamin went into captivity in 606 B.C. to the Babylonians. Judah remained captive for seventy years as prophesied by Jeremiah (Jer. 25:11), but under Ezra, Nehemiah and Zerubbabel they began returning to their homeland in 536 B.C.

3) The third time Israel was removed out of their land was in A.D. 70 by the invading Roman armies under the Roman General Titus. The Jews in Palestine began scattering throughout all the world.

During the time Israel was dispersed throughout the world, many different peoples have been in control of the holy land. In A.D. 637, the Arabs ruled this area until the sixteenth century. Palestine was trampled under foot by Gentile armies during the Crusades of the twelfth and thirteenth centuries only to be defeated by Saladin in 1187. The Ottoman Turks ruled this area between 1517 until Turkey's defeat in World War 1.

THE ZIONIST MOVEMENT—1917

In 1871, a few Jews began migrating back to their homeland and by 1881 nearly twenty-five thousand Jews had returned to their land. But it wasn't until 1897 that the Zionist movement formally began, as Theodore Herzl stated the goal of reclaiming the land of Palestine as a home for the Jews before the first Zionist Congress. This proclamation captured the attention of Jews the world over. By 1914, the number of Jews that had returned to Jerusalem was nearly eighty thousand.

The British occupation of the holy land began in 1917 when General Allenby conquered Jerusalem. It was at this time that the British Foreign Declaration stated approval of Israel's goal of establishing a national homeland for Jews. This was done as a

THE KINGDOM RESTORED

gesture to show support for the Jewish war effort.

However, due to growing Arab pressure, Britain failed to keep it's commitment and very little was achieved until 1939 when World War 11 started. But nonetheless, 400,000 wandering Jews found their way back to their birthright land despite harsh immigration laws.

THE STATE OF ISRAEL CREATED—1948

The holocaust of the Jews by Hitler's stormtroppers during World War 11 led to world empathy for the Jews. People the world over began to realize that Jews needed a homeland like everyone else.

After World War 11, the United Nations, with the approval of the United States and Russia, agreed to establish a homeland for the Jews despite an Arab league opposition.

According to the proclamation, Palestine was to be divided into a Jewish state and an Arab state, with five thousand square miles assigned to the newly formed state of Israel on May 14, 1948.

This newly formed nation contained 650,000 Jews and hundreds of Arabs. The Jews were not in their homeland very long before a war broke out between them and the dissenting Arab world in 1948-1949. Israel was victorious in this war which included Egypt, Jordan, Iraq, Syria, Lebanon and Saudi Arabia. Although Israeli casualties were heavy, they extended their territory to eight thousand square miles.

Ironically, this date calculates out to be exactly 2520 biblical years from the Babylonian captivity in 536 B.C. According to historical and Biblical scholars, Judah's captivity began in 606 B.C. and ended in 536 B.C. Flavius Josephus confirms this fact.

Therefore, if we count 2520 biblical years from this 536 B.C. ($2520 \times 360 = 907,200$ days). This translates out to be a total of 2,483.8 calendar years of 365.25 days (907,200 divided by 365.25 = 2,483.8 years. Adding 1 year when going from B.C. to A.D. brings us to 1948!

THE SIX DAY WAR—1967

As a result of the spectacular Six-day War of 1967, the nation of Israel found itself in full control of the city of Jerusalem for the

THE RESTORATION OF ISRAEL

first time since their dispersion in A.D. 70. Besides occupying the city of Jerusalem, Israel's territory expanded to include the territory of the west bank of the Jordan river.

THE YOM KIPPUR WAR—1973

On Yom Kippur, the most solemn Holy day of the Jews, Egypt and Syria attacked Israel. If it wasn't for Russian and United States intervention, Israel would have stormed into Cairo. The cease fire came at a time when advancing Israeli armies almost surrounded the Egyptian third army. This would have allowed the Israeli army and air force to advance deep into Egypt and eventually Syria.

As a result of this war, Israel annexed territory into Egypt and Syria.

THE FINAL DISPERSION OF ISRAEL

4) The fourth and final dispersion of Israel is yet future, but the stage is now set for the prophecy Jesus spoke of in Luke 21:20 to be fulfilled. This occurs just prior to the return of Jesus Christ to the earth, notice:

> **And when you see Jerusalem compassed [surrounded] with armies, then know that the desolation is nigh [near]. Then let them which are in Judea flee [disperse] to the mountains; and let them which are in the midst of it depart out...**

After 3 1/2 years of captivity, Jesus will return to the earth and start the New Covenant with a repentant and obedient Israel as Moses recorded:

> **When thou art in *tribulation*, and all these things are upon thee, *even in the latter days*, if thou turn to the LORD thy God, and shalt be obedient unto his voice; [For the LORD thy God is a merciful God] he will not forsake thee, neither destroy thee, nor forget the covenant of thy fathers which he sware unto them (Deut.**

THE KINGDOM RESTORED

4:29-31).

It will be at this time that Jesus Himself will lead Israel out of captivity (Ezek. 37:12,14,21; 38:8; 39:27,28) of the heathen nations for the final dispersion of Israel, and begin to RESTORE THE KINGDOM TO ISRAEL as His model nation!

DANIEL'S 70TH WEEK AND 2520 YEARS

We have read the prophecies in Daniel regarding an image depicting four Gentile governments that would rule the world for 2520 years *until* the second coming of Christ—when the government, church and state, shall be *restored* to Israel!

After seventy years of servitude, a partial return of the nation of Judah was allowed to return to their homeland by king Cyrus the Persian in 536 B.C. Therefore, if we count 2520 prophetic years from 536 B.C. we would arrive at the very significant year of 1948—the year in which Israel was "reborn" as a nation and established in their homeland!

We also saw how Daniel's prophecy of 483 years from the time the commandment or decree given to restore and to rebuild Jerusalem—or after the "threescore (60) and two weeks", which follows the first seven weeks (69 weeks) the Messiah would make His triumphant entry into Jerusalem and present Himself as the Messiah of Israel, and shortly thereafter would be "cut off" or be crucified.

If we use the traditional date of 457 B.C. as the Persian decree and count 483 calendar years, we would arrive at the date of Christ's beginning ministry in A.D. 27. This would make the crucifixion (3 1/2 years later) in A.D. 31.

Thus far we have seen the incredible accuracy of Daniels prophecy concerning the death of our Savior and the resurrection and rebirth of the nation of Israel in 1948. But did the prophecy clock stop in 1948 regarding the 70 weeks prophecy? Was there an approximate 2,000 year interim before the 70th week would start "Jacob's Trouble" and the Great Tribulation?

Recall that the first 69 weeks were fulfilled in the Messiah's death. But what about the rest of the prophecy regarding His return and the fulfillment of the 70th week?

Daniel's seven weeks and the seven times punishment of the nation of Israel for 2520 prophetic years was fulfilled in 1948. But

THE RESTORATION OF ISRAEL

the rest of the prophecy foretells of the return of the Messiah.

Using typology as our guide, it is as though what happened to God's spiritual Son (Jesus) and Physical National son (Israel) have many parallels. But are there any parallel types we can find in the Bible that demonstrate how God uses his mathmatecal punishment for the nation of Israel?

Recall, after leaving their Egyptian bondage and upon their arrival at Kadesh Barnea, which bordered the Promised Land of Canaan, they sent out twelve spies to survey the land and its people (Numbers 13:18-25). But what did the spies say to Moses as they returned from Promised Land. They reported that the land was indeed a good land "flowing with milk and honey." Except for Joshua and Caleb the 10 spies told the people that there was no way they could defeat the people living in the land as they were like giants and too strong.

We read of the account in Numbers 13:30-32: "Then Caleb quieted the people before Moses and said, We should by all means go up and take possession of it, for we will *surely* overcome it. But the men who had gone up with him said, We are not able to go up against the people, for they are too strong for us."

Because of the Isralites lack of faith and unbelief that God would help them conquer the promised land, He was now going to punish them using His day for a year principle. For every day the spies were on lookout (40) God was going to punish them 40 years in the wilderness before they could enter the promised land

But when did the actural counting of the 40 years begin? Did it start from the time the Israelites came back from their spying mission? No, it actually started two years previous from the time they entered Kadesh Barnea.

JESUS IN THE WILDERNESS

There are many parallels between Moses as a type of Jesus but we will focus only upon the wilderness experience.

Immediately after Jesus' baptism, the Holy Spirit "drove him out into the wilderness" (Mark 1:12). What followed was our Lord's temptation by Satan. Anyone familiar with the Old Testament will quickly see the many parallels between Jesus' time in the wilderness and the history of Israel.

Israel's testing for forty years in the wilderness and Jesus' being tempted for forty days in the same place (Deut. 8:1–2; Mark

THE KINGDOM RESTORED

1:13) is yet another parallel.

Moses, the representative of Israel, spent forty days on Mount Sinai at a critical point in his ministry. Jesus also spent forty days in the wilderness at a critical point in His ministry (Ex. 24:15-18; Mark 1:13).

Moses chose 12 spies to explore Canaan, and Jesus chose 12 disciples. Moses appointed 70 rulers over Israel, and Jesus sent 70 disciples out to share the gospel.

Moses interceded on behalf of the disbelieving Israelites (Num. 14:11; 28-29) and Jesus pleaded to the Father to forgive the Israelites who chose to release Barabbas over Him (Lk. 23:34).

Israel was punished for their unbelief and was not allowed to enter the promised land in both situations, under Moses and the generation of unbelievers and the Jews of Jesus' day. The pattern then is the same.

Jesus spoke of a fig tree generation that would not pass till all things prophesied in Matthew 24, Mark 13 and Luke 21 be fulfilled, "Now learn a parable of the fig tree; When his branch is yet tender, and puts forth leaves, ye know that summer is nigh" (Matt. 24:32-34). Clearly, Jesus was offering the Kingdom to the nation of Israel and His generation. But they rejectyed His message as they did in Moses' day.

Could it be that the counting of Israel's punishment and the return of our Savior can be counted using the same principle? In other words the prophetic time clock according to some interpretors did not stop at the 69th week of Daniel even though there is a 2,000 year time lapse. Could it be that the prophetic clock has continued just as the counting of the Israelites punishment did not start after the spies came back, but two years previously. In other words, God added time on the clock instead of stopping the clock.

Most Bible scholars believe the starting point of the 70 weeks was the decree to restore and rebuild Jerusalem by King Artaxerxes the Persian in 457 B.C. (Dan.9:25; Ezra 7:11-26).

There is a theory that suggests that the counting of the 40 years in the wilderness did not officially begin when the spies had returned from scouting out the land for 40 days, but 2 years previous when Israel was not wandering for 40 years in the desert but spent two years in Kadesh Barnea which was just outside the border of Canaan. Therefore, the theory suggest the counting should start backwards from 457 B.C. and counting 2520 days or prophetic years to when Jacob's Trouble or the Great Tribulation would begin. But which calendar should we use?

In order to understand any aspect of prophecy relating to prophetic days or years, it is vital to understand the Hebrew Calendar.

For over two centuries the Israelites had been in severe bondage in Egypt—forced to work with cruel taskmasters over them. There was no Bible—no written Word of God. They were not permitted to worship God as He had ordained. They were forced to work seven days a week.

It appears that God first revealed His religious calendar to the nation of Israel prior to their first Passover observance in Egypt. At this time, God set His civil calendar approximately six months backwards, as the first month of the religious calendar became the seventh month of the civil calendar.

The Sabbath day had established the days of the week, the new moons had established the months in proper sequence. Once Israel set foot in their new land, the Sabbatical cycles and Jubilee Year were established (Lev. 25:2-12).

Our modern world calendar is based on the solar cycle, and consists of 365.25 days. The calendar that God gave the Israelites was calculated according to both lunar and solar cycles.

Therefore, counting 2520 biblical years from this 457 B.C. (2520 x 360 = 907,200 days divided by 365.25 calendar years = 2,483.8 years when the 70th week of Daniel begins! Adding 1 year when going from B.C. to A.D. brings us to 2028 A.D.; the possible return of our Savior. If that date is correct, the Tribulation would start seven years prior in 2021. This is pure speculation and only time will tell!

Chapter Nineteen

> *Then I saw an angel coming down from heaven, having the key to the bottomless pit and a great chain in his hand. He laid hold of the dragon, that serpent of old, who is the Devil and Satan, and bound him for a thousand years; and he cast him into the bottomless pit, and shut him up, and set a seal on him so that he should deceive the nations no more till the thousand years were finished. But after these things he must be released for a little while.*
> —*(Rev. 20:1-3).*

SATAN CHAINED FOR 1,000 YEARS

Satan, known throughout the Bible as the Serpent, the Wicked one, the Devil, the Adversary, the Dragon, the father of lies, the Tempter, etc., is finally to be chained and bound for a duration of 1,000 years! This is the time Jesus Christ will rule on the earth with His Saints, and the Millennium of peace and prosperity will begin.

The Devil has been the root cause of all the world's evils, and only when he is restrained will deception of religious worship cease! This cunning adversary has lured mankind into sin by appealing to human nature. Through deceit, he has influenced man's carnal mind to lust, and kill, and steal, and connive, and fraud, and lie, etc., etc! Now he will be temporarily removed for

THE RESTORATION OF ISRAEL

one thousand years!

Coupled with the fact that now God's Holy Spirit will be written upon the hearts and minds of those who willingly accept God's way of life—happiness, joy and love will prevail in a near utopia world!

SAINTS TO REIGN WITH CHRIST

And I saw thrones, and they sat on them. and judgment was committed to them. And I saw the souls of those who had been beheaded for their witness to Jesus and for the word of God, who had not worshipped the beast or his image, and had not received his mark on their foreheads or on their hands. And they lived and reigned with Christ for a thousand years (Rev. 20:4; 5-6).

The Church age pictured by Pentecost will be the resurrected Bride of Jesus Christ. Together, they will work in harmony with the nation of Israel in converting the entire earth, notice:

And he that overcometh, and he that keepeth my works unto the end, *to him will I give authority over the nations:* **and he shall rule them with a rod of iron... Rev. 2:26-29).**

Israel will have been gathered into their land, and God will then circumcise their heart with His Holy Spirit. Saints will be governing the nation of Israel and the earth from Jerusalem, the new capital of the world!

Power will be given these Saints to enforce God's laws—and all nations who disobey them, will be severely punished by natural phenomena such as droughts!

God has *never* made any promise that the reward of the Saints will be a place in heaven. Contrariwise, the inheritance of the Saints will be the Kingdom of God on earth (Rev. 5:10).

ALL NATIONS TO KEEP THE FEAST OF TABERNACLES

And it shall come to pass that everyone who is left of all the nations which came against Jerusalem shall go up from year to year to worship the King, the LORD of hosts, and to keep the Feast of Tabernacles. And it shall be that whichever of the families of the earth do not come up to Jerusalem to worship the King, the LORD of hosts, on them there will be no rain...This shall be the punishment of Egypt and the punishment of all the nations that do not come up to keep the Feast of Tabernacles (Zech. 14:16-19).

Once the Kingdom of God is established on the earth—all the nations that were Israel's oppressors will be required to keep the Feast of Tabernacles! The Feast will be kept as a *memorial* of the time God saved Israel out of the north country! The miraculous return of Israel out of captivity will be acknowledged and remembered by all nations!

Eventually, the entire earth will keep the Feast of Tabernacles—which commemorates the return of God's people to their land out of captivity! Under a one world government, and a universal religion—all peoples of the earth will rejoice in keeping this Feast, memorializing the fame and renown of the great miracle the Eternal performed!

Severe punishment in the form of drought will accompany any nation who refuses to observe this most glorious Feast!

Once Jesus sets up His throne in Jerusalem—the Aaronic sacrificial system will be restored:

...Yes, every pot in Jerusalem and Judah shall be holiness to the LORD of hosts. *Everyone who sacrifices shall come* **and take them and cook in them. In that day there shall no longer be a Canaanite in the house of the LORD of hosts (Zech. 14:21—see also Ezek. 44:9-31).**

These sacrifices will be instituted as memorials, like the feast days—to teach the newly enlightened nations God's ways! God will teach the world His ways and laws from ground one.

Our Master Teacher is going to convert the world through the nation of Israel. Once before He taught them the meaning of sin through the sacrificial system, and He will start His plan of salvation through them again. This is God's kindergarten method for converting the world!

Because the nations of the earth will not come to the Eternal willingly at first, as obedience will not be by *faith* as it is in the sacrifice of Jesus Christ today—it will be therefore necessary for God to enforce His laws with *a strong hand*!

Unlike the other nations, Israel will eventually walk by *faith* and not by sight, as God's laws will be written upon their hearts and minds! They will have learned by now to trust in the Eternal, and that His laws are right and good! The analogy of the Church to the world now—will be the same as Israel to the world then!

GOG AND MAGOG ATTEMPT ANOTHER COUP

Now the word of the LORD came to me, saying, Son of man, set your face against Gog, of the land of Magog, the prince of Rosh, Meshech, and Tubal, and prophesy against him, and say, 'Thus says the Lord GOD: Behold, I am against you, O Gog, the prince of Rosh, Meshech, and Tubal...After many days you will be visited. *In the latter years you will come into the land of those brought back from the sword and gathered from many people on the mountains of Israel, which had long been desolate; they were brought out of the nations, and now all of them dwell safely...* **On that day it shall come to pass that thoughts will arise in your mind. and you will make an evil plan: You will say,** *I will go up against a land of unwalled villages; I will go to a peaceful people who dwell safely, all of them dwelling without walls, and having neither bars nor gates,* **to take plunder and to take booty, to stretch out your hand against the waste places that are again inhabited, and against a people**

> **gathered from the nations, who have acquired livestock and goods, who dwell in the midst of the land' (Ezek. 38:1-12).**

Almost all Bible dictionaries, commentaries, and scholars agree that the names *Gog* and *Magog* refer to the nation of Russia. The ancient capital cities of Russia were *Meshech* and *Tubal*, from which the modern cities of *Moscow* and *Tobolsk* are derived.

Gog was ruler of the land of Magog. In (Genesis 10:2), Magog, Meshech, Tubal, and Gomer are named the sons of Japheth, and founders of the northern group of nations. The clincher as to the identity of modern-day Magog is found in the book of Ezekiel. Three times he speaks of them dwelling in the "Northern parts" (Chapters 38:6, 15; 39:2).

The *King James* version distorts the real meaning of the original Hebrew, and is translated "uttermost" or "extreme" north in the *Revised Standard* and *Amplified Versions*. Any world map will clearly show the nation to the "uttermost" or "extreme" north of Israel is Russia!

After Jacob's trouble is over, they will be led out of captivity, and brought back to their land. God will have mercy on them and they will be a blessed and prosperous nation. They will have acquired a great deal of material wealth from their oppressors—in a similar manner as their ancestors did after being led out of Egypt during the first exodus.

Israel will be a barren and desolate people during their enslavement—losing their wealth and world power. But God will gather them out of the nations *one by one* and restore them in the Promised Land. Even Israel's desert land that had been a continual waste for many centuries, will be made to blossom.

When envious nations see the accumulated opulence of Israel—they will want to take the spoil. They will think it is their opportunity to fulfill their dreams of conquering the whole earth! How ironic, that after all of the plagues that have been poured out, and all the miracles performed by God—the evil plot of world domination would still prevail!

This only proves that miracles are not enough to convince anyone that God's way of life is best. Miracles did not convince the nation of Israel to be more righteous and have more faith in God! Think about all the fantastic miracles the Eternal performed for Israel in Egypt, and in the wilderness. Did Israel become more faithful, more loyal?—no, they became more rebellious! In fact, within a year of the Exodus, they rebelled against God on ten different occasions (Num. 14:22).

And what about the time of Christ's ministry? If ever there was a time of signs and wonders to convince the nation of Israel—this was it! Jesus performed unbelievable healings before their very eyes, and gave them the sign of Jonah—that He would be in the heart of the earth for three days and nights after being crucified. Did this lead to the conversion of the nation of Israel—absolutely not! What did they do? They killed Christ's disciples!

In Jesus' own words, He said it was, **"An evil and adulterous generation that seeketh after a sign [miracle]..." (Matt. 12:39).** Jesus also said that: **"Many will say to me in that day, Lord, Lord, have we not prophesied in thy name? and in thy name have cast out devils? and in thy name done many wonderful works [miracles]? And then will I profess unto them, I never knew you: depart from me, ye that work iniquity [lawlessness]" (Matt. 7:21-23).**

Clearly, miracles are outward signs designed to appeal to the spiritually weak or carnally minded who have no faith in the laws of God. Furthermore, even if people execute miracles in Christ's name, this is no guarantee that they are teaching and abiding by the laws of God! The "False Prophet" will perform tremendous [false miracles] and lead people astray!

Because Israel will be dwelling without fortifications or armed troops—the attack of the north will think they are easy prey! Israel will be living peacefully, trusting in her God to defend her—now that she has a new heart and mind! But her newly acquired wealth from her captors will cause the poorer nations to lust after her.

GOG AND MAGOG'S PUNISHMENT

> **On that day when My people Israel dwell safely, will you not know it? Then you will come from your place out of the far north, you and many peoples with you, all of them riding on horses, a great company and a mighty army. You will come up against My people Israel like a cloud, to cover the land. It will be in *the latter days* that I will bring you**

> **against My land, so that the nations may know Me, when I am hallowed in you, O Gog, before their eyes...I will call for a sword against Gog throughout all My mountains, says the Lord God. Every man's sword will be against his brother. And I will bring him to judgment with pestilence and bloodshed; I will rain down on him. on his troops, and on the many peoples who are with him, flooding rain, great hailstones, fire, and brimstone (Ezek. 38:14-23).**

The time setting in which Gog and Magog will attack Israel is in the *latter days*. Israel will have been brought back out of bondage and will be dwelling securely without walls or gates when the nations from the "uttermost parts of the north" will invade them. This may be 15 to 20 years after the return of Christ—prior to the actual start of the Millennium for cities are already built and seed planted (Ezek. 38:11).

This time however, Israel will let Jesus Christ personally fight their battles for them—and He will destroy them with overwhelming hailstones, fire and brimstone! From that time onward, the nations will know the God of Israel, who magnifies Himself and sanctifies Himself!

The entire army of Gog and Magog will be wiped out by Jesus Christ by the rod of His mouth! There will be such a tremendous slaughter of Israel's enemies, that it will require seven months to bury their dead. Ravenous birds and wild beasts will devour their flesh. This army from the north will be so prodigious, that the material from their weapons will be used to furnish Israel's fuel supply for seven years! (Ezek. 39:1-16).

Gog and all his followers will be buried in the valley of Hamongog, which means *the multitude of Gog* (Ezek. 39:11-16). The valley of Hamongog is also referred to as the valley of Jehoshaphat, the plain of Esdraelon, Jezreel and Megiddo.

THE NATIONS TO LEARN WAR NO MORE

Prior to Christ's return, scripture indicates the earth is to be utterly *destroyed*, notice:

THE RESTORATION OF ISRAEL

> **Behold, the LORD maketh the earth empty, and maketh it waste, and turneth it upside down, and scattereth abroad the inhabitants thereof. And it shall be, as with the people, so with the priest; as with the servant, so with his master; ...The land shall be *utterly emptied, and utterly spoiled*: for the LORD hath spoken this word (Isa. 24:1,3).**

The earth is to be *devoured* and *few* men left:

> **Therefore hath the curse devoured the earth, and they that dwell therein are desolate: therefore the inhabitants of the earth are burned, and *few men left* (Isa. 24:6). See also (Revelation 16:8).**

This is most likely the 1290 day period or 45 days after Christ returns, in which **"one shall be taken and one left."** At this time, the earth will be totally cleansed of all the ungodly, and prepared to begin the Millennium!

However, unbelievable as it may seem, even after all this destruction and pain to the inhabitants of the earth, Gog & Magog will attack the peaceful and prosperous Israelites now dwelling safely at Jerusalem.

But this time Jesus intervenes so that all the heathen nations may know Him:

> **And thou shalt come up against my people of Israel, as a cloud to cover the land; it shall be in *the latter days*, and I will bring thee against my land, THAT THE HEATHEN MAY KNOW ME, when I shall be sanctified in thee, O Gog, before their eyes (Ezek. 38:16).**

Let's read more of this event in Ezekiel 39:6-7:

> **And I will send a fire on Magog, and among them that dwell carelessly in the isles; and they shall know that I am the LORD. So will I make my holy name**

> known in the midst of my people Israel; and I will not let them pollute my holy name any more: and the heathen shall know that I am the LORD, the Holy One in Israel.

The weapons of Gog are then to be destroyed and burned for 7 years:

> **And they that dwell in the cities of Israel shall go forth, and shall set on fire and burn the weapons, both the shields and the bucklers, the bows and the arrows, and the handstaves, and the spears, and they shall burn them with fire seven years (Ezek. 39:9).**

Israel, will then bury the dead for seven months:

> **And seven months shall the house of Israel be burying of them, that they may cleanse the land (Ezek. 39:12).**

Finally, the nations will learn war no more, when God's House is established in Jerusalem:

> **But in the last days, it shall come to pass, that the mountain of the house of the LORD shall be established in the top of the mountains, and it shall be exalted above the hills; and people shall flow unto it [mountains and hills are symbolic for great nations and small nations]. And many nations shall come, and say, Come, and let us go up to the mountain of the LORD, and to the house of the God of Jacob; and he will teach us of his ways, and we will walk in his paths: for the law shall go forth of Zion, and the word of the LORD from Jerusalem. And he shall judge among many people, and rebuke strong nations afar off; and they shall beat their swords into plowshares and their spears into pruninghooks: nation shall not lift**

THE RESTORATION OF ISRAEL

up sword against nation, **NEITHER SHALL THEY LEARN WAR ANY MORE** (Micah 4:1-3).

ISRAELITES TO BUILD THE OLD WASTE PLACES

Perhaps only 10% of the remaining 1/3 of the nation of Israel who goes into captivity will live to begin the Millennium, notice:

> **And I will cause you to pass under the rod, and I will bring you into the bond of the covenant: And I will purge out from among the rebels, and them that transgress against me: I will bring them forth out of the country where they sojourn, and they shall not enter into the land of Israel: and ye shall know that I am the LORD (Ezek. 20: 37-38).**

Notice, God is going to "purge out" the REBELS of Israel! This is God's method of weeding out the tares! The expression **"pass under the rod"** is God's method of scrutinizing those He wants. This was His instruction to the Levites in taking a *tithe* of the peoples flocks (Lev. 27:30-32).

This same prophecy is repeated in Amos 5:3:

> **For thus saith the LORD GOD; The city that went out by a thousand shall leave an hundred (10%), and that which went forth by an hundred shall leave ten, (10%) to the house of Israel.**

The Eternal will begin rebuilding the nation of Israel, then the entire world by gathering the wealth of the heathen nations and giving it to Judah:

> **And Judah also shall fight at Jerusalem; and the wealth of all the heathen round about shall be gathered together, gold, and silver, and apparel, in great abundance (Zech. 14:14).**

Isaiah 60 describes how this wealth will be gathered from the heathen nations. The ships of Tarshish shall bring silver and gold as well as Sheba and other nations (vss. 6-9). Isaiah 61 describes the rebuilding of the nation of Israel from captivity:

> **And they shall build the old wastes, they shall raise up the former desolations, and they shall repair the waste cities, the desolations of many generations (Isa. 61:4).**

The other nations will tend Israel's flocks, and tend their vineyard's:

> **And strangers shall stand and feed your flocks, and the sons of the alien shall be your plowmen and your vinedressers (Isa. 61:5).**

THE ACCEPTABLE YEAR OF THE LORD

Israel will once again be a physical nation of kings and priests (Ex. 19:5-6). They will be a **"peculiar treasure unto God"**, just as the New Testament Church (1 Pet. 2:9). The entire nation of physical Israelites will be **"a kingdom of priests"**, not just the tribe of Levi! They will be a nation of priests! (Isa. 66:21). Israel will then have God's laws written in their hearts to fulfill His purpose on earth (Jer. 31:31). This will be the fulfillment of Isaiah's prophecy, as Jesus declared in Luke 4:18-19:

> **...he hath sent me to heal the brokenhearted, to preach deliverance to the captives, and recovering of sight to the blind, to set at liberty them that are bruised, to preach the ACCEPTABLE YEAR OF THE LORD...(see Isaiah 61).**

That's why the Messenger [Christ] comes to His Temple to *purify* the sons of Levi (Mal. 3:3). This is a *dual* prophecy for the spiritual priesthood [the Church] but also begins the RESTORATION of the ancient Levitical priesthood, as God did after they left Egypt when the *rebels* were sorted out, notice:

THE RESTORATION OF ISRAEL

> To appoint unto them that mourn in Zion...the oil of joy for mourning, the garment of praise for the spirit of heaviness; that they might be called **TREES OF RIGHTEOUSNESS, the planting of the LORD, that he might be glorified...But ye shall be named the Priests of the LORD: men shall call you the Ministers of our God: ye shall eat the riches of the Gentiles, and in their glory shall ye boast yourselves (Isa. 61:3-6).**

At this time, the PURIFIED nation of physical Levites will give the Eternal an offering. This will be a repeat of what God gave the nation of Israel to do in the first place:

> **And he shall sit as a refiner and purifier of silver: and he shall purify the sons of Levi...that they may offer unto the LORD an offering in righteousness. Then shall the offering of Judah and Jerusalem be pleasant unto the LORD, as in the days of old, and as in the former years (Mal. 3:3-4; Isa. 66:20-21).**

It will be at this time that Gog and Magog will come against the once again *prosperous* nation of Israel who are now dwelling safely in Jerusalem, after being brought back from captivity (Ezek. 38:8).

Sheba, Dedan and the merchants of Tarshish, who brought back the vast wealth to Israel, will be allied with Gog and Magog to take the spoil.

Israel will be dwelling in "unwalled villages" (vs. 11) as God in the presence of Jesus Christ will be Israel's "walls of salvation," and her "gates of praise" (Isa. 60:18). Israel will now TRUST her great God, instead of taking things into her own hands.

Jesus will destroy these heathen nations, and they will spend seven months burying their dead!

ISRAEL—A "LIGHT" TO THE WORLD

Originally, it was God's intended purpose that the nation of Israel be a shining light to the world around them, even as the parable of The Lamp Under A Bushel, notice:

> **Ye are the light of the world. A city [Jerusalem] that is set on an hill cannot be hid. Neither do men light a candle, and put it under a bushel, but on a candlestick; and it giveth light unto all that are in the house (Matt. 5:16).**

Anciently, the Eternal gave Israel the basic outline of His master plan for converting the human race—but they failed! It was always God's desire that ancient Israel teach the nations around them His ways and laws by their example, notice:

> **Behold, I have taught you statutes and judgments, even as the LORD my God commanded me, that ye should do so in the land whither ye go to possess it. Keep therefore and do them; for this is your wisdom and your understanding in the sight of the nations, which shall hear all these statutes, and say, Surely this great nation is a wise and understanding people (Deut. 4:5-6).**

Many nations will come up to the mountain of the Lord and to the house of Jacob from Jerusalem (Micah 4:1-2). Once the nation of Israel repents and turns to God, and lives the way of life they should have—the heathen nations will recognize Israel's blessings and respect her. They will be the model example or "light" and emissary of God that they should have been—and will once they seek God's will:

> **Thus saith the LORD of hosts: it shall yet come to pass, that there shall come people, and the inhabitants of one city shall go to another, saying, Let us go speedily to pray before the LORD, and to seek the LORD of hosts: I will go also. Yea, many people and strong nations shall come to seek the LORD of hosts in Jerusalem, and to pray before the LORD. Thus saith the LORD of hosts; In those days it shall come to pass, that ten men**

> shall take hold out of all languages of the nations, even shall *take hold of the skirt of him that is a Jew, saying, We will go with you: for we have heard that God is with you* (Zech. 8:20-23).
>
> **And the Gentiles shall come to thy light, and kings to the brightness of thy rising. Then thou shalt see, and flow together, and thine heart shall fear, and be enlarged; because the abundance of the sea shall be converted unto thee, the forces of the Gentiles shall come unto thee (Isa. 60:3,5). See also (Isa. 62:2)**

God will use the physical nation of Israel to be a part of His Kingdom government, working along side of the resurrected Saints! Israel will be the physical example to the world, working side by side with the Church!

A point of clarification must be made here in regards to the distinction between "the Government or Kingdom of God" and "the Millennium."

The Millennium is not the Kingdom of God, rather it is a 1,000 year period of time in which those physical beings living on earth will have an opportunity to qualify to be a part of God's government, for **"...flesh and blood cannot inherit the kingdom of God" (1 Cor. 15:50).** Those who have been changed into spirit beings, will comprise the Government of God!

The converted nation of Israel will be like the Church today—unable to convert anyone without God's help. They will bring the nation of Egypt to repentance, notice Isaiah 19: 18-21:

> **In that day shall five cities in the land of Egypt shall speak the language of Canaan, and swear to the LORD of hosts: one shall be called, The city of destruction. In that day shall there be an altar to the LORD in the midst of the land of Egypt, and a pillar at the border thereof to the LORD. And it shall be for a sign and for a witness unto the LORD of hosts in the land of Egypt: for they shall cry unto the LORD because of the oppressors, and HE SHALL SEND THEM A SAVIOR, and a**

> great one, and he shall deliver them. And the LORD shall be known to Egypt, and the Egyptians shall know the LORD in that day, and shall do sacrifice and oblation: yea they shall vow a vow unto the LORD, and perform it.

The Hebrew word for "Savior" in this verse means, ("delivers one from danger or distress", "help out of danger", "give aid", "set them at liberty"). This refers to the resurrected Church that will provide assistance in knowing God's Law, and providing teaching and instruction. They will provide language assistance in Hebrew and will solve their problems by a God family ambassador who will teach, instruct and guide the nation of Egypt in God's new government that has the answers!

Egypt, will be called "God's people", and Assyria, "the work of God's hands." Along with Israel, they will be the three leading nations God will use at the beginning of the Millennium to bring the rest of the nations to repentance, as God's government disseminates from Jerusalem:

> In that day shall there be a highway out of Egypt to Assyria, and the Assyrian shall come into Egypt, and the Egyptian into Assyria, and the Egyptians shall serve with the Assyrians. In that day shall Israel be the third with Egypt and with Assyria, even a blessing in the midst of the land: Whom the LORD of hosts shall bless, saying, Blessed be Egypt my people, and Assyria the work of my hands, and Israel mine inheritance (Isa. 19:23-25).

ALL NATIONS TO KNOW GOD'S GLORY

> I will set My glory among the nations; all the nations shall see My judgment which I have executed, and My hand which I have laid on them. So the house of Israel shall know that I am the LORD their God from that day forward. The Gentiles shall know that the house of Israel went into captivity for their iniquity; because they were unfaithful to Me, therefore I hid My face from them. I gave them into

> the hand of their enemies, and they all fell by the sword. According to their uncleanness and according to their transgressions I have dealt with them, and hidden My face from them (Ezek. 39:21-24).

The Eternal will make His name known in the midst of Israel—and from then on He will reign upon the earth. He will rule with a strong hand, and His Holy Name shall no more be profaned by the nations:

> So I will make My holy name known in the midst of My people Israel, and I will not let them profane My holy name anymore. Then the nations shall know that I am the LORD, the Holy One in Israel. Surely it is coming, and it shall be done, says the Lord God, This is the day of which I have spoken (Ezek. 39:7-8).

Jerusalem will be a holy city that only the redeemed of the earth can enter:

> And an highway shall be there, and a way, and it shall be called The way of holiness; the unclean shall not pass over it; but it shall be for those: the wayfaring men, though fools, shall not err therein. No lion shall be there, nor any ravenous beast shall go up thereon, it shall not be found there; but **THE REDEEMED** shall walk there: And the ransomed of the LORD shall return, and come to Zion with songs and everlasting joy upon their heads...(Isa. 35:8-10).

When Jesus Christ destroys the enemies of Israel from the north country—all nations will know He is the Holy One of Israel! From that day foreword, the nation of Israel will know that Jesus Christ is their Lord!

The second Passover *pictured* the intervention of Jesus Christ in the affairs of Israel—pouring out plagues upon Israel's captors. The Feast of Unleavened Bread was *reminiscent* of their repentance during the time of Jacob's trouble. The Day of

SATAN CHAINED

Atonement *foreshadowed* Israel's forgiveness of sin—followed by the *symbolic* meaning of Trumpets as Israel is gathered "one by one" out of captivity,

Israel will have been given a new heart to keep God's laws, *envisioned* by Pentecost and the pouring out of God's Holy Spirit. The Feast of Tabernacles *typifies* Israel's deliverance from their enemies and being led back to the Promised Land. They will have inherited tremendous wealth and promised blessings from God that will cause the armies of Gog and Magog to come up against them to take their booty.

But Jesus Christ will devour Israel's foes—and from that day forward, all nations will know what God has done for His people! After Israel has a converted heart—the entire world will follow her example.

THE MILLENNIUM'S BEGINNING

Exactly how will the Millennium begin? How do you reestablish the boundaries of nations and economic systems of the shambled nations?

The Millennium will last for 1,000 years, and Satan will be chained during this time (Rev. 20). He will not have any power to tempt or deceive the world as He did during the previous 6,000 years. It will be a period of re-education to true values! It will be a Kingdom run the way it should have been run with Israel as God's leading nation!

However, when Christ returns, the earth will be laying in a state of chaos and turmoil, waste, scattered, desolate, and empty with few men left (Isa. 24:1,3,6).

There is no human being on earth today that can solve the prodigious problems we face, and that is precisely why the world will ultimately head toward the conditions of (Isaiah 24), and the return of Jesus Christ.

But we must ask ourselves yet another question, "How is the Millennium going to begin?" Once Satan is bound, is his influence going to cease? Will human nature be eradicated so that no human being will ever sin again?

Man has bungled it for 6,000 years and is incapable of restructuring even one nation, let alone the entire world! When it is all over and done, we will see as a human race, that man, without God ruling him would ultimately fail!

THE RESTORATION OF ISRAEL

God's Word states that man's earthly wisdom without His Holy Spirit is foolish, and he is incapable of understanding spiritual things (Isa. 29:9-14; 1 Cor. 1:18; 2:11-16). Truly, man in all his earthly knowledge does not know how to solve his problems!

The Eternal knew this would happen 6,000 years ago, and began His new government and system with a handful of "firstfruits" that would restore peace to the human race as opposed to the way man has been ruling for the past 6,000 years.

Through God's immortal "firstfruits" the world will learn how to deal with the land by observing God's land rest. They will educate the world about the environment, and the earth will yield abundant food.

Once the world begins to understand this vital missing knowledge, man is still going to have to utilize this knowledge and do the actual building. The Church is being taught this foundational material so they can teach others in God's kingdom!

God's divine Government will be overseered by faithful and loyal Christians, who will be "resurrected" or changed into spirit beings upon Christ's return. They will be given God's holy and righteous character upon being resurrected. Therefore, they will be fully qualified to teach an eager and unconverted world God's ways!

SATAN LOOSED AFTER 1,000 YEARS

After the 1,000 years have elapsed, Satan will again be loosed upon the earth (Rev. 20:7-8). Once again, He will gather and deceive the nations of Gog and Magog and make war against God's chosen nation!

But this time Israel will have learned to trust their heavenly Father, and He will personally devour their armies by raining fire from heaven upon them (Rev. 20:9).

Here we find that Satan never gives up! First, he attacked God's creation in the universe as the rebellious Lucifer. Then as Satan the devil, he deceived Eve in the garden, he assaulted Jesus Christ personally, he confronted God's hosts at Armageddon in a final coup before the end of the age, and then he attacks God's new headquarters at Jerusalem shortly into the Millennium. In one final effort he attacks God's Government again in a final effort just after the Millennium.

SATAN CHAINED

How could this happen you ask? How could Satan deceive mankind so very easily after Jesus sets up His government for 1,000 years, consisting of kings and priests who would enforce and teach all nations God's laws? (Isa. 2:1; 9:6-7; 11; 1 Pet. 2:9-10; Rev. 5:10; Dan. 2:44; 7:13).

Because the carnal mind is against God's laws! (Rom. 8:7). Even though God gave mankind 1,000 years of world peace during the Millennium—mankind's rebellious nature does not change! This conclusively demonstrates once and for all—that without God's full measure of the Holy Spirit—mankind is incapable of worshiping God! Human beings void of God's Holy Spirit will not observe His laws—even though they were placed under a perfect government! Plain and simple!

MILLENNIAL LIFE

Exactly, what is it going to be like as a physical human being living during the Millennium? This is going to be a utopia world free of Satan's influence, when God's knowledge will be readily available to all of mankind, and God's Holy Spirit will unlock their minds to these new truths!

But what will peoples attitudes and lifestyles be like as we progress through the Millennium without Satan's influence? Is everyone going to keep God's way of life perfectly? Consider, if the garden of Eden is a *type* of millennial life—Adam sinned without any help or "hook" from Satan! Realize also, that the Church today, also a *type* of millennial life, is not deceived—God's truth is readily available to them, and Satan for the most part has not influenced them, yet Christians continue to sin!

If these examples are a *foretaste* of millennial life, sin is still going to last for at least 1,000 years! The Bible tells us that, "All human beings have sinned, and come short of the glory of God." As human beings, God's law will continue to be broken throughout the Millennium—and therefore in this state, it will be impossible to please God! The Millennium is not going to be a pollyanna world!

Interestingly, the Millennium ends the same way it began—with war between Gog and Magog! It doesn't take Satan very long to once again deceive mankind, even though God's government has been in power for 1,000 years!

Why, you ask?

The world will be full of prosperity, abundance of food, clothing, free of war, pollution and crime will be under control for 1,000 glorious years! Why then, will God allow Satan to be loosed for a short time afterward to deceive mankind again?

Could there be another purpose beyond peace and prosperity, a perfect way of life and a perfect government?

Absolutely!

All of this new found opulence, perfection of government with peace and prosperity—WILL NOT PRODUCE PERFECT HUMAN BEINGS!

Human beings, as perfect as they can be, while still in the flesh will still sin! Just as true as today, man's heart will still be deceitful above all things (Jer. 17:9), he will still be incapable of directing his own path (Jer. 10:23), all will still sin and come short of the glory of God (Rom. 3:23), none will be righteous, (Rom. 3:10), none will do good [all the time] (Rom. 3:12), and the carnal mind will still be rebellious towards God's laws (Rom. 8:7).

That's the way man was created!

Every single human carnal fleshly human being will still have to repent of sin (Acts 2:38). Every human being will need the Comforter to teach them God's laws and to remember them (Jn. 14:26).

Even as God has made known to His Church today, the mystery of His will as to *who* Christ was and *why* He had to die—when the dispensation of the fullness of times come, the entire world will be reeducated to these truths (Eph. 1:9-10).

The human race is going to have to go through the same conversion process as the Church does today! But how many perfect Christians do you know?

Truly, the apostle Paul echoed God's sentiments concerning them that are in the flesh: **"So then they that are in the flesh cannot please God" (Rom. 8:8).** Human weakness is in the flesh, and we all have it! As converted as the apostle Paul was, he knew that in his flesh was no good thing, and he could not control it 100% of the time (Rom. 7:13-25).

During the Millennium, human beings with the spirit of God will have to grow in grace and knowledge, and overcome sin just as every Christian must during his lifetime.

SATAN CHAINED

Therefore, it is imperative and paramount for Satan to be loosed once again at the Millennium's conclusion to deceive the nations one more time! Every human being must be absolutely convinced before entering the family of God, that with or without prosperity [the Millennium], and with or without a perfect government—that no flesh should glory in himself!

Human beings are going to learn that, **"the Foolishness of God is wiser than man,"** and that **"no flesh should glory in his [own] presence" (1 Cor. 1:25-29).** Every human being must learn that no flesh of and by itself can glory in it's own self, and that they cannot produce the Kingdom of God—but must instead realize that of and by ourselves **"we can do nothing"** without God!

Human beings will come to realize that **"man in his best state is altogether vanity,"** and destined to fail! We will have learned that money, good food, peace, perfect government, Christian husbands and Christian wives still cannot please God!

The only individuals who will enter God's kingdom when Christ presents His spotless Bride to the Father—are those who will have learned that their POWER comes from God and that the flesh fails!

Isn't it ironic that only after the Millennium ends and God the Father dwells with His immortal children in a new heaven and new earth do we find no more sea (Rev. 21:1). After the earth had been rebuilt and the seas purified—they are still unfit for God the Father and His children to inherit forevermore! This only goes to prove that the Millennial life was still imperfect for God's perfect family.

Only after the Millennium do we find no more tears, death, sorrow, crying, or pain: **"for the former things are passed away" (Rev. 21:4).** Absolutely, human beings have nothing to glory in, and it is only through God's grace that we can overcome and make it into His eternal ruling family!

SATAN'S FATE

In (Revelation 20:1-3) we read that Satan is to be BOUND and cast into an abyss at the beginning of Christ's millennial rule over the nations upon His return. This condition of restraint will last during the thousand years, and then the devil will be momentarily allowed freedom to deceive the nations again for a little season (Rev. 20:3).

After Satan is allowed to deceive the nations for a little while, he will be cast into the "lake of fire" where the Beast and the False Prophet were cast and shall be tormented day and night for ever and ever (Rev. 20:10). Some Bibles use italics to show that the word "are" in this verse was supplied by the translators. It is not found in the Greek manuscripts.

The phrase should read: After Satan is allowed to deceive the nations for a little while, he will be cast into the "lake of fire" "where the Beast and the False Prophet *were* [remember they were cast into the "lake of fire" at the beginning of the Millennium]. The *Amplified Bible* has this verse correct. These two mortal individuals will have been destroyed over 1,000 years before the time Satan is put into these flames.

That is why Jesus said in Matthew 25:41, **"Depart from me, ye cursed, into everlasting fire, prepared for the devil and his angels."** The Greek word used here for "everlasting" is *aionion*, the root word is "*aion*" meaning "age." Therefore, the more proper translation would read, "into age-lasting fire prepared for the devil and his angels."

HOW A SPIRIT CAN SUFFER

Fire is a physical, chemical thing! Fire is the combustion of physical objects with oxygen which changes the physical objects into ashes and gaseous vapor! But Satan is a SPIRIT being and spirit beings are not affected by physical fire! They are not material!

Since Satan and his angels cannot be destroyed physically by fire, how else can they be punished? A disembodied spirit—is an uncomfortable, miserable spirit! Jesus described this condition of MENTAL TORMENT when He said, **"...when the unclean spirit is gone out of a man, he walketh through dry places, seeking rest; and finding none, he saith, I will return unto my house whence I came out"** (Lk. 11:24).

This is further illustrated by the account of Christ's experience with the many demons who had entered a man in the country of the Gadarenes. Jesus commanded the spirits to come out of the man, and they **"...brought him much that he would not send them away out of the country" (Mk. 5:10). "And all the devils [demons] besought him, saying, Send us into the swine, that we may enter into them"** (verse 12).

When Philip was performing miracles at Samaria, he cast out

many demons, who came out of people, "crying with loud voice" (Acts 8:7) showing their utter frustration and anger at being deprived of their dwelling place! (Lk. 8:28).

RESERVED UNTO JUDGMENT

Satan and his angels know that they have a little time left (Rev. 12:12) and stand in fear of their judgment and tremble! (Jas. 2:19; Mk. 1:24; Matt. 8:29).

A vital part of the job of each of God's children will be judges. The apostle Paul tells us in 1 Corinthians 6:2-3: **"Do ye not know that the saints shall judge the world? And if the world shall be judged by you, are ye unworthy to judge the smallest matters? Know ye not that WE SHALL JUDGE ANGELS?"**

Yes, Christians are to judge angels! Remember the wicked spirits, including Satan, are presently being reserved, being kept in restraint, unto judgment! The judging is yet to be done by God's children who will become kings and priests with Christ, and RULE THIS EARTH! (Rev. 5:10).

The Bible plainly reveals Satan will be cast into the lake of fire, but the lake of fire will end when the new heavens and new earth are established. It also shows his torment while in that fire is going to be MENTAL, at seeing all he has strived toward, worked for, plotted for, burned up!

Jude gives a slight indication of the possible mental anguish and nature of punishment for Satan and his demons as he describes the **"raging waves of the sea, foaming out their own shame; WANDERING STARS [see Rev. 1:20), where stars are symbols of angels] to WHOM IS RESERVED THE BLACKNESS OF DARKNESS FOREVER"! (Jude 13).**

As a point of speculation, the Greek word used here for "forever" can mean "age lasting" and therefore may not apply to Satan's final fate. In other words, after the millennial age, Satan may be completely destroyed!

Chapter Twenty

'THE NEW HEAVENS' AND 'NEW EARTH'

Imagine if you can, 1,000 years from now into eternity—what will you be doing?

With the passing of time, we have journeyed like Israel in *type* from Egypt to the Promised Land. We have fulfilled the feast days of God spiritually, as we have experienced Passover to Tabernacles.

Spiritually, we have come from the outer courtyard of the Temple, into His gates, cleansed ourselves in the laver, entered the holy place—and are now ready to enter the Holy of Holies forever! We are ready to experience eternity, *symbolized* by the Last Great Day—as we start a "new beginning" in eternity!

Now we come to the grand finale of God's plan, the crescendo—the creme de'la creme if you will! God has been waiting for this incredible moment for 7,000 agonizing years! If you thought that salvation, spirit bodies, marriage feast, Millennium, was all there is to look forward to—you are in for a surprise!

Here we shall expand our minds to explore "the mysteries of the universe" in eternity!

THE MARRIAGE OF THE CHURCH

At this point I suggest you review the Parable of the Royal Marriage Feast, in which the basic wedding pattern between Christ and His Church will transpire.

Recall the three stages of the Hebrew wedding pattern that *parallel* the Church, namely: 1) the *betrothal period* in which the Bride is chosen by the groom's parents (God the Father has chosen us), without the groom's prior knowledge. A formal contract (the New Testament) is then written up, 2) the *wedding feast* begins lasting anywhere between a day to a week (the Millennial Feast), and 3) finally, the *marriage is consummated* when the groom takes the bride to his home (at the end of the Millennium).

Currently, the Church is in the *betrothal* stage. After Christ returns with His *resurrected* Bride, the 1,000 year "marriage feast" will take place. Then the marriage will be *consummated* between Christ and His Bride [New Jerusalem], beginning the "New Heavens" and "New Earth"!

By understanding the Hebrew custom of marriage in *type*, and also God's numerical system—it makes sense that the spiritual *consummation* of the Church would come, not after 6,000 years of human history, but after 7,000 years of perfection! The number 7 being indicative of "spiritual perfection" when Christ would present His spotless Bride to Himself!

THE OVERCOMERS COMPRISE "NEW JERUSALEM"

Granted, that the Bride of Christ, "New Jerusalem" will be presented to Christ as a spotless Bride *after* the Millennium, when the *marriage* will be consummated—WHO will comprise the Lamb's Wife?

Will Christ's Wife be comprised of the nation of Israel, the New Testament Church, the 144,000 Tribulation Saints, or Millennial Saints?

Reflecting back to (Revelation 21:1-7) in regards to *whom* comprises "New Jerusalem" after the Millennium we read:

> **And I saw a new heaven and a new earth...And I saw the holy city *New Jerusalem*, coming down from God out of heaven, *prepared as a bride* adorned for her husband [notice she is prepared to get married]... And I heard a great voice out of heaven saying, Behold, the tabernacle of God is with men, and he will dwell with them, and they shall be his people,**

THE NEW HEAEN AND EARTH

> **and God himself shall be with them, and be their God...He that OVERCOMETH shall inherit all things, and I will be his God, and he shall be my son.**

Read that again!

God says the *overcomers* shall inherit New Jerusalem! Lest there be any doubt that the "overcomers" will inherit *all things,* including "New Jerusalem"—read the following verses in Revelation concerning Christ's promises to His seven Churches (Rev. 2:7,11,17,26; 3:5,12,21).

Here we find that only *overcomers* will "eat of the tree of life" (2:7), "not be hurt by the second death" (2:11), "will be given hidden manna" (2:17), "will be given a new name" (2:17), "will be given authority over the nations" (2:26), "shall rule the nations with a rod of iron" (2:27), "shall be clothed in white garments, and shall not have his name erased from the book of life" (3:5), "will be made a pillar in the Temple of God, and will not go out of the Temple, and Christ will write the name of the city of His God [New Jerusalem] and His [Christ's] new name" (3:12), "will be granted to sit with Christ in His throne" (3:21).

Another point in hammering down the final nail on this subject, is that the first Adam and his wife Eve were a *type* of the second Adam [Christ] and His Bride.

Did you ever wonder *why* God created Eve out of one of Adam's ribs instead of making her out of the dust of the ground like Adam? It was because He wanted to form Adam's bride out of a part of Adam's body!

Likewise, Christ's Bride comprising all *overcomers* will be fashioned out of His body or the very substance of which He was made—SPIRIT!

Conclusively, the foundation for the future holy city is built upon Jesus Christ, and *overcomers* from the N.T Church composed of both Jew and Gentile.

THE RESTORATION OF ISRAEL

TABERNACLES AND GOD'S ETERNAL DWELLING HOUSE

God's *resting* after the 7th day of the creation week is *typical* of His eternal resting with His creation! The main theme of the Bible is that of God abiding and *dwelling* with His people—and we with Him!

This is the central issue of the concept of the "New Jerusalem" of God—that of God *tabernacling* with His creation FOREVER! "New Jerusalem" is the Father's house that is being fashioned out of "spiritual jewels." It will be the Lamb's Wife and the eternal dwelling place of God among His people. Notice the many scriptural references that make this concept abundantly clear:

Jn. 14:23	"Jesus answered and said unto him, if a man love me, he will keep my words: and my Father will love him, and we will come to him, and make *our abode with him*."
Jn. 17:21	"That they all may be one; as thou, Father art in me, and *I in thee,* that they also may be *one in us*..."
Jn. 6:56	"He that eateth my flesh, and drinketh my blood, *dwelleth in me, and I in him*."
Jn. 15:4	"*Abide in me, and I in you.* As the branch cannot bear fruit of itself, except it abide in the vine; no more can ye, *except ye abide in me*."
Gal. 2:20	"I am crucified with Christ: nevertheless I live; yet not I, but *Christ liveth in me*..."
Col. 2:9	"For in him dwelleth all the fulness of the *Godhead* bodily."
Eph. 3:17	"That Christ may *dwell in your hearts* by faith..."

THE NEW HEAEN AND EARTH

Rev. 3:20 "Behold, I stand at the door, and knock: if any man hear My voice, and open the door, *I will come in to him,* and will sup with him, and he with me."

HIDE AND SEEK

Ever since the Garden of Eden, it was God's intended purpose to *dwell* among His creation. But Adam and Eve disobeyed their Creator by eating of the tree of the knowledge of good and evil, and then hid themselves from God's face!

Mankind has been doing precisely the same thing for the past 6,000 years—that is, *hiding* from God's ways while He is *seeking* to convert us!

God showed Himself to His people once again upon Mt. Sinai—but God's awesome presence accompanied by thunder and smoking, terrified the fearful Israelites! They showed their discontent by making a "golden calf" to worship instead!

Again, God tried to *dwell* among His people as Jesus came to His own—but the Jewish people chose to kill Him! In fact, one of Jesus' names "Emanuel" means "God with us!" God tried earnestly to *dwell* among His people in Eden, Sinai and Galilee—but mankind would not have it!

In His wisdom, God chose another way to *dwell* among His people—by creating a "spiritual house" composed of "spiritual stones", with Jesus Christ at the apex, being the Chief Corner Stone. God will yet *dwell* among His creation in a great SPIRITUAL TEMPLE that He is now molding together through the mortar of His Holy Spirit!

Notice the many scriptures to this effect:

Ex. 25:8 "And let them make me a sanctuary; *that I may dwell among them.*"

Ps. 132:13 "For the LORD hath chosen Zion; *he hath desired it for his habitation.*"

Ps. 132:14 "This is my rest for ever: *here will I dwell:* for I have desired it."

THE RESTORATION OF ISRAEL

Acts 7:49	"Heaven is my throne, and earth is my footstool: what house will ye build me? saith the LORD: or *what is the place of my rest?*"
Eph. 2:22	"In whom ye also are builded together for *an habitation of God through the Spirit.*"
1 Jn. 4:13	"Hereby know we that *we dwell in him, and he in us, because he hath given us of his Spirit.*"
11 Cor. 6:16	"...ye are the temple of the living God; as God hath said, *I will dwell in them,* and walk in them; and I will be their God, and they shall be my people."

After the Millennium, never again will God (Jesus/Son) live in a Temple made with hands (Acts 7:48). Presently, the God family is in a tabernacle [temporary dwelling] but the entire God family of Father, Son and Holy Spirit will finally *dwell* with their children at the end of the Millennium for ever more!

The God family is now *perfecting the* Church, the Bride of Christ to be joined in perfect holy matrimony! This perfect union between Christ and His Church will make them ONE in Christ, as they become **"bone of His bone, and flesh of His flesh"**—just as Jesus is ONE with the Father! Then, the Bride and Groom can bear children, as the nations of the earth can be brought into this beautiful fruitful union!

THE ETERNAL TABERNACLE OF GOD

When we read of the description of the "New Jerusalem" of God, there is no Temple or light there—for the city itself is the eternal Temple of God, as God the Father and God the Son are the light of it!

The *overcoming Saints* will be the pillars of the Temple structure who carry out God's government to the nations. The River of Life [God's Holy Spirit] will flow freely to all nations to drink abundantly of the Tree of Life which is Jesus Christ, who will provide healing for the nations of the earth in this eternal spiritual city!

Solomon's Temple, in all its glory, was a *type* of the spiritual Temple of God. Each stone of this magnificent edifice was prepared and shaped at their quarries, rather than at the Temple location. These beautiful stones were made so precisely, that, **"...there was neither hammer nor axe nor any tool or iron heard in the house, while it was in building" (1 Kings 6:7).** Likewise, God's "spiritual stones" are being fashioned in advance of their placement, notice:

Jn. 14:2	"In my Father's house are *many mansions:* if it were not so, I would have told you, I go to prepare a place for you..."
Eph. 2:20-22	"And are *built upon the foundation of the apostles and prophets,* Jesus Christ himself being the chief corner stone; In whom *all the building fitly framed together groweth unto an holy temple in the Lord:* In whom ye also are builded together for an habitation of God through the Spirit."
Eph. 4:16	"From whom *the whole body fitly joined together* and compacted by that which every joint supplieth, according to the effectual working in the measure of every part, maketh increase of the body unto the edifying of itself in love."
1 Pet. 2:5	"Ye also, as lively [living] stones, are built up a *spiritual house,* an holy priesthood, to offer up spiritual sacrifices, acceptable to God by Jesus Christ."
1 Cor. 3:9	"For we are labourers together with God: ye are God's husbandry, *ye are God's building."*
1 Cor. 3:16	"Know ye not that *ye are the temple of God,* and that the Spirit of God *dwelleth* in you?"

THE RESTORATION OF ISRAEL

Heb. 3:6   "But Christ as a son over his own house; *whose house are we,* if we hold fast the confidence and the rejoicing of the hope firm unto the end."

1 Tim. 3:15   "*...the house of God, which is the church of the living God,* the pillar and ground of the truth."

The Church is the affianced Bride or the Holy City of "New Jerusalem" that is the Body of Christ. But the Body of Christ is the Father's gift to His Son, as every member of that Body is "hand picked" by the Father (Jn. 6:37), just like every stone of Solomon's Temple was chosen in advance!

Here is another *mystery* revealed by Christ's names. Did you notice that the Bride in (Revelation 19:7) is called the "Lamb's Wife", instead of "Christ's Wife", or "Jesus' Wife", or the "Word's Wife", or the "Wife of the Son of God"?

Remember, names have deep spiritual significance in the Word of God, and this particular terminology has specific connotation. The reason the Church is called "the Lamb's Wife" is because it was Christ coming as a *lamb* to be slaughtered for the sins of His Bride.

During the last Passover that Jesus celebrated on earth, He instituted the New Testament symbols of the bread and wine. As the Church eats His body and drinks His blood *symbolically* during this commemoration—they meditate upon what the Passover lamb did for them and therefore the Church will be *married* to the Passover Lamb!

GOD DESIRES TO DWELL WITH US

Most definitely, the Eternal desires to *dwell* with His people. This is a major lesson of the Feast of Tabernacles.

Numerous Bible passages point to the fact that God wants to be with the people through whom He is working.

For example, God moved the great cloud between the host of Israel and the warriors of Egypt to protect the Israelites (Ex. 14:19-20). When the Tabernacle in the wilderness was finished, the presence of God filled it (Ex. 40:34-35). The glory of God also filled the Temple in Jerusalem (11 Chron. 7:1-2). The apostle John said that the hope of all those who *purify* themselves spiritually is to see God "as He is" (1 Jn. 3:2-3).

Anciently, the Feast of Tabernacles, was kept "in the place which He [God] choose" and was to remind Israel of God's desire to *dwell* with them (Deut. 14:23, 16:15). New Testament Christians renew our hope of seeing God "as He is" in the place God has chosen.

EZEKIEL'S MESSAGE

Ezekiel, whose name meant "God strengthens," was a prophet in exile. From a priestly family (Ezek. 1:3), he grew up in Judea during the last years of Judah's independence. He was deported to Babylon with King Jehoiachin in 597 B.C.

A main message of the book of Ezekiel vividly illustrates God's desire to be with His people.

Ezekiel lived with the Jewish exiles by the River Chebar (Ezek. 1:1, 3:15). He was called to be a prophet in the fifth year of his captivity. The last date mentioned in the book of Ezekiel is the 27th year (Ezek. 29:17); therefore we may deduce that Ezekiel's work lasted 22 years, from about 593 to 571 B.C.

Ezekiel began his prophecies at a time when the nation of Israel was at the lowest ebb of its history, spiritually and nationally.

On the day the final siege of Jerusalem began, Ezekiel's wife suddenly became sick and died. In this, Ezekiel became a *sign* to the people of greater sorrow coming. Ezekiel wasn't allowed to mourn.

Ezekiel's last prophecies were uttered after Jerusalem had fallen and the Temple had been destroyed. Only a pitiful *remnant* was left in the land. Israel's spirit was broken.

But a prophecy centuries before had detailed what would happen if Israel broke the covenant with God. God predicted that the Israelites would say, **"Are not these evils come upon us, because our God is not among us?" (Deut. 31:17).**

God warned, **"And I will surely hide my face in that day for all the evils which they shall have wrought" (verse 18)**.

Ezekiel recorded God's departure from the Temple and the midst of the people (Ezek. 10:4, 18-19, 11:22-24). Only a few brief centuries after God entered the Temple, He reluctantly left *dwelling* with His chosen nation. The destruction of the city and deportation of the remaining tribes was imminent.

THE RESTORATION OF ISRAEL

But Ezekiel received and delivered prophecies that pointed toward the Kingdom of God and the return of the presence of God to earth! These were prophecies of hope and consolation on a grand scope. The close relationship between God and His creation will yet be restored!

The book of Ezekiel concludes with a name of God given only in the book of Ezekiel. This appears to be the last name by which God reveals Himself and His character in the Old Testament. The last words of Ezekiel are *Yahweh-shammah*, meaning **"God is there" (Ezek. 48:35).** It is a fitting name!

This name represents God's promise that He will finish His plan for mankind. God is going to once again dwell among His people. This is the fabulous time for which we look forward!

GOD AND MAN RECONCILED

Jesus Christ is coming, as King of kings, to rule the entire earth and set up the Kingdom of God (Rev. 19:16). He is going to replace this world's present evil governments and establish an everlasting kingdom. God's presence will never again be removed from that Kingdom.

When God again *dwells* among His chosen people, what will it be like? As nations begin to see the positive results of the righteous and living rule of God's government, they will seek Christ and ask for instruction in God's way of life (Isa. 61:1). The prophet Micah wrote that people will flow to the government of God to be educated in the art of peace (Micah 4:1-3).

Isaiah wrote, **"Cry out and shout, thou inhabitant of Zion: for great is the Holy One of Israel in the midst of thee" (Isa. 12:6).**

Jeremiah says, **"At that time they shall call Jerusalem the throne of the Lord" (Jer. 3:7).** This hope stirred the minds of the prophets and patriarchs (Ps. 140:13).

Ezekiel prophesied about God's return to His spiritual Temple:

> **And behold, the glory of the God of Israel came from the way of the east: and his voice was like a noise of many waters: and the earth shined with his glory...and, behold, the glory of the Lord filled the house (Ezek. 43:2,5). Neither will**

THE NEW HEAEN AND EARTH

I hide my face any more from them (Ezek. 39:29). I will dwell in the midst of the children of Israel for ever (Ezek. 43:7,9).

Ezekiel put the crowning touch on this subject of God's presence when he spoke of the time we shall see God "as he is": **"And the name of the city from that day shall be, The Lord is there" (Ezek. 48:35).**

THE EIGHTH DAY AND ETERNITY

The spiritual significance of the number *eight* is that of "a new beginning"—and therefore it is highly probable that the eighth day of the Feast of Tabernacles also *pictures* the first day of the new week of eternity!

After the Millennium, when the "New Heavens" and "New Earth" with a "New Jerusalem" are created—the eighth day of the Feast of Tabernacles will most likely find its fulfillment in the eternal week which has no end! Although such a supposition cannot be easily proved, it should not be regarded as unlikely.

The first seven days of the Feast of Tabernacles *pictures* the first seven days of the creation week, after which God will finally *rest* with His people! Thus, redemption will have been completed in man as God now *dwells* with him as we enter into His eternal rest! Then the "first day" of eternity will begin as *symbolized* by the eighth day of the Feast of Tabernacles!

It is here that "New Jerusalem" comprising the Wife of Christ will expand the family of God as they reign as Kings and Priests over the nations!

Recall how earthly marriage is a *type* of the heavenly between the Lamb and His Wife. Also realize that the Hebrew nuptial custom *parallels* the marriage of Christ to the Church. Therefore, the reason God the Father does not come to *dwell* with His people until after the Millennium—is because the Lamb's Bride, even though made immortal through the resurrection, will not be spiritually mature until *after* the Millennium!

Just like any human courtship—it takes time to become mentally adjusted for marriage! Throughout the 1,000 years of priestly service, undoubtedly the Bride will become increasingly refined!

Similarly, the Feast of Tabernacles *pictures* the maturing of the Lamb's Bride, even as the fruits and vegetables harvested during this time have come to full succulent maturity! *Figuratively,* that is why the Feast of Tabernacles was to be observed in the Land of Promise! It was there that the harvest [picturing the Church] would grow to full "spiritual maturity!"

Perhaps that is why "New Jerusalem" does not descend as the Lamb's Wife as a sparkling diadem until after the Millennial Jubilee has been completed?

ENTERING THE "HOLY OF HOLIES"

The Old Testament Tabernacle and Temple, with their various offerings, were merely *types* of the progression to "spiritual maturity" in the life of a Christian. The spiritual concept of Christians progressing from the outer court to the Holy of Holies will now be discussed.

To refresh your memory, recall how the outer court was where the people brought their animals to be sacrificed. Inside the Tabernacle was the holy place where only the ordinary priests could go, but not the rest of the people. The holy place was separated by the Holy of Holies, where God *dwelt* and where only the high priest could only enter once a year on the Day of Atonement.

Spiritually speaking, the Holy of Holies could only be entered by Christian priests through Christ—the door [Veil] that leads us to God's throne. All those outside the perimeters of the Tabernacle's sanctuary were in the "court of the Gentiles." Spiritually speaking, this stood for all those unrepentant sinners who were not even allowed in the inner courtyard to offer up sacrifices.

The golden altar in the holy place, where only the priests could enter, pointed to the *holiness* in the New Testament Church. The brazen altar in the *courtyard* outside the Tabernacle was for the sacrifices of the people.

Between the door of the Tabernacle and the altar in the courtyard stood a brass laver or pot of water. Before administering to the people, the priests had to wash in it, *personifying* the "cleansing" or purifying of sin through water baptism!

The anointed priests stood for the New Testament Church, as they must **"come out of the world"** by repenting of sin (*symbolic* of those sacrifices in the courtyard). Thus, spiritually speaking, only those who have repented of sin, and are filled with God's Holy Spirit can enter the door of the Tabernacle, and move from the holy place into the Holy of Holies!

However, before we can enter the Holy of Holies as Christian priests, we must utilize God's Holy Spirit in full and dedicated service to Him. To be baptized, and allow God's Holy Spirit to remain dormant without exercising it in service—is to stop at the holy place spiritually!

But there is a great giant step that must be taken before one can enter the Holy of Holies—and that is in becoming an *overcomer* or a bond-servant for Christ!

To begin our spiritual life at the Passover, after accepting the precious blood of Jesus Christ, and end spiritually at Pentecost, would mean to miss out on the Feast of Tabernacles and the Last Great Day spiritually!

It would be like the nation of Israel coming out of Egypt and remaining in the wilderness forever! It would only have been a half way point in our spiritual journey, and spiritually like remaining at the feast of Pentecost forever!

After Israel was delivered from Egypt, God led them through the wilderness and fought their battles for them. He fed them and clothed them and protected them as their husband! Likewise, when one becomes a Christian, God does most of our fighting for us!

The wilderness was a training experience to see if the Israelites would be faithful to God's laws and government. Israel's wilderness training spiritually *parallels* Pentecost in that after we receive the Holy Spirit we must walk in *obedience* to God—before we can proceed to the Feast of Trumpets and spiritually *conquer* the Promised Land!

The next phase of God's plan is the Feast of Trumpets *picturing* our "conquering" and fighting for victory in becoming an *overcomer!* Only when we become an overcomer can we enter the Promised Land or the Holy of Holies in the Tabernacle!

"New Jerusalem" is the *consummation* of God's *spiritual building*, and all *overcomers* will comprise Jesus' Bride and become this spiritual jewel of a city! Then this entire spiritual city will become ONE GREAT HOLY OF HOLIES! The apostle Paul put it so very succinctly in 11 Corinthians 5:1, when he said: **"For we know that if our earthly house of this tabernacle were dissolved, we have a building of God, an house not made with hands, *eternal in the heavens.*"**

THE RESTORATION OF ISRAEL

"SPIRITUAL FIRSTFRUITS"

Let's stop and analyze these deep concepts and expand our minds a little more into enternity. Consider the fact that "firstfruits" or "overcomers" are going to have **"better promises"** being in the first resurrection (Heb. 8:6).

But what were these better promises?

The marriage Covenant and the Old Covenant was one and the same! It was this marriage, then, that established *organization* and *government* among God's people! The 10 Commandments, God's statutes and judgments were the terms and conditions—the basis—of that marriage contract. The Eternal [Lord] of the Old Covenant, as the Husband, promised to provide for and protect the nation or congregation of Israel. The nation of Israel in turn agreed to remain faithful always to Him.

God agreed to perform the duties of a husband, to provide for and bless her. The people of Israel accepted the terms that God gave them. They bound themselves by the Old Covenant to refrain from any adulterous or whorish relations with the false gods of other nations—and to remain chaste and acceptable to their own "husband" (Ex. 34:12-17).

But the Israelites, being without the Spirit of God, were constantly rebelling—sinning—against their "husband"—and the 10 Commandment Law He had given them (Ezek. 20:13), and so the Eternal then added temporary "ritualistic laws" for them to keep because of their rebellion, to impress upon them the weakness of their own inherent *human nature* in respect to keeping God's Law (Lev. 1:1-9).

But ancient Israel continued to be disobedient and UNFAITHFUL to her husband and turned from worshipping God, and followed the customs of the heathen—serving other gods! She broke her part of the marriage covenant by committing *spiritual adultery*!

Jesus' disciples understood that the *Kingdom*, with all authority to govern, whether civil or church government, had been taken away from their people, and turned over to Gentiles. You'll remember how they asked Him, **"Lord, wilt thou at this time restore again the kingdom to Israel?" (Acts 1:6).**

Jesus came to His own [the nation of Israel] first, or to His wife! (Jn. 1:11). Realize, all the apostles were Jews! The gospel was to go to the Jew first (Rom. 1:16). Jesus said He was sent unto *the house of Israel*! (Matt. 15:24). He told His disciples not to go to the Gentiles or the Samaritans—but to *the house of Israel*! (Matt. 10:5).

The early Church was composed solely of Jews on the day of Pentecost! (Acts 2:5). See also (Acts 3:25, 26; 13:36). The parable of the Vineyard in (Matthew 21) is very graphic in explaining the transfer of the Kingdom to another nation [the Church].

The promises of all spiritual blessings, and of eternal life, revealed in the gospel, and made sure through Christ, are of infinitely greater value, better promises. The Old Covenant promises were mainly of earthly, temporal promises, contrary to the heavenly blessings of the New Testament. The Old Covenant's original design of a ritual system was, a schoolmaster leading and preparing us for our true High Priest, Jesus, the Christ.

The book of Hebrews explains that there was a fault with the Old Covenant, otherwise there wouldn't have been a need for the new. What was the fault? Hebrews 8:7-8 helps us understand why Israel failed and what was the fault of the Old Covenant, notice: **"For if that first covenant had been faultless, then no place would have been sought for a second. Because *finding fault with them.*"**

God determined to make a new covenant. In this crucial indictment, God says plainly where He found fault: not with the law, not with the Ten Commandments, not with the statutes and judgments, but *with the people themselves!*

Although the book of Hebrews says that God found fault "with them [Israelites]," the apostle Paul readily recognized the problem was not with just the nation of Israel, but Sin. Paul states a universal problem for all humanity—Jews and gentiles are all under sin (Romans 3; Galatians 3:22). This was Israel's dilemma under the Old Covenant, and it is the dilemma of all human beings. Sin is easy. It is a way of life that comes naturally to us (Romans 7:13-23).

The solution God revealed to Jeremiah for the problem of sin was the same one proclaimed hundreds of years later in the book of Hebrews:

> **Behold, the days are coming says the Lord, when I will make a new covenant with the house of Israel and with the house of Judah—not according to the covenant that I made with their fathers in**

> the day that I took them by the hand to bring them out of the land of Egypt, My covenant which *they broke*, though I was a husband to them, says the Lord" (Heb.8:8-10; Jeremiah 31:31-32).

God inspired Jeremiah to proclaim that a New Covenant would be established that would have a better outcome than the Old Covenant established at Mount Sinai, notice:

> But this is the covenant that I will make with the house of Israel after those days, says the Lord: I will *put My law in their minds and write it on their hearts;* and I will be their God, and they shall be my people. No more shall every man teach his neighbor and every man his brother, saying, 'Know the Lord,' *for they all shall know Me* from the least of them to the greatest of them, says the Lord. *For I will forgive their iniquity, and their sin I will remember no more* (verses 33-34).

This New Covenant would have an additional dimension, an extra ingredient. The Holy Spirit would make the difference!

The New Covenant is a better covenant because God's way of life, reflected in the Ten Commandments, *becomes a part of our very being.* People in whose lives the work of writing the law upon their hearts and minds is completed are given a promise—not just physical blessings as with the Old Covenant, but *eternal life.* Then, throughout eternity, they will reflect God's way of life, summarized by love, in everything they think, say and do.

The promises in the first covenant as outlined in Exodus 20-24 pertained mainly to the present life. They were promises of length of days; of increase of numbers; of seed time and harvest; of national privileges, and of extraordinary peace, abundance, and prosperity, etc. But looking for the promise of eternal life, one cannot find it! In the new Testament, however, the promise of spiritual blessings becomes the principal objective. The mind is directed toward heavenly things!

But what else are going to be the better promises of those "firstfruits" in God's Kingdom? God had promised the Israelites that they would be "a kingdom of priests" and a "holy nation" if they would be faithful to Him (Ex. 19d:6). But they were not faithful and so God called a spiritual people to be "kings and priests" *ruling* over His Kingdom during the Millennium.

TO RULE OVER NATIONS

Now realize that those who are "firstfruits" will be rulers over the nations during the millennial reign of Jesus Christ (Rev. 2:26,27), and forever!

True, the word translated "forever" in the Bible can refer to the time period designated to fulfill a particular dispensation—but realize also there are going to be nations on the newly created earth (Rev. 21:24,26; 22:2; Isa. 65:17-25; 66:22).

These nations do not dwell in Jerusalem, but their kings may visit it (Rev. 21:24). *Who* then are these nations existing on the newly created earth, and *who* are the kings ruling over them?

Recall the promise Christ made to the *overcomers* in (Revelation 22:5) was to reign for ever and ever. Those qualifying as *overcomers* will rule from Jerusalem, the headquarters for eternity and their eternal residence where the Father and Son comprising the Temple *dwell* (Rev. 3:12; 21:22).

Over *what* nations of the earth will the overcomers reign? Whoever these nations are, they will need healing of sickness, for the leaves of the tree of life are for their healing (Rev. 22:2). Therefore, these nations that need healing cannot be those qualified as "overcomers," for "overcomers" will never be in need of healing again (Rev. 21:4).

Could it be that the Millennium will be a *prototype* for all eternity? What a marvelous work our great God has done, and Christians can look forward to a wonderful fuiture!

CONCLUSION

Based upon the forgoing dissertation of facts, probability and possibility, we may deduce the following observations:

- There is definitely going to be a time that God will restore again the kingdom [the ability to rule] to the nation of Israel and reestablish them in their promised land. This truth is expressed over and over again in the prophecies, parables, and feast days.

THE RESTORATION OF ISRAEL

- The apostle Paul referred to this time as a "grafting in" of the nation of Israel as God's natural branches (Romans 11). Paul is stating here that God is going to bring Israelites, who have the knowledge of Jesus Christ into His vineyard as a wild olive tree that has been pruned. Though these branches were broken off at one time — they will be grafted back into the olive tree once they accept Jesus Christ as their personal Savior.

- The nation of Israel was restored to their rightful land in 1948 fulfilling the 70 Weeks Prophecy of **"to finish the transgression."** Soon Israel will be restored as a ruling power!

- There is coming a time in the "last days" that "old men of Israel will dream dreams, and young men shall have visions [of the Messiah's imminent return], as the sons and daughters of Israel will prophesy. This is the time that apostle Peter spoke of as fulfilling Joel's prophecy of sending the Holy Spirit, and would occur prior to the 6th seal in which the sun will be turned dark, and the moon into blood, before the return of our Savior (Acts 2:14- 22; Matt. 24:29; Rev.6:12). This event occurs between the 6th and 7th Seal. The 5th Seal is the Great Tribulation, and the 7th Seal is our Lord's return.

- Indications are that there will be a "sealing" of 144,000 physical Israelites just after the Great Tribulation and prior to our Lord's return (Rev. 7).

- The nation of Israel will be brought out of captivity as a whole by Jesus Christ, and returned back to their land as Israel's fulfills Daniel's 70th Week and the Day of Atonement, **"to make an end of sins, and to make reconciliation for iniquity"** (Hosea 12:9; Jer. 16:14; Isa. 30).

- The Eternal will rebuild the nation of Israel to be His model nation, as a "light to the Gentile nations" in assisting in their conversion throughout the Millennium

THE NEW HEAEN AND EARTH

(Isa. 61; Mal. 3:1-4; Ezek. 38, 39; Deut. 4:5-6; Micah 4:1-2; Zech. 8:20-23). This event will fulfill Daniel's 70th Week prophecy of **"to bring in everlasting righteousness."**

- In the last days, the city of Jerusalem is going to be the focus of world attention. All the people of the earth will be against the nation of Israel (Zech. 12:3). It is the city where sacrifices will start again, where a rebuilt Temple may be erected, where the Saints (converted Jews) will flee from in the winter and on the Sabbath (Matt. 24:20), where the "Beast Power" will enter and kill the "Two Witnesses" (Rev. 11) — in short, it is where God will **restore again the kingdom to Israel!**

THE RESTORATION OF ISRAEL

Books by Ronald Wlodyga
Now available from Amazon or Barnes & Noble

Ronald R. Wlodyga

The Foolishness of God

Is wiser than men (I Cor. 1:25)

God's Master Plan of Salvation through Typology, Parables, Prophecy, and Feast Days

Volume 1

✝ **In the Beginning**
✝ **Satan becomes God of the World**
✝ **God's Plan of Duality**
✝ **Types of the True Church**
✝ **Types of Satan**
✝ **Types of Christ and Satan**
✝ **Types of the Holy Spirit**
✝ **Types of Baptism**
✝ **Types of the Two Witnesses**
✝ **Types of Sin**
✝ **God' Government of Numbers**
✝ **God's Plan of Names**
✝ **God's many Names**
✝ **The Seven Stages of Sonship**
✝ **God's Plan in the Old Covenant**
✝ **God's Plan in the First Five Books**

Ronald R. Wlodyga

The Foolishness of God

Is wiser than men (I Cor. 1:25)

God's master plan of salvation through
prophetic numbers and parables of Israel's
History. God's many Professions

Volume 2

✝ **God's Trades**

✝ **God's Businesses**

✝ **His Recreations**

✝ **His Professions**

✝ **The Galilean Parables**

✝ **Parables of Israel's History**

✝ **Evangelistic Parables**

✝ **Prophetic Parables**

✝ **Parables of Christian**

✝ **Admonition**

✝ **The Futility of Riches**

✝ **Spiritual Numbers**

✝ **Prophetic Numbers**

✝ **Daniel's Seventy WeeksProphecy**

Ronald R. Wlodyga

The Foolishness of God

Is wiser than men (1 Cor. 1:25)

God's master plan of salvation through the Feast Days, Melchizedek Priesthood, and the eight Sanctuaries of God

Volume 3

† **Passover**

† **Who Killed Christ**

† **Unleavened Bread**

† **Pentecost**

† **Trumpets**

† **Atonement**

† **Tabernacles**

† **Eight Sanctuaries of God**

† **Melchizedek Priesthood**

† **The Law of the Offerings**

† **The Tabernacle**

† **God's Spiritual Temple**

† **Neglect Not the Spirit**

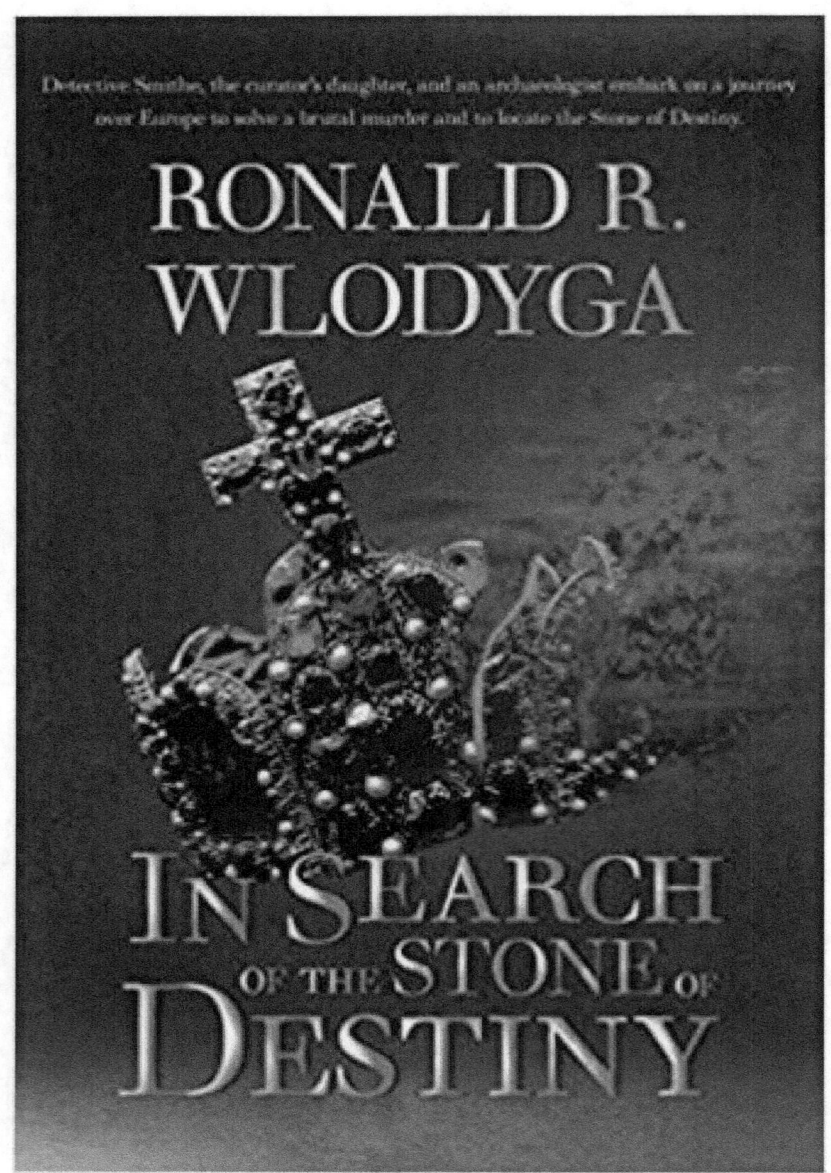

When the curator at Westminster Abbey is bludgeoned to death one fateful night, it sets into motion a string of events that will alter the world forever. The Stone of Destiny, has fired the passion for the coronation of Irish, Scottish, and English monarchs for centuries, has been stolen. According to legend, the Patriarch Jacob used the Stone of Destiny as a pillow and saw God in a dream who promised Jacob that many kings would come out of his legacy through King David. Whoever has possession of the stone, has supernatural power! Detective Smithe, a rational and cold-hard-facts type of man, is thrown into the investigation of his lifetime. Together, he, archaeologist Robert McNair, and the curator's daughter

Sara Flanders embark on a journey all over Europe to locate the Stone of Destiny and to counter the Antichrist. As they race against the clock they unearth a powerful secret using DNA of the true perpetrator of evil and deception culminating in a world despot enforcing "the mark of the beast." An unsuspecting world awaits their solution as the past and present collide. Will they have enough time to stop him and triumph over evil before it's too late?

www.ingramcontent.com/pod-product-compliance
Lightning Source LLC
Chambersburg PA
CBHW070523010526
44118CB00012B/1057